Theories of Psychotherapy
Origins and Evolution

Edited by

Paul L. Wachtel *and*
Stanley B. Messer

American Psychological Association

Washington, DC

First printing July 1997
Second printing July 1998
Third printing January 2003

Published by
American Psychological Association
750 First Street, NE
Washington, DC 20002

Copies may be ordered from
APA Order Department
P.O. Box 92984
Washington, DC 20090-2984

In the United Kingdom and Europe, copies may be ordered from
American Psychological Association
3 Henrietta Street
Covent Garden
London WC2E 8LU
England

Typeset in Goudy by EPS Group Inc., Easton, MD

Printer: Data Reproductions Corporation, Auburn Hills, MI
Cover designer: Minker Design, Bethesda, MD
Technical / production editor: Valerie Montenegro

Cover photo courtesy of the Clark University Archives.

Library of Congress Cataloging-in-Publication Data
Theories of psychotherapy : origins and evolution / edited by
    Paul L. Wachtel and Stanley B. Messer.
        p.   cm.
    Includes bibliographical references and index.
    ISBN 1-55798-435-2 (pbk. : acid-free paper)
    1. Psychotherapy. 2. Psychotherapy—Philosophy. I. Wachtel, Paul L.,
1940- . II. Messer, Stanley B.
RC480.T442 1997
616.89'14—dc21   97-20793
                                                                     CIP

British Library Cataloguing-in-Publication Data
A CIP record is available from the British Library.

Printed in the United States of America

*This book is dedicated to the memory of
our good friend and colleague Perry London.*

CONTENTS

List of Contributors vii

Preface ix

Chapter 1   The Contemporary Psychotherapeutic Landscape:
Issues and Prospects 1
Stanley B. Messer and Paul L. Wachtel
    Symptoms, Character, and Values 3
    Brief Psychotherapy 6
    Modernist Versus Postmodernist Approaches to
        Psychotherapy 11
    Pharmacotherapy and Psychotherapy 17
    The Controversy Over Empirically Validated
        Treatments 21
    Managed Care and Psychotherapy 27

Chapter 2   Psychoanalytic Theories of Psychotherapy 39
David L. Wolitzky and Morris N. Eagle
    Freudian Drive Theory 41
    Psychoanalytic Ego Psychology 43
    Object Relations Theory 55
    Interpersonal Psychoanalysis 61
    Other Contributions to Psychoanalytic Theory
        and Treatment 70
    Most Recent Developments: Reflections
        on Theories and Techniques
        in Psychoanalysis 78
    Conclusion 85

Chapter 3   Humanistic Approaches to Psychotherapy 97
                 Leslie S. Greenberg and Laura N. Rice
                        Origins 99
                        The Therapeutic Processes 104
                        Recent Decades 113
                        Future Developments 116
                        Most Recent Developments: Evidence-Based
                            Experiential Psychotherapy 118
                        Conclusion 121

Chapter 4   The Conceptual Evolution of Behavior Therapy .. 131
                 Daniel B. Fishman and Cyril M. Franks
                        History 133
                        Definition of Behavior Therapy 143
                        A Metatheoretical Framework for Characterizing
                            Contemporary Behavior Therapy 146
                        Behavior Therapy in Action 153
                        Behavior Therapy in Contemporary Context ... 160
                        Conclusion 169

Chapter 5   Development of Family Systems Theory 181
                 Philip J. Guerin, Jr., and David R. Chabot
                        Communication Theorists 183
                        Psychoanalytic Multigenerational Theorists 192
                        The Structural Family Therapy Theorists 206
                        Comment on Behavioral Family Therapy 210
                        Summary of the Years 1950–1990 211
                        Most Recent Developments 212
                        Conclusion 221

Chapter 6   Integrative Theories of Therapy 227
                 Hal Arkowitz
                        What Is Psychotherapy Integration? 228
                        Psychotherapy Integration: A History of Ideas .. 229
                        Why Integration Now? 254
                        Psychotherapy Integration: Contributions,
                            Problems, and Promises 256
                        Psychotherapy Integration Comes of Age:
                            Recent Developments 258
                        Conclusion 272

Author Index 289

Subject Index 299

About the Editors 309

CONTRIBUTORS

Hal Arkowitz, PhD, associate professor of psychology at the University of Arizona, is coeditor of *Psychoanalytic Therapy and Behavior Therapy: Is Integration Possible?* (with S. B. Messer, 1984). Currently, he is editor of the *Journal of Psychotherapy Integration.*

David R. Chabot, PhD, is associate professor of clinical psychology and was formerly the director of the clinical psychology program at Fordham University.

Morris N. Eagle, PhD, is professor of psychology at the Derner Institute for Advanced Psychological Studies, Adelphi University. He is the author of *Recent Developments in Psychoanalysis: A Critical Evaluation* (1987).

Daniel B. Fishman, PhD, is professor of clinical psychology in the Graduate School of Applied and Professional Psychology, Rutgers University. He is past president of the Society for Studying Unity Issues in Psychology, senior editor of *Paradigms in Behavior Therapy: Present and Promise* (1988), and author of *Foundations for a New, Pragmatic Psychology: Getting Down to Cases* (in press).

Cyril M. Franks, PhD, Distinguished Professor, Emeritus at Rutgers University, is cofounder and was first president of the Association for Advancement of Behavior Therapy. He is also the founding editor of the journal *Behavior Therapy* and founding and current editor of *Child and Family Behavior Therapy.*

Leslie S. Greenberg, PhD, is professor at York University. He is a past president of the Society for Psychotherapy Research, coeditor of *Empathy Reconsidered: New Directions in Psychotherapy* (with A. C. Bohart, 1997), and coauthor of *Emotion in Psychotherapy* (with J. D. Safran, 1987).

Philip J. Guerin, Jr., MD, is director of the Center for Family Learning and adjunct professor of psychology at Fordham University. He edited *Family Therapy: Theory and Practice* (1976) and coauthored *The Evaluation* *and Treatment of Marital Conflict* (1987). Most recently, he coauthored *Working with Relationship Triangles: One, Two, Three of Psychotherapy* (1996).

Stanley B. Messer, PhD, is professor and chairperson in the Department of Clinical Psychology at the Graduate School of Applied and Professional Psychology, Rutgers University. He is coauthor of *Models of Brief Psychodynamic Therapy: A Comparative Approach* (with C. S. Warren, 1995) and coeditor of *Essential Psychotherapies: Theory and Practice* (with A. S. Gurman, 1995), among other works. He has written extensively about the prospects for psychotherapy integration as well as philosophical issues in psychotherapy, and he conducts research on psychotherapy process. Dr. Messer maintains a clinical practice in Highland Park, New Jersey.

Laura N. Rice, PhD, Professor Emeritus in psychology at York University, is coeditor of *Patterns of Change: Intensive Analysis of Psychotherapy Process* (with L. S. Greenberg, 1984).

Paul L. Wachtel, PhD, is CUNY Distinguished Professor at City College and the Graduate Center of the City University of New York. He has coauthored *Family Dynamics in Individual Psychotherapy* (with E. F. Wachtel, 1986) and authored *Psychoanalysis, Behavior Therapy, and the Relational World* (1997), *Therapeutic Communication: Principles and Effective Practice* (1993), and *Action and Insight* (1987), among other works. He was a cofounder of the Society for the Exploration of Psychotherapy Integration.

David L. Wolitzky, PhD, associate professor of psychology at New York University (NYU), is also director of the NYU Psychology Clinic and codirector of the NYU Postdoctoral Program in Psychotherapy and Psychoanalysis.

PREFACE

The chapters in this book originated in a volume, *History of Psychotherapy: A Century of Change*, designed to celebrate the 100th anniversary of the American Psychological Association (APA). Published in 1992, under the sponsorship of APA Division 29 (Division of Psychotherapy), *History of Psychotherapy* was edited by Donald K. Freedheim with the participation of six associate editors: Herbert J. Freudenberger, Jane W. Kessler, Donald R. Peterson, Hans H. Strupp, and ourselves. Each associate editor took primary responsibility for one section of the book—Jane Kessler for the introductory overview setting the social and historical context, Hans Strupp for the section on psychotherapy research, Herb Freudenberger for the section on practice, Don Peterson for the section on education and training, and we took primary responsibility for the section on theoretical perspectives in psychotherapy.

We wish to express our appreciation to Don Freedheim and the other associate editors for their work in making *History of Psychotherapy* a success. It was in part as a result of the very positive reception of that volume that the present book was conceived. *History of Psychotherapy* offered a comprehensive overview of many facets of the evolution of psychotherapy over the past 100 years, and we believe that it remains a reference volume of enduring value. But it was, by its very nature, too large and expensive to be purchased by most students or used as a central reading for courses in universities and other training institutions.

The present volume, in contrast, is designed for precisely those uses. It is a relatively brief and affordable introduction to the major points of view in the field of psychotherapy and is suitable for graduate courses in clinical and counseling psychology, psychiatry, psychiatric nursing, social work, and related fields, as well as for some advanced undergraduate courses in clinical psychology or psychotherapy. Rather than present a large number of chapters depicting the various "brands" of psychotherapy that claim separate allegiances, we have chosen to represent the predominant conceptual thrusts of the field of psychotherapy, examining more deeply the fundamental ways of thinking that unite and characterize broad segments of the therapeutic profession and the ways in which these points of view have evolved. Thus, the chapters are organized to represent psychodynamic, experiential, cognitive–behavioral, family systems, and integrative approaches.

All of the chapters have been significantly updated and expanded from their versions in the earlier volume, with a section on new developments bringing the evolution of key ideas in our field right up to the present. The chapter by Fishman and Frank has been even more thoroughly reorganized and revised in order to gear it more to the intended purposes of this book. Our own introductory chapter is completely new and, we hope, makes a useful addition in presenting to readers a number of key issues and themes that cut across the various theoretical perspectives and are of central concern to most psychotherapists.

Although the chapters in this volume originated in the previous book's section on theoretical perspectives, it will be evident to the reader that most of them have considerable relevance for clinical practice and also address in significant ways the findings of psychotherapy research. Moreover, although they originated in a volume concerned with the 100-year history of psychotherapy in the United States, they are all decidedly oriented to the particular ways that psychotherapy has evolved in recent years, and they address the most current developments in each broad approach. It is our hope that these chapters will provide the reader with an up-to-the-minute appreciation of the status of the key approaches to psychotherapy, of how those approaches have evolved, and of how the methods and theories of the present compare with those of earlier eras.

1

THE CONTEMPORARY PSYCHOTHERAPEUTIC LANDSCAPE: ISSUES AND PROSPECTS

STANLEY B. MESSER AND PAUL L. WACHTEL

As Jerome Frank (1973) elucidated in his influential book, *Persuasion and Healing*, psychotherapy is an institution with roots that are both broad and deep. Historically, its development can be traced to the shamans, priests, rabbis, and faith healers that have responded to the spiritual and psychological needs of humankind at least since the dawn of recorded history. More currently, Frank suggested, it has strong affinities not only with the continuing application of those earlier practices but also with placebo processes in medicine and with a variety of practices of persuasion, including some—such as the "thought reform" practiced by totalitarian regimes—that are far from benign.

Frank's intention was not to tar psychotherapy with the brush of political repression, nor simply to declare that it is "nothing new." Rather, he was attempting to offer a degree of historical and cultural perspective that was (and still is) rare in the discourse about psychotherapy in our professional journals. He also aimed to address a phenomenon that could be seen as one more example of such cultural and historical influences: the proliferation of "brands" of psychotherapy, each claiming to be more effective and to have discovered an important and theretofore unrecognized or suppressed truth.

This proliferation of therapeutic schools—one estimate runs as high as 400 (Karasu, 1986)—is itself a cultural phenomenon because psychotherapy as a business and as a form of secular counseling is one of the defining characteristics of the culture. Although its influence may already be waning in certain respects (see later in this section), it must nonetheless be noted that works such as *The Triumph of the Therapeutic* (Rieff, 1966), *The Psychological Society* (Gross, 1978), *The Culture of Narcissism* (Lasch, 1979), *The Repression of Psychoanalysis* (Jacoby, 1983), *Habits of the Heart* (Bellah, Madsen, Sullivan, Swidler, & Tipton, 1985), and *The Modes and Morals of Psychotherapy* (London, 1986) are but a sampling of the critical works that have examined the evolution and social significance of the professionalization of psychotherapy and its rapid growth in influence in this century.

The various schools of psychotherapy, to be sure, differ in significant ways. They differ in practice, in values, in the training and temperaments of their practitioners and advocates, and in the intellectual traditions to which they link themselves. Some of those differences will become apparent in the chapters that follow. And yet, Frank argued, they also have much in common.

To begin with, these various approaches all seem to achieve roughly comparable results (see, e.g., Lambert & Bergin, 1994). Frank began his first chapter by quoting the Dodo in Lewis Carroll's *Alice in Wonderland:* "Everybody has won and all must have prizes." This so-called Dodo verdict has been requoted frequently in the ensuing years of debate over the differential effectiveness of different forms of psychotherapy (see, e.g., Luborsky et al., 1993), although it is by no means accepted by all reviewers (e.g., Chambless, 1996; Giles, 1993). To date, although there is indeed evidence that certain procedures have particular success with certain specific, narrowly defined disorders (e.g., Barlow, 1993; Bellack & Hersen, 1993; Giles, 1993; Nathan & Gorman, in press), for the broad range of problems that clients bring to psychotherapists there is still no convincing evidence that one approach is any better than the others (Elliott, Stiles, & Shapiro, 1993; Lambert & Bergin, 1994; Luborsky et al., 1993).

For Frank, the most likely reason for the comparable effectiveness of these various therapeutic schools is that despite surface differences, they all mobilize the same basic set of processes and experiences. Patients come to psychotherapy, Frank argued, because they are discouraged and demoralized about some aspect of their lives, and psychotherapists engage in what is essentially a persuasive exercise that helps them overcome that demoralization. Crucial to the successful overcoming of the demoralization, according to Frank, are four features shared by virtually all approaches to psychotherapy: (a) a relationship in which the patient has confidence that the therapist is competent and cares about his welfare; (b) a practice setting that is socially defined as a place of healing; (c) a rationale or "myth" that explains the patient's suffering and how it can be overcome; (d) a set of procedures that require the active participation of both patient and therapist and that both believe to be the means of restoring the patient's health. Frank (1973) stated,

> In short, when successful, all forms of psychotherapy relieve dysphoric feelings, rekindle the patient's hopes, increase his sense of mastery over himself and his environment, and in general restore his morale. As a result, he becomes able to tackle the problems he had been avoiding and to experiment with new, better ways of handling them. These new capabilities decrease the chance that he will become demoralized again and, with good fortune, enable him to continue to make gains after psychotherapy has ended. (p. 330)

SYMPTOMS, CHARACTER, AND VALUES

It is worth noting that the discussion thus far is very largely couched in moral and value terms. For various reasons that we will elaborate, psychotherapy has become to a large degree (and in certain respects to its detriment) assimilated into a medical, health–sickness institutional framework—but its focus in actual daily practice tends to be much more on value questions than on medical ones. As Frank's formulation implies, the comparison of psychotherapy to medicine may be drawn not only because both are "modern," "scientific" enterprises but because medicine, too—if covertly—largely partakes of the tradition of the "healer." It often depends for its effectiveness on evoking age-old attitudes and experiences of faith as much as on discoveries in physiology or biochemistry.

As Perry London (1986) especially illuminated, psychotherapy addresses not just (or even primarily) symptoms of disease but also moral conflicts and choices about the good life. The rhetoric of "symptom" reduction may be a useful tactical maneuver: In the language of our discussion that follows about the role of narrative constructions in psychotherapy, it is a kind of new narrative that reframes people's conflicts over value and moral questions as sequelae of "disease" or "disorder," thereby bringing into play the prestige (and hence curative potential) accruing to medicine and technology in our society. But however useful this rhetoric may be in a significant number of cases—we will also consider some of its drawbacks —we should not overlook the rhetorical dimension in this choice of terminology. It may well be a useful way of talking about people's difficulties, but it *is* a way of talking about them, not simply defining them. (See the section Modernist Versus Postmodernist Approaches to Psychotherapy.)

The "medicalization" of psychotherapy is not a recent phenomenon. Indeed, the redefining of problems that were once the province of priests or friends, or were endured in silent despair, as issues to be brought to a doctor represents the very birth of the modern profession of psychotherapy. The reason Frank could compare psychotherapy *to* faith healing is that it had emerged *from* it, had become something that, as society saw it, was different. Few would disagree that Freud was the dominant figure in the emergence of this new profession, and it was far from irrelevant that Freud was a physician. Although many now see psychotherapy as a profession more appropriately tied to psychology than to medicine, it would have been difficult for psychologists (such as there were in Freud's day) to wrest the problems now labeled as psychological from the priesthood. It required the idea that they belonged to the realm of the body to counter the idea that they were of the realm of the soul.

But if, to begin with, the aim of psychotherapy was to cure the client of "symptoms," it was not long before the focus shifted to "character." Character is a much more frankly psychological concept, but it also has roots in the moral realm that have never really been very far from the concerns clients present in that new confessional booth called the consulting room. It is a peculiarity of clinicians' currently dominant diagnostic scheme—which, like Super Bowls and sequels to *Rocky*, appears regularly in versions with Roman numerals (e.g., *DSM-III, DSM-IV,* for *Diagnostic and Statistical Manual of Mental Disorders,* third and fourth editions, respectively [American Psychiatric Association, 1980, 1994])—that it labels *character disorders* or *personality disorders* as specific diagnostic entities apart from the rest of psychiatric symptomatology. As far back as the writings of Wilhelm Reich (1933) and Karen Horney (1939) and extending into more recent work such as that of David Shapiro (1965, 1981, 1989), psychotherapists have argued persuasively that virtually *all* psychological difficulties are characterological, that symptoms are rooted not so much in disease as in character (cf. the section The Controversy Over Empirically Validated Treatments).

Interestingly, much as Freud's work began with a narrow focus on symptoms and led increasingly to a concern with the analysis of broader features of character, so too did behavior therapy begin with a symptom focus and move toward addressing the broader thrust of the person's way of living in and adapting to the world. Psychoanalysts who dismissed behavior therapy as merely concerned with symptoms forgot that Freud, too, at first staked his claims on the basis of symptom relief. In any event, they were focusing their barbs on a moving target. As Fishman and Lubetkin (1983) noted, over time the clinical emphasis of behavior therapists evolved from a narrow focus on particular techniques addressing specific symptoms and narrowly defined problems to a broader focus on developing the coping skills and capacities to deal effectively with the problems life presents. Reflecting on the development of outpatient behavior therapy, Hersen (1983) pointed out that although behavior therapy began as a brief and focused treatment, ultimately, behavioral treatments became "lengthier, more comprehensive in scope, and considerably more sophisticated" (p. 5).

More recently, narrower concern with symptom relief has reemerged in almost all therapeutic orientations in response to economic pressures and the "corporatization" of health care that has so significantly changed the climate within which psychotherapy is practiced. (We return to this sea change in the final pages of this chapter.) Today's remedicalization of psychological distress has different roots than the original turn to medical models of psychological disorder. Less than any conceptual or social advance, it reflects very largely the effort simply to spend less money on human services. Here again, value questions cannot be separated from the evolution of psychological treatments.

This is not to say that there has not been some merit in the turn toward examination of the medical dimension of psychological disorder or in the increased emphasis on briefer, more focused forms of psychotherapy. With regard to the former, important advances have been made, for example, in understanding the biochemical and genetic bases of disorders such as schizophrenia and bipolar affective disorders, and the increasing availability of antipsychotic and mood-stabilizing medications has contributed significantly to the relief of human suffering. Even in the milder disorders, new medications have aided therapeutic efforts and added to the range of ways of intervening in troubling symptoms and life patterns. Although there are some voices in psychiatry who would largely *replace* psychotherapy with psychopharmacology, the evidence suggests that medication is best viewed as a complement or adjunct to psychotherapy rather than as a substitute, and that indeed in many instances it does not make a measurable additional contribution beyond what psychotherapy alone can achieve (see the section Pharmacotherapy and Psychotherapy). In general, earlier attitudes on the part of psychotherapists that viewed medication as antithetical to psychotherapy are increasingly being modified, and therapists are finding ways to include medication in their treatment efforts without abandoning the essential aims and methods of the psychotherapeutic relationship.

Turning to the greater focus on symptoms and on briefer therapies, we once again encounter a mixture of value issues on the one hand and considerations deriving from new discoveries, observations, and innovations on the other. Focusing therapeutic efforts on brief rather than long-term approaches can be viewed from rather varied value perspectives, and sorting out the hidden motivations that underlie this trend is extremely difficult. On the one hand, the turn toward briefer therapies points toward more rapid relief of suffering, a goal that in itself is certainly viewed positively by the vast majority of therapists and patients. As the field of psychotherapy evolved, and especially in the more psychodynamic approaches, the assumption did become widespread that meaningful change inevitably required a rather long-term treatment, and this very likely became a kind of self-fulfilling prophecy that interfered with the possibility of helping people more expeditiously. The rapidly developing field of brief psychodynamic therapy is contributing to changing the attitudes even of therapists who work according to more long-term, intensive models and increases the likelihood of patients' achieving gains more quickly. The focus on brief therapy serves as well the goal of making mental health services more widely available. When therapists work with patients in a more long-term model, they necessarily can see fewer patients over the course of their careers. There is thus a kind of democratization of psychological services when brief therapy models are in the ascendancy (Messer & Warren, 1995; see also the section Brief Psychotherapy).

On the other hand, the emphasis on briefer therapies also reflects an implicit social decision to devote fewer resources to psychological well-being on the whole. There can be a temptation to make treatments "quick and cheap" and an acceptance of more superficial understanding and more superficial goals. One must ask where the resources saved on mental health services will go instead. In a nation that spends extraordinary amounts of money on luxury goods and on items such as cosmetics and new wardrobes every year, one must wonder if the "savings" are worthwhile. There is good reason to suggest that our society's thinking about economic matters is already too skewed toward material goods and insufficiently attentive to quality of life (Wachtel, 1989; see also the section Managed Care and Psychotherapy).

Further consideration of the implications of the growing trend toward briefer forms of psychotherapy requires a more detailed examination of this trend and its clinical and empirical foundations. It is to this topic that we now turn.

BRIEF PSYCHOTHERAPY

Psychotherapy theory and practice do not develop in a vacuum. The prevailing economic, political, and ideological climate can have a marked effect on what kinds of psychotherapy theory or practice predominate in a particular time period or place (cf. Cushman, 1992). For example, it is not surprising that psychoanalytic and existential therapies, which encompass a tragic view of life's difficulties and possibilities, developed in this century in Europe—the scene of both World Wars, major revolutions, and many local conflicts. Behavior therapy and person-centered therapy, the former with its more pragmatic stance and the latter with its more optimistic outlook on human nature and possibility, developed in America, on whose soil no major war has been fought since the Civil War and where a spirit of optimism and "can do" has prevailed.

In similar fashion, the current economic reality of corporate downsizing and greater reluctance to pay for health services has fostered the practice of time-limited (or what might be termed "cost-limited") therapies. The ubiquity of the two-career family—a consequence of changing economic conditions and the women's liberation movement—has also decreased the time people are willing to make available for treatment. Another factor that has increased the practice of brief therapy, and one that is related to the same economic changes in the United States, is the advent of managed care organizations (MCOs). They have grown with astonishing rapidity over the past 10 years, so that by the end of 1993, 45.2 million members were enrolled (Belar, 1995). An MCO typically contracts with a company or institution to oversee and administer employees' treatment. Just as it hires physicians to offer health services, it employs psychotherapists to deliver mental health treatment at set fees. In an effort to reduce costs, most MCOs severely limit the number of sessions they will pay for, and they require reports from therapists at frequent intervals to be sure that as few sessions as possible are being used. Referred to as "the rape of psychotherapy" (Fox, 1995), there is probably no more controversial movement on the current psychotherapy scene than managed care (although lurking in the wings is the question of prescription privileges for psychologists). We will return to this topic later in the chapter.

It is not so much that the brief therapies are new as that they are being practiced more widely. In fact, it has long been the case that most people seeking therapy have remained in treatment for only a relatively short time, which is brief therapy by default if not by design. In the National Medical Expenditures Survey, for example, in which over 38,000 individuals were sampled about their use of psychotherapy (Olfson & Pincus, 1994), 34% had 1 to 2 visits, 37% had 3 to 10, 13% had 11 to 20, and only 16% had more than 20 visits. If we define brief therapy as encompassing fewer than 20 sessions, these data inform us that 84% received brief therapy. The attrition figures from studies dating back 10 to 20 years are strikingly similar to these, and they seem to apply regardless of diagnosis, age, sex, presenting complaints, and the length of therapy offered (Phillips, 1985).

What is brief therapy? Although any effort to specify its span of sessions is somewhat arbitrary, it can be said to range from 1 to 40 sessions, with 10 to 20 being more typical. The *time limit* is usually known and set from the start, which places into motion a certain train of expectations that has an effect on both the content of the material that clients bring to therapy and on the length of time they may be willing to remain. Apropos of the latter, in a study comparing therapy with a set time limit with both brief and open-ended therapy conducted without a limit, the dropout rate in the time-limited therapy was half of that in a brief therapy where the time limit was not set in advance, and it was half of that in the open-ended, long-term therapy (Sledge, Moras, Hartley, & Levine, 1990).

In brief therapy, *a focus* is set that may be alleviation of a disorder such as depression, an interpersonal problem, a negative feeling about the self, an underlying conflict, a family issue, and so forth. The point is that not all of a client's difficulties can be taken up in a short time period; rather, there is a narrowing of the work. Related to the focus, *goals* are often set at the start that may or may not be directly communicated to the client but that also serve to guide the therapy. Unlike the practice in some traditional models of therapy, the therapist tends to be relatively *active* in engaging the client in dialogue. There are also criteria for *client suitability* for this modality that are probably observed as much in the breach as in the practice because of the pressure in most clinics to offer all clients brief therapy only. (For a comprehensive overview of the brief therapies, see Bloom, 1992; Hoyt, 1995; Wells & Giannetti, 1990).

There is extensive research support for the value of brief therapy (e.g., Koss & Shiang, 1994). We will cite the conclusions that Messer and Warren (1995, pp. 35–36) reached on the basis of their review of this literature. Stated in the most general terms, time-limited therapy is helpful to a substantial proportion of clients and is often as helpful as time-unlimited therapy. Its effects seem to be as lasting as those of time-unlimited treatment. These global conclusions must be qualified, however, in several ways.

First, the dose-effect studies (which track the percentage of patients improved or the symptoms alleviated as a function of number of sessions) suggest that, although time-limited therapy is helpful to a majority of clients (e.g., 60% improved by 13 sessions; 75% by 26 sessions), the percentage increases the longer that therapy continues (e.g., 85% after 1 year). Similarly, the breadth of change may be greater for long-term therapy. In a sense, it can be said both that brief therapy is helpful and that longer term therapy can be even more helpful. The latter finding parallels the level of satisfaction for different lengths of therapy reported by psychotherapy clients in a recent retrospective survey ("Mental Health," 1995; Seligman, 1995).

Second, we cannot say that any one form of brief therapy is clearly superior to another, to medication, or to some types of nonpsychiatric treatment.

Third, clients diagnosed as depressed or anxious improve faster than do borderline patients. Reasonable proportions of the latter, however, also make gains in a relatively brief time period (2 to 6 months, depending on the source of measurement). Similarly, acute symptoms (e.g., anxiety, depression) and more chronic problems (e.g., cognitive disturbances and interpersonal problems) improve sooner than does more severe psychopathology (e.g., paranoid ideation, schizoid traits).

Fourth, measures of well-being and symptoms show earlier improvement than does general life functioning, including interpersonal relationships.

Fifth, the results of time-limited versus time-unlimited therapy are dependent on the outcome measures employed. Therapist-measured outcome often yields superior results for time-unlimited therapy, especially compared to outcomes gauged by tests or behavioral measures.

Finally, clients in time-limited psychotherapy tend to maintain their gains. Thus, overall, the research supports the value of both brief and moderate-term psychotherapy.

Turning to the theoretical perspectives covered in this volume, each has produced its own brand of short-term therapy, which we will mention briefly. In the *psychoanalytic* domain, therapies that derive primarily from drive and ego psychology tend to be focused on formulations that emphasize aggressive, sexual, and dependent impulses and defenses against them, as well as oedipal conflicts (e.g., the brief therapies of Malan, Davanloo, Sifneos). There are also brief psychodynamic therapies based largely on object relations and interpersonal perspectives, which formulate problems in terms of maladaptive interpersonal patterns (Binder & Strupp, 1991); client wishes, the response of the other, and the subsequent response of self (Luborsky & Mark, 1991); pathogenic beliefs and the way they are manifested in relation to the therapist (Weiss & Sampson, 1986); and schemas and role relationships (Horowitz et al., 1984). In addition to incorporating these theoretical approaches, Mann (1992) has described a time-limited, 12-session therapy that includes concepts from self psychology, particularly the use of empathy to heal clients' chronically endured pain.

Behavior therapy, once exclusively short-term, became longer as behavior therapists began to treat clients with characterological difficulties and dual diagnoses (Robins & Hayes, 1993). Nevertheless, because behavior therapists tend to advocate specific techniques oriented to the alleviation of symptoms (or disorders) such as phobias, panic, anorexia, compulsions, and depression, or to changing behaviors such as smoking, drug addiction, or overeating, behavior therapy remains largely a brief therapy. That is, problems are viewed within behavior therapy in such a way as to make brief therapy more possible (see chap. 4 in this volume). In a sense, brevity was a defining feature of behavior therapy when it first arrived on the therapy scene, and this remains largely so (Wilson, 1981). Perhaps for this reason, chapters on behavioral, cognitive, and cognitive–behavioral therapy in handbooks on brief therapy often do not include the descriptor *brief* because there is no distinction made in theory or practice between short- and long-term therapy (e.g., Lehman & Salovey, 1990; Moretti, Feldman, & Shaw, 1990).

Little has been written about brief therapy in *humanistic/experiential therapy* traditions, perhaps because it can seem inimical to its person-centered versus task- or problem-oriented tradition. Nevertheless, a differentiation exactly along these lines has been made recently by two major proponents and theorizers of experiential therapy (Elliott & Greenberg, 1995):

> The process-experiential approach is appropriate as either a brief therapy or a long-term treatment, although the balance between task and relationship elements will probably vary with the treatment length. As a brief therapy, the treatment will usually be more active and emphasize task interventions appropriate to the client. As a long-term (i.e., 50+ sessions) treatment of chronic personality or interpersonal difficulties, a process-experiential approach will tend to emphasize relationship aspects, although task interventions are certainly used where appropriate. (p. 136)

Family therapy so regularly tends to be brief and problem-focused that relatively few publications particularly stress this dimension. Like other forms of therapy, family therapy, too, tends to be briefer when the focus is narrower and to take more time when the goals are more vague or more ambitious. Bergman (1985), for example, considers his brief systemic family therapy as akin to emergency road service designed to get families back on the road. In a combined strategic/systems approach, de Shazer (1988; de Shazer & Molnar, 1984) defines brief family therapy as an attempt to help family members reframe their problems so that these can be reacted to differently. De Shazer's therapy is solution focused and strategic insofar as it stresses the need for the family to do something different. Rather than exploring the present problem, he looks for the "exceptions," that is, times when the problem does *not* occur; such an approach is seen as holding the key to its rapid solution. The influential model of brief therapy that has come out of the Mental Research Institute in Palo Alto, CA (Fisch, Weakland, & Segal, 1983) also manifests a strategic approach to therapeutic change, emphasizing the ways in which "the solution becomes the problem" and employing reframings and therapeutic paradoxes to interrupt the family's repeated efforts to do more of what has not worked.

Finally, there are *integrative and eclectic* short-term therapies that can be thought of as paralleling the division of this area into common factors, technical eclecticism, and theoretical integration (see chap. 6 in this volume; Messer & Warren, 1995). Proponents of a *common factors* approach believe that what moves therapy forward is not what is unique to each therapy but, rather, those factors that cut across treatment modalities. In this tradition, Garfield (1989) catalogued a range of common factors, such as the therapeutic relationship, insight, emotional release, and reinforcement, showing how these can be harnessed in a brief therapy. *Technically eclectic* therapists draw on techniques from whatever source when they seem indicated. Bellak (1992), for example, combined interpretations with advice, medication, and reassurance in a six-session therapy. They also try to match a particular mode of therapy to the patient. Gustafson (1986) offered a partial *theoretical integration* of brief therapy in bringing together psychoanalytic and family systems conceptions of therapy. More recently, McCullough (1993) proposed a brief therapy that draws on several theoretical traditions. For other integrative brief therapy models, see Budman and Gurman (1988), Garske and Molteni (1985), Hoyt (1995), Lazarus (1997), Reid (1990), and Segraves (1990).

It is interesting to note that practitioners do not regard length of therapy as a particularly significant factor in its success and that the importance they attribute to it decreases with therapist experience (Mahoney & Craine, 1991). It seems clear that brief therapy is on the ascendance. We predict that there will be new models appearing in the near future and an increased emphasis placed by training programs on this modality in its various forms.

MODERNIST VERSUS POSTMODERNIST APPROACHES TO PSYCHOTHERAPY

For much of its 100-year history, the field of psychotherapy has approached its task via a point of view that has come to be labeled—largely by its critics—as "modernist" (Safran & Messer, 1997). This perspective emphasizes empirical approaches—especially controlled experimentation —in concert with hypothetico–deductive or formal–computational logic. These methods, properly applied, help to reveal universal laws, general principles, and truths, not only about the physical universe but also about the psychological and social domains. Just as there has been an accumulation of knowledge about the physical world, so there can be assembled a fund of facts within psychology, sociology, and other social sciences that build on each other in a step-by-step, progressive manner. These facts are presumed to be free of both values and ideological outlook. This view grew out of the Enlightenment, whose thinkers believed in "linear progress, absolute truths, and rational planning of ideal social orders" (Harvey, 1989, p. 27).

In accordance with this sensibility, the traditional role of psychotherapy theory has been to guide empirical investigators to those areas most likely to reveal the underlying laws that will explain the process of behavioral and personality change. (In reciprocal fashion, the theory of change is also shaped by such empirical results.) For example, Rogerian or person-centered theory posits, as the major therapeutic change agent, the quality of the client–therapist relationship. Rogers hypothesized that therapist empathy, unconditional positive regard for the client (or nonpossessive warmth), and genuineness (or congruence) of manner—all as perceived by the client—were the necessary and sufficient conditions for therapeutic personality change to take place.

Scores of studies have been conducted on these variables with generally positive results (Orlinsky & Howard, 1986). Similarly, and in accordance with the psychoanalytic theory of therapy, the role of therapist interpretations has been the subject of extensive empirical research and has been found to be an effective mode of intervention (Orlinsky, Grawe, & Parks, 1994). Within a modernist view, such empirical research will be the ultimate arbiter among the many competing theories of therapy, converging increasingly on a singular truth.

From a postmodern perspective, however, the world is a decidedly less certain and orderly place than that portrayed by modernism. It claims no possibility of uncovering general principles, laws, or truths about human nature. In fact, postmodernism rejects the modernist notion that one theory can ever have an exclusive claim to the truth. Thus, postmodernism embraces pluralism, in which several theories can have truth value, and lends legitimacy to diverse methodologies such as ethnographic field study, phenomenological observation, case studies, and qualitative approaches in addition to traditional experimental studies.

Our object here is to show what effect postmodernism has had on one important trend in the way psychotherapy is currently being conceptualized. To do so, however, we must elaborate further on what is meant by postmodernism. Polkinghorne (1992) highlighted four themes: foundationlessness, fragmentariness, constructivism, and neopragmatism.

Foundationlessness refers to the postmodern emphasis that we do not view the world "as it is" but only as a product of our cognitive operations. That is, we impute meaning to our perceptions rather than apprehending pure impressions or sensations that reflect a consensual reality. Because we are adding meaning to our perceptions, there is no knowledge free of our presuppositions. Thus, according to this view, the fundamental data of the social sciences are meanings, intentions, plans, goals, and purposes, all of which are subject to multiple interpretations (Messer, Sass, & Woolfolk, 1988).

Fragmentariness means that our reality is not unified. Modernism stresses regularities and commonalities in the world, whereas postmodernism focuses on that which is unique. Knowledge is concerned with the local, the individual, and the specific, not with a search for context-free laws.

The social, historical, and linguistic contexts in which events occur take on new importance because it is these variables that determine our understanding of such events. Regarding linguistic contexts, language stands between reality and experience (Rorty, 1989). That is to say, language, which is a conveyor of meaning, is not neutral but filters experience through its particular structure.

Constructivism tells us that human experience is not a mirrored reflection of reality but is constructed based on the way our cognitive processes operate and on our interactions with both the material and relational worlds. The world appears organized and meaningful because we operate in such a way as to use things in the world to accomplish our purposes. We constantly invent new ways of seeing the world. Social constructionism, a variant of constructivism, posits that the commonality among our constructions of the world come about through the common social, cultural, linguistic, and historical period we share.

Whereas modernism focuses on generating knowledge by trying to describe accurately what is out there, *neopragmatism* describes, in practical terms, actions that accomplish intended ends. The test for pragmatic knowledge is not whether it corresponds to "the real" but whether it successfully guides human actions to fulfill certain intentions. That is, does a particular action (or therapeutic intervention) work? Neopragmatism does recognize the value of scientific effort, not as producing universal laws, but as documenting which practices produce intended results.

The influence of postmodernism on the development of one stream of psychotherapy can be illustrated by what has come to be called the narrative therapy movement (e.g., White & Epston, 1990) or, more broadly, constructivist therapies (e.g., Mahoney, 1995a, 1995b).

Psychotherapy as Narrative or Story Construction

When clients come to a therapist, they tell a story—of their lives, their problems, their symptoms, their relationships, their desires, as well as their construals of all of these. According to the therapy-as-narrative outlook, such stories do not necessarily correspond accurately to real current or past events, but rather reflect the clients' own interpretations of this reality. In a sense, the narrative is the person's life insofar as it organizes and guides the way he or she remembers events and acts in the present. It is akin to a script for a play in which the client is the protagonist. What one believes and says to oneself about one's life is transformed into how one lives. Drawing on Spence's (1982) distinction between narrative truth and historical truth, Omer and Strenger (1992) wrote, "The story of clients' lives, which develops in therapy, is not the real history, archaeologically reconstructed, but is one possible narrative: perhaps more orderly, detailed, and coherent than the pretherapeutic one, but not necessarily more true" (p. 253). Psychotherapy, by these lights, is a narrating and renarrating of one's story, in the process of which the story gets elaborated, transformed, and repaired (Howard, 1991; Strenger & Omer, 1992). Let us now examine how this description matches the characteristics of postmodernism as we have outlined them.

Foundationlessness

As described by narrative therapists (e.g., White, 1993), neither they nor clients possess an objective and unbiased account of reality. It is not an objectively true story that clients narrate but only their subjective perspective on their lives. It is one of many possible narratives. That is, there are no referents outside the story itself against which it can be validated, and in this sense it is foundationless. Meaning is *created* in the interaction between therapist and client.

Fragmentariness

Postmodernists look to the unique rather than the general (Rosenau, 1992). "The narrative therapist seeks no deeper truth or meta-level according to which to compare or understand someone's story of her experiences. Each person's experience is explicitly responded to as her unique perspective on a given situation" (Parry, 1991, p. 38). Note that unique stories do not give any general or objective truths about human nature (Held, 1995), and, in this sense, narrative approaches are fragmented, rather than unified by a common theoretical outlook.

The medium of therapy is language; it is carried out through conversation. According to postmodern writers such as Polkinghorne (1992), "Each language has its own particular way of distorting, filtering and constructing experience" (p. 150). Indeed, he suggested, it is not reality that creates language but language that creates our reality. Furthermore, "Many within the movement argue that language, including the language of therapy, does not reflect, represent, correspond to, or give us any (extralinguistic) reality that is independent of the knower, or the knower's theory/language/narrative/story" (Held, 1995, p. 95). Once again, this suggests that there can be no unified outlook or theory that guides therapy.

Constructivism

Social constructionists argue that clients are active agents who invent their realities in conjunction with the culture in which they live and then act in accordance with the resulting script or story. The therapeutic task is to help them author alternative stories that liberate them from their self-defeating scripts (White & Epston, 1990). From a narrative perspective, the various therapies practiced within a modernist framework tend to provide set narratives or templates (Omer & Strenger, 1992). Postmodernist therapists in the narrative tradition criticize modernist therapies for imposing such predetermined story lines on clients, be they oedipal issues, separation anxiety, the double-bind, or irrational cognitions. "According to those narrative therapists, all therapists must replace general, predetermined dominant discourses with a story that is ever more personalized and unique to each client" (Held, 1995, p. 109). The new story should supersede predetermined discourses that may be sexist, racist, or otherwise oppressive.

Neopragmatism

Just as there can be no single, correct theory of therapy within a postmodernist outlook, there is no single, authorized methodology and no single criterion that can be used to determine the correctness of the theory. Because there is no one true meaning to be ascribed to the client's problem and its resolution, there is no universal indicator of its success. Postmodernism, then, fosters the view that each theoretical approach must determine its own criteria of change consistent with its outlook. Increasingly, we see calls for research to be carried out in this vein (e.g., Barber, 1994; Messer & Warren, 1990).

Another solution to the absence of a true, single measure of the validity of a therapeutic construct is to use instead a multiplicity of pragmatic criteria. Strenger and Omer (1992), for example, have proposed evaluation of therapeutic constructs by the degree to which they are acceptable to four relevant groups: clients, clinicians, the academic community, and the lay public. Thus, with regard to the utility of a therapeutic construct or intervention, clients should show increased willingness to perform therapeutic tasks, clinicians would note whether the construct or intervention activates important therapeutic processes, academics would apply accepted research criteria, and laymen would judge improvement in terms of commonsense variables such as cost-effectiveness and improvement in daily living. The greater the agreement among these perspectives, Strenger and Omer argued, the more useful the construct, and hence the greater its validity.

Constructivist Trends in Schools of Therapy

There are constructivist trends within each of the major theoretical schools, and we will offer brief examples for illustrative purposes.

The traditional approach to *cognitive therapy* has been to spot clients' irrational cognitions, dispute them, and eliminate them. The object is to help clients revise their beliefs in accordance with a presumed consensual reality. Cognitive therapists with a constructivist bent reject the correspondence theory of truth and the assumption that clients suffer because some of their beliefs fail to correspond to objective reality and therefore are, by definition, dysfunctional (e.g., Mahoney, 1991, 1995a, 1995b; Neimeyer & Harter, 1988). Instead, as Neimeyer (1993) put it, "They hold that the viability of any given construction is a function of its consequences for the individual or group that provisionally adopts it (cf. von Glasersfeld, 1984), as well as its overall coherence with the larger system of personally or socially held beliefs into which it is incorporated" (p. 222). Note here both the pragmatic criterion for construct validity as well as the emphasis on validity as internal coherence rather than external correspondence. Constructivist cognitive therapists, then, strive to help clients develop their constructions rather than prompting them to revise or eliminate irrational or dysfunctional cognitions. Therapist interventions are more likely to be reflective and elaborative than analytical and instructive. (For an overview of the cognitive and constructivist psychotherapies, see Mahoney, 1993, 1995b.)

Meichenbaum (1993) sets out the implications of narrative/constructivist thinking for *cognitive–behavioral therapy*. It is not the symptoms of depression and anxiety that interfere with functioning, he says, but the "story" that clients tell themselves about these symptoms. This storytelling is viewed as part of a normal, rehabilitative, adaptive process. The therapist's job is to discern the story line and help transform it by building new ways for clients to see themselves and the world.[1]

Family therapy authors and practitioners have been leaders in the constructivist therapy movement. For example, Hoffman (1988) pointed out that whereas earlier systems therapists focused on pathological *behavior* to explain the function of a symptom, contemporary constructivist family therapists focus on the *ideas and beliefs* around which and the process by which families construct and negotiate their shared reality. Family premises, stories, or "contractual arrangements" (Efran, Lukens, & Lukens, 1990) are said to be determined by language. The role of the therapist is to draw out and challenge those stories that bring about family members' dysfunctional relationships with one another. Family therapists use a variety of ways, such as ritual prescription, to bring to light different family members' interpretations of events or symptoms. The idea is to show that there is more than one way to construe a problem, that each may be viable, and that each has consequences for family members' behavior (Neimeyer, 1993). This pluralistic outlook is part and parcel of postmodernism.

Within *psychoanalysis*, Ricoeur (1981) pointed out that psychoanalytic accounts are a narrative unfolding that produces coherence and unity in the description of people's lives. In a similar vein, Spence (1982) argued that the psychoanalyst is not an archaeologist unearthing actual events and memories from the past. Thus, it is not the recall or discovery of an ac-

---

[1] Another trend in the behavioral realm that reflects postmodernist thinking is the *radical behavior therapy* of authors such as Hayes, Follette, and Follette (1995) and Kohlenberg & Tsai (1991). Their work is characterized not so much by constructivism, but contextualism, another key concept in postmodern thought. Contextualism posits that an event must be studied in the context of its specific setting.

curate memory (that is, its correspondence with some actual event) or some other truth in the client's life that is therapeutic, but the creation of new meaning through interpretation, which includes the interpretation's aesthetic quality, resonance, and appeal.

In this sense, the analyst is more like an artist or writer "lending form and coherence to the fragments of memory, fantasy and association that the patient has produced. . . . What we discover in psychoanalysis are not pieces of personal history so much as meanings, filtered through memory and through language—that is, through the conversation of analyst and patient" (Woolfolk, Sass, & Messer, 1988, p. 10). Schafer's (1983, 1992) outlook is also in accordance with postmodernist understandings insofar as he views the task of therapy as one of helping the analysand construct new and better nonneurotic stories. And there is more than one way to construct the story. In sum, "Psychoanalysis can only be concerned with reinterpretation, and not reconstruction; presentation, and not representation" (Leary, 1994, p. 448).

Finally, we make mention of the *humanistic approaches to psychotherapy*, which, in their unique way, have always had more of a postmodernist flavor than the other therapies. Greenberg and Rice (see chap. 3 in this volume) list "fostering the construction of new meaning" as one of the four central principles of the humanistic therapies. For example, *existential therapy* is principally about individuals seeking meaning in a meaningless world (Yalom, 1981). The type of meaning pursued in existential therapy involves such basic matters as love, courage, freedom, and aesthetic fulfillment (Bugental & Sterling, 1995), as well as anxiety over one's mortality, awareness of the future, and guilt at not having fulfilled one's potential (e.g., Frankl, 1963; Maslow, 1968; May, 1961). In *Gestalt therapy*, meaning is said to flow directly from vivid experience from which the client creates meaning (Polster & Polster, 1973). Finally, *client-centered therapy* "engages the client in a process of experiential search which involves attending to, differentiating, and integrating an inner referent in order to construct new meanings" (see p. 110 in this volume).

Postmodernist views within psychology, psychoanalysis, and psychotherapy are not without their critics (e.g., Chaiklin, 1992; Held, 1995; Sass, 1992). We expect that the next decade will see ongoing debate and argument between modernist and postmodernist outlooks and a continuing impact of this debate on the conceptualization of the therapeutic enterprise.

PHARMACOTHERAPY AND PSYCHOTHERAPY

Since the 1950s there have been substantial advances in understanding brain mechanisms underlying several mental disorders, as well as a proliferation of medications to treat them. In fact, the mind-altering drugs, especially the antianxiety and antidepressant agents, are probably among the most frequently prescribed of all medications in use. To read the popular press these days, as well as some psychiatric texts, one might wonder whether psychotherapy is in danger of being overshadowed by medication as a treatment for psychological disorders. To indicate just one professional implication of the trend to medicate, psychologists are now debating the merits of obtaining the privilege to prescribe psychotropic drugs, which is currently reserved for physicians. For these reasons, the evidence for the benefits of medication versus psychotherapy are worth examining, as well as their value compared with that of a placebo.

Because there are particularly copious data pertaining to the efficacy of antidepressants, we will focus on the treatment of depression, which is probably the most frequently diagnosed and treated of the mental disorders. Its prevalence is variously estimated at between 3% and 13% (Amenson & Lewinsohn, 1981; Glick, 1995; Kessler et al., 1994) and its lifetime incidence for any individual between 20% and 55% (Antonuccio, Danton, & DeNelsky, 1995).

Antidepressant Medication Compared With Psychotherapy

Antonuccio et al. (1995) reviewed studies of the effects of three types of cognitive–behavioral treatment compared with antidepressant medication: increasing pleasant activities, changing maladaptive cognitions, and improving social skills. They were all found to compare favorably with antidepressant medication in the treatment of depression. Wexler and Cicchetti (1992) conducted a meta-analysis of psychotherapy versus medication in treating depression. Using dropout rate and treatment success rate as outcome indicators, they found that pharmacotherapy was much less effective than psychotherapy. Based on their extensive review of the data regarding outcomes, Antonuccio et al. (1995) concluded that "several meta-analyses—reported in both psychiatry and psychology journals—covering multiple studies with thousands of patients are remarkably consistent in support of the perspective that psychotherapy is at least as effective as medication in the treatment of depression" (p. 577). This result also held when the depression was severe, especially for patient-rated measures of outcome. (However, it should be added that there is no evidence that psychotherapy is an effective treatment for psychotic depression or for treating depression in inpatients; Persons, Thase, & Crits-Christoph, 1996.)

Even if this general conclusion is correct, if medication is simpler to administer and often less costly than psychotherapy, why should it not be the treatment of choice for depression? Part of the cost of using antidepressants, especially the tricyclics (such as Elavil), is their frequent side effects, which may include dry mouth, blurred vision, urinary retention, constipation, and delirium (Settle, 1992). Such side effects are particularly prominent in elderly people, who are major consumers of antidepressants. More serious yet is the risk of patients' using the cyclic antidepressants to commit suicide. For example, "About a one-week supply of imipramine [Tofranil] at therapeutic doses is sufficient to do most patients in" (DeBattista & Schatzberg, 1995). Although psychotherapy can also produce negative effects, it is relatively benign compared with drugs. Another factor that suggests caution in using antidepressants as the treatment of choice is the evidence suggesting that drug treatments are less effective than psychotherapy at follow-up (Antonuccio et al., 1995, p. 578). In other words, psychotherapy appears to have longer lasting effects.

Psychotherapy or Medication Alone Compared With Psychotherapy and Medication Combined

Psychiatrists frequently combine psychotherapy with medication in the treatment of depression in outpatients. The logic is that if each is helpful, the combination may be even more helpful, or helpful in different respects, such as medication alleviating symptoms while psychotherapy enhances social adjustment and alters negative cognitions (Rush & Hollon, 1991). According to Frank, Karp, and Rush (1993), there are few data to guide clinicians regarding when or if to combine drug therapy and psychotherapy in treating depression. Furthermore, Manning and Frances (1990), after reviewing the relevant evidence, concluded that although combining the two did no harm, neither did one enhance the effects of the other.

This area is clearly a controversial one, with different authors or reports coming to different conclusions. The American Psychiatric Association (1993) guidelines, for example, recommended that most patients are best treated with a combination of antidepressants and psychotherapy. Similarly, Thase and Glick (1995), two experts in psychopharmacology, stated that "there is little doubt about the effectiveness of combining pharmacotherapy and the new forms of time-limited psychotherapy in major depression" (p. 201).

On the other hand, the Depression Guideline Panel of the Agency for Health Care Policy and Research (Depression Guideline Panel, 1993) stated that "combined treatment may have no unique advantage for patients with uncomplicated nonchronic major depressive disorder" (p. 41). (They added, however, that the combination may have an advantage for those patients who respond only partially to either treatment alone, those who have a chronic history of depression, or those who recover poorly between episodes.) Persons et al. (1996) argued, on the basis of their review of this literature, that the empirical evidence for combining drugs and psychotherapy provides little support for the American Psychiatric Association recommendations but does support the AHCPR conclusions. They added that psychotherapy alone deserves greater weight in the description of treatment options for major depression in both sets of guidelines. In accordance with this perspective, a recent survey of the satisfaction of a large number of consumers with their outpatient mental health treatment ("Mental Health," 1995; Seligman, 1995) found no difference for any disorder between psychotherapy alone and psychotherapy plus medication.

Medication Compared With Placebo

Greenberg, Bornstein, Greenberg, and Fisher (1992) performed a meta-analysis of 22 studies of antidepressant outcome effects, making a special effort to decrease sources of clinician bias. When a study contains just one drug group compared with a placebo group, it is relatively easy for clinicians to become unblinded (because clients report side effects of the drug) and to rate the drug group higher according to their vested interests. Therefore, Greenberg et al. included only those studies that included *two* antidepressant groups—one given the standard, older drugs (i.e., the tricyclics imipramine or amitriptyline) and the other, the newer drugs (i.e., amoxapine, maprotiline, or trazadone)—along with a placebo control group. Having two drug groups makes it harder for clinicians to identify one of the drug groups as taking their favored medication and to rate it better than the placebo control group.

The effects of antidepressant medication were quite modest and were considerably less than those reported when the identity of those who were taking drugs was more discernible. In fact, client ratings of outcome revealed no advantage for antidepressants when compared with placebo. The authors concluded that nonspecific psychological factors play a large role in determining the outcome of antidepressant treatment.

In a more recent article, Greenberg, Bornstein, Zborowski, Fisher, and Greenberg (1994) conducted a meta-analysis of all the double-blind placebo-controlled efficacy trials of the antidepressant fluoxetine (Prozac). "Results produced a relatively modest overall effect size that was no greater than effect sizes obtained by previous meta-analyses of tricyclic antidepressants" (p. 547). Given the considerable publicity surrounding Prozac, these results are quite sobering. The greater the percentage of patients with side effects, the better the outcome ratings, suggesting to the authors of the study that outcome may be artifactually enhanced as a function of clinicians' and clients' becoming unblinded by clients' experiencing and reporting side effects.

Finally, Sommers-Flanagan and Sommers-Flanagan (1996) reviewed all double-blind placebo-controlled studies of the efficacy of tricyclic antidepressant drugs as well as the group-treatment studies of fluoxetine (Prozac) with depressed youth. Neither type of drug "demonstrated greater efficacy than placebo in alleviating depressive symptoms in children and adolescents, despite the use of research strategies designed to give antidepressants an advantage over placebo" (p. 145).

The combined impact of all these reviews and studies is that antidepressant medication may be overprescribed and that psychotherapy ought to be the initial treatment of choice in most instances of depression (but not all; see Frank et al., 1993), especially for those who wish to pursue it and who are able to work productively in it (Persons et al., 1996). More and better research is needed, however, before definitive conclusions can be drawn, as pointed out by many of the cited authors.

Lest we be misunderstood, none of this is to say that medication is not effective in the treatment of some mental disorders, particularly the more severe ones such as schizophrenia and bipolar disorder. The case example of depression, however, which was widely assumed to be remarkably improved via the physiological effects of medication, should give one pause as to the purely biological effects of taking medication. In this connection, Beitman (in press) has recommended that the meaning of medication to the patient should be incorporated in research designs. Medication can sometimes serve as a blank screen onto which patients project meaning that can illuminate their patterns of emotional, cognitive, and behavioral dysfunction. "Prescription in itself is a dynamic intervention with transference and countertransference implications" (Beitman, Hall, & Woodward, 1992, p. 535). That is, the psychological and not only the biological effect of taking medication merits careful study. In a recent example of this kind of study, Krupnick et al. (1996) found that client contributions to the therapeutic alliance had a significant effect on the alleviation of depression not only for interpersonal and cognitive–behavioral therapies but for active and placebo pharmacotherapy as well.

THE CONTROVERSY OVER EMPIRICALLY VALIDATED TREATMENTS

A committee of the Division of Clinical Psychology of the American Psychological Association (Task Force on Promotion and Dissemination of Psychological Procedures, 1995) recently published a report listing those therapies that they viewed as effective for various psychological disorders, as supported by empirical research. In part, the impetus for this task force was to provide balance to similar reports published by other groups with more of a biomedical orientation (e.g., the American Psychiatric Association; the Agency for Health Care Policy and Research). Insofar as clinical psychology regards itself as a scientific, data-based profession, the efforts of this committee, on the face of it, are unremarkable, even laudatory. The implementation of their goals, however, has been more questionable, and serious criticisms have been raised on political, conceptual, and method-ological grounds.

Political Issues

The political concern is that the list will be used by insurance and managed care companies (that is, third-party payers) to dictate to practitioners what therapies they should use in treating their clients. That is, this list would parallel a medical text or physician's desk reference, which provide fairly circumscribed guidelines prescribing a specific treatment for a specific disorder. For a variety of reasons that we will discuss, many practitioners—and researchers—question the wisdom and the validity of such a way of thinking about meeting the needs of psychotherapy clients. Similarly, the list could lead to an overemphasis on so-called empirically validated treatments (EVTs) in training and even in accreditation of clinical and counseling psychology programs, which would be premature (to say the least), given the current state of knowledge (Shoham, 1996).

Another semipolitical issue is that the large majority of sanctioned therapies are short-term (vs. long-term) and cognitive–behavioral (vs. psychodynamic, experiential, etc.), most probably because the majority of research (especially the narrow band of research that the committee limited itself to) falls within these rubrics. Thus, the list of EVTs contrasts sharply with therapy as it is usually practiced in the field, where most therapists base their work on psychodynamic or integrative approaches (Jensen, Bergin, & Greaves, 1990). In part, this discrepancy reflects the better fit between briefer, more cognitive–behavioral approaches and the research paradigms that EVT research tends to follow; it is *easier* to do such research on those approaches than on longer term and psychodynamic or experiential therapies. As the controversial Division 12 committee has recognized and acknowledged, however, ease of doing efficacy research on a given approach is not the same as that approach's being more effective. Moreover, the very definitions of effectiveness vary among therapeutic approaches, and the criteria often employed in EVT research are covertly value laden, reflecting definitions of therapeutic success more congenial to some approaches than others. Often left out or unable to fit within the research paradigm currently in favor for EVT research are not only such considerations as character change, genuineness, integrity, or depth of feeling (in contrast to a narrow focus on symptoms or readily measurable social behavior) but also a concern (for some psychodynamic and experiential therapists) with the *process* by which change is achieved (Gold, 1995). Within this view, therapy crucially involves such processes as exploration, self-discovery, and learning to be more empathic with oneself and others, all of which contribute significantly to symptom reduction and behavioral change but are not reducible to those dimensions of outcome alone.

EXHIBIT 1
Criteria for Empirically Validated Treatments

Well-Established Treatments

I. At least two good between group design experiments demonstrating efficacy in one or more of the following ways:
   A. Superior to pill or psychological placebo or to another treatment.
   B. Equivalent to an already established treatment in experiments with adequate statistical power (about 30 per group; cf. Kazdin & Bass, 1989).

OR

II. A large series of single case design experiments (n > 9) demonstrating efficacy. These experiments must have:
   A. Used good experimental designs and
   B. Compared the intervention to another treatment as in I.A.

FURTHER CRITERIA FOR BOTH I AND II:

III. Experiments must be conducted with treatment manuals.
IV. Characteristics of the client samples must be clearly specified.
V. Effects must have been demonstrated by at least two different investigators or investigatory teams.

Probably Efficacious Treatments

I. Two experiments showing the treatment is more effective than a waiting-list control group.

OR

II. One or more experiments meeting the Well-Established Treatment Criteria I, III, and IV, but not V.

OR

III. A small series of single case design experiments (n > 3) otherwise meeting Well-Established Treatment Criteria II, III, and IV.

From Chambless et al. (1996), p. 16. Copyright 1996 by the Division of Clinical Psychology, American Psychological Association.

Conceptual Issues

Exhibit 1 presents the criteria asserted by the task force for a therapy to be included in the list of empirically validated treatments (Chambless et al., 1996). One of the most frequent criticisms of these criteria and the findings regarding EVTs (e.g., Stricker, 1996) is that they sacrifice on the altar of scientific exactitude (internal validity) the generalizability or applicability of the results to the world of real practice (external validity). The way this is commonly stated is that the research is largely oriented to *efficacy*, whereas the practitioner is interested in the therapy's *effectiveness* in the field; these are not the same. In conducting efficacy research (which is intended to prove that a treatment works), one seeks patients who (a) fit neatly into one particular *DSM* category, (b) will be treated by manual-driven (i.e., carefully specified) therapies, and (c) are assigned randomly to the different treatment conditions (randomized control trials). To be considered effective, a therapy has to be shown to work in the less controlled environment of everyday clinical practice.

Use of DSM

Practitioners and researchers question the validity and utility of *DSM* diagnoses used in efficacy research, arguing that they do not describe their clients fully or well (e.g., Fensterheim & Raw, 1996). Clients frequently present with a mixture of Axis I and Axis II (personality disorder) diagnoses or with personality and cultural characteristics not captured by *DSM* but that influence the conduct, length, and outcome of treatment (Goldfried & Wolfe, 1996). Practitioners typically cannot be as choosy as researchers about whom they treat, nor do—or should—they limit their treatment efforts to one isolated characteristic of what troubles the individual.

In this vein, critics such as Seligman (1995) have questioned the relevance to practice of efficacy research on pure diagnostic types, on which the list of EVTs largely rests. Responding to this criticism, Wilson (1995) pointed out that it is possible to overstate the uniqueness of patients seen in practice versus those recruited for clinical trials. Drawing on research studies of bulimia nervosa, he argued that patients enrolled in research studies frequently have multiple problems and relatively poor prognoses because controlled clinical research is often their last resort after they have failed to improve in previous attempts at therapy. Nonetheless, even where these multiple problems exist, they do not typically enter into the criteria for success in the so-called EVT studies; the ideology of EVT proponents tends to minimize such assessment.

A variant on the theme of the limitations of *DSM* categorization is that there is a gap between the recommendations stemming from the research findings (e.g., "use interpersonal or cognitive therapy for depression") and the more nuanced nature of clinical problems to which the EVTs are to be applied. Summarizing relevant literature on the psychopathology of depression, Blatt (1995), for example, described two quite different types of problems underlying depression: (a) dependency issues based on a fear of abandonment ("anaclitic") and (b) self-critical thoughts and feelings based on negative self-evaluation and guilt ("introjective"). These subtypes of depression are said to require different treatment approaches. Efficacy research rarely captures such variants of psychopathology or attends sufficiently to individual client characteristics, either of which, it is asserted, can affect both the process of psychotherapy and its outcome (Messer, 1994; Persons, 1991; Raw, 1993). To deal with patients' idiosyncrasies and their multiple problems, practitioners frequently assimilate techniques from other therapies into their favored approach (Jensen et al., 1990; Messer, 1992; Stricker & Gold, 1996; Wachtel, 1991, 1997), and this, too, is not part of EVT research protocols.

Wilson (1995), however, saw a downside to the call for idiographic assessment and assimilative therapy. He questioned whether personal clinical experience, which he claimed guides assimilative integration, will help in selecting and implementing effective techniques. To support this concern, he cited research on confirmatory bias (in which clinicians find relationships among variables on the basis of what they expect to find rather than on what relationships actually exist) and on how the availability of more diagnostic information, while increasing judges' confidence in their decisions, does not affect their accuracy (O'Donahue & Szymanski, 1994). Clinicians, he argued, may tend to be mistakenly guided in their formulation and techniques by the intricacies of a compelling case history rather than by more valid information from well-controlled studies.

Use of Manuals

The requirements the task force has devised for efficacy research and their criteria for EVTs include use of a manual specifying the content of the techniques and the process of implementing them (see Sanderson & Woody, 1995, for a list of available manuals). Among the arguments for using manuals are that one knows better—although certainly not definitively—how clients were treated, which allows for replication of the procedures in a standardized way and checking therapists' adherence to the procedures. Moreover, because a manual provides a careful description of what is involved in conducting a particular therapy, it may be a good training device, and one which can be readily disseminated (Shoham, 1996).

Nevertheless, there are potential pitfalls when using manuals. Goldfried and Wolfe (1996) pointed out that manuals can function as straitjackets, constraining the nature of the therapist's responses too rigidly. In fact, there is research that has confirmed the negative effects of overly close adherence to a manual (e.g., Henry, Strupp, Butler, Schacht, & Binder, 1993). This may occur because manuals pay more attention to techniques than to how these are to be implemented, such as the interpersonal sensitivity and skillful timing of the therapist (e.g., Silverman, 1995). Also, manuals usually focus on the therapist's activities with less regard for patient responses (Stricker, 1996).

Wilson (1995) countered that a well-constructed manual does not neglect the broader aspects of treatment, including the therapeutic relationship or the timing of interventions. He gave examples of how one can set aside the manual for treatment of a specific disorder if other client problems become more pressing (preferably switching to another manual-based treatment) and then return to the original manual when these problems subside. He was not persuaded by any empirical literature that clinical judgments, tailor-made for individual cases, are superior to following an empirically supported, manual-based treatment.

Random Assignment

It has also been pointed out that efficacy research assigns patients randomly to conditions, which does not parallel how patients get assigned in public clinics or how they go about choosing therapists in independent practice. By employing clinical judgment in assigning clinic clients to therapists or by allowing clients to choose therapists based on theoretical orientation or reputation, the probability of a successful outcome may be increased.

Methodological Issues

Wampold (in press), in a sophisticated article on the methodological problems of identifying uniquely efficacious psychotherapies, argues that finding that Therapy A is efficacious does not mean that the results are due to the specified theory or procedures. Rather, because the bulk of extant studies do *not* reveal differences among therapies (e.g., Lambert & Bergin, 1994), it is likely that common factors are at play. "The presence of this alternate explanation detracts from the position of adherents of particular treatments who seek to claim that *the unique components of their treatments led to therapeutic change* and that their treatment should be classified as empirically validated" (p. 15, italics added). He agrees that results *could* be due to specific factors but that comparative studies, on which the list of EVTs depends, are not suitable to answer this question. It is also possible that common factors may function differently in different therapies. For example, therapeutic alliance, a frequently cited common factor, was related to outcome only for one of the four therapies in the National Institute of Mental Health treatment study of depression (Krupnick, Elkin, Collins, Simmens, & Sotsky, 1994).

One upshot of Wampold's argument is that listing a particular treatment as an EVT says nothing about whether it is any better than one of the other bona fide (that is, nonplacebo) treatments, and, on the basis of the empirical literature, the likelihood is very great that it is not. This is one reason that it is inappropriate for EVTs to be imposed as required treatments by third parties. At the same time, the presence of a therapy on the EVT list is some reassurance that something about it is working well, although it is misleading to suggest that only the therapies on the list have been supported by empirical evidence.

Regarding manuals, Wampold notes that even if the elements required by the manual were present in the therapy, this does not say that they were administered skillfully. Nor is there much evidence linking adherence to manuals to therapy outcome. Research, says Wampold, would be better focused on such variables as differences in therapist skill and client characteristics and their relationship to outcome than on comparative outcome studies. Given the lack of differences among bona fide therapies, he concludes that "The criteria presently proposed by Division 12 have the appearance of being scientific, but in fact do not reflect either the logic of efficacy research or the present status of outcome research in psychotherapy" (p. 31).

We agree with these conclusions and, before leaving this topic, will add one final perspective on EVTs to the several that we have described. As already mentioned, the majority of EVTs derive from a behavioral or cognitive framework. It is important to note that theoretical allegiance of the researcher is a strong predictor of the findings of studies claiming differences in efficacy among classes of treatment (e.g., Robinson, Berman, & Neimeyer, 1990; Stiles, Shapiro, & Elliott, 1986). When allegiance is controlled for, differences between treatments typically disappear. This has led some to speculate that a favored therapy is administered more faithfully in such research than is a nonfavored therapy.

MANAGED CARE AND PSYCHOTHERAPY

For most of the history of psychotherapy, psychotherapists were either independent practitioners or staff members of clinics or hospitals that, although they obviously could not be oblivious to matters of cost and funding, had as their mission primarily to provide service. In recent years, however, psychotherapy has increasingly been practiced within the framework of "managed health care," a framework that has greatly reduced therapists' autonomy. Not all therapists have opted to become involved with managed care corporations, but except for those who are relatively well established or who have especially strong convictions, the economic pressures to do so have been very strong. Those who have thus far resisted involvement with managed care are a minority; for most therapists today, at least some portion of their practice—and for many, a very large portion—must be conducted within guidelines set not by their own clinical judgments but by a large corporation external to the clinical enterprise.

What is psychotherapy likely to look like if this trend continues? In part, the effect may be to motivate therapists to achieve their goals more quickly and effectively. The contingencies under which fee-for-service psychotherapy has been practiced did in some ways encourage longer treatments and less immediate concern for promoting concrete changes in the client's life. Patients may similarly benefit from the emphasis on objective and demonstrable results that have been associated with the managed care movement; clinical impressions that "what we are doing helps people" are not the most trustworthy criteria.

Clearly, however, the main force driving the managed care movement is not clinical but economic. It is certainly true that health care in general has become more expensive, both in absolute terms and as a percentage of the gross national product (GNP). Limits on spending for mental health care are part of a larger societal effort to cut the costs of health care in general. Up to a point, that is a reasonable and even salutary goal. Spending more on health care than we need to limits the money available for other purposes. If we can deliver the same level of care more efficiently, all to the good.

Difficult questions arise, however, when we look more closely at what is meant by "efficiency." Efficiency is not a value-free concept. In general medicine, for example, is it wasteful to do an extra thousand tests to detect one treatable cancer? Economists may be able to tell us what the cost (in dollars) is of doing this, but they cannot tell us whether it is worthwhile. And one's perspective on whether or not it is worthwhile will surely be different if one is the CEO of a managed care company that will have to pay for the tests or, if one is the individual whose life is saved. Correspondingly, what is more wasteful—the CEO's huge salary, lavish office, and costly perks, or the medical and psychotherapeutic procedures, the availability of which he or she is being paid to reduce? Values cannot be excluded in considering such questions.

Almost everyone would agree that offering the same level of service for lower cost is an increment in efficiency. But what is meant by same level of service? Advocates for managed care companies claim that they are eliminating only "wasteful" or "ineffective" services, and even that patients are better served by requiring greater documentation of effectiveness before a procedure (medical or psychotherapeutic) is permitted. Up to a point, this is true. There *is* a virtue in accountability, and practitioners do have a stake in proceeding as they always have. Clearly, however, practitioners are not the only ones with biases or a stake in the outcome. Executives and scientists for cigarette manufacturers somehow manage to find data indicating that cigarettes are not harmful, and executives and evaluators for managed care companies are similarly motivated to find that expensive procedures are unnecessary or unproven. As our discussion of postmodernist perspectives has made clear, value-free, objective vantage points for such inquiry are not readily at hand.

To be sure, the biases of clinicians are not a priori or inherently superior to those whose guiding concern is the corporate bottom line. Some way of integrating the competing perspectives that lead to important societal decisions is required. Perhaps at one time practitioners did have too much autonomy, too much unchecked reliance on their clinical judgments alone. It seems to us, however, that the pendulum has swung too far in the opposite direction and that clinical and client welfare decisions have increasingly taken second place to cost cutting as the primary criterion.

It is sometimes pointed out that, as an argument against the narrow cost-cutting philosophy that has at times characterized the managed care movement, the "savings" produced by the stringencies of managed care are often false or misleading. Many studies suggest that money is ultimately *saved* by providing generous mental health services, because a high proportion of (more expensive) medical visits and procedures derive from psychological distress rather than actual medical necessity. This point is well taken, but seems to us insufficient, for it largely accedes to the general notion that our nation is spending too much for medical care. In fact, a good case can be made that this is *not* the case: In part, we are spending a higher proportion of our GNP on medical care because a civilized society *should* do so as its wealth increases. One reason health costs have gone up as a percentage of the GNP is that other costs have gone down; that is, as a product of the economic growth that has taken place in recent decades—even during periods we have experienced as entailing recession or stagnation (see Wachtel, 1989, in press)—it takes a smaller percentage of our earnings to put food on the table, clothes on our backs, and a roof over our heads.

Yes, we are spending more on health care, but if we subtract what we spend on health care, what we are left with is considerably more than what we had before health costs supposedly "exploded." It may be possible to obtain the same level of health care at lesser cost, but before we make cost cutting the driving engine for our decisions, it is worth our asking whether better health care—including greater access to psychotherapy than managed care companies would like to see us have—may not be a more valuable "luxury" than the luxury items we would buy instead if health care costs were in fact driven down.[2] Moreover, even with regard to the mythical "worried well," whom managed care efficiencies are supposed to distinguish from the truly needy in the mental health realm, we might well ask whether a new kitchen, a boat, or a video game would increase their sense of well-being more than psychotherapy. We find it highly unlikely that the answer to that question will turn out to be yes.

---

[2]The rhetoric supporting the reduction of health care costs usually does not point to luxury goods as the alternative. Rather, what is often discussed is more money for education, child nutrition, and the like. The current political and cultural climate, however, makes it very unlikely that these are the areas to which such savings would really be directed.

REFERENCES

Amenson, C. S., & Lewinsohn, P. M. (1981). An investigation into the observed sex differences in prevalence of unipolar depression. *Journal of Abnormal Psychology, 90*, 1–13.

American Psychiatric Association. (1980). *Diagnostic and statistical manual of mental disorders* (3rd ed.). Washington, DC: Author.

American Psychiatric Association. (1993). Practice guidelines for major depressive disorder in adults. *American Journal of Psychiatry, 150*(Suppl. 4), 1–26.

American Psychiatric Association. (1994). *Diagnostic and statistical manual of mental disorders* (4th ed.). Washington, DC: Author.

Antonuccio, D. O., Danton, W. G., & DeNelsky, G. Y. (1995). Psychotherapy versus medication for depression: Challenging the conventional wisdom with data. *Professional Psychology: Research and Practice, 26*, 574–585.

Barber, J. P. (1994). Efficacy of short-term dynamic psychotherapy. *Journal of Psychotherapy Practice and Research, 3*, 108–121.

Barlow, D. H. (Ed.). (1993). *Clinical handbook of psychological disorders* (2nd ed.). New York: Guilford Press.

Beitman, B. D. (in press). Reciprocal relationship between pharmacotherapy and psychotherapy. In H. Levenson, S. F. Butler, & B. D. Beitman, *A concise guide to brief dynamic psychotherapy*. Washington, DC: American Psychiatric Association.

Beitman, B. D., Hall, M. J., & Woodward, B. (1992). Integrating pharmacotherapy and psychotherapy. In J. C. Norcross & M. R. Goldfried (Eds.), *Handbook of psychotherapy integration* (pp. 533–560). New York: Basic Books.

Belar, C. D. (1995). Collaboration in capitated care: Challenges for psychology. *Professional Psychology: Research and Practice, 26*, 139–146.

Bellack, A. S., & Hersen, M. (1993). *Handbook of behavior therapy in the psychiatric setting.* New York: Plenum.

Bellah, R., Madsen, R., Sullivan, W., Swidler, A., & Tipton, S. (1985). *Habits of the heart: Individualism and commitment in American life.* Berkeley, CA: University of California Press.

Bellak, L. (1992). *Handbook of intensive brief and emergency psychotherapy* (2nd ed.). Larchmont, NY: C.P.S. Inc.

Bergman, J. S. (1985). *Fishing for barracuda: Pragmatics of brief systemic therapy.* New York: Norton.

Binder, J. L., & Strupp, H. H. (1991). The Vanderbilt approach to time-limited dynamic psychotherapy. In P. Crits-Christoph & J. P. Barber (Eds.), *Handbook of short-term dynamic psychotherapy* (pp. 137–165). New York: Basic Books.

Blatt, S. J. (1995). The destructiveness of perfectionism: Implications for the treatment of depression. *American Psychologist, 50*, 1003–1020.

Bloom, B. L. (1992). *Planned short-term psychotherapy.* Needham Heights, MA: Allyn & Bacon.

Budman, S. H., & Gurman, A. S. (1988). *Theory and practice of brief therapy*. New York: Guilford Press.

Bugental, J. F. T., & Sterling, M. M. (1995). Existential–humanistic psychotherapy: New perspectives. In A. S. Gurman & S. B. Messer (Eds.), *Essential psychotherapies: Theory and practice* (pp. 226–260). New York: Guilford Press.

Chaiklin, S. (1992). From theory to science and back again: What does postmodern philosophy contribute to psychological science? In S. Kvale (Ed.), *Psychology and postmodernism* (pp. 194–208). Thousand Oaks, CA: Sage.

Chambless, D. L. (1996). In defense of dissemination of empirically supported psychological interventions. *Clinical Psychology: Science and Practice, 3*, 230–235.

Chambless, D. L., Sanderson, W. C., Shoham, V., Bennett Johnson, S., Pope, K. S., Crits-Christoph, P., Baker, M., Johnson, B., Woody, S., Sue, S., Beutler, L., Williams, D. A., & McCurry, S. (1996). An update on empirically validated therapies. *The Clinical Psychologist, 49*, 5–18.

Cushman, P. (1992). Psychology to 1992: A historically situated interpretation. In D. Freedheim (Ed.), *History of psychotherapy: A century of change* (pp. 21–64). Washington, DC: American Psychological Association.

DeBattista, C., & Schatzberg, A. F. (1995). Somatic therapy. In I. D. Glick (Ed.), *Treating depression* (pp. 153–181). San Francisco: Jossey-Bass.

Depression Guideline Panel. (1993). *Clinical practice guideline number 5: Depression in primary care: 2. Treatment of major depression* (AHCPR Publication No. 93-0551). Rockville, MD: U.S. Department of Health and Human Services, Agency for Health Care Policy and Research.

de Shazer, S. (1988). *Clues: Investigating solutions in brief therapy*. New York: Norton.

de Shazer, S., & Molnar, A. (1984). Four useful interventions in brief family therapy. *Journal of Marital and Family Therapy, 10*, 297–304.

Efran, J. S., Lukens, M. D., & Lukens, R. J. (1990). *Language structure and change*. New York: Norton.

Elliott, R., & Greenberg, L. S. (1995). Experiential therapy in practice. In B. Bongar & L. E. Beutler (Eds.), *Comprehensive textbook of psychotherapy* (pp. 123–139). New York: Oxford University Press.

Elliott, R., Stiles, W. B., & Shapiro, D. A. (1993). Are some psychotherapies more equivalent than others? In T. R. Giles (Ed.), *Handbook of effective psychotherapy* (pp. 455–477). New York: Plenum.

Fensterheim, H., & Raw, S. D. (1996). Psychotherapy research is not psychotherapy practice. *Clinical Psychology: Science and Practice, 3*, 168–171.

Fisch, R., Weakland, J. H., & Segal, L. (1983). *The tactics of change: Doing therapy briefly*. San Francisco: Jossey-Bass.

Fishman, S. T., & Lubetkin, B. S. (1983). Office practice of behavior therapy. In M. Hersen (Ed.), *Outpatient behavior therapy: A clinical guide* (pp. 21–41). New York: Grune & Stratton.

Fox, R. E. (1995). The rape of psychotherapy. *Professional Psychology: Research and Practice, 26*, 147–155.

Frank, E., Karp, J. F., & Rush, A. J. (1993). Efficacy of treatments for major depression. *Psychopharmacology Bulletin, 29*, 457–475.

Frank, J. D. (1973). *Persuasion and healing: A comparative study of psychotherapy* (Rev. ed.). Baltimore: Johns Hopkins University Press.

Frankl, V. (1963). *Man's search for meaning: An introduction to logotherapy*. New York: Pocket Books.

Garfield, S. L. (1989). *The practice of brief therapy*. New York: Pergamon Press.

Garske, J. P., & Molteni, A. L. (1985). Brief psychodynamic psychotherapy: An integrative approach. In S. J. Lynn & J. P. Garske (Eds.), *Contemporary psychotherapies* (pp. 69–115). Columbus, OH: Merrill.

Giles, T. R. (Ed.). (1993). *Handbook of effective psychotherapy*. New York: Plenum.

Glick, I. D. (1995). Introduction. In I. D. Glick (Ed.), *Treating depression* (pp. xiii–xviii). San Francisco: Jossey-Bass.

Gold, J. (1995). The place of process-oriented psychotherapies in an outcome-oriented psychology and society. *Applied and Preventive Psychology, 4*, 61–74.

Goldfried, M., & Wolfe, B. (1996). Psychotherapy practice and research: Repairing a strained alliance. *American Psychologist, 51*, 1007–1016.

Greenberg, R. P., Bornstein, R. F., Greenberg, M. D., & Fisher, S. (1992). A meta-analysis of antidepressant outcome under "blinder" conditions. *Journal of Consulting and Clinical Psychology, 60*, 664–669.

Greenberg, R. P., Bornstein, R. F., Zborowski, M. J., Fisher, S., & Greenberg, M. D. (1994). A meta-analysis of fluoxetine outcome in the treatment of depression. *Journal of Nervous and Mental Disease, 182*, 547–551.

Gross, M. L. (1978). *The psychological society: A critical analysis of psychiatry, psychotherapy, psychoanalysis, and the psychological revolution*. New York: Random House.

Gustafson, J. P. (1986). *The complex secret of brief psychotherapy*. New York: Norton.

Harvey, D. (1989). *The condition of postmodernity: An enquiry into the origin of cultural change*. Cambridge, MA: Basil Blackwell.

Hayes, S. C., Follette, W. C., & Follette, V. M. (1995). Behavior therapy: A contextual approach. In A. S. Gurman & S. B. Messer (Eds.), *Essential psychotherapies: Theory and practice* (pp. 128–181). New York: Guilford Press.

Held, B. S. (1995). *Back to reality: A critique of postmodern theory in psychotherapy*. New York: Norton.

Henry, W. P., Strupp, H. H., Butler, S. F., Schacht, T. E., & Binder, J. L. (1993). Effects of training in time-limited dynamic psychotherapy: Changes in therapist behavior. *Journal of Consulting and Clinical Psychology, 61*, 434–440.

Hersen, M. (1983). Perspectives on the practice of outpatient behavior therapy. In M. Hersen (Ed.), *Outpatient behavior therapy: A clinical guide* (pp. 3–20). New York: Grune & Stratton.

Hoffman, L. (1988). A constructivism position for family therapy. *Irish Journal of Psychology, 9,* 110–129.

Horney, K. (1939). *New ways in psychoanalysis.* New York: Norton.

Horowitz, M., Marmar, C., Krupnick, J., Kaltreider, N., Wallerstein, R., & Wilner, N. (1984). *Personality styles and brief psychotherapy.* New York: Basic Books.

Howard, G. S. (1991). Culture tales: A narrative approach to thinking, cross-cultural psychology, and psychotherapy. *American Psychologist, 46,* 187–197.

Hoyt, M. F. (1995). Brief psychotherapies. In A. S. Gurman & S. B. Messer (Eds.), *Essential psychotherapies: Theory and practice* (pp. 441–487). New York: Guilford Press.

Jacoby, R. (1983). *The repression of psychoanalysis.* New York: Basic Books.

Jensen, J. P., Bergin, A. E., & Greaves, D. W. (1990). The meaning of eclecticism: New survey and analysis of components. *Professional Psychology: Research and Practice, 21,* 124–130.

Karasu, T. B. (1986). The specificity versus nonspecificity dilemma: Toward identifying therapeutic change agents. *American Journal of Psychiatry, 143,* 687–695.

Kazdin, A. E., & Bass, D. (1989). Power to detect differences between alternative treatments in comparative psychotherapy outcome research. *Journal of Consulting and Clinical Psychology, 57,* 138–147.

Kessler, R. C., McGonagle, K. A., Zhao, S., Nelson, C. B., Hughes, M., Eshelman, S., Wittchen, H., & Kendler, K. S. (1994). Lifetime and 12-month prevalence of *DSM-III-R* psychiatric disorders in the United States. *Archives of General Psychiatry, 51,* 8–19.

Kohlenberg, R. J., & Tsai, M. (1991). *Functional analytic psychotherapy.* New York: Plenum Press.

Koss, M. P., & Shiang, J. (1994). Research on brief psychotherapy. In A. E. Bergin & S. L. Garfield (Eds.), *Handbook of psychotherapy and behavior change* (pp. 664–700). New York: Wiley.

Krupnick, J. L., Elkin, I., Collins, J., Simmens, S., & Sotsky, S. M. (1994). Therapeutic alliance and clinical outcome in the National Institute of Mental Health Treatment of Depression Collaborative Research Program. *Psychotherapy, 31,* 28–35.

Krupnick, J. L., Sotsky, S. M., Simmens, S., Moyer, J., Elkin, I., Watkins, J., & Pilkonis, P. A. (1996). The role of the therapeutic alliance in psychotherapy and pharmacotherapy outcome: Findings in the National Institute of Mental Health Treatment of Depression Collaborative Research Program. *Journal of Consulting and Clinical Psychology, 64,* 532–539.

Lambert, M. J., & Bergin, A. E. (1994). The effectiveness of psychotherapy. In A. E. Bergin & S. L. Garfield (Eds.), *Handbook of psychotherapy and behavior change* (4th ed., pp. 143–189). New York: Wiley.

Lasch, C. (1979). *The culture of narcissism.* New York: Norton.

Lazarus, A. A. (1997). *Brief but comprehensive psychotherapy.* New York: Springer.

Leary, K. (1994). Psychoanalytic "problems" and postmodern "solutions." *Psychoanalytic Quarterly, 63*, 433–465.

Lehman, A. K., & Salovey, P. (1990). An introduction to cognitive–behavior therapy. In R. A. Wells & V. J. Giannetti (Eds.), *Handbook of the brief psychotherapies* (pp. 239–259). New York: Plenum.

London, P. (1986). *The modes and morals of psychotherapy* (2nd ed.). Washington, DC: Hemisphere.

Luborsky, L., Diguer, L., Luborsky, E., Singer, B., Dickter, D., & Schmidt, K. A. (1993). The efficacy of dynamic psychotherapies: Is it true that "Everyone has won and all must have prizes"? In N. E. Miller, L. Luborsky, J. P. Barber, & J. P. Docherty (Eds.), *Psychodynamic treatment research* (pp. 497–516). New York: Basic Books.

Luborsky, L., & Mark, D. (1991). Short-term supportive–expressive psychoanalytic psychotherapy. In P. Crits-Christoph & J. P. Barber (Eds.), *Handbook of short-term dynamic psychotherapy* (pp. 110–136). New York: Basic Books.

Mahoney, M. J. (1991). *Human change processes: The scientific foundations of psychotherapy*. New York: Basic Books.

Mahoney, M. J. (1993). (Ed.). Special section: Recent developments in cognitive and constructivist psychotherapies. *Journal of Consulting and Clinical Psychology, 61*, 187–275.

Mahoney, M. J. (Ed.). (1995a). *Cognitive and constructive psychotherapies*. New York: Springer.

Mahoney, M. J. (1995b). Theoretical developments in the cognitive and constructive psychotherapies. In M. J. Mahoney (Ed.), *Cognitive and constructive psychotherapies* (pp. 3–19). New York: Springer.

Mahoney, M. J., & Craine, M. H. (1991). The changing beliefs of psychotherapy experts. *Journal of Psychotherapy Integration, 1*, 207–221.

Mann, J. (1992). Time-limited psychotherapy. In P. Crits-Christoph & J. P. Barber (Eds.), *Handbook of short-term dynamic psychotherapy* (pp. 17–44). New York: Basic Books.

Manning, D. W., & Frances, A. J. (1990). Combined therapy for depression: Critical review of the literature. In D. W. Manning & A. J. Frances (Eds.), *Combined pharmacotherapy and psychotherapy for depression* (pp. 3–33). Washington, DC: American Psychiatric Association.

Maslow, A. H. (1968). *Toward a psychology of being*. Princeton: Van Nostrand.

May, R. (1961). *Existential psychology*. New York: Random House.

McCullough, L. (1993). An anxiety-reduction modification of short-term dynamic psychotherapy (STDP): A theoretical "melting pot" of treatment techniques. In G. Stricker & J. R. Gold (Eds.), *Comprehensive handbook of psychotherapy integration* (pp. 139–149). New York: Plenum.

Meichenbaum, D. (1993). Changing conceptions of cognitive behavior modification: Retrospect and prospect. *Journal of Consulting and Clinical Psychology, 61*, 202–204.

Mental health: Does therapy help? (1995, November). *Consumer Reports*, pp. 734–739.

Messer, S. B. (1992). A critical examination of belief structures in integrative and eclectic psychotherapy. In J. C. Norcross & M. R. Goldfried (Eds.), *Handbook of psychotherapy integration* (pp. 130–165). New York: Basic Books.

Messer, S. B. (1994). Adapting psychotherapy outcome research to clinical reality: A response to Wolfe. *Journal of Psychotherapy Integration, 4,* 280–282.

Messer, S. B., Sass, L. A., & Woolfolk, R. L. (Eds.). (1988). *Hermeneutics and psychological theory: Interpretive perspectives on personality, psychopathology, and psychotherapy.* New Brunswick, NJ: Rutgers University Press.

Messer, S. B., & Warren, C. S. (1990). Personality change and psychotherapy. In L. A. Pervin (Ed.), *Handbook of personality: Theory and research* (pp. 371–398). New York: Guilford Press.

Messer, S. B., & Warren, C. S. (1995). *Models of brief psychotherapy: A comparative approach.* New York: Guilford Press.

Moretti, M. M., Feldman, L. A., & Shaw, B. F. (1990). Cognitive therapy: Current issues in theory and practice. In R. A. Wells & V. J. Giannetti (Eds.), *Handbook of the brief psychotherapies* (pp. 217–237). New York: Plenum.

Nathan, P. E., & Gorman, J. M. (Eds.). (in press). *Psychotherapies and drugs that work: A review of the outcome studies.* New York: Oxford University Press.

Neimeyer, R. A. (1993). An appraisal of constructivist psychotherapies. *Journal of Consulting and Clinical Psychology, 61,* 221–234.

Neimeyer, R. A., & Harter, S. (1988). Facilitating individual change in personal construct therapy. In D. G. Dunnette (Ed.), *Working with people* (pp. 174–185). London: Routledge & Kegan Paul.

O'Donahue, W., & Szymanski, J. (1994). How to win friends and not influence clients: Popular but problematic ideas that impair treatment decisions. *The Behavior Therapist, 17,* 30–33.

Olfson, M., & Pincus, H. A. (1994). Outpatient psychotherapy in the United States: II. Patterns of utilization. *American Journal of Psychiatry, 151,* 1289–1294.

Omer, H., & Strenger, C. (1992). The pluralist revolution: From the one true meaning to an infinity of constructed ones. *Psychotherapy, 29,* 253–261.

Orlinsky, D. E., Grawe, K., & Parks, B. P. (1994). Process and outcome in psychotherapy—*nach einmal.* In A. E. Bergin & S. L. Garfield (Eds.), *Handbook of psychotherapy and behavior change* (4th ed., pp. 270–376). New York: Wiley.

Orlinsky, D. E., & Howard, K. I. (1986). Process and outcome in psychotherapy. In S. L. Garfield & A. E. Bergin (Eds.), *Handbook of psychotherapy and behavior change* (3rd ed., pp. 311–381). New York: Wiley.

Parry, A. (1991). A universe of stories. *Family Process, 30,* 37–54.

Persons, J. B. (1991). Psychotherapy outcome studies do not accurately represent current models of psychotherapy: A proposed remedy. *American Psychologist, 46,* 99–106.

Persons, J. B., Thase, M. E., & Crits-Christoph, P. (1996). The role of psycho-therapy in the treatment of depression. *Archives of General Psychiatry, 53,* 283–290.

Phillips, E. L. (1985). *Psychotherapy revised: New frontiers in research and practice.* Hillsdale, NJ: Erlbaum.

Polkinghorne, D. E. (1992). Postmodern epistemology of practice. In S. Kvale (Ed.), *Psychology and postmodernism* (pp. 146–165). Thousand Oaks, CA: Sage.

Polster, E., & Polster, M. (1973). *Gestalt therapy integrated.* New York: Brunner/Mazel.

Raw, S. (1993). Does psychotherapy research teach us anything about psycho-therapy? *The Behavior Therapist, 16,* 75–76.

Reich, W. (1933). *Character analysis.* New York: Farrar, Straus & Giroux.

Reid, W. J. (1990). An integrative model for short-term treatment. In R. A. Wells & V. J. Giannetti (Eds.), *Handbook of the brief psychotherapies* (pp. 55–77). New York: Plenum.

Ricoeur, P. (1981). *Hermeneutics and the human sciences.* Cambridge, England: Cambridge University Press.

Rieff, P. (1966). *The triumph of the therapeutic.* New York: Harper & Row.

Robins, C. J., & Hayes, A. M. (1993). An appraisal of cognitive therapy. *Journal of Consulting and Clinical Psychology, 61,* 205–214.

Robinson, L. A., Berman, J. S., & Neimeyer, R. A. (1990). Psychotherapy for the treatment of depression: A comprehensive review of controlled outcome research. *Psychological Bulletin 108,* 30–49.

Rorty, R. (1989). *Contingency, irony, and solidarity.* Cambridge, England: Cambridge University Press.

Rosenau, P. M. (1992). *Post-modernism and the social sciences: Insights, inroads, and intrusions.* Princeton, NJ: Princeton University Press.

Rush, A. J., & Hollon, S. D. (1991). Depression. In B. D. Beitman & G. L. Klerman (Eds.), *Integrating pharmacotherapy and psychotherapy.* Washington, DC: American Psychiatric Association.

Safran, J. D., & Messer, S. B. (1997). Psychotherapy integration: A postmodern critique. *Clinical Psychology: Science and Practice, 4,* 142–154.

Sanderson, W. C., & Woody, S. R. (Eds.). (1995). Manuals for empirically vali-dated treatments. *The Clinical Psychologist, 48,* 7–11.

Sass, L. A. (1992). The epic of disbelief: The postmodern turn in contemporary psychoanalysis. In S. Kvale (Ed.), *Psychology and postmodernism* (pp. 166–182). Thousand Oaks, CA: Sage.

Schafer, R. (1983). *The analytic attitude.* New York: Basic Books.

Schafer, R. (1992). *Retelling a life: Narratives and dialogue in psychoanalysis.* New York: Basic Books.

Segraves, R. T. (1990). Short-term marital therapies. In R. A. Wells & V. J. Giannetti (Eds.), *Handbook of the brief psychotherapies* (pp. 437–459). New York: Plenum.

Seligman, M. E. P. (1995). The effectiveness of psychotherapy: The Consumer Reports study. *American Psychologist, 50,* 965–974.

Settle, E. C. (1992). Antidepressant side effects: Issues and options [Monograph]. *Journal of Clinical Psychiatry, 10,* 48–61.

Shapiro, D. (1965). *Neurotic styles.* New York: Basic Books.

Shapiro, D. (1981). *Autonomy and rigid character.* New York: Basic Books.

Shapiro, D. (1989). *Psychotherapy of neurotic character.* New York: Basic Books.

Shoham, V. (1996, April). *The promise (?) of empirically validated psychotherapy integration.* Paper presented at the annual meeting of the Society for the Exploration of Psychotherapy Integration, Berkeley, CA.

Silverman, W. H. (1995, August). *Cookbooks, manuals, and paint-by-numbers: Psychotherapy in the 1990s.* Paper presented at the annual convention of the American Psychological Association, New York, NY.

Sledge, W. H., Moras, K., Hartley, D., & Levine, M. (1990). Effect of time-limited psychotherapy on patient dropout rates. *American Journal of Psychiatry, 147,* 1341–1347.

Sommers-Flanagan, J., & Sommers-Flanagan, R. (1996). Efficacy of antidepressant medication with depressed youth: What psychologists should know. *Professional Psychology: Research and Practice, 27,* 145–153.

Spence, D. P. (1982). *Narrative truth and historical truth.* New York: Norton.

Stiles, W. B., Shapiro, D. A., & Elliott, R. (1986). Are all psychotherapies equivalent? *American Psychologist, 41,* 165–180.

Strenger, C., & Omer, H. (1992). Pluralistic criteria for psychotherapy: An alternative to sectarianism, anarchy, and utopian integration. *American Journal of Psychotherapy, 46,* 111–130.

Stricker, G. (1996, April). *Empirically validated treatment, psychotherapy manuals, and psychotherapy integration.* Paper presented at the annual meeting of the Society for the Exploration of Psychotherapy Integration, Berkeley, CA.

Stricker, G., & Gold, J. R. (1996). Psychotherapy integration: An assimilative, psychodynamic approach. *Clinical Psychology: Science and Practice, 3,* 47–58.

Task Force on Promotion and Dissemination of Psychological Procedures. (1995). Training in and dissemination of empirically validated psychological treatments. *The Clinical Psychologist, 48,* 3–23.

Thase, M. E., & Glick, I. D. (1995). Combined treatment. In I. D. Glick (Ed.), *Treating depression* (pp. 183–208). San Francisco: Jossey-Bass.

von Glasersfeld, E. (1984). An introduction to radical constructivism. In P. Watzlawick (Ed.), *The invented reality* (pp. 17–40). New York: Norton.

Wachtel, P. L. (1989). *The poverty of affluence: A psychological portrait of the American way of life.* Philadelphia: New Society Publishers.

Wachtel, P. L. (1991). From eclecticism to synthesis: Toward a more seamless psychotherapeutic integration. *Journal of Psychotherapy Integration, 1,* 43–54.

Wachtel, P. L. (1997). *Psychoanalysis, behavior therapy, and the relational world.* Washington, DC: American Psychological Association.

Wachtel, P. L. (in press). Overconsumption: Lessons from psychology for politics and economics. In D. Bell, L. Fawcett, R. Keil, & P. Penz (Eds.), *Political ecology: Global and local perspectives.* New York: Routledge.

Wampold, B. E. (in press). Methodological problems in identifying efficacious psychotherapies. *Psychotherapy Research.*

Weiss, J., & Sampson, H. (1986). *The psychoanalytic process.* New York: Guilford Press.

Wells, R. A., & Giannetti, V. J. (Eds.). (1990). *Handbook of the brief psychotherapies.* New York: Plenum.

Wexler, B. E., & Cicchetti, D. V. (1992). The outpatient treatment of depression: Implications of outcome research for clinical practice. *Journal of Nervous and Mental Disease, 180,* 277–286.

White, M. (1993). Deconstruction and therapy. In S. Gilligan & R. Price (Eds.), *Therapeutic conversations* (pp. 22–61). New York: Norton.

White, M., & Epston, D. (1990). *Narrative means to therapeutic ends.* New York: Norton.

Wilson, G. T. (1981). Behavior therapy as a short-term therapeutic approach. In S. H. Budman (Ed.), *Forms of brief therapy* (pp. 131–166). New York: Guilford Press.

Wilson, G. T. (1995). Empirically validated treatments as a basis for clinical practice: Problems and prospects. In S. Hayes, V. M. Follette, R. M. Dawes, & K. E. Grady (Eds.), *Scientific standards of psychological practice: Issues and recommendations* (pp. 163–196). Reno, NV: Context Press.

Woolfolk, R. L., Sass, L. A., & Messer, S. B. (1988). Introduction to hermeneutics. In S. B. Messer, L. A. Sass, & R. L. Woolfolk (Eds.), *Hermeneutics and psychological theory* (pp. 2–26). New Brunswick, NJ: Rutgers University Press.

Yalom, I. (1981). *Existential psychotherapy.* New York: Basic Books.

2

PSYCHOANALYTIC THEORIES OF PSYCHOTHERAPY

DAVID L. WOLITZKY AND MORRIS N. EAGLE

To a significant extent, the history of theoretical developments in psychoanalysis can be understood as a series of successive reactions to Freudian drive theory, with its emphasis on libidinal and aggressive wishes as the primary motives for behavior. Thus, following Pine (1990), the main foci of theorizing in psychoanalysis subsequent to drive theory—ego, object, and self—can be meaningfully viewed as entailing modification or abandonment of that drive theory. These theoretical developments gave greater primacy to interpersonal and social determinants of personality development and psychopathology.

The extension of drive theory to include ego psychological considerations was begun quite early by Freud himself with the concept of defense (Freud, 1894/1962), continued with his paper, "On Narcissism" (1914/1957a) where consideration of self and object and of pre-oedipal periods of development came to the fore, and culminated with the exposition of

This chapter is a revised and expanded version of "Psychoanalytic Theories of Psychotherapy," by M. N. Eagle and D. L. Wolitzky, 1992, in *History of Psychotherapy: A Century of Change* (pp. 109–158), edited by D. K. Freedheim, Washington, DC: American Psychological Association.

the tripartite, structural theory of the mind (Freud, 1923/1961, 1926/1959). Generally speaking, the period from 1900 to 1914 can be considered the era of "id psychology" (partly initiated by Freud's [1897/1954c] abandonment of the seduction theory) and the period from 1914 to 1939 can be regarded as the era in which "ego psychology" was developed (A. Freud, 1936; S. Freud, 1923/1961, 1926/1959; Hartmann, 1939/1958). In the United States, the three decades from 1940 to 1970 were strongly dominated by psychoanalytic ego psychology. Although much of their work was roughly contemporaneous with the literature on ego psychology, it is mainly in the past 20 years that the contibutions of the British object relations theorists (Balint, 1965, 1968; Fairbairn, 1941, 1952; Guntrip, 1969; Klein, 1948; Winnicott, 1958) have heavily influenced American psychoanalysts. In the past two decades, Kohut's (1971, 1977, 1984) presentation of self psychology has also had a profound impact on the theory and practice of psychoanalysis. Many psychoanalysts (e.g., Pine, 1990; Silverman, 1986) believe that each of these perspectives is vital to a comprehensive and clinically useful account of human experience. In fact, at no time in the history of psychoanalysis have we seen as great a theoretical diversity and pluralism within what might be called the mainstream or common ground of psychoanalytic thought (Wallerstein, 1988a, 1990b). Given this current theoretical pluralism, it is not accurate to talk of *the* psychoanalytic theory of psychopathology or of treatment.

The topics and authors covered in this chapter will generally follow the historical sequence we have briefly outlined. First, we will discuss traditional Freudian drive theory, followed by a section on its ego psychological extensions. We will then present object relations theory, interpersonal theory (which, as Guntrip [1969] suggests, can be viewed as an American version of object relations theory), self psychology, and a sampling of other recent developments (by Mahler, Kernberg, and Weiss and Sampson). Roughly parallel with these theoretical changes, conceptions of therapeutic action have shifted from a primary and near-exclusive emphasis on insight into unconscious conflicts (primarily oedipal ones) to an increasing stress on relationship factors in treatment and their efficacy in ameliorating the maladaptive impact of early defects, deficits, and developmental arrests. This latter emphasis reflects a shift from the drive discharge model to the person point of view (Gill, 1983), or what Greenberg and Mitchell (1983) called the "drive/structure" versus the "relational/structure" model. Others (e.g., Modell, 1984) have referred to the same distinction as being between a "one-person" versus a "two-person" psychology.

These models of therapeutic action focus mainly on psychoanalysis and, by extension and modification, to psychoanalytic psychotherapy. The issue of the similarities and differences between these two forms of treatment has been a topic of continuing discussion and lively debate (Gill, 1954, 1984; Wallerstein, 1983, 1986, 1990a). The distinction between them is generally drawn less sharply today than it has been in the past, and for the purposes of this chapter we will treat them as more overlapping than different.[1]

FREUDIAN DRIVE THEORY

Roots in Prepsychoanalytic "Dynamic Psychiatry"

One of the core set of ideas that Freud inherited from the prepsychoanalytic thinking of Charcot (1882) and Janet (1889, quoted in Ellenberger, 1970) was that certain mental contents (i.e., ideas, memories, thoughts) cannot be integrated into one's dominant self-organization and therefore exist outside normal consciousness; furthermore, by virtue of their "underground," unintegrated status, these contents exert powerful pathogenic influences upon one's behavior, thoughts, and feelings.

It is clear that Freud picked up the preceding set of ideas and soon gave them a special psychoanalytic cast. In his early work, however, his position was quite similar to Charcot's and Janet's. He identified the associative isolation of certain ideas and traumas as the proximate causes of hysteria. In *Studies on Hysteria* (Breuer & Freud, 1895/1955), affect and the beginnings of a more distinctively psychoanalytic formulation enter the explanatory picture and are added to the associative isolation account. Every experience, according to Freud, is accompanied by a "quota of affect" which is normally discharged through conscious experience (including labelling and talking about the experience) and is worn away through associative connection with other mental contents. Freud also tells us that it is especially difficult for ideas accompanied by large amounts of affect to achieve associative connection with other ideas. Because traumas are, by definition, affectively intense experiences, they present a special challenge for the tasks of discharge and associative connection. In hysteria, neither of these tasks is carried out effectively, with the result that the affect remains in a "strangulated" state, and the memory of the experience is cut off from associative connection with other mental contents. The ultimate result of affect strangulation and associative isolation is the development of hysterical symptoms.

It follows quite logically that perhaps the symptoms can be removed through *abreacting* (so to speak, unstrangulating) the affect by an adequate response, including a verbal response, and by bringing the memory of the

---

[1]Note that we will not include separate discussions of the theories of Adler, Jung, Horney, and Fromm. This will undoubtedly disappoint some readers, but any chapter must recognize realistic limitations. Our decision regarding which material to cover and which to omit is based on limitations on our knowledge and areas of competence and on our judgment of what appear to be the main areas of interest in a large part of the current psychological and psychoanalytic communities.

trauma into associative connection with other ideas. As Breuer and Freud (1895/1955, p. 17) put it, psychotherapy allows "strangulated affect [of the idea] to find a way out through speech; and also subjects the idea to associative correction by introducing it into normal consciousness."

Much of the early history of psychoanalytic theories of treatment can be understood as being organized around the question of how best to bring traumatic memories and their accompanying affect into conscious experience and how best to permit them to achieve expression and associative connection with the other ideas of normal consciousness. Of course, once free association became the standard technique for psychoanalytic treatment, the primary purposes for which it was being employed had changed; the earlier goals of abreaction of strangulated affect and "associative correction" had been replaced by later process goals such as making the unconscious conscious and insight. However, one can see the rather direct line from the earlier concepts of strangulated affect and associative isolation, embedded in prepsychoanalytic theory, to the more modern conception of psychoanalytic treatment.[2] Furthermore, these earlier ideas were never entirely relinquished, but were instead absorbed and integrated into later formulations.

In "The Neuro-Psychoses of Defense," Freud (1894/1962) explicitly and specifically disputed Janet's claim that hysterical symptoms are a consequence of the hysteric's innate weakness in the capacity for psychic synthesis. Although he continued to employ such terms as "splitting of consciousness" and "the formation of separate psychical groups," he maintained that splitting of consciousness is not the result of innate weakness, but "*of an act of will on the part of the patient* [Freud's emphasis]; that is to say, it is initiated by an effort of will whose motive can be specified" (p. 46). In *defense hysteria*, which is caused by "an incompatibility . . . [in the patient's] ideational life," the ego is faced with an experience, idea, or feeling "which aroused such a distressing affect that the subject decided to forget about it because he had no confidence in his power to resolve the contradiction between that incompatible idea and his ego by means of thought activity" (1894/1962, p. 47). Freud observes that in females it is mainly sexual experiences and sensations that constitute the source of incompatible ideas.

One finds in this 1894 paper, then, the beginnings of a distinctively psychoanalytic formulation of hysteria. Hysterical symptoms are held to be, not a matter of constitutional weakness, but *motivated* expulsion (forgetting) of distressing material from consciousness. Here are the essential elements of the core idea of repression, which Freud later called "the cornerstone on which the whole structure of psycho-analysis rests" (Freud, 1914/1957b, p. 16).

---

[2]As Freud (Breuer & Freud, 1895/1955) acknowledges, Breuer and his patient, Anna O., are due a great deal of credit for "discovering" free association and the "talking cure."

What are the implications for treatment of this shift from a prepsychoanalytic to a distinctively psychoanalytic theory of psychopathology? To the extent that the expulsion of certain mental contents from consciousness (which, it will be recalled, was held to be fraught with pathogenic significance) is not a matter of a constitutionally based inability to integrate expelled ideas or to discharge large quotas of affect, but, rather, is motivated (by such motives as the desire to avoid pain or to protect one's picture of oneself), it follows that mere mechanical abreaction of affect or associative connection of ideas will not suffice as therapeutic goals. Rather, the therapist will have to deal with the motives for repression themselves, with such questions as why the patient is so intent on expelling a particular set of mental contents from consciousness and with the general issue of the relation between these mental contents and the rest of the personality.

This seemingly simple, but in fact critical, explanatory shift from constitutional weakness to motivated expulsion opens the door to a whole host of therapeutic implications. One must now deal not only with the patient's motives for expulsion as well as the expulsion itself, but also with what the patient is passionately trying to hide from himself or herself, with the self-image the patient is desperately trying to protect, and with the relation between the patient's neurotic symptoms and the expelled ideas. Also, it can be seen that simply bringing expelled memories and ideas to consciousness through hypnosis (or through suggestion or pressure techniques) is not likely to be therapeutically adequate. For if the patient is actively trying to hide certain memories, ideas, and desires from himself or herself, then it is necessary to come to terms with the act of hiding, with the reasons for hiding, and with the aspects of self that he or she is trying to hide and protect. In short, one must deal, above all, with the unconscious personal meanings of the patient's memories, ideas, and desires in their relation to unconscious conflicts.

PSYCHOANALYTIC EGO PSYCHOLOGY

The concept of unconscious conflict is central to the traditional Freudian model and to its ego-psychological extensions by Hartmann (1939/1958, 1964); Hartmann, Kris, and Lowenstein (1946); Rapaport (in Gill, 1967); Arlow and Brenner (1964); and many others. The components of an intrapsychic, unconscious conflict are an unacceptable or threatening wish (or so-called drive derivative), an anticipation of danger or anxiety associated with awareness of and expression of the wish, defenses against the wish, and a compromise between the wish and the defense. The compromise may be more or less adaptive and more or less ego-alien. It may take the form of a symptom, a character trait or style, or an inhibition (Freud, 1926/1959).

Signals of anxiety trigger the activation of defense, currently understood to include not only the classic mechanisms of defense (such as projection, denial, repression, reaction formation, etc.), but any aspect of ego functioning that can be used for defensive purposes (Brenner, 1982). The primary anxieties or danger situations of childhood are loss of the object, loss of the object's love, castration anxiety, and super ego anxiety (guilt). The failure of signal anxiety to activate adequate defenses leads to traumatic anxiety and an extreme state of unpleasure in which the ego is totally overwhelmed and rendered helpless. It is this traumatic situation of overstimulation that some (e.g., A. Freud, 1936; Waelder, 1960) regard as the basic, bedrock anxiety (cf. Hurvich, 1985, on annihilation anxiety). Brenner (1982) has extended this formulation to include depressive affect as a trigger for defense.

As is well known, a core contribution of psychoanalytic ego psychology was an emphasis on the autonomy of certain ego functions such as memory, thinking, and intelligence. What Hartmann (1939/1958) calls "primary autonomy" refers to the claim that certain ego functions have an inborn basis that, in an average expectable environment, will develop relatively independently of the vicissitudes of drives. "Secondary autonomy" refers to the fact that, although certain ego functions may have originally developed in the context of conflict and may have originally served defensive functions, they may subsequently develop a secondary autonomy in the sense of becoming relatively conflict-free and carried out for their own sake. For example, although intellectualization may have originally served mainly defensive purposes, intellectual activities and pursuits may achieve a relatively conflict-free and autonomous status. (Hartmann's concept of secondary autonomy is very similar to Allport's (1950) concept of "functional autonomy.")

In short, one of the main clinical and theoretical contributions of psychoanalytic ego psychology was to soften and modulate the sweeping claim of Freudian instinct theory that virtually all behavior was energized by, and directly or indirectly, overtly or covertly, in the service of, drive gratification. Following the theoretical emendations of ego psychology, there was now room in psychoanalytic theory for behavior and functions relatively autonomous of the vicissitudes of drive. At the same time, one of the main treatment implications of ego psychology is that, because patients can be unaware of both their wishes and their defenses against them, a central focus of interpretation is on the patient's defensive strategies.

For patients with neurotic personality organization, repressed conflicts involving libidinal and aggressive drive derivatives are understood in terms of Freud's structural, tripartite theory of id, ego, and superego and its ego-psychological extensions by A. Freud (1936), Hartmann (1939/1958), Arlow and Brenner (1964), and others. The most common neurotic conflict is considered to be an unresolved oedipal struggle. Unconscious conflicts over the gratification of unacceptable oedipal longings are expressed not only in symptomatic behavior, but also in the maladaptive, self-punitive characterological patterns to which this conflict can give rise (e.g., those "wrecked by success," work inhibitions). For more detailed accounts of basic psychoanalytic theory, see Brenner (1982), Meissner (1980), and Waelder (1960).

The theoretical understanding and treatment of more severe forms of psychopathology (e.g., borderline conditions) is a matter of controversy. Some clinicians (Abend, Porder, & Willick, 1983; Arlow & Brenner, 1964) rely primarily on traditional psychoanalytic ego psychology in understanding these patients while other clinicians (see Greenberg & Mitchell, 1983) minimize the importance of oedipal and pre-oedipal conflicts and emphasize the role of ego defects and deficits. Opinions regarding the proper therapeutic approach to borderline patients range from support (Knight, 1953; Zetzel, 1971) to standard psychoanalysis (Segal, 1967), with some clinicians modifying their standard psychoanalytic technique at the start of treatment but allowing it to evolve into psychoanalysis in later stages (Kernberg, 1975, 1976).

We should note that, although the theory of psychoanalytic treatment was built on the model of the moderately neurotic, oedipally conflicted patient, analysts have always treated a wide range of psychopathology. Freud had distinguished among psychoneuroses, actual neuroses, and narcissistic neuroses, believing that only the first group was suitable for analytic treatment. Several of Freud's own cases, however, were clearly beyond the neurotic range, and other psychoanalytic pioneers (e.g., Abraham, 1927) treated very disturbed patients.

In the early 1950s one began to see more frequent, explicit discussions of the so-called widening scope (Stone, 1954) of psychoanalytic treatment, that is, the treatment of more severely disturbed patients. The adaptations of classical technique considered necessary to treat such patients have been a frequent topic of discussion for the past 40 years. Alterations in the basic analytic stance have been discussed under the heading of "parameters," a term introduced by Eissler (1953) to refer to a deviation from sole reliance on interpretation and strict adherence to the principle of abstinence. Such deviations were considered necessary for patients who could not tolerate the rigors of the standard psychoanalytic situation due to ego defects and deficits originating in traumas of early childhood.

Treatment Implications of Traditional Freudian Theory

The main features of the traditional psychoanalytic theory of treatment can be summarized as follows:

1. The patient is suffering from pathological compromise formations (e.g., symptoms and maladaptive character traits) based on repressed conflicts.
2. These conflicts are based on instinctual wishes originating in early childhood, especially oedipal wishes, and they are subject to fixation and regression. They become expressed in the context of the therapeutic relationship, particularly in the form of resistance and transference.
3. The emergence of the patient's readiness for transference reactions is facilitated when the treatment situation is unstructured and fosters free associations that will allow the unconscious, unresolved conflicts to be expressed via dreams, memories, reactions to the therapist, and so on.
4. The analyst listens with free-floating or evenly hovering attention and a neutral (i.e., nonbiased), nonjudgmental, empathic attitude, which facilitates the "therapeutic alliance" — that is, the patient's desire to cooperate despite conflicting attitudes about wanting to recover (Curtis, 1980; Greenson, 1965).
5. The analyst generally adheres to the principle of abstinence. That is, deliberate transference gratifications normally are withheld. The process proceeds on the principle of optimal frustration on the grounds that this approach will most efficaciously stimulate the patient's conflicts and fantasies and center them on the person of the analyst. It will help the patient to experience and to understand the intrapsychic basis of his or her interpersonal problems.
6. These conditions promote the development of an analyzable transference, defined and discussed later. However, deviations from these conditions (parameters, per Eissler, 1953) may be required in order to maintain the therapeutic alliance under various circumstances.
7. The analyst's interpretations of the patient's unconscious conflicts and resistances, as they are manifested in the transference, will yield insights into the origin and nature of these conflicts and into the anxieties associated with them.
8. Through the repetitive experience and interpretation of longstanding conflicts, in the context of affectively vivid "here-and-now" transference reactions, the patient gradually "works through" (Greenson, 1978a) his or her difficulties by shifting to more adaptive emotional and behavioral patterns inside and outside the treatment situation. Repeated insight into and increased tolerance and acceptance of disavowed, split-off, anxiety-laden wishes, conflicts, and fantasies (in Freud's

terminology, the id or drive derivatives) allows them to become more integrated into the ego, particularly when the insights are accompanied by behavioral changes that convince patients that they will not be overwhelmed by their fears. This goal is expressed in Freud's (1933/1964b, p. 80) famous epigram, "Where id was, there shall ego be," an alteration of the earlier goal, based on the topographic model, of making the unconscious conscious (Freud, 1905/1953, p. 266).

There are other important, noninterpretive ingredients in the therapeutic relationship that are considered to facilitate change (Stone, 1981). Although these allegedly curative factors are considered important by many analysts who regard themselves as Freudians, these factors nonetheless take us beyond the traditional Freudian account with its overriding emphasis on insight as the primary curative agent (Blum, 1979). Freudian clinicians who also find aspects of an object relations or a self-psychology approach useful tend, relatively speaking, to deemphasize insight in favor of the other factors or conditions. We shall list these elements here and explicate them later in the chapter in our discussion of different authors who represent more recent trends in the history of psychoanalysis.

1. The actual experience and internalization (Loewald, 1960) of a new, benign relationship with a nonjudgmental parental figure helps reduce the harshness of the patient's superego. This element was discussed by Strachey as early as 1934.
2. The patient has an opportunity to form a new identification; the patient can form an identification with the analyst's approach (i.e., with the analytic attitude) and with the analyst's conception of the patient's potential for growth (Loewald, 1960) and can introject and later identify with the analyst as a person.
3. The analyst and the analyst–patient relationship can provide a safe, supportive base, a "holding environment" (Modell, 1976; Winnicott, 1958) that can foster the patient's progressive urges toward greater autonomy and individuation (as against regressive longings to merge and to cling to infantile dependence).
4. In Kohut's view (1984), the analyst serves a critical function by allowing the patient to use him or her to aid in the patient's efforts to regulate his or her own tension states. The therapist's empathy, as experienced by the patient, is held to be a vital element in this process and in therapeutic change in general. This component is stressed particularly by Kohut (1984) and his followers, who regard feeling that one is un-

derstood (and its positive implications for the experience of affirmed selfhood) as the ultimately curative factor, the one that gives insight its impact.

Variations in the way analysts apply these principles are mainly a function of their theoretical persuasion and the type of patient they are treating. These differences allow three main generalizations: (a) Among sicker patients, especially those manifesting borderline and narcissistic pathology, the various ways in which the therapeutic relationship can help are considered relatively more important than insight. However, among healthier patients (i.e., those with neuroses), the relationship factors are seen as secondary, as primarily a background to insight which retains its earlier preeminence as the mutative therapeutic agent. (b) Regardless of levels and types of pathology, Freudian clinicians accord greater weight to insight into unconscious conflicts, while analysts espousing an object relations or self psychology view place relatively more stress on aspects of the therapeutic relationship that they claim have curative properties in their own right (e.g., by facilitating the belated acquisition of a more cohesive sense of self). (c) Those who stress insight tend to see oedipal conflicts as primary, whereas those who focus more on the relationship concentrate more on pre-oedipal developmental arrests and worry less about issues of transference gratification.

When such transference gratifications are mutative in their own right, when they facilitate interpretive work which the patient could not otherwise tolerate, and when they fail to facilitate the treatment in any manner or impede it are questions to which we do not have answers. These are also questions that go back at least as far as Ferenczi and Rank's (1956) controversial experiments with "active techniques." The generalizations just offered, of course, fail to do justice to important nuances discernible among those who share similar views, but they do seem to us accurate in their broad outlines. It should also be noted that, even within the Freudian tradition, the relative emphasis on insight versus relationship factors has varied over the years. (See Friedman, 1978, for an excellent account of trends in the psychoanalytic theory of treatment.)

A complete statement of the necessary and sufficient conditions for therapeutic personality change as a function of psychoanalytic treatment would have to include a specification of the patient and therapist variables (and their interaction) which facilitate or impede improvement. It would, of course, also have to address what is meant by change, particularly "structural" change (Wallerstein, 1988b; Weinshel, 1988). (For the most recent attempts to conceptualize the psychoanalytic process, see the special issue of The Psychoanalytic Quarterly, Erle, 1990.)

Having presented general principles and concepts of psychoanalytic psychotherapy, we will now elaborate on some of the key aspects of the traditional Freudian treatment model. An oft-quoted definition of classical psychoanalysis is that given by Gill (1954, p. 775), who stated, "Psychoanalysis is that technique which, employed by a *neutral* analyst, results in the development of a *regressive transference neurosis* and the ultimate resolution of this neurosis by techniques of *interpretation* alone" [emphasis added; original entirely in italics]. Let us consider each of these concepts in turn.

Neutrality, Empathy, Countertransference, and the Analytic Attitude

As indicated previously, *neutrality* means that the analyst takes a position equidistant from the various components of the patient's conflicts. Neutral also means nonjudgmental; it does not mean indifferent or uncaring. It requires that analysts' countertransference reactions not interfere with their understanding of the patients' conflicts nor with their interpretations and other interventions.

The concept of technical neutrality is closely linked to Freud's (1912/1958, 1937/1954a) proscription that the analysis be conducted in a state of *abstinence*. This technical precept has been the subject of lengthy, often passionate debate in the history of psychoanalytic treatment. The rule of abstinence refers to the idea that the analyst should not deliberately provide the patient with any gratifications other than those intrinsic to the analytic process. Abstinence protects analysts from their proclivity to change the analytic relationship into an ordinary relationship, including sexual contact with patients; fosters analytic neutrality by avoidance of selective transference gratifications; facilitates the patient's motivation for analytic work; and highlights in the transference the ways that patients deal with past and current conflicts by centering them regressively on the person of the analyst. Abstinence avoids the partial solutions to be gained from direct gratification of unmet needs and wishes. Such gratification would be a temporary expedient; it would impede insight and the possibility of structural change. This is not to say that the patient experiences no gratification in the relationship. Rather, as already indicated, it is the inherent features of the relationship (i.e., the analyst's listening, nonjudgmental attitude, the regularity and dependability of the relationship, etc.) which provide significant and necessary support.

The so-called classical analytic attitude that we have been describing (Stone, 1981) also requires analysts to retain relative anonymity in an effort not to "contaminate" the transference. As has been noted, primarily by Stone (1961), there is a danger that this attitude could be overdone (e.g., a callous, aloof, arbitrary, withholding attitude). Such a stance clearly includes the risk of inducing an iatrogenic regression. This attitude is not inherent in Freud's theory of treatment, but is a caricature of it.

The notions of technical neutrality and the rule of abstinence are closely linked to the concepts of empathy, countertransference, and the analytic attitude. Analysts listen with an attitude of "evenly hovering attention" as a way of apprehending the unconscious fantasies and conflicts within the patient. They want to enter the patient's frame of reference in order to understand in a cognitive and affective manner, through partial, transient identifications, what it feels like to be the patient and how the patient deals with psychic conflicts. This is what is meant by *empathy* (Greenson, 1978b; Schafer, 1959; Schwaber, 1981).

Ideally, psychoanalysts are participant-observers (see Sullivan, 1953). By effecting an oscillating split in their ego between an experiential mode and an observational mode (observing their own experience, that of the patient, and their interaction), they engage in a "regression in the service of the ego" (Kris, 1952) similar to that which they hope to encourage in the patient. In order to accomplish this difficult task, analysts monitor the presence and potential intrusiveness of their own feelings, attitudes, and conflicts to keep them from interfering in their ability to understand the patient and to offer interventions. This is referred to as the detection and management of the *countertransference*. The training analysis is said to aid in this process, supplemented by the analyst's ongoing self-analysis. This is a constant challenge, and success is variable. Countertransference reactions are considered a vital source of information about the psychology of the patient. However, undetected, and therefore unmanaged, countertransference can seriously impede the treatment. In fact, Langs (1982) boldly asserts that this is the primary cause of treatment failure.

In summary, a neutral analyst, as defined in the preceding text, is one who listens with evenly hovering attention, recognizes and tries to control personal biases, applies the rule of abstinence with appropriate tact and dosage, is genuinely nonjudgmental, safeguards the "working alliance" (Greenson, 1965), recognizes his or her stimulus value to the patient (including behaviors which are a standard part of the technique, such as silence), and creates an atmosphere of safety for the patient. These are some of the main components of what is referred to as the analytic attitude (Schafer, 1983) or the basic analytic stance and are regarded as necessary conditions for a favorable therapeutic outcome.

Transference

Transference, according to Greenson's commonly cited definition, is the

> ... experiencing of impulses, feelings, fantasies, attitudes, and defenses with respect to a person in the present which do not appropriately fit that person but are a repetition of responses originating in regard to significant persons of early childhood, unconsciously displaced onto persons in the present. The two outstanding characteris-

tics of transference phenomena are (1) it is an indiscriminate, non-selective repetition of the past, and (2) it ignores or distorts reality. It is inappropriate. (Greenson & Wexler, 1969, p. 28)

There are problems with this definition. First, the patient may be aware, even before an interpretation, of certain displaced transference feelings and attitudes. Second, not all transference reactions are repetitions of the past in any simple, literal, or isomorphic sense. To take one obvious example, patients often engage in attempts at role reversal. In an effort to master an experience which they endured passively in childhood, they try to make the analyst the victim and seek the role of the active, dominant partner. For instance, a patient who was constantly kept waiting by his mother and who, in virtually every way, felt coerced by her, kept his analyst waiting by frequently showing up late for sessions.

With these qualifications, traditional Freudian analysts would accept Greenson's definition of transference. It should be noted, however, that in actual practice, what one regards as transference is a matter of judgment and theoretical preference. For example, a not particularly intense or inappropriate erotic wish directed toward the analyst is apt to be regarded as transference, although it does not meet the definitional criteria indicated above (Schimek, 1983).

The "regressive transference neurosis," now considered unnecessary by some (e.g., Gill, 1984) and a misleading term by others (e.g., Brenner, 1982), refers to the intense, emotional revival in the relationship with the analyst of important aspects of the infantile neurosis. As Macalpine (1950) observed, the transference neurosis is not simply due to the patient's readiness to develop transferences. It develops by virtue of the features of the psychoanalytic situation which encourage it—the freedom to free associate, the supine position, the absence of visual cues from the analyst, the analyst's relative silence, the frequency of visits, and the open-endedness of the treatment which give rise to a sense of timelessness. As Gill (1984) and others (Cooper, 1987, 1989; Modell, 1989) have noted, this formulation is based on a one-person, as opposed to a two-person, psychology and thereby fails to consider adequately the ways in which the analyst's personality shapes the patient's transference.

Although we cannot take the space to discuss in detail the various altered conceptions of Freud's views of transference, we will briefly present and comment on Gill's (1982) position because it has received considerable attention in the past decade and will cite Cooper's (1987) overview of the changing conception of transference.

Gill's Conception of Transference

In recent years, the traditional view of transference has been severely criticized by Gill (1982) who objects to the conceptualization of transference as a distortion because it implies an assumption of arbitrary power which places the analyst in the position of the final arbiter of reality. Gill argues for a relativistic position in which the analyst does not judge what is distorted or inappropriate, but adopts a perspectival view of reality and attempts to understand how the patient's behaviors constitute plausible reactions to aspects of the analyst's real behavior. Transference for Gill is very broadly conceived and seems to be virtually synonymous with the patient's experience of the relationship. His view is a welcome corrective to the tendency of some analysts to lose sight of the fact that what they regard as normative analytic behaviors (e.g., silence, offering interpretations) are not simply neutral, technical devices but have meanings to patients in light of their own experiences.

Related Conceptions of Transference

Cooper (1987) presents a useful overview of changes in the conceptualization of transference by contrasting what he calls the *historical* and the *modernist* views of transference, acknowledging that this distinction is oversimplified. The historical model which refers to Freud's view of the transference, expressed previously in Greenson's definition, is that it is the reproduction of essential elements of important, early relationships in the relationship with the analyst (as well as with others in the patient's current life). Insofar as the patient constructs his relationship to the analyst on the basis of these past prototypes, ". . . what he takes to be new in real life is a reflection of the past" (Freud, 1940/1964a, p. 177). From this perspective, the value of interpreting the transference neurosis is that it allows the patient to "reexperience and undo the partially encapsulated, one might say 'toxic,' neurotogenic early history" (Cooper, 1987, p. 81). In this view, the "here-and-now" transference is the royal road to the infantile neurosis. The affective immediacy of the here-and-now transference is vital because, as Freud (1912/1958, p. 108) noted, one cannot slay anyone *in absentia* or *in effigie*.

The modernist view, according to Cooper (1987, p. 81), "regards the transference as a new experience rather than an enactment of an old one." In this view, the purpose of transference interpretation "is to help the patient to see, in the intensity of the transference, the aims, character, and mode of his current wishes and expectations as influenced by the past." Resolving the here-and-now transference is tantamount to dissipating the neurosis (see Gill, 1984).

Whether these are matters of emphasis or they constitute a new paradigm is a matter of debate. Our inclination, following Wallerstein (1984), is to regard these conceptions of transference not as basic theoretical differences but as differences of emphasis, with the so-called modernist view allowing clinicians more technical latitude in working with more disturbed patients.

Interpretation

We come now to the third main element in Gill's (1954, p. 775) definition, "... by techniques of interpretation alone." The emphasis on interpretation recognizes that there are many other verbal and nonverbal interventions employed by the analyst (cf. Bibring, 1954). These interventions (e.g., confrontations, clarifications, questions, etc.) are regarded as preparatory to interpretations and as not having any mutative effect of their own. Broadly speaking, the term, interpretation, is used to encompass not only the attribution of meanings to discrete aspects of the patient's experience and behavior but also constructions which entail a more comprehensive account of aspects of the patient's history, an evolving narrative of the patient's neurosis.

According to the theory, the most effective interpretations are those which offered, with suitable tact, dosage, and timing, focus on the transference and its links to the patient's current and past unconscious conflicts and fantasies. In other words, a focus on the dynamics of the here-and-now transference, coupled with reconstructions of the dynamic and genetic basis (the "then-and-there") of the current transference, facilitates mutative insights that lead to the resolution of the transference. Some clinicians (e.g., Limentani, 1975) assert that interpretations other than of the transference are, at best, a waste of time, if not actually deleterious, while others (e.g., Blum, 1983) claim that extra-transference interpretations have a definite place in treatment, not only as preparation for transference interpretations but in their own right.

An important point to be made here is that a primary feature of psychoanalysis (as opposed to psychoanalytic psychotherapy and, even more so, other therapies) is the minimization of suggestion through deliberate manipulation of the transference (as in the case of Alexander's [1948] corrective emotional experience) or by more subtle directives. In this context, it is worth noting Stein's (1981) concern that the so-called unobjectionable positive transference (Freud, 1912/1958) often is a tacit, tenacious form of resistance. The patient's contribution to the "working alliance" (Greenson, 1965) has to be scrutinized for indications of excessive compliance in accepting the analyst's interpretations.

In fact, the major focus of psychoanalytic interpretation is on the patient's resistance. Resistance is a central concept in the theory of treatment. It can be defined, following Gill (1982), as defense expressed in the transference, both as resistance to the awareness of transference and to its resolution (Gill, 1982).

Resistance, though it often has had a pejorative connotation (Schafer, 1983), is a necessary and inevitable aspect of treatment. As Freud (1912/1958, p. 103) put it, "The resistance accompanies the treatment step by step. Every single association, every act of the person under treatment must reckon with the resistance and represents a compromise between the forces that are striving towards recovery and the opposing ones." Resistance thus includes opposition to free association, to the procedures of analysis, to recall, to insight, and to change. The sources and forms of resistance have been written about extensively, and resistances have been classified in various ways (A. Freud, 1936; S. Freud, 1926/1959, 1937/1954a; Greenson, 1967; Reich, 1949; Wachtel, 1982). According to Freud (1937/1954a), the causes and motives for resistance include the constitutional strength of the drives, particularly aggression, impaired ego plasticity, the "adhesiveness of the libido," the so-called negative therapeutic reaction and its connection to unconscious guilt, the repetition compulsion, castration anxiety and passive/homosexual wishes in men, and penis envy in women.

The therapist's task in a traditional analysis, and to a lesser extent in psychoanalytic psychotherapy, is to clarify and interpret that the patient is resisting, how and what the patient is resisting, and why. A detailed discussion of the typical clinical signs of resistance and the techniques for dealing with it can be found in Greenson (1967) and Wachtel (1982).

Psychoanalysis and Psychoanalytic Psychotherapy (Expressive and Supportive)

In the past we have seen passionate debates (Alexander, 1954; Bibring, 1954; Gill, 1954; Rangell, 1954; Stone, 1954) regarding whether we should or can make a clear distinction between psychoanalysis and psychoanalytic psychotherapy. As noted earlier, psychoanalysis and psychoanalytic psychotherapy, particularly of the expressive variety, currently are considered by most clinicians as overlapping rather than as sharply distinct from one another, as was the case 40 years ago when classical analysts were at great pains to distance their therapeutic approach from Alexander's (1948) corrective emotional experience. Nonetheless, there still is considerable controversy concerning the proper criteria for what is to be rightly regarded as psychoanalysis. Some clinicians stress the criteria of frequency of sessions, the use of the couch, and free association. We agree with Gill (1982, 1984) who, among others, emphasizes the centrality of a focus on the transference as the defining, intrinsic characteristic of psychoanalysis and psychoanalytic psychotherapy, as distinct from other forms of psychotherapy.

It has long been believed, if not always explicitly asserted, that, all things being equal, psychoanalysis is the treatment of choice. Expressive therapy and particularly supportive therapy have been regarded as less effective. Yet, Freud (1919/1955) had long ago recognized the necessity of combining the "pure gold" of psychoanalysis with the "copper" of direct suggestion in order to create a therapy of wider applicability. For many years the clinical rule of thumb has been to offer as much support as is needed but as little as necessary (Luborsky, 1984; Wallerstein, 1986). More recently, it has been recognized that different forms of psychoanalytically informed treatment appear suitable for different kinds of patients.

The basis for the alleged superiority of psychoanalysis is that it would more likely lead to so-called structural change by virtue of the insights it could offer into the patient's conflictual and defensive behavior. Structural change, a thorny concept which we cannot discuss here, implies greater stability, generalizability, and resistance to new stressors (Wallerstein, 1988b; Weinshel, 1988). However, if structural change can occur on grounds other than insight (e.g., the partial undoing of ego deficits as a result of a benign, new therapeutic relationship), the preeminence of insight as the curative agent is thrown into question, as is the alleged superiority of psychoanalysis compared with psychoanalytic psychotherapy. This is what Wallerstein (1986) had to conclude after a very detailed, long-term study of patients in the Menninger Foundation's Psychotherapy Research Project. (For the most recent, comprehensive account of the history of this issue see Wallerstein, 1990a.)

OBJECT RELATIONS THEORY

Just as ego psychology established relative autonomy for the domain of ego functions, so similarly did object relations theory attempt to establish autonomy for the domain of object relations. An assertion of the autonomy of object relations is most succinctly expressed in Fairbairn's (1952) claim that "libido is object-seeking, not pleasure-seeking." Just as Hartmann (1939/1958) argued that certain ego functions are primary and not a secondary derivative of drive gratification, so Fairbairn claimed that our interest in and attachment to objects have a primary inborn basis and are not secondary derivatives of the libidinal (and aggressive) drive-gratifying functions that objects serve. This basic claim is most fully articulated and elaborated in Bowlby's (1969) attachment theory.

Although many of the writings of ego psychology and object relations theory were roughly contemporaneous, it is meaningful to think of object relations theory *following* ego psychology in at least two senses: First, as far as North American psychoanalysis is concerned, the popularity and influence of ideas taken from object relations theory (or the so-called English School) followed the assimilation of ego psychology into psychoanalytic theory. Second, compared with ego psychology, object relations theory represents a more radical break with and transformation of traditional psychoanalytic theory.

As noted earlier, virtually every theoretical development in psychoanalytic theory entails either a substantial modification or outright rejection of Freudian instinct theory. This is also the case for object relations theory, the subject of this section.

The historical and theoretical origins of object relations theory or the English School are clear. They began with Ferenczi and include Hermann, the Balints, and Melanie Klein (who, collectively, can be referred to as the "Budapest School"). Mainly through Klein's direct influence, these origins found expression in the work of Fairbairn, Winnicott, and Guntrip. Bowlby's attachment theory, although it has developed along somewhat independent lines and was strongly influenced by ethological theory, can also broadly be seen as an expression of object relations theory.

Although Klein's (1948) work strongly influenced the English School, Kleinian theory and Kleinian adherents have retained a sufficiently separate identity to be distinguished from the English School. In addition, there are central aspects of Kleinian theory (primarily those having to do with Klein's instinct theory) that are rejected by the object relations theorists. Hence, while acknowledging the influence of Klein, object relations theory will be discussed separately from Kleinian theory. Finally, we want to note that we will be dealing mainly with the work of Fairbairn (1941, 1952) as representative of object relations theory because he presents the most systematic and comprehensive account of object relations theory.

Basic Tenets of Object Relations Theory

From a broad, theoretical perspective, what most clearly distinguishes object relations theory from Freudian theory is captured by Fairbairn's (1952) dictum that "libido is object seeking, not pleasure seeking" (p. 82) (and by Balint's [1965] concept of "primary object-love"). In this dictum Fairbairn is disputing Freud's interrelated claims that (a) behavior is primarily motivated by the push for sexual and aggressive instinctual gratification and discharge and (b) our interest in and relation to objects is based primarily on the object's role in serving instinctual discharge.

With regard to our relation to actual external objects, the issue seems quite clear. The evidence strongly suggests that we are inherently object-seeking creatures and that our interest in objects is not a secondary derivative of some presumably more basic drive (Eagle, 1987). However, a significant part of object relations theory deals with *internalized objects* and *internalized object relations*. In contrast to Freud's psychic world, which is populated by unconscious wishes and defenses against those wishes, Fairbairn's psychic world is populated by internalized objects and internalized object relations.

The essential idea that is conveyed by the concept of internalized object (as well as by the concept of introject) is that aspects of the other (prohibitions, evaluations, characteristics, etc.) are taken in *but are not fully metabolized and integrated* into one's self-organization, with the result that these aspects are experienced as felt "presences" (Schafer, 1968) rather than as natural and unquestioned parts of oneself. As Fairbairn informs us, the notion of internalized object can be traced to Freud's concept of the superego. According to that concept, punishments, prohibitions, evaluations, rules, and so on, whose original source was external objects, are eventually internalized as a psychic structure. However, frequently the internalization is not complete, as expressed in the common tendency to experience and describe the internalized prohibitions as a homunculus standing outside oneself and observing or directing what one does and in such locutions as "my conscience tells me . . ." (rather than "I believe . . ."). The incomplete internalization suggests that the superego often has the status of an introject rather than of a fully and smoothly assimilated identification.

As a rather clear example of what we believe is meant by the concept of internalized object, we cite a patient who, before each occasion of sexual intercourse, would experience the obsessive thought, "If they could see me now." The patient reported that the "they" were her parents and also that the feeling accompanying the thought was one of defiance. Thus, to each sexual occasion, this patient brought representations of her parents and played out her internal object relations with them. Further, the ego-alien, obsessive quality of the thought—it is there almost as a felt presence— bespeaks the unintegrated status of these internal representations. The thought is her thought, but it is unbidden, as if it had a life of its own.

According to Fairbairn, objects are internalized for two basic reasons: (a) Incorporation and internalization are natural psychological modes for the young infant; and (b) the infant assumes and takes in the badness of the environment in order to make the latter more benevolent and controllable. As Fairbairn (1952, p. 66) stated, "It is better to be a sinner in a world ruled by God than to live in a world ruled by the Devil." Implied in this latter point is the idea that it is mainly under the impact of negative depriving and frustrating experiences that objects are internalized.

Fairbairn's (1952) concepts of internalized objects and internalized object relations are embedded in a complex and somewhat arcane metapsychological structure of splits in the object correlated with splits in the ego. There is not sufficient space to cover this material (and we are far from certain that it repays the efforts necessary to understand it).

Implications of Object Relations Theory for Treatment

Before discussing the implications of object relations theory for psychotherapy, one general comment that also applies to other theoretical developments in psychoanalysis is in order. Because most of the writing in this area is highly theoretical, it is often difficult to determine what therapists of different theoretical persuasions actually do and to what extent and in what specific ways their therapeutic activities differ from each other (Sandler, 1983). Detailed clinical data (as would be available, for example, from tape recorded sessions) are simply not available. The result is that, although we know a great deal about Fairbairn's theory, we know very little about how and to what extent his theory was expressed and implemented in his treatment. What we can do, however, is note some implications of object relations theory for the practice of psychotherapy.

1. To the extent that interpretation continues to be a main activity of object relations therapists, one would certainly expect that the *content* of interpretations would tend to differ from those provided by traditional analysts.[3] One would expect, for example, much less emphasis on sexual and aggressive wishes and on oedipal issues and correspondingly greater attention to so-called pre-oedipal issues and to issues such as early infant–mother interaction, relationships with internalized objects, merging fantasies, fears of loss of an object world, and feelings of ego weakness and fragility.

   As a specific example of differences in the content of interpretations, contrast Fairbairn's (1952) understanding of agoraphobia with that of traditional theory. According to the latter, the *fear* of walking in the streets is related to the unconscious *wish* to street-walk. That is, unconscious prostitution wishes and fantasies are held to be a key element underlying the agoraphobic symptom (Freud, 1954b). One would expect that the content of interpretations given to patients in treatment by a traditional analyst would reflect this particular way of understanding the nature of the agoraphobic syndrome. Contrast this interpretation of agoraphobia with Fairbairn's (1952, p. 43) claim that it represents a conflict between "the regressive lure of identification" and "the progressive urge of separation." In short, Fairbairn understands agoraphobia, not in terms of conflict around sexual wishes, but in terms of what Mahler (1968) would refer to as a separation-individuation inner conflict. (See Eagle, 1979, for a comparison of traditional and object relational conceptions of phobias.)
2. Along with other clinical and theoretical developments in

---

[3]We are aware that interpretations offered by therapists of any theoretical persuasion should really be determined by the patient's productions rather than by theoretical predilection. However, it is clear that the therapist's theoretical orientation does influence his or her interpretations, particularly when patients' productions are susceptible to different interpretations, as they very often are. There is a critical issue of the degree to which the therapist's theoretical point of view is *imposed* upon the patient. (See Peterfreund, 1983, for a discussion of "stereotyped" versus "heuristic" therapists.)

psychoanalytic theory, object relations theory deemphasizes a number of therapeutic factors that are central to traditional theory—for example, insight, making the unconscious conscious, transforming id into ego, and analysis of the transference—and instead places primary emphasis on the therapeutic relationship which is understood as a therapeutic agent in its own right. This focus on the relationship is summed up by Fairbairn's statement that an overriding goal of treatment is to replace the "bad object" with a "good object."

Although he does not employ the same terminology, Fairbairn clearly suggests that, to use Alexander and French's (1946) term, "corrective emotional experiences" with the therapist are the vehicle for change. However, much remains unclear in this formulation. Although ideas such as replacing bad objects with good objects are evocative and one has a general sense of what they mean, they are far from precise. And Fairbairn does not attempt to make them more precise.

3. As noted above, the therapeutic goal of "dissolution," or what Fairbairn (1952) refers to as "exorcism," of internalized objects is quite consistent with his object relations theory. This goal, more than any other, highlights important theoretical differences between object relations theory and traditional theory. According to traditional theory, one central goal of treatment is to claim or own what was disclaimed and disowned, as expressed in Freud's (1933/1964b) dictum, "Where id was, there ego should be" (p. 80). One way of putting this is to say that one makes personal and internal what was defensively expelled and made impersonal and external (see Eagle, 1987). A central therapeutic goal in object relations theory is precisely the opposite—to render impersonal and external (that is, to exorcise) that which, under the impact of trauma, was improperly and defensively *internalized*. One wants to reduce the degree to which one's psychic life is dominated by these internalized objects.

There is a parallel between the therapeutic goal in traditional theory of softening the harshness of the superego (Strachey, 1934) and the goal of exorcising internalized objects. The superego is the one psychic structure in traditional theory that is based entirely on internalizing that which was initially and inherently external. In a certain sense the idea of softening the harshness of the superego can be understood as generally synonymous with the notion of exorcising the internal saboteur. That is to say, in contrast to a mature conscience, a primitive and harsh superego can be understood as an internalized object (or archaic introject) that needs to be exorcised or, at least, tempered and modulated.

In certain respects, however, the idea of exorcising internalized objects goes further than softening the superego. What the former suggests on the clinical-behavioral level is that patients are driven by unconscious fantasies in which the exciting object will finally be available, loving, and accepting rather than elusive and rejecting. Thus, to say that these internalized objects need to be exorcised seems to us to be tantamount to the relinquishment of the above fantasy. As Fairbairn (1952, p. 73) stated, the difficult task in treatment is "the overcoming of the patient's devotion to his repressed [internalized] object." Evidence for this sort of change would be reflected in such areas as alterations in object choice (e.g., interest in actual caring and available objects), different patterns in intimate interpersonal relations (mainly a modulation of the tendency to induce and create interactions in which the object combines the lure of excitement with rejection) and, of course, changes in transference reactions. Indeed, the main vehicle for such changes would likely consist in a living out and a persistent examination of the ways in which the patient "transforms" the therapist and experiences him or her as an exciting and rejecting object.

Note that different theoretical language notwithstanding, the object relations approach does not seem very different from the traditional and familiar idea of analysis of the transference. Even the idea of experiencing the therapist as an exciting and rejecting object may not be too different, in practice, from the traditional conception of transferring one's instinctual wishes on to the therapist. Certainly, the idea of internalizing the other as an object with exciting and rejecting (read also, forbidden) features is consistent with an oedipal account in which enticement, excitement, rejection, and prohibition are all components of the object as well as of the oedipal triangle.

4. Object relations theorists place a great deal of emphasis on the role of *regression* in treatment. It is true that in classical Freudian treatment, partial and circumscribed regression is induced by the analytic setting. However, in object relations theory, particularly in the writings of Winnicott (1958) and Guntrip (1969), regression has a different and more directly therapeutic role. Both Winnicott and Guntrip refer to the importance of the patient returning to an earlier point at

which psychological development went askew and to that point at which development turned in the direction of a "false self" (Winnicott, 1958). The basic idea behind these various formulations seems to be that under the impact of trauma, certain defensive and defective structures (e.g., false self, a pseudo-adult self masking an underlying ego weakness) developed that are at the heart of the patient's pathology. According to this view, what needs to be accomplished in treatment is a regression to the point at which these structures developed and a resumption of developmental growth along new and better pathways.

The basic idea that successful treatment makes possible a return to some earlier point of trauma at which development began its pathological course and that one can resume development on a new basis characterizes not only object relations theory, but also, as we shall see, self psychology. As is true of other ideas in object relations theory, it is evocative and even compelling. It certainly feeds into fantasies of a rebirth and of starting all over again. However, it is also a very vague idea and does not tell us very much regarding the specific processes and the specific changes that are involved in successful treatment.

INTERPERSONAL PSYCHOANALYSIS

As noted earlier, Greenberg and Mitchell (1983) distinguish two main paradigms in psychoanalytic thinking. One is Freud's drive theory (which they refer to as the drive/structure model) in which "all facets of personality and psychopathology are understood essentially as a function, a derivative, of drives and their transformations" (p. 3). In this view, object relations are drive vicissitudes. The other model is one they term a "relational/structure" model in which "relations with others constitute the fundamental building blocks of mental life. The creation, or re-creation, of specific modes of relatedness with others replaces drive discharge as the force motivating human behavior" (p. 3).

Interpersonal psychoanalysis refers to theories which subscribe to the relational/structure model. Historically, the main proponents of this model have been Sullivan (1953), Horney (1945, 1950), Fromm-Reichmann (1950), and Fromm (1941). More recent, research-oriented versions of interpersonal psychoanalytic psychotherapy have been presented by Strupp and his colleagues (Strupp & Binder, 1984) and by Klerman and his coworkers (Klerman, Rounsaville, Chevron, & Weissman, 1984). Space limitations preclude an account of all of these authors' theories of treatment.

We shall restrict ourselves to the work of Sullivan because he was the originator of, and the most ardent, influential spokesperson for, this point of view. As noted earlier, Sullivan's (1953) theory can be seen as the first important American version of an object relations theory.

Sullivan's Theory

Central to Sullivan's conception of personality development and psychopathology is his overriding emphasis on the interpersonal field beginning with the infant–mother dyad. The organism has two main needs—biological satisfaction and psychological and interpersonal security—the latter playing a vital role in personality development and psychopathology. In Sullivan's (1953) theory, anxiety originates from a disturbance in the emotional connection ("empathic linkage") between mother and infant. Anxiety in the mother induces anxiety in the infant. The reduction of this anxiety generates a feeling of interpersonal security. The relative freedom from anxiety is crucially dependent on parental tenderness and empathy. Infants learn to regulate their conscious experience, their behavior, and their developing conceptions of themselves in accord with an anxiety gradient in order to avoid anxiety and thereby maximize their feelings of security. In this process, experiences linked with a reduction of anxiety and, therefore, a sense of "good mother" become internalized and represented as "good me." Experiences associated with "bad mother" (i.e., disapproving or anxious mother) lead to the conceptions of "bad me" and "not me," the latter referring to disowned, unintegrated realms of experience associated with truly intense anxiety.

Without being explicit about it, Sullivan appears to have a two-factor theory of anxiety induction (anxiety in the mother and maternal disapproval). The developing child constructs a "self-system" which assesses the probability of anxiety (similar to Freud's notion of signal anxiety) and tries to avoid it through the triggering of "security operations" (analogous to defenses in Freud's theory, although Levenson [1985, p. 50] points out what is defended against is a "... contagious terror set in motion *by the other person*" rather than by unconscious drive derivatives). It is in this sense that the self is said to be constructed from "reflected appraisals." A detailed account of these and other important aspects of the theory can be found in Sullivan (1953). See Zucker (1989) for a statement of the key premises of interpersonal theory.

Treatment Implications of Sullivan's Theory

As far as we can tell there has been no systematic development of Sullivan's theory and therefore no coherent, current core of interpersonal theory shared by analysts who trace their lineage to Sullivan. It is, therefore, not possible to present *the* interpersonal theory of treatment. Although they rely on Sullivan as their theoretical common ground, many contemporary interpersonal psychoanalysts depart from him in their clinical approach. We cannot hope to do justice to the considerable range of theory and technique within contemporary interpersonal psychoanalysis. As Levenson (1985, p. 53) points out, a wide variety of positions exist "under the loose rubric of 'interpersonal.'" He notes that "Interpersonalists range from extreme interactionalists through viewpoints largely indistinguishable from object-relations theorists, especially Winnicott and Fairbairn, and even on to some closet 1930s Freudians." We can, however, indicate the main orienting assumptions and treatment implications stemming from a Sullivanian perspective.

Perhaps the main bond that unites Sullivanians is their emphasis on the concept of the participant-observer (Witenberg, 1974). Recall that Sullivan (1953, pp. 110–111) defined personality as "the relatively enduring pattern of recurrent interpersonal situations which characterize a human life." According to Sullivan, it is misleading to talk about personality traits or states as though they were self-contained, intrapsychic entities. Nursing at the breast is first and foremost an interpersonal situation for both mother and infant. Applied to the analytic situation, the idea of a participant-observer has come to mean (Levenson, 1988) that the therapist is always as much a participant in the interaction as is the patient. For example, the therapist's restraint (e.g., in the form of silence or relative anonymity) is a communication which may be experienced by the patient in various ways. The therapist is not simply an observer focusing on the patient's predominant modes of interaction, but is an integral part of the interpersonal field as both subject and object.

Within this perspective, a central feature of Sullivan's theory of treatment is the elucidation of the patient's interpersonal interactions with significant others, including the therapist. Interactions fraught with overt and covert anxiety and misunderstanding obviously are the most important ones in need of attention and clarification. The "security operations" the patient uses to avoid anxiety are a major focus of exploration. Awareness of the archaic nature of the self-system, its selectively unattended "bad-me" and dissociated "not-me" aspects, and its detrimental impact on the patient's interpersonal relationships provide a major impetus for change. The therapist, through a "detailed inquiry" (Sullivan, 1954), helps the patient unpack current and past anxiety-laden experiences which were avoided through "selective inattention" at the time they occurred. Experiences of demystification have therapeutic power. Clarification through language leads to what Levenson (1982) calls "semiotic competence." He reminds us that Sullivan said that "no one has grave difficulties in living if he has a very good grasp of what is happening to him" (quoted in Levenson, 1985, p. 49).

The emphasis on participant-observation, with its stress on the overt and covert mutual influence of the two participants and the idea that the act of observation alters the phenomena observed, has been contrasted with the classical psychoanalytic position which is seen as static and as implying that the observer could somehow stand outside the interaction. Witenberg (1974, p. 852), for example, claims that in classical psychoanalysis the analyst is a detached observer and that the notion of the therapist as a participant-observer "puts at the disposal of the therapist more of the relevant clinical data, and it frees him from the inhibition imposed by classical theory of the use of his emotional reactions in treatment." We might point out here that revisions of the traditional psychoanalytic theory of treatment (e.g., Gill, 1982; Kernberg, 1975, 1980; Kohut, 1984; Muslin & Gill, 1978) by those who began in the Freudian tradition have brought the traditional Freudian view closer to the concept of participant-observation. This shift is evident, for example, in Cooper's (1987) depiction of the modernist view of transference, outlined earlier, and in the discussions of a one-person versus a two-person psychology (Gill, 1983; Modell, 1984). It has been prompted in part by the focus on the nonclassical analytic patient and by enlarged conceptions of the nature of countertransference (Racker, 1968). As Gill (1983) pointed out, there is no necessary connection between the analyst's subscribing to the drive discharge paradigm versus the interpersonal paradigm and the degree to which the analyst believes that he or she is participating in the analytic situation.

In any case, it is our impression that there is a considerable range of therapeutic approaches among those who regard themselves as Sullivanians, as well as significant deviations from Sullivan's own treatment methods. First, although inspired by Sullivan, many therapists depart from him in their stress on transference interpretations and vary among themselves regarding how vital they believe such interpretations to be. Second, interpersonalists seem to differ a great deal in the degree to which they emphasize relationship factors versus insight in their conceptualization of therapeutic action. Third, they differ in the degree to which they advocate revealing their countertransference feelings and reactions to their patients. With regard to the last point, Ehrenberg (1982), for example, in the course of asserting the value of active engagement and participation by the analyst, advocates the explicit acknowledgment to the patient of his or her emotional impact on the analyst, that is, disclosure of the countertransference, broadly defined. For example, in response to a patient's detached and disinterested attitude about everything, including the sessions, the analyst made it plain that she was concerned that the sessions be useful and that she "did not like to feel useless" (Ehrenberg, 1982, p. 551).

While interpersonalists vary in the extent to which they share their countertransference reactions with their patients, they repeatedly stress that they are very much in the interaction they are attempting to analyze and that this focus is itself an important aspect of the interaction. Thus, for Levenson (1988, p. 140), "the analysis of the relationship between what is being said and who is saying it to whom and how it is being said and heard—the classic linguistic formula of message and metamessage—is at the core of the psychoanalytic process." Levenson (1988, p. 101) believes that "*the power of psychoanalysis may well depend on what is said about what is done* [italics as in original] as a continuous, integral part of the therapy." As suggested above, this is a view increasingly shared by many traditional Freudians who also emphasize the importance of an oscillation between the enactment and experiencing of the here-and-now transference and countertransference configurations and their analysis.

While Levenson's (1988) conception of recursive patterning is consistent with a Freudian view, he does point to what he believes to be a sharp demarcation of Freudian and interpersonal approaches to dealing with this patterning. He sees the Freudian position as "*the search for the truth behind appearances*" and the interpersonal position as "*search for the truth inherent in appearances*. For the Freudian, the key question is, what does it truly mean? For the interpersonalist, the question is, what's going on around here?" (Levenson, 1985, p. 53).

Kohut's Self Psychology

Freud's (1914/1957a) "On Narcissism" represents an important point of departure for those theoretical orientations that give central consideration to the self, the object, and the relations between them. Nowhere is this clearer than in Kohut's self psychology. In his essay, "On Narcissism," Freud (1914/1957a) looked at psychological development, not so much from the point of view of drive, psychosexual stages, and growth of ego functions, but from the perspective of increasing differentiation between self and object. It is this perspective that Kohut (e.g., 1971, 1977, 1984) began with and developed into a psychoanalytic self psychology in which the narcissistic line of development is the central dimension of psychological growth and in which a unitary, cohesive self is the central developmental achievement.

As noted elsewhere (Eagle, 1987), in his earlier work, Kohut (e.g., 1971) presented self psychology as an outgrowth and supplement to traditional Freudian theory. In the earlier writings, traditional Freudian theory is held to be applicable to the "structural neuroses," which are characterized by conflict between intact structures, while self psychology is applicable to those conditions, such as narcissistic personality disorders, in which defects and disorders of the self are at the core of pathology. In the course of time, however, this two-factor apportionment of domains came to be increasingly replaced by an outright rejection of traditional Freudian theory and its thoroughgoing replacement by self psychology. Thus, in all pathology, intrapsychic conflict regarding sexual and aggressive wishes was always secondary to the issue of self-cohesiveness. In short, although self psychology emerged from traditional Freudian theory, its further development led to a splitting away from mainstream psychoanalytic theory. Further, there appears to be little interest or faith in the possibility of integrations of the two perspectives. Thus, Ornstein (1978, p. 98) wrote: "The essential advance made . . . is the development of a self psychology that is conceptually independent from and has moved beyond drive theory and ego psychology."

Finally, one sociological note: Largely because, for the most part, self psychologists did not break with existing psychoanalytic training institutes and did not go on to establish their own training institutes, in a political sense they have continued to be viewed as a perspective *within* mainstream psychoanalysis in contrast, say, to followers of Adler, Jung, and Horney who are viewed as *outside* mainstream psychoanalysis.

Kohut's self psychology diverges from traditional psychoanalytic theory in a number of ways. From a broad theoretical point of view, Kohut's main departure from traditional psychoanalytic theory is his positing of a separate line of development along the dimension of narcissism. According to Freud, normal development is characterized by a *decreasing* investment of libido in the ego and an *increasing* investment of libido in the object. In short, according to traditional theory, in normal development we move from self love to object love (although Freud noted that a certain minimal degree of self love is necessary for psychological health). Furthermore, given the limited supply of libido, there is a *reciprocal* relation between self interest and object interest. Too much absorption in the self is necessarily at the expense of interest in the other, and conversely, too much absorption in the other is at the expense of the interest of the self.

One of Kohut's main objections to the Freudian theoretical treatment of narcissism is that it is viewed as inherently pathological and regressive —a state or condition one grows away from in the normal course of development. Kohut rejects this view and argues instead that narcissism is a separate line of development that, as a function of the vicissitudes of early experiences, can proceed in either a healthy or a pathological direction. Healthy narcissism is marked, above all, by the development of a cohesive self and by the productive and joyful carrying out of one's "nuclear program," that is, by the exercise of one's talents and skills in the pursuit of one's basic ambitions and goals, and culminating in the development of a set of ideals and values. By contrast, narcissistic personality disorders, a primary expression of pathological narcissism, are characterized by self-defects, a proneness to "disintegration anxiety," archaic grandiosity and exhibitionism (a pathological expression of ambitions and goals), and marked failures in the carrying out of one's nuclear program.

According to Kohut, one can lead a productive, meaningful, and even joyful life without the pursuit of object love being at its center. As Kohut

(1984, p. 7) puts it, "There are ... good lives, including some of the greatest and most fulfilling lives recorded in history, that were not lived by individuals whose psychosexual organization was heterosexual-genital or whose major commitment organization was to unambivalent object love." In a recent book, *Solitude*, Storr (1988) makes a similar point, with an illustration from the life of the historian Gibbon, the author of *The Decline and Fall of the Roman Empire*. Storr (1988) writes:

> Modern insistence that true happiness can only be found in intimate attachments, more especially in sexual fulfillment, does not allow a place for a character like Gibbon. It is clear that, although his friendships were many, his chief source of self-esteem and of pleasure was his work. (p. xi)

Implied in Kohut's position on object love is his rejection of Freudian instinct theory. That is, contrary to Freud, Kohut does not believe that instinctual gratification and the need to find the object(s) through which such gratification can occur are superordinate motives governing behavior and mental life. In self psychology, the need for self-cohesiveness and self-esteem are the superordinate motives that replace instinctual gratification. For Kohut, being compelled or driven by sexual and aggressive drives is not a normal expression of our psychobiological nature, but is rather a "disintegration product," reflecting failures in self-cohesiveness.

Both as a developmental—etiological theory and in the context of treatment, Kohut's main emphasis is on the achievement of a cohesive self. According to Kohut, the development of a cohesive self requires the parental provision of empathic mirroring and the later availability of a parental figure permitting idealization. Such early mirroring and later idealization are held to facilitate the smooth development of the normal and necessary narcissistic phase of grandiosity and exhibitionism and the construction of an "idealized parent image." The experience of grandiosity and the availability of an idealized parental image enable the child to feel powerful and full rather than powerless and empty in the face of the unavoidable shortcomings and frustrations of reality.

The traumatic failure to provide empathic mirroring and adequate conditions for idealization are, according to Kohut, the primary etiological factors in the generation of pathological narcissism or, more specifically, in the development of a noncohesive self (or self defects). As noted earlier, clinically, the markers of pathological narcissism include archaic grandiosity and exhibitionism, proneness to disintegration anxiety, sensitivity to narcissistic injury, and narcissistic rages.

Pathological narcissism is also manifested in the individual's relations to others. And here Kohut introduces a term that plays a special role in self psychology, namely, *selfobject*. As the term suggests, the selfobject is neither fully self nor fully other. Broadly speaking, it is a response to the other, not as a separate other, but primarily in terms of the other's role in sustaining one's self-cohesiveness. In narcissistic personality disorders, the individual establishes primarily archaic self–selfobject bonds with others. The psychological importance of the other lies mainly in the others' role in providing self-aggrandizement, the regulation of self-esteem, and the maintenance of self-cohesiveness. That is, the other carries out functions that, in healthy development, one would eventually carry out oneself.

In Kohut's earlier writings, he gives the impression that, in normal development along the line of narcissism, one moves from a reliance on selfobjects to carry out self-regulation and self-sustaining functions to an increasing ability to execute these functions oneself. However, in his 1984 book, in rejecting the desirability or even possibility of autonomy as a developmental goal, Kohut argues that we continue to need selfobjects all our lives. (So vital is this need for selfobjects in Kohut's view that he compares it to a lifelong need for oxygen.) The issue, according to Kohut, is not presence or absence of selfobjects, but a move from an archaic self-object (based, for example, on merging) to more mature self–selfobject bonds which are based on "empathic resonance."

To sum up, in contrast to traditional psychoanalytic theory, in which pathology (as well as a wide range of normal behavior) is viewed from the perspective of intrapsychic conflict, the primary emphasis in self psychology is on developmental *defects*, in particular, self defects. In this sense, self psychology is one expression of what might generally be referred to as a mini-paradigm shift (Kuhn, 1962) from a psychology of conflict to a psychology of developmental defects and arrests that has characterized recent developments in psychoanalysis.

Implications of Kohut's Theory for Treatment

It seems to us that more than other psychoanalytic developments, self psychology is primarily a theory of treatment, with an etiological theory of pathology and a theory of personality development grafted on. Indeed, Kohut (1979) himself tells us that an important impetus for the development of self psychology was his experience in the two analyses of the patient he called Mr. Z. Very briefly, the second analysis of Mr. Z was more successful than the first, according to Kohut, largely because Kohut shifted from understanding Mr. Z's sense of "entitlement" as an expression of a clinging to infantile wishes, to understanding this behavior as a response to lack of self-cohesiveness.

According to Kohut, a theory that interprets a patient's narcissistic attitudes and demands as resistances against relinquishing infantile wishes, as "clinging to outdated drive-pleasures that must be opposed by the reality principle and the strictures of adult morality" (1984, p. 89), will communicate a "censorious and disapproving" attitude to the patient. By contrast, the self psychology analyst, Kohut tells us, tends to be more accepting of such behaviors because he or she understands them, not as clinging to infantile gratification, but as reflecting "faulty structures responsible for [the] faulty functioning" (1984, p. 86). In short, from a self psychology perspective, much of the patient's behavior in and out of treatment is understood, not as the covert and conflicted pursuit of infantile wishes, but as the consequence of self-defects and lack of self-cohesiveness.

How are such self-defects dealt with in self psychology treatment? According to Kohut, narcissistic patients spontaneously form mirroring and idealizing transferences. Other kinds of transferences are also discussed in the self psychology literature, but it is the mirroring and idealizing transferences that are the primary innovative emphases of self psychology. The core expressions of these transferences are, respectively, a need to be perfectly mirrored and to merge with an idealized figure. Kohut views these transferences, not as clinging to infantile wishes, but as expressions of the patient's poignant attempt to resume developmental growth. In that sense, these transference expressions are not regressive but *progressive*. Or perhaps one can say that its aim for progressive growth is pursued through regressive means. Because the patient's basic fear is retraumatization at the hands of the therapist, for a period of time resistances against the full formation of mirroring and idealizing transferences are likely to operate. These resistances are dealt with by interpretations regarding the patient's motives and sources. No therapist, of course, can provide perfect empathic understanding or provide a perfect figure for idealization. In other words, the therapist will fail the patient's needs for perfect mirroring and idealization. Such failures will often be met with rage, despair, withdrawal, and regression, as if they did indeed retraumatize the patient. However, as long as the therapist's failures are not, in fact, of traumatic proportions and as long as the therapist acknowledges them, interprets the patient's regressive retreats, and continues to attempt to understand the patient, these failures will function as "optimal failures" or "optimal frustrations."

According to Kohut, after each optimal failure "new self structure will be acquired and existing ones will be firmed" (1984, p. 69). He also notes that following the working through of optimal failure the patient will become more resilient and, finally, "empathic resonance" will replace the bondage of archaic self–selfobject relationships. For Kohut, empathic understanding and the repeated working through of optimal failures in empathy constitute "the basic therapeutic unit" of treatment.

Why should feeling understood be such a potent therapeutic agent, ultimately playing the critical role in the repair of self-defects and the building up of psychic structure?[4] Clearly, understanding and feeling un-

---

[4]We are using Kohut's language in referring to "repair" of self-defects and building up of psychic structure. The precise meaning and referents of these terms are not at all clear to us.

derstood are general *desiderata* in virtually every context of human communication, including that of psychotherapy. But why the special role that it is given in the self psychology conception of treatment? In order to answer this question adequately, one must turn to Kohut's etiological theory of pathology. Very simply, and briefly, underlying the therapeutic role given to feeling understood are the implicit assumptions that (a) being understood (empathic mirroring) is a universal developmental need; (b) traumatic failures in this area lead to self-defects; (c) mirroring transferences bespeak the poignant efforts of a person with a defective self to complete his or her development and finally to have his or her need for empathic mirroring met; and, finally, (d) the meeting of this need by the therapist serves as a critical contribution to the repair of self-defects, the building up of psychic structures, and the resumption of developmental growth. In short, the provision of empathic understanding is so critical because it meets a traumatically unfulfilled developmental need and thereby facilitates the resumption of developmental growth. As Friedman (1986) characterized it, "being understood is a maturing environment."

OTHER CONTRIBUTIONS TO PSYCHOANALYTIC THEORY AND TREATMENT

We now turn to a brief summary of some of the more recent developments in psychoanalytic theories of psychopathology and treatment. We limit our discussion to the work of Mahler, Kernberg, and Weiss and Sampson. If space permitted, we would have included the work of other important contributors such as Jacobson, Winnicott, Loewald, Sandler, Modell, Gedo, Gill, Schafer, and Brenner, among others. We would also have discussed the development of brief psychoanalytic psychotherapy (Budman, 1981).

The work of Mahler (1968), the work of Kernberg (1975, 1976, 1980, 1984), and the "unconscious-control" theory of Weiss and Sampson (1986) and their colleagues (the Mt. Zion Group)—are a representative sample of contemporary theoretical developments in psychoanalysis that do not as readily lend themselves to categorization in terms of Pine's (1990) four different foci of drive, ego, object, and self.

We begin with a few introductory comments concerning these three approaches. Mahler's theory represents a combination of a number of different psychoanalytic perspectives. Although many of her formulations are presented in the language of drive theory, her theory focuses on the differentiation between self and object, the development of concepts of self and of object, and the relation between the two. In an important sense,

Mahler's work on separation-individuation is both an object relations theory and a self psychology.

Kernberg acknowledges the influence both of Mahler and of Jacobson (1964). His work represents an early psychoanalytic mainstream version of an object relations theory and self psychology. Kernberg's (1975, 1976, 1984) clinical and theoretical efforts have been explicitly directed toward an attempted integration of aspects of Freud's drive theory and object relations theory. Although much of Kernberg's theory has been directed toward an understanding of borderline conditions, his formulations have broader application. He presents a picture of psychological development in which self and object representations are initially organized in accord with the dominant affective tone (i.e., gratification versus frustration) of self and object interactions in which a major developmental challenge is the integration of opposite self-object-affect structural units.

Finally, from a certain perspective, Weiss and Sampson's (1986) unconscious-control theory can be seen as an extension and elaboration of ego psychology, in the sense that a major emphasis is placed on unconscious ego processes of belief, judgment, testing, and so on. However, unconscious control theory is also interactional and object relational, in the sense that unconscious pathogenic beliefs are acquired through interactions with and communications from parental figures and are tested in treatment through interaction with the therapist. In addition, unconscious-control theory can also be understood as a psychoanalytic expression of a zeitgeist in which cognitive processes (including unconscious cognitive processes) and cognitive psychology have come to occupy center stage in the behavioral sciences.

Mahler

The first, recent contribution we consider is the work of Mahler and her colleagues. Unfortunately, we cannot cover Mahler's rich formulations with the detail they deserve. We will focus on the essentials of her theory and its implications for treatment.

Mahler places separation-individuation as a core and separate dimension of psychological development, which, while related to and even overlapping with the dimensions of psychosexual and ego development, is both sufficiently different and important to warrant a central place in a psychoanalytic theory of development. Further, severe psychopathology involves deformation in this dimension of development.

Mahler characterizes the infant's early extrauterine life as a state of *normal autism*. In this stage, which is concerned mainly with attempts to achieve homeostasis, the infant cannot differentiate between the mother's need-reducing ministrations and its own efforts at getting rid of unpleasurable tension (through defecating, urinating, regurgitating, etc.) mainly because there is no concept yet of an object or a self.

From the second month on, "dim awareness of the need-satisfying object marks the beginning of the phase of *normal symbiosis*, in which the infant behaves and functions as though he and his mother were an omnipotent system—a dual unity in their one common boundary" (Mahler 1968, p. 8; italics added). During this stage, the infant requires the help of the "auxiliary ego" of the mother in order to maintain homeostasis. In this state of fusion, the "I" is not differentiated from the "not I," and "inside and outside are only gradually coming to be sensed as different" (Mahler, 1968, p. 9). According to Mahler, in "symbiotic child psychosis," the ego regresses to this state of delusional omnipotent fusion. From the more traditional perspective, this is a stage of an undifferentiated id–ego matrix.

According to Mahler, the infant must experience "optimal human symbiosis" (1968, p. 14) in order to successfully negotiate the separation-individuation process and achieve both a clear sense of identity and libidinal object constancy. Stated in more metapsychological terms, in the course of normal development the child achieves differentiation between self-representations and object representations "from the hitherto fused symbiotic self-plus-object representations" (Mahler, 1968, p. 18). From another perspective, one can describe the separation-individuation process in terms of "the child's achievement of separate functioning in the presence and emotional availability of the mother" (Mahler, 1968, p. 20).

Finally, we note the distinction made between the two complementary processes of separation and individuation. "Separation consists of the child's emergence from a symbiotic fusion with the mother . . . and individuation consists of the achievements making the child's assumption of his own individual characteristics" (Mahler, Pine, & Bergman, 1975, p. 4).

We have attempted to provide a general description of Mahler's theory rather than a detailed account, which would include a description of the various subphases of separation-individuation (e.g., the differentiation, practicing, and rapprochement subphases). The detailed account is readily available elsewhere (e.g., Bergman & Ellman, 1985; Mahler 1968; Mahler, Pine, & Bergman, 1975).

Mahler distinguishes between autistic and symbiotic psychoses, with most of her attention given to the latter. Very briefly and crudely, in autistic psychosis the child is unable to experience and enter the symbiotic mother–infant dual unity. He or she is unable to respond to stimuli emanating from the mother and reacts with rage or panic when threatened with human intrusion. In symbiotic psychosis, the child is unable to *leave* the state of symbiotic unity or fusion and reacts with panic and disorganization at any hint of separateness. In both cases, there is a severe disturbance of identity, "not in a sense of *who* I am but *that* I am" (Mahler,

Bergman, & Pine, 1975, p. 8). Also in both cases, the child is unable to use the mother as a basis for developing a sense of separate identity and of relatedness to the world. As Mahler (1968) states it, "In the psychotic child, ... there seems to be a limitation to his inner capacity to utilize the mother, as a result of which he does not obtain the gratification and relief of tension that are preconditions for progressive development" (p. 231).

Implications of Mahler's Theory for Treatment

In considering the implications of Mahler's theory for treatment, one must distinguish between the direct implications for the treatment of severe childhood pathology (mainly, infantile autism and symbiotic psychosis) and the more indirect and implicit implications for the conceptualization and treatment of adult pathology (mainly, borderline conditions). We shall consider only the latter. One important implication of Mahler's work is that at the center of adult pathology, particularly severe pathology, are issues having to do with differentiation and separation-individuation. That is, many lives are made or broken as a function of one's ability or inability to achieve the differentiation between self and other needed to develop a clear sense of one's identity and a clear and stable sense of an object to whom one can relate libidinally and affectively.

It will be recognized that this emphasis on the development of a sense of self, of object representations, and of the relation between the two is also central to Kohut's self psychology and to object relations theory. For example, Fairbairn's (1952, p. 43) earlier noted characterization of agoraphobia in terms of a conflict between "the regressive lure of identification and the progressive urge for separation" is entirely consistent with Mahler's developmental theory of symbiosis and separation-individuation. Despite her frequent use of the language of Freudian drive theory and metapsychology, Mahler's theory, in many respects, is a version of object relations theory.

As we shall see, Mahler's influence on conceptions of adult pathology is especially evident in Kernberg's work, particularly his formulations of borderline personality organization. For example, Kernberg's developmental stages quite closely parallel Mahler's subphases of separation-individuation. As another example, in both Mahler's and Kernberg's work, excessive aggression, particularly failures in the neutralization of aggression, plays a central role in understanding pathology. And more generally, in both Mahler and Kernberg's formulations, at the heart of pathology lie failures in the achievement of both a stable and integrated sense of self and sense of the object. Mahler writes in regard to borderline patients, "In essence, in these adult patients, as with the children, it is the object and self-representation that seem particularly vulnerable to distortion and obliteration" (Mahler, 1968, pp. 235–236).

It is easier to write about the implications of Mahler's theory for *conceptualization* than for *treatment* of adult pathology. This is often the case in the psychoanalytic literature. For example, one can say a great deal more about the conception of pathology in object relations theory than its prescriptions for treatment. Nevertheless, Mahler's developmental theory does have certain implications for the treatment of adult pathology. It seems to us that there are two broad and related ways in which these implications are manifested. One is the emphasis on the therapeutic relationship, and the other is the emphasis on self and object representations in treatment.

A central idea in Mahler's description of treatment of psychotic children is that the therapist must provide the child with a set of experiences that were not available, indeed that were traumatically unavailable, in the course of development. This is summed up by Mahler in her concept of the "corrective symbiotic experience." It seems to us that this basic idea, that the treatment provides what was not available in the course of development, is also central to many current conceptions of treatment of adults. Thus, in self psychology the therapist provides the empathic mirroring that was traumatically unavailable in the patient's early life. And in object relations theory, the therapist attempts to replace a "bad object situation" with a "good object situation." All of these ideas show obvious links to Alexander and French's (1946) concept of the "corrective emotional experience," a concept which can also be traced back to the influence of Ferenczi and Rank (1925/1956).

As for the emphasis on self and object representations, common to both Mahler's treatment of psychotic children and much current work with adult patients is the idea that central therapeutic tasks in treatment have to do with modifications in self representations, object representations, and relations between the self and objects. Although there are different nuances and somewhat different languages among the different theoretical approaches of, say, self psychology, object relations theory, and Kernberg's formulations, there is convergence on the common emphasis in treatment on the importance of self and object representations and the relations between them.

Kernberg

Kernberg has contributed in a number of different but related areas: (a) He has attempted to integrate object relations, ego psychology, and drive theories (e.g., Kernberg, 1976), along with the contributions of M. Klein and Mahler, in a psychoanalytic developmental theory of psychopathology. (b) He has developed a theory of "borderline personality organization" and has presented ways of diagnosing and assessing such organization (e.g., Kernberg, 1975, 1984). (c) He and his colleagues have offered guidelines for the psychoanalytic treatment of borderline patients (Kernberg, Selzer, Koenigsberg, Carr, & Applebaum, 1989). (d) He has attempted to apply his approach to hospital treatment and other group settings.

According to Kernberg, a central characteristic clearly observed in the transference patterns of borderline patients is the alternation or *splitting* of contradictory affective responses and object relations—from idealization and admiration (love) to devaluation and rage (hate). Furthermore, the borderline patient's reaction to being confronted with the existence of these contradictory ego states is characteristically one of anxiety. For Kernberg (1976, p. 25), these alternating and contradictory states are "the pathologically fixed remnants of the normal processes of early introjection."

In order to understand this quoted phrase, one must examine Kernberg's developmental theory. It is a complex and dense theory, and we do not have sufficient space to do it justice here. However, we can describe some of its key features. A central feature of Kernberg's developmental theory is an emphasis on internalization processes, the basic components being (a) self representations, (b) object representations, and (c) affective states associated with different self-object interactions. One can refer to the organization of the above components as S(self)-O(object)-A(affect) units. Early in development, S-O-A units of opposite affective valences are unintegrated, initially as a function of immaturity (i.e., normal age-appropriate limitations in integrative capacity), and then as a defensive process of splitting. Later in development, the more primitive defense of splitting is normally replaced by repression and other higher level defenses. For borderline patients, this maturational process does not occur, and splitting as well as other primitive defenses (e.g., projective identification) predominate. Introjections that take place under the positive valence of libidinal gratification are organized as the "good internal object" and introjections that take place under the negative valence of the aggressive drive are organized as the "bad internal object." In splitting, these two psychic organizations are kept apart, with the result that an integrated organization of the object and one's relation to the object, an organization that includes ambivalent and complex feelings and perceptions, is not achieved. Because intense anxiety is experienced when the person confronts the existence side-by-side of contradictory positive and negative affective organizations, splitting as a defense is instituted and maintained.

Why should the confrontation with contradictory ego states elicit intense anxiety? Kernberg's answer, clearly derived from the work of Klein and Fairbairn, appears to be that the patient fears that his or her aggression will destroy the good internal object and thus leave him or her living in an inner world with no benevolent objects and at the mercy of bad internal objects.[5] According to Kernberg (1975), the borderline patient is especially susceptible to this danger because of intense oral aggression which is the result of early extreme frustration or a constitutional predisposition. This "excessive pregenital and particularly oral aggression tends to be projected and causes a paranoid distortion of the early parental images, especially of the mother. Through the projection of predominantly oral-sadistic but also anal-sadistic impulses, the mother is seen as potentially dangerous" (p. 41).

Recently, Kernberg et al. (1989) have provided a handbook for the psychoanalytically oriented treatment of borderline patients. The treatment recommendations are based on Kernberg's conception of the nature of borderline personality organization, according to which the borderline patient attempts to avoid conflict by "unrealistically cleaving loving and hating aspects of both self and others into separate parts" (p. 9). The result of this "dissociative act that completely separates aggression from love" is that relations between self and others are "either totally idealized or totally persecutory" (p. 9). As we understand Kernberg, the aim of the treatment is to clarify, through interpretation, the dissociated or split-off components of the patient's self and object representations, as they are expressed in the transference; and, then help the patient integrate these components "into more realistic and stable [self and object] images" (Kernberg et al., 1989, p. 50). The emphasis in the treatment is on interpretation of here-and-now primitive defensive operations as they are expressed in the transference. Just as these primitive defensive operations weaken the ego, so will interpretation of them strengthen the ego.

Weiss, Sampson, and Their Colleagues (The Mt. Zion Group)

One of the noteworthy recent developments in psychoanalysis is a theory of treatment (and, to a certain extent, an accompanying theory of psychopathology) put forth by Weiss and Sampson at Mt. Zion Hospital in San Francisco. In the past, they have referred to their approach as "control-mastery theory," but more recently have labelled it "the unconscious-control hypothesis" (Weiss, 1990). The Mt. Zion group is unique in the psychoanalytic community in that they have attempted to evaluate their hypothesis (which is pitted against a more traditional Freudian hypothesis) through the relatively rigorous use of clinical data and through testing out specific predictions in systematic research.

What is the unconscious-control hypothesis? One can begin by contrasting it to what Weiss (1990) refers to as Freud's "dynamic hypothesis." According to the latter, whether or not material reaches consciousness is

---

[5]The specific defensive functions served by splitting or keeping apart "good" and "bad" object representations are not always entirely clear. According to Klein as well as Fairbairn, the main defensive function served by splitting is to preserve the good object, that is, to keep it from being infiltrated and destroyed by the bad object.

entirely an automatic consequence of the relative strengths of the (sexual and aggressive) impulses seeking gratification and the repressive forces opposing these impulses. By contrast, according to the unconscious-control hypothesis, people exert some control over unconscious functioning and make unconscious decisions regarding the conditions under which they will keep impulses and ideas repressed versus permitting them to reach consciousness. In general, mental contents are kept repressed when an unconscious assessment is made that expressing them would be dangerous; ideas and impulses are experienced or expressed when an assessment is made that conditions of safety obtain.

According to this view, patients come to treatment, not to gratify infantile wishes, but to find conditions in which it is safe to bring forth repressed material and to master the conflicts, anxieties, and traumas that are associated with them.

In contrast to the dynamic hypothesis, Weiss and Sampson maintain that pathology is rooted not in repressed impulses but in unconscious pathogenic beliefs. The essence of pathogenic beliefs is that developmentally normal, desirable goals are experienced as endangering oneself and are fraught with anxiety, guilt, and fear. These pathogenic beliefs can be understood as taking an if-then form: If I pursue such and such a goal, then I will be punished or I will endanger a vital relationship, or I will be hurting someone important to me. One person might have the pathogenic belief that "if I pursue the goal of leading an independent life, it can only be at the expense of my parent(s)," thus engendering intense separation guilt (versus separation anxiety). Another person may suffer from a pathogenic belief that "if I pursue my ambitions and desire to be successful, I will be severely punished for surpassing my parents or siblings," thus resulting in the experience of survivor guilt and the inhibition of ambitious strivings. (Note that this last example is essentially a restatement of the Freudian concept of castration anxiety in the context of Weiss and Sampson's theory.)

In order to determine whether it is safe to bring forth repressed material, patients unconsciously present tests to the therapist. If these tests are passed, the patient is more likely to bring forth repressed material. If tests are failed, the patient is less likely to lift repressions. Much of the clinical richness of Weiss and Sampson's model is expressed in the accounts of what constitutes test-passing and test-failing for particular patients. In general, test-passing can be understood to occur when the therapist's interventions are in accord with the patient's unconscious plan as to how to lift repressions and master anxieties, conflicts, and traumas. Test-failing can be understood to occur when the therapist's interventions are not in accord with or are contrary to the patient's unconscious plan.

An example of a patient presenting tests in treatment is taken from a recent paper by Weiss (1990, pp. 107–108). "A woman who feared she would hurt her parents and her male therapist by becoming independent might experiment with independent behavior in her sessions by disagreeing with the therapist's opinions and then unconsciously monitoring him to see if he feels hurt." Obviously, the therapist's tolerance and acceptance of disagreement would constitute test-passing, while his or her anger or attempts to direct or control the patient would constitute test-failing. Test-passing and the conditions of safety that this implies will, according to Weiss and Sampson, both facilitate the patient's insight into his or her pathogenic beliefs and serve to disconfirm them.

MOST RECENT DEVELOPMENTS: REFLECTIONS ON THEORIES AND TECHNIQUES IN PSYCHOANALYSIS

Our aim in this brief section is to offer, in light of developments in the field in the past several years, some reflections on the theories and techniques of psychoanalytic therapy that we covered in this chapter. We will limit our focus to the reasons for the current theoretical pluralism in psychoanalytic approaches to treatment and its implications for the relationship between theories and techniques of treatment. Our emphasis on theories of psychoanalytic treatment rather than on different etiological theories of psychopathology or general theories of personality development and human nature reflects the current tendency toward therapeutic eclecticism, despite sharp differences in broader theoretical outlook.

First, however, we need to point out more clearly that our chapter does not include all of the extant major theoretical models. Most notably absent, although not in any particular order, are a consideration of intersubjectivity (Stolorow & Atwood, 1992) and social–constructivist (Hoffman, 1991, 1992) theorists; Kleinian theory, both the Latin American versions and the contemporary neo-Kleinians of London (Schafer, 1994); other variants of object relations theories (e.g., Guntrip, 1969; Winnicott, 1958); Loewald's (1980) attempt to integrate object relations conceptions into Freudian theory; Modell's (1984, 1990) similar efforts; and the earlier neo-Freudian approaches (e.g., Jung, Adler, Horney). Space does not permit us to present these theorists now, either. We note, however, that the main themes of the discussion that follows are also applicable to these theories.

Theoretical Pluralism in Contemporary Psychoanalysis

We will discuss several related reasons for the current multiplicity of theories of psychoanalytic treatment. First, there is a dearth of systematic research evidence that clearly directs a choice among rival approaches. Controversies concerning the relative efficacy of different treatment methods are dealt with in the psychoanalytic literature primarily by appeal to authority and to carefully selected clinical vignettes intended to bolster the writer's assertions. Many analysts still try to maintain that the consulting room is a laboratory and that hypotheses can be generated and confirmed (or disconfirmed) within the clinical context. However, the trenchant criticism by Grunbaum (1993), among others, makes this position very difficult to defend. (See, however, a spirited defense of the case study method by Edelson, 1988.)

Our mention of the paucity of systematic studies of the process and the outcome of long-term treatment is not to argue that an accumulated body of research findings necessarily leads to any reliable conclusions about the relative superiority of a particular mode of treatment. We might learn, for example, that, all other things being equal (e.g., therapists' level of competence and experience, type of patient), treatment outcomes are quite comparable and that therefore there is no warrant for preferring one treatment approach and its corresponding theory over another. It might be, as appears to be in the case of research on the outcome of various short-term psychotherapies, that the meta-analyses (e.g., Smith, Glass, & Miller, 1980) would show that it is the common elements of different treatment approaches (e.g., the level of therapist empathy or the strength of the therapeutic alliance) that account for most of the variance in outcome. (Actually, it should be noted that few, if any, of the studies covered in the meta-analyses investigated the effects of variations in the content and focus of the interpretations [e.g., oedipal vs. pre-oedipal interpretations, or transference vs. nontransference interpretations] in long-term treatment.)

Even if it were to be shown that, on average, one kind of theoretically derived interpretations produced better therapeutic outcomes, one might still argue that such a finding would not necessarily confirm that the interpretations were more accurate and that the theory from which they derived was more valid, since "inexact" interpretations (Glover, 1931) can have a therapeutic benefit. And, to obtain independent evidence of the accuracy of interpretations is a formidable if not impossible task. (See, however, Luborsky's [1988] findings of a correlation between positive therapeutic outcome and a focus on the patient's core conflictual relationship themes, as formulated by independent judges.) To cite another example of a challenging research problem, it would be extremely difficult to tease apart the relative therapeutic impact of insight per se versus the relationship (in any empirical study). Clinicians have made strong claims about the relative efficacy of these elements, although as we have argued elsewhere (Eagle & Wolitzky, 1982), the dichotomy between these two oftcited therapeutic elements is not a meaningful one.

Our point in raising these considerations is to indicate that even in the context of research it will be difficult to resolve controversial issues about the complex factors that seem integral to the therapeutic process.

These thorny issues, however, can never be resolved in case conferences or case studies. Systematic empirical data can at least point in the direction of a greater clarity on these matters. Some investigators have begun to tackle the methodological issues involved in doing meaningful research on long-term psychoanalytic treatment (e.g., Bucci, 1994; Caston, 1993; Caston & Martin, 1993; Dahl, 1994; Luborsky, 1996; Messer, Tishby, & Spillman, 1992; Spence, 1994; Weiss & Sampson, 1986).

Another reason for the pluralism in psychoanalytic theories of treatment is the fact that Freud's claim that interpretations that "tallied with something real" in the patient were curative turned out to be fraught with difficulties and hardly as simple a matter as this claim suggested. For example, it was clear to many analysts that a wide range of interpretations, *as well as other aspects* of the treatment situation, could be therapeutically effective. In view of such considerations it became difficult to maintain that anyone had claim to a superior view of the patient's intrapsychic reality or a superior means of alleviating human suffering. In the face of these realizations, Freud's theory became more vulnerable to competing models.

The way was thus paved for a variety of theories, including the currently popular view of the psychoanalytic situation in which it is stressed that there are two interacting "subjectivities" who are "creating" new meanings rather than "discovering" fixed, objective meanings. From this perspective, the older Freudian view that the observer could somehow stand outside the field of observation while engaged in interaction with the patient is an incorrect perpetuation of a so-called one-person psychology focused on the intrapsychic processes within the patient's mind—when only a two-person psychology emphasizing the interactions of patient and therapist can adequately characterize the creation of a negotiated, narrative "truth."

One influential expression of two-person psychology has been referred to as a "social constructivist" position, articulated by Hoffman (1991, 1992) and wholeheartedly embraced by Gill (1982, 1994) in his influential writings on transference. Implied in this position is the idea that we should be less ready to consider the patient's reaction a transference "distortion" as though we had a lock on what is "really" going on. Instead, Gill (1994) urged that we should view the patient's response as a "plausible" reading of our behavior or intentions. Even if we consider that the patient's response is based on a selective reading of the therapist's behavior, we should realize that it is based on some cues emitted by the therapist. At times, Gill (1994) can be read not so much as urging a new conceptual paradigm but as claiming that his approach is a more effective means of enabling both patients and analysts to acknowledge their respective contributions to the interaction. As stated by Gill (1987), "The first step in the resolution of such transference is the analyst's interpretation of how the patient's experience is plausible in the light of what the analyst has said and done. *Only then* is it likely that one can successfully pursue the patient's contributions, first in the present, and then in the past" (p. 252, italics added). This position would seem especially important with patients who readily feel resentful when they believe that there is an implication that they have constructed a response from "whole cloth." In any case, Gill's emphasis is strongly in accord with the idea that there is more than one reality to consider and that the analyst's perspective is not automatically to be taken as superior to that of the patient.

Another reason for the current theoretical pluralism is the increasing dissatisfaction with the alleged limitations and constricted perspective of traditional Freudian theory combined with the appeal and allegedly greater clinical relevance both of object relations theories and of Kohut's self psychology (Eagle, 1987), particularly for the treatment of borderline and narcissistic disorders. As noted in the chapter, most of these theories reject Freud's drive theory in favor of one that places greater explanatory weight on environmental factors, particularly parental failure, than on any inherent incompatibility between the person and the environment that creates inevitable intrapsychic conflict. With respect to its implications for technique, both object relations theorists and Kohutians believe that the emphasis on oedipal conflicts is overdone theoretically and that it interferes with effective treatment, at least with narcissistic and borderline patients. Compared with the so-called classical neurotic, these patients, it is argued, often require a greater relaxation of the principle of abstinence, greater attention to the therapeutic alliance, and stronger sensitivity to the patient's fear of retraumatization. As put by Modell (1987), to cite but one author with this view, "Matters of the safety and preservation of the self must take precedence before the analysis of erotic and oedipal themes" (p. 235).

For purposes of the present discussion we are deliberately grouping all versions of object relations theory under the same rubric, even though we recognize that there are important differences among them. We are doing this to highlight one key feature that seems to unite most object relations theories, and that is their emphasis on the motivational primacy of a need to relate to and connect with objects. This emphasis is contrasted with the Freudian view of "drive discharge" as the principal motivational thrust of behavior. As we noted in this chapter, Fairbairn (1952) put it in epigrammatic form by claiming that "libido is object-seeking not pleasure-seeking" (p. 82). We also want to note as a recent trend the emergence of what has been referred to as a relational point of view bearing certain similarities to, but not identical with, the British object relations theories. One can perhaps describe this perspective as an integration of interpersonal and object relations theories. Mitchell (1988, 1993) has been a leading figure in developing and articulating this point of view.

Thus, the Freudian depiction of man as a pleasure-seeking animal insisting on immediate drive gratification whenever possible stands in contrast to the various object relations, interpersonal, and relational theories that portray the human as seeking connectedness with others. Yet, in our view, these latter positions can potentially be integrated with the traditional Freudian model if we assume that the seemingly inherent drive toward objects makes evolutionary sense in that the biological helplessness of the infant requires a caregiver to regulate and reduce the infant's tension states.

The Relationship Between Theory and Technique

To what extent do these different theoretical models actually dictate differences in technique? According to some (e.g., Richards & Richards, 1995), the different theories of pathogenesis and their corresponding implications for a theory of therapeutic action and cure make for important differences in technique. Wallerstein (1990b, 1995), in contrast, takes the position that our theoretical diversity exists largely in "our experience-distant 'general theories,' our theoretical explanatory systems created to give coherence and order and a sense of psychological understanding . . . to the phenomena observed in the consulting room" (1995, p. 528). These systems are seen as useful metaphors rather than as different constructs that can be validated through empirical study. He preferred to emphasize our "common ground," which "exists in our experience-near clinical theory, encompassing the discernible clinical events of conflict, resistance, and transference−countertransference interplay palpable in our daily clinical encounters" (p. 528). He also believed, contrary to Richards and Richards (1995), that there usually is a loose, elastic link between theory and technique. This, of course, is an empirical question that has been little studied, but at least one study (Fine & Fine, 1990) showed that proponents of different theories offer discriminably different interpretive interventions.

Wallerstein's (1992, 1995) position seems to us to come close to Frank's (1973) suggestion that any reasonably coherent, plausible explanation will facilitate therapeutic progress. It seems to suggest further that the goals analysts share (i.e., an interest in alleviating human suffering and in promoting positive personality growth through a focus on conflict, defense, transference, etc.) are far more important than any differences in technique or in the theoretical explanations of the clinical phenomena. It is not altogether clear that Wallerstein believed that being guided by one or more psychoanalytic models is essential to effective treatment, although he obviously recognized that analysts value their theories: "Our chosen explanatory *metaphors* [are] heuristically exceedingly useful to us, in terms of our varying intellectual value commitments in explaining the primary clinical data of our consulting rooms" (Wallerstein, 1992, p. 205). We believe that he can be read as implying that although clinicians subjectively regard their theories as important, if not vital, it might be that a commonsense, implicit theory of personality could suffice, particularly if it is reasonably sophisticated (i.e., if it went beyond obvious ideas such as people's tendency to defend themselves against awareness of unacceptable impulses and included notions such as an unconscious desire to fail).

In his most recent effort to articulate his notion of a common ground, Wallerstein (1995) stated, "The analyst, of whatever theoretical allegiance, who is empathetically tracking the patient's shifting psychic state is or should be necessarily resonating to the same clinical phenomena . . . and should be dealing with these clinical phenomena in comparable enough ways" (p. 541). He added that this is more likely the case for seasoned practitioners than for neophytes. He concluded with the implication that "differences in personal style, sociocultural context, personality structure, and temperament" (p. 541) ultimately are more important than allegiance to one or another psychoanalytic model.

Many analysts (e.g., Richards, 1990; Richards & Richards, 1995) would disagree with Wallerstein (1992), claiming that the emphasis on the common ground obscures the fact that theoretical differences have significant consequences for technique. Adherents of a given school of thought naturally have a narcissistic investment in the idea that their perspective offers the most comprehensive, coherent, accurate, and therapeutically useful approach to clinical work. Thus, Kohutians will accuse Freudians of being unnecessarily adversarial in ways that impede therapeutic progress (e.g., Lachmann, 1986; Wile, 1984) or of not really listening to the patient but being too intent on imposing their theoretical model on the patient (e.g., Peterfreund, 1983, 1990). Some Freudians, by the same token, believe that other approaches are seriously misguided. Richards and Richards (1995), for example, have claimed that self psychologists would fail to introduce ideas different from what the patient expresses and therefore would not teach the patient anything of new value or significance. As they put it, "We believe that this technical consequence makes self psychology nothing more than friendly comfort" (Richards & Richards, 1995, pp. 439–440).

Other analytic writers are willing to consider that clinicians representing different theoretical approaches might have comparable rates of therapeutic success, even if their theories do lead to different technical approaches. This position is in line with Wallerstein's (1992, 1995) claim that experienced clinicians of whatever theoretical stripe are substantially similar with respect to what they actually do with patients, even where their different theories might be "telling" them to do different things. Many years ago, Fiedler (1950) reported that experienced clinicians (i.e., analytic, Rogerian, Adlerian) were more similar in their actual therapeutic tactics than were inexperienced clinicians of the same theoretical persuasion.

Almost a half-century later, Pulver (1993) claimed that "psychoanalytic schools are not as different from one another as they are commonly supposed to be, particularly in matters of technique" (p. 339). He wrote that "in their daily practice, most analysts do not adhere strictly to the precepts of a specific school, even though they profess to be adherents of that school. Instead, they . . . adopt those technical procedures and principles that fit their own personalities and prove the most efficacious with their patients, regardless of the school from which they come" (p. 339). He applauded this eclectic trend and tried to demonstrate its benefits to his patients.

Pulver (1993) cited Sandler (1983) in support of his observation that analysts are moving in a more eclectic direction. Sandler (1983) asserted that in the privacy of their consulting rooms, analysts draw on useful concepts from rival schools of thought, even though they publicly identify with a single approach. Obviously, all these possible combinations of theory and practice make it difficult to know precisely what percentage of analysts do what and what difference it makes, if any.

Another prominent example of an eclectic trend in the context of treatment is Pine's (1990) influential *Drive, Ego, Object, and Self*. As the very title of his book indicates, Pine maintained that at different points in treatment, the analyst will need to focus on different aspects of personality highlighted by different psychoanalytic theories. Thus, for Pine—in the treatment situation, at least—psychoanalytic theories that emphasize drive, ego, object relations, or self do not oppose but *complement* each other. He suggested that the use of multiple models enhances therapeutic effectiveness (see also Silverman, 1986). Pine did not consider, nor was he interested in considering, the question of the degree to which at least certain aspects of different psychoanalytic theories—seen as broad theories of personality development or of human nature rather than primarily as guides to treatment—contradict one another. For example, the claims that sex and aggression are paramount in generating pathology and that they are not paramount clearly contradict each other. Or, as another example, the claim that the oedipal conflict is universal and that it plays a central role in pathology and the counter-claim that oedipal *conflicts* (as contrasted with *entering* the oedipal period) arise only when parents are overly seductive, competitive, and consumed with generational envy clearly contradict each other. The move toward therapeutic eclecticism does not eliminate these theoretical differences. It should be noted that in this section we are focusing almost entirely on the degree to which these theoretical differences have an impact on therapeutic technique and outcome rather than on the differences per se.

These considerations point to a sense of uncertainty about the validity of previously cherished theoretical beliefs and technical precepts regarding treatment. Although we still see evidence of heated debate, we also see a greater sense of modesty about what we think we know. We are now more apt to hear, "That's not how I do analysis" (perhaps still carrying the implication that the way *I* do it is better) rather than the bald proclamation, "You call *that* an analysis!" In a similar vein, Weinshel (1990) "advances the thesis that in the past 35 years there has been a relatively silent but nonetheless significant movement within the mainstream of American psychoanalysis toward a more 'modest' position" (p. 275). Among the trends he noted are (a) a focus on therapeutic changes rather than on "cures," (b) a focus on a shift in compromise formations rather than on the elimination of psychological conflict or on a "complete" analysis or resolution of the transference (see Kantrowitz, Katz, & Paolitto, 1990), (c) a lessened emphasis on insight as the sine qua non of a successful analysis, and (d) a greater acknowledgment of the analyst as a participant in the therapeutic process rather than as a passive mirror.

As a final, recent trend, it appears for the most part that the earlier, very sharp distinction between psychoanalysis and psychoanalytic psychotherapy has been softened. This is perhaps due in part to the relative paucity of patients being treated four to five times a week and to the insistence, most forcefully articulated by Gill (1982, 1984), that the distinction should rest on the degree to which the transference is the treatment focus rather than on whether the patient is sitting up and facing the analyst or supine on the couch, or whether the frequency of sessions is four times or less per week. On the other hand, the issue of frequency of sessions (generally focused on three versus four or more sessions per week) seems to continue to consume endless debate and organizational energy, even though we simply do not know in any scientifically defensible or even ordinarily reliable way whether or under what circumstances three versus four sessions per week (or any other frequency) makes any discernible difference at treatment outcome or at follow-up points. The absence of any reliable evidence permits this debate to continue unabated.

These somewhat informal reflections on the current state of the field stand in contrast to the systematic presentation of different schools of thought in the main body of our chapter. It is intended both to indicate some recent trends and to make more evident the gaps between the theories as stated and the realities of clinical practice.

CONCLUSION

Historically, an important general trend in psychoanalytic theory and practice has been the clear and steady shift from Freud's emphasis on instinctual wishes and on conflicts and defenses in relation to these wishes, to the increasing centrality of issues having to do with the development of self representations, of object representations, and of the relationship between them. Although in traditional theory, lives were believed to founder around issues of instinctual gratification and conflict, particularly oedipal conflict, in the more contemporary view, relative success or failure in the achievement of separation-individuation, self-cohesiveness, and supportive object relations is the hallmark of pathology versus health. As Jones put it some time ago, in his Preface to Fairbairn's (1952) *Psychoanalytic Studies of the Personality*:

> If it were possible to condense Dr. Fairbairn's new ideas into one sentence, it might run somewhat as follows. Instead of starting, as Freud did, from stimulation of the nervous system proceeding from excitation of various erotogenous zones and internal tension arising from gonadic activity, Dr. Fairbairn starts at the center of the personality, the ego, and depicts its strivings and difficulties in its endeavor to reach an object where it may find support. (p. v)

Also characterizing contemporary psychoanalytic theory is a relative shift from a psychology of conflict to one of defects, deficits, and arrests, although some contemporary psychoanalytic theorists have broadened the traditional Freudian concept of conflict so that it also is applicable to object relational issues (e.g., see Eagle, 1987; Mitchell, 1988; Weiss & Sampson, 1986).

Finally, changes in concepts of psychological development and of psychopathology have also been accompanied by changes in conceptions of treatment. There has been a shift involving a relative deemphasis on the therapeutic role of interpretation and insight and an increasing emphasis on the importance of the therapeutic relationship as the effective therapeutic agent. In the course of this shift, certain key concepts such as transference and countertransference have been reconceptualized to reflect the more interactional, two-person view of treatment. Thus as noted earlier, in Gill's (1982) writings, transference is not understood as a patient distorting a "blank screen" therapist, but as a patient responding to the therapist's cues and giving them his or her personal meanings.

For a good part of its history, the mainstream psychoanalytic community reacted to opposing views as heresies that needed to be uprooted and condemned. What seems to be distinctive about the contemporary psychoanalytic scene is the tolerance for and assimilation of formulations that were once viewed as deviant and heretical. In short, more than at any other period of its history, contemporary psychoanalysis is characterized by pluralism and theoretical diversity, and it is clear that our current conceptualizations of the nature of therapeutic change are more complex and multifaceted than ever. But to what extent the theoretical perspectives and treatment models presented here (and others which were omitted) are actually associated with different therapist behaviors and attitudes (Gray, 1982) and to what extent the use of one or another or some combination of these models is in fact associated with variations in the effectiveness of treatment outcome are among the important questions we need to answer in the future.

In the previous section, Most Recent Developments (written as an addendum to the chapter as it was originally published), we focused on some of the reasons for the present theoretical diversity and on the related issue of the use of multiple models in clinical work. In this context, we referred both to Wallerstein's (1992) emphasis on the idea of a "common ground" in psychoanalysis and to Pine's (1990) endorsement of the use of multiple theoretical perspectives as implying that therapeutic eclecticism is now fairly prevalent and desirable as long as certain basic psychoanalytic assumptions are maintained. We also noted that there are discrepancies between formal statements of the nature of therapeutic action and actual clinical practice. These trends pose a formidable challenge to gauging therapeutic effectiveness, particularly in view of an important, unchanged characteristic of clinical theory and practice, namely the paucity of systematic process and outcome studies of long-term psychoanalytic treatment. Thus, even though we see a somewhat greater tolerance of theoretical differences and more modest claims of therapeutic efficacy, the ways of resolving controversial issues that do still exist depend almost exclusively on persuasion and confident assertion—frequently but not always illustrated and buttressed by selected case vignettes—and on appeal to experience and authority. What is often presented in the psychoanalytic literature in lieu of evidence is a reference to an earlier stated authoritative claim or assertion. When this happens often enough, the assertion is taken as fact rather than opinion. This pattern of argumentation and theorizing persists, and as long as it does, we cannot really know whether innovations in theory and practice are merely shifts in fashion or constitute genuine progress.

REFERENCES

Abend, S. M., Porder, M. S., & Willick, M. S. (1983). *Borderline patients: Psychoanalytic perspectives*. Madison, CT: International Universities Press.

Abraham, K. (1927). *Selected papers on psychoanalysis*. London: Hogarth.

Alexander, F. (1948). *Fundamentals of psychoanalysis*. New York: Norton.

Alexander, F. (1954). Psychoanalysis and psychotherapy. *Journal of the American Psychoanalytic Association, 2*, 722–733.

Alexander, F., & French, T. M. (1946). *Psychoanalytic therapy: Principles and application*. New York: Ronald Press.

Allport, G. W. (1950). *The nature of personality: Selected papers* (pp. 79–91). Cambridge, MA: Addison-Wesley.

Arlow, J., & Brenner, C. (1964). *Psychoanalytic concepts and the structural theory.* Madison, CT: International Universities Press.

Balint, M. (1965). *Primary love and psychoanalytic techniques.* New York: Liveright.

Balint, M. (1968). *The basic fault.* New York: Brunner/Mazel.

Bergman, A., & Ellman, S. (1985). Margaret S. Mahler: Symbiosis and separation-individuation. In J. Reppen (Ed.), *Beyond Freud* (pp. 231–256). Hillsdale, NJ: Analytic Press.

Bibring, E. (1954). Psychoanalysis and the dynamic psychotherapies. *Journal of the American Psychoanalytic Association, 2,* 745–770.

Blum, H. P. (1979). The curative and creative aspects of insight. *Journal of the American Psychoanalytic Association, 27*(Suppl.), 41–65.

Blum, H. P. (1983). The position and value of extratransference interpretation. *Journal of the American Psychoanalytic Association, 31*(3), 587–618.

Bowlby, J. (1969). *Attachment and loss* (Vol. 1). New York: Basic Books.

Brenner, C. (1982). *The mind in conflict.* Madison, CT: International Universities Press.

Breuer, J., & Freud, S. (1955). Studies on hysteria. In *Standard edition of the complete psychological works of Sigmund Freud* (Vol. 2). London: Hogarth. (Original work published 1895)

Bucci, W. (1994). The multiple code theory and the psychoanalytic process: A framework for research. *Annual of Psychoanalysis, 22,* 239–259.

Budman, S. H. (Ed.). (1981). *Forms of brief therapy.* New York: Guilford Press.

Caston, J. (1993). Can analysts agree? The problems of consensus and the psychoanalytic mannequin: I. A proposed solution. *Journal of the American Psychoanalytic Association, 41*(2), 493–511.

Caston, J., & Martin, E. (1993). Can analysts agree? The problems of consensus and the psychoanalytic mannequin: II. Empirical tests. *Journal of the American Psychoanalytic Association, 41*(2), 513–548.

Charcot, J. M. (1882). Physiologie pathologique: Sur les divers etats nerveux determines par l'hypotization chez les hysteriques [Pathological physiology: On the different nervous states hypnotically induced in hysterics]. *CR Academy of Science Paris, 94,* 403–405.

Cooper, A. M. (1987). Changes in psychoanalytic ideas: Transference interpretation. *Journal of the American Psychoanalytic Association, 35,* 77–98.

Cooper, A. M. (1989). Concepts of therapeutic effectiveness in psychoanalysis: A historical review. *Psychoanalytic Inquiry, 9,* 4–25.

Curtis, H. C. (1980). The concept of therapeutic alliance: Implications for the "widening scope." In H. Blum (Ed.), *Psychoanalytic explorations of technique* (pp. 159–192). Madison, CT: International Universities Press.

Dahl, H. (1994). The characteristics, identification, and applications of FRAMES. *Psychotherapy Research, 4,* 253–276.

Eagle, M. (1979). Psychoanalytic formulations of phobias. In L. Saretsky, G. D.

Goldman, & D. S. Milman (Eds.), *Integrating ego psychology and object relations theory* (pp. 97–118). Dubuque, IA: Kendall/Hunt.

Eagle, M. (1987). *Recent developments in psychoanalysis: A critical evaluation.* Cambridge, MA: Harvard University Press.

Eagle, M., & Wolitzky, D. L. (1982). Therapeutic influences in dynamic psychotherapy: A review and synthesis. In S. Slipp (Ed.), *Curative factors in dynamic psychotherapy* (pp. 321–348). New York: McGraw-Hill.

Edelson, M. (1988). *Psychoanalysis: A theory in crisis.* Chicago: University of Chicago Press.

Ehrenberg, D. (1982). Psychoanalytic engagement: The transaction as primary data. *Contemporary Psychoanalysis, 18,* 535–555.

Eissler, K. R. (1953). The effect of the structure of the ego on psychoanalytic technique. *Journal of the American Psychoanalytic Association, 1,* 104–143.

Ellenberger, H. (1970). *The discovery of the unconscious.* New York: Basic Books.

Erle, J. (1990). Studying the psychoanalytic process: An introduction. *Psychoanalytic Quarterly, 59*(4), 527–531.

Fairbairn, W. R. D. (1941). A revised psychopathology of the psychoses and psychoneuroses. *International Journal of Psychoanalysis, 22,* 250–279.

Fairbairn, W. R. D. (1952). *Psychoanalytic studies of the personality.* London: Tavistock Publications and Kegan Paul, Trench, & Trubner.

Ferenczi, S., & Rank, O. (1956). *The development of psychoanalysis.* New York: Dover Publications. (Original work published 1925)

Fiedler, F. (1950). A comparison of therapeutic relationships in psychoanalytic, nondirective, and Adlerian therapy. *Journal of Consulting Psychology, 14,* 436–445.

Fine, S., & Fine, E. (1990). Four psychoanalytic perspectives: A study of differences in interpretive interventions. *Journal of the American Psychoanalytic Association, 38,* 1017–1047.

Frank, J. D. (1973). *Persuasion and healing* (Rev. ed.). Baltimore: Johns Hopkins University Press.

Freud, A. (1936). *The ego and the mechanisms of defense.* Madison, CT: International Universities Press.

Freud, S. (1953). On psychotherapy. In J. Strachey (Ed. and Trans.), *The standard edition of the complete psychological works of Sigmund Freud* (Vol. 7, pp. 255–268). London: Hogarth. (Original work published 1905)

Freud, S. (1954a). Analysis terminable and interminable. *Standard edition* (Vol. 23, pp. 209–253). London: Hogarth. (Original work published 1937)

Freud, S. (1954b). *The origins of psychoanalysis: Freud's letters to Wilhelm Fliess, 1887–1902.* New York: Basic Books.

Freud, S. (1954c). *The origins of psychoanalysis,* (Letter 69). New York: Basic Books. (Original work written in 1897)

Freud, S. (1955). Lines of advance in psycho-analytic therapy. *Standard edition* (Vol. 17, pp. 157–168). London: Hogarth. (Original work published 1919)

Freud, S. (1957a). On narcissism. *Standard edition* (Vol. 14, pp. 67–102). London: Hogarth. (Original work published 1914)

Freud, S. (1957b). On the history of the psychoanalytic movement. *Standard edition* (Vol. 14, pp. 2–66). London: Hogarth. (Original work published 1914)

Freud, S. (1958). The dynamics of transference. *Standard edition* (Vol. 12, pp. 97–108). London: Hogarth. (Original work published 1912)

Freud, S. (1959). Inhibitions, symptoms, and anxiety. *Standard edition* (Vol. 20, pp. 77–174). London: Hogarth. (Original work published 1926)

Freud, S. (1961). The ego and the id. *Standard edition* (Vol. 19, pp. 3–68). London: Hogarth. (Original work published 1923)

Freud, S. (1962). The neuro-psychoses of defense. In J. Strachey (Ed. and Trans.), *Standard edition* (Vol. 3, pp. 43–61). London: Hogarth. (Original work published 1894)

Freud, S. (1964a). An outline of psychoanalysis. *Standard edition* (Vol. 23, pp. 141–207). London: Hogarth. (Original work published 1940)

Freud, S. (1964b). New introductory lectures. *Standard edition* (Vol. 22, pp. 3–182). London: Hogarth. (Original work published 1933)

Friedman, L. (1978). Trends in the psychoanalytic theory of treatment. *Psychoanalytic Quarterly, XLVII*(4), 524–567.

Friedman, L. (1986). Kohut's testament. *Psychoanalytic Inquiry, 6*, 321–347.

Fromm, E. (1941). *Escape from freedom.* New York: Holt, Rinehart & Winston.

Fromm-Reichmann, F. (1950). *Principles of intensive psychotherapy.* Chicago: University of Chicago Press.

Gill, M. M. (1954). Psychoanalysis and exploratory psychotherapy. *Journal of the American Psychoanalytic Association, 2*, 771–797.

Gill, M. M. (1967). *The collected papers of David Rapaport.* New York: Basic Books.

Gill, M. M. (1982). Analysis of the transference. In H. J. Schlesinger (Ed.), *Psychological Issues* [Monograph 53]. Madison, CT: International Universities Press.

Gill, M. M. (1983). The point of view of psychoanalysis: Energy discharge or person. *Psychoanalysis and Contemporary Thought, 6*, 523–551.

Gill, M. M. (1984). Psychoanalysis and psychotherapy: A revision. *International Review of Psychoanalysis, 11*(2), 161–179.

Gill, M. M. (1987). The analyst as participant. In, How theory shapes technique: Perspectives on a clinical study [Special issue]. *Psychoanalytic Inquiry, 7*(2), 249–259.

Gill, M. M. (1994). *Psychoanalysis in transition.* Hillsdale, NJ: Analytic Press.

Glover, E. (1931). The therapeutic effect of inexact interpretation. *International Journal of Psychoanalysis, 12*, 397–411.

Gray, P. (1982). "Developmental lag" in the evolution of technique for psychoanalysis of neurotic conflict. *Journal of the American Psychoanalytic Association, 30*, 621–655.

Greenberg, J. R., & Mitchell, S. A. (1983). *Object relations in psychoanalytic theory.* Cambridge, MA: Harvard University Press.

Greenson, R. R. (1965). The working alliance and the transference neurosis. *Psychoanalytic Quarterly, 34,* 155–181.

Greenson, R. R. (1967). *The technique and practice of psychoanalysis,* Vol. 1. Madison, CT: International Universities Press.

Greenson, R. R. (1978a). The problem of working through. In R. R. Greenson (Ed.), *Explorations in psychoanalysis* (pp. 255–267). Madison, CT: International Universities Press.

Greenson, R. R. (1978b). Empathy and its vicissitudes. In R. R. Greenson (Ed.), *Explorations in psychoanalysis* (pp. 147–161). Madison, CT: International Universities Press.

Greenson, R. R., & Wexler, M. (1969). The non-transference relationship in the psychoanalytic situation. *International Journal of Psycho-Analysis, 50,* 27–39.

Grunbaum, A. (1993). Validation in the clinical theory of psychoanalysis: A study in the philosophy of psychoanalysis. *Psychological Issues* [Monograph 61]. Madison, CT: International Universities Press.

Guntrip, H. (1969). *Schizoid phenomena, object relations and the self.* Madison, CT: International Universities Press.

Hartmann, H. (1958). *Ego psychology and the problem of adaptation.* Madison, CT: International Universities Press. (Original work published 1939)

Hartmann, H. (1964). *Essays on ego psychology: Selected problems in psychoanalytic theory.* Madison, CT: International Universities Press.

Hartmann, H., Kris, E., & Lowenstein, R. M. (1946). Comments on the formation of psychic structure. *Psychoanalytic Study of the Child, 2,* 11–38.

Hoffman, I. Z. (1991). Discussion: Toward a social constructivist view of the psychoanalytic situation. *Psychoanalytic Dialogues, 1,* 74–105.

Hoffman, I. Z. (1992). Some practical implications of a social–constructivist view of the psychoanalytic situation. *Psychoanalytic Dialogues, 2,* 287–304.

Horney, K. (1945). *Our inner conflicts.* New York: Norton.

Horney, K. (1950). *Neurosis and human growth.* New York: Norton.

Hurvich, M. (1985, May). *Traumatic moment, basic dangers, and annihilation anxiety.* Paper presented to the New York Freudian Society, New York.

Jacobson, E. (1964). *The self and the object world.* Madison, CT: International Universities Press.

Kantrowitz, J., Katz, A. L., & Paolitto, F. (1990). Followup of psychoanalysis file to ten years after termination: III. The relation between the resolution of the transference and the patient–analyst match. *Journal of the American Psychoanalytic Association, 38*(3), 655–678.

Kernberg, O. F. (1975). *Borderline conditions and pathological narcissism.* New York: Jason Aronson.

Kernberg, O. F. (1976). *Object relations theory and clinical psychoanalysis.* New York: Jason Aronson.

Kernberg, O. F. (1980). *Internal world and external reality*. New York: Jason Aronson.

Kernberg, O. F. (1984). *Severe personality disorders*. New Haven, CT: Yale University Press.

Kernberg, O. F., Selzer, M. A., Koenigsberg, H. W., Carr, A. C., & Applebaum, A. H. (1989). *Psychodynamic psychotherapy of borderline patients*. New York: Basic Books.

Klein, M. (1948). *Contributions to Psychoanalysis (1921–1945)*. London: Hogarth Press.

Klerman, G. L., Rounsaville, B., Chevron, E., & Weissman, M. (1984). *Interpersonal psychotherapy of depression*. New York: Basic Books.

Knight, R. P. (1953). Management and psychotherapy of the borderline schizophrenic patient. *Bulletin of the Menninger Clinic, 17*, 139–150.

Kohut, H. (1971). *The analysis of the self*. Madison, CT: International Universities Press.

Kohut, H. (1977). *The restoration of the self*. Madison, CT: International Universities Press.

Kohut, H. (1979). The two analyses of Mr. Z. *International Journal of Psychoanalysis, 60*, 3–27.

Kohut, H. (1984). *How does analysis cure?* Chicago: University of Chicago Press.

Kris, E. (1952). *Psychoanalytic explorations in art*. Madison, CT: International Universities Press.

Kuhn, T. (1962). *The structure of scientific revolutions* (2nd ed.). Chicago: University of Chicago Press.

Lachmann, F. M. (1986). Interpretation of psychic conflict and adversarial relationships: A self-psychological perspective. *Psychoanalytic Psychology, 3*(4), 341–355.

Langs, R. (1982). *The psychotherapeutic conspiracy*. New York: Jason Aronson.

Levenson, E. (1982). Language and healing. In S. Slipp (Ed.), *Curative factors in dynamic psychotherapy* (pp. 91–103). New York: McGraw-Hill.

Levenson, E. (1985). The interpersonal (Sullivanian) model. In A. Rothstein (Ed.), *Models of the mind* (pp. 49–67). Madison, CT: International Universities Press.

Levenson, E. (1988). Show and tell: The recursive order of the transference. In A. Rothstein (Ed.), *How does treatment help?—On the modes of therapeutic action in psychoanalytic psychotherapy*. Madison, CT: International Universities Press.

Limentani, A. (1975). Discussion. *Psychoanalytic Forum, 5*, 288–294.

Loewald, H. (1960). On the therapeutic action of psychoanalysis. *International Journal of Psycho-Analysis, 2*, 17–33.

Loewald, H. (1980). *Papers on psychoanalysis*. New Haven, CT: Yale University Press.

Luborsky, L. (1984). *Principles of psychoanalytic psychotherapy: A manual for supportive-expressive treatment*. New York: Basic Books.

Luborsky, L. (1988). The accuracy of therapists' interpretations and the outcome of dynamic psychotherapy. *Journal of Consulting and Clinical Psychology, 56,* 490–495.

Luborsky, L. (1996). Theories of cure in psychoanalytic psychotherapies and the evidence for them. *Psychoanalytic Inquiry, 16,* 257–264.

Macalpine, I. (1950). The development of the transference. *Psychoanalytic Quarterly, 19,* 501–539.

Mahler, M. (1968). *On human symbiosis and the vicissitudes of individuation. Vol. I: Infantile psychosis.* Madison, CT: International Universities Press.

Mahler, M., Pine, F., & Bergman, A. (1975). *The psychological birth of the human infant.* New York: Basic Books.

Meissner, W. W. (1980). Theories of personality and psychopathology: Classical psychoanalysis. In H. J. Kaplan, A. M. Freedman, & B. J. Sadock (Eds.), *Comprehensive textbook of Psychiatry: Vol. 1* (pp. 631–728). Baltimore: Williams and Wilkins.

Messer, S., Tishby, O., & Spillman, A. (1992). Taking context seriously in psychotherapy research: Relating therapist interventions to patient progress in brief psychodynamic psychotherapy. *Journal of Consulting and Clinical Psychology, 60,* 678–688.

Mitchell, S. A. (1988). *Relational concepts in psychoanalysis: An integration.* Cambridge, MA: Harvard University Press.

Mitchell, S. A. (1993). *Hope and dread in psychoanalysis.* New York: Basic Books.

Modell, A. H. (1976). "The holding environment" and the therapeutic action of psychoanalysis. *Journal of the American Psychoanalytic Association, 24,* 285–307.

Modell, A. H. (1984). *Psychoanalysis in a new context.* Madison, CT: International Universities Press.

Modell, A. H. (1987). An object relations perspective. In, How theory shapes technique: Perspectives on a clinical study [Special issue]. *Psychoanalytic Inquiry, 7*(2), 233–240.

Modell, A. H. (1989). The psychoanalytic setting as a container of multiple levels of reality: A perspective on the theory of psychoanalytic treatment. *Psychoanalytic Inquiry, 9*(1), 67–87.

Modell, A. H. (1990). *Other times, other realities: Toward a psychoanalytic theory of treatment.* Cambridge, MA: Harvard University Press.

Muslin, H., & Gill, M. M. (1978). Transference in the Dora case. *Journal of the American Psychoanalytic Association, 26,* 311–328.

Ornstein, P. (Ed.). (1978). *The season for the self: Selected writings of Heinz Kohut: 1950–1978.* Madison, CT: International Universities Press.

Peterfreund, E. (1983). *The process of psychoanalytic therapy.* Hillsdale, NJ: Analytic Press.

Peterfreund, E. (1990). On the distinction between clinical process and clinical content theories. *Psychoanalytic Psychology, 7*(1), 1–12.

Pine, F. (1990). *Drive, ego, object, and self: A synthesis for clinical work.* New York: Basic Books.

Pulver, S. (1993). The eclectic analyst: or the many roads to insight and change. *Journal of the American Psychoanalytic Association, 41*(2), 339–357.

Racker, H. (1968). *Transference and countertransference.* Madison, CT: International Universities Press.

Rangell, L. (1954). Similarities and differences between psychoanalysis and dynamic psychotherapy. *Journal of the American Psychoanalytic Association, 2,* 734–744.

Reich, W. (1949). *Character analysis* (3rd ed.; T. P. Wolfe, Trans.). New York: Noonday Press.

Richards, A. D. (1990). The future of psychoanalysis: The past, the present, and the future of psychoanalytic theory. *Psychoanalytic Quarterly, 59*(3), 347–369.

Richards, A. D., & Richards, A. K. (1995). Notes on psychoanalytic theory and its consequences for technique. *Journal of Clinical Psychoanalysis, 4,* 429–456.

Sandler, J. (1983). Reflections of some relations between psychoanalytic concepts and psychoanalytic practice. *International Journal of Psychoanalysis, 64*(1), 35–45.

Schafer, R. (1959). Generative empathy in the treatment situation. *Psychoanalytic Quarterly, 28,* 342–373.

Schafer, R. (1968). *Aspects of internalization.* Madison, CT: International Universities Press.

Schafer, R. (1983). *The analytic attitude.* New York: Basic Books.

Schafer, R. (1994). The contemporary Kleinians of London. *Psychoanalytic Quarterly, 63,* 409–432.

Schimek, J. G. (1983). The construction of the transference: The relativity of the "here and now" and the "there and then." *Psychoanalysis and Contemporary Thought, 6,* 435–456.

Schwaber, E. (1981). Empathy: A mode of analytic listening. *Psychoanalytic Inquiry, 1,* 357–392.

Segal, H. (1967). Melanie Klein's technique. In B. Wolman (Ed.), *Psychoanalytic techniques: A handbook for the practicing psychoanalyst* (pp. 168–190). New York: Basic Books.

Silverman, D. K. (1986). A multi-model approach: Looking at clinical data from three theoretical perspectives. *Psychoanalytic Psychology, 3,* 121–132.

Smith, M. L., Glass, G. V., & Miller, T. I. (1980). *The benefits of psychotherapy.* Baltimore: Johns Hopkins University Press.

Spence, D. P. (1994). Monitoring the analytic surface. *Journal of the American Psychoanalytic Association, 42,* 43–64.

Stein, M. H. (1981). The objectionable part of the transference. *Journal of the American Psychoanalytic Association, 29*(4), 869–892.

Stolorow, R. D., & Atwood, G. E. (1992). *Contexts of being: The intersubjective foundations of psychological life.* Hillsdale, NJ: Analytic Press.

Stone, L. (1954). The widening scope of indications for psychoanalysis. *Journal of the American Psychoanalytic Association, 2,* 567–594.

Stone, L. (1961). *The psychoanalytic situation: An examination of its development and essential nature.* Madison, CT: International Universities Press.

Stone, L. (1981). Notes on the noninterpretive aspects of the psychoanalytic situation and process. *Journal of the American Psychoanalytic Association, 29,* 89–118.

Storr, A. (1988). *Solitude: A return to the self.* New York: Ballantine Books.

Strachey, J. (1934). The nature of the therapeutic action of psycho-analysis. *International Journal of Psychiatry, IV,* 127–159.

Strupp, H. H., & Binder, J. L. (1984). *Psychotherapy in a new key.* New York: Basic Books.

Sullivan, H. S. (1953). *The interpersonal theory of psychiatry.* New York: Norton.

Sullivan, H. S. (1954). *The psychiatric interview.* New York: Norton.

Wachtel, P. L. (Ed.). (1982). *Resistance.* New York: Plenum.

Waelder, R. (1960). *Basic theory of psychoanalysis.* Madison, CT: International Universities Press.

Wallerstein, R. S. (1983). *Psychoanalysis and psychotherapy: Relative roles reconsidered.* Presented as a plenary address at the Boston Psychoanalytic Society and Institute Symposium on "Psychoanalysis Today: The Interpretation of Theory and Practice." Boston, MA, October 29, 1983.

Wallerstein, R. S. (1984). The analysis of transference: A matter of emphasis or of theory reformulation. *Psychoanalytic Inquiry, 4*(3), 325–354.

Wallerstein, R. S. (1986). *Forty-Two lives in treatment. A study of psychoanalysis and psychotherapy.* New York/London: Guilford Press.

Wallerstein, R. S. (1988a). One psychoanalysis or many? *International Journal of Psychoanalysis, 69,* 5–21.

Wallerstein, R. S. (1988b). Assessment of structural change in psychoanalytic therapy and research. *Journal of the American Psychoanalytic Association,* 36(Suppl.), 241–261.

Wallerstein, R. S. (1990a). Psychoanalysis and psychotherapy: An historical perspective. *International Journal of Psychoanalysis, 70*(4), 563–592.

Wallerstein, R. S. (1990b). Psychoanalysis: The common ground. *International Journal of Psychoanalysis, 71,* 3–20.

Wallerstein, R. S. (Ed.). (1992). *The common ground of psychoanalysis.* Northvale, NJ: Aronson.

Wallerstein, R. S. (1995). The relation of theory to technique. *Journal of Clinical Psychoanalysis, 4,* 527–542.

Weinshel, E. M. (1988). Structural changes in psychoanalysis. *Journal of the American Psychoanalytic Association* (Suppl. 36), 263–280.

Weinshel, E. M. (1990). How wide is the widening scope of psychoanalysis and how solid is its structural model? Some concerns and observations. *Journal of the American Psychoanalytic Association, 32*(2), 275–296.

Weiss, J. (1990). Unconscious mental functioning. *Scientific American, 262* (no. 3), 103–109.

Weiss, J., & Sampson, H. (1986). *The psychoanalytic process: Theory, clinical observations, and empirical research.* New York: Guilford Press.

Wile, D. B. (1984). Kohut, Kernberg, and accusatory interpretations. *Psychotherapy, 21*(3), 353–364.

Winnicott, D. W. (1958). *Through pediatrics to psychoanalysis.* London: Tavistock Publications.

Witenberg, E. G. (1974). American Neo-Freudian schools—A. The interpersonal and cultural approaches. In S. Arieti (Ed.), *American Handbook of Psychiatry* (2nd ed.). New York: Basic Books.

Zetzel, E. R. (1971). A developmental approach to the borderline patient. *American Journal of Psychiatry, 127,* 867–871.

Zucker, H. (1989). Premises of interpersonal theory. *Psychoanalytic Psychology,* 6(4), 401–419.

3

HUMANISTIC APPROACHES TO PSYCHOTHERAPY

LESLIE S. GREENBERG AND LAURA N. RICE

The theories of psychotherapy designated as humanistic share beliefs and principles that differentiate them clearly from other major orientations such as cognitive–behavioral and psychodynamic. As we explain in this chapter, the ways in which these principles are implemented in the actual therapy sessions vary substantially in the different humanistic approaches. Nevertheless, all share an emphasis on subjectivity and awareness in understanding behavior, and a resistance against the view of the person as an object, to be seen objectively from an external vantage point that ignores the individual's existential reality. The position of Kierkegaard (1843/ 1954), as well as that of Sartre (1943/1956), was that both objective reality and one's uniquely human subjective reality must be respected in order to grasp the more complete reality underlying both the subjective and the objective. The European philosophers Husserl (1925/1977), Heidegger (1949/1962), Jaspers (1963), and Marcel (1951) were all influential in explicating and extending this position.

This chapter is a revised and expanded version of "Humanistic Approaches to Psychotherapy," by L. N. Rice and L. S. Greenberg, 1992, in *History of Psychotherapy: A Century of Change* (pp. 197–224), edited by D. K. Freedheim, Washington, DC: American Psychological Association.

Humanistic theorists, often spoken of as the "third force" in psychology, have written extensively on the nature of human existence, on methods by which uniquely human modes of functioning can be studied and grasped, and on implications of humanistic assumptions for the goals and processes of psychotherapy (Bugental, 1967; Buhler, 1967; Jourard, 1968; Lewin, 1951; Maslow, 1968; May, 1961).

A number of authors have attempted to characterize the core beliefs of humanistic psychology (e.g., McWaters, 1977, and Sutich & Vich, 1969). The most recent comprehensive attempt (Tageson, 1982) has focused in detail on a number of major themes of humanistic psychology. We consider four of these to be of primary importance in all the humanistic psychotherapy approaches.

1. The first and most central characteristic of humanistic psychology and psychotherapy is the commitment to a phenomenological approach. This approach is grounded in the belief in the uniquely human capacity for reflective consciousness, and in the belief that it is this capacity that can lead to self-determination and freedom. Tageson (1982) states the core assumption in a way that is especially relevant to psychotherapy. "Whatever terminology is preferred, all seem agreed on the inescapable uniqueness of human consciousness and on the importance of understanding *this* person's perception of reality if we are ever completely to understand his or her behaviour" (p. 33).

2. The operation of some form of actualizing or growth tendency is a second highly significant issue for humanistic therapists, although it is one on which they take somewhat different positions. All would agree with the importance of the antihomeostatic view of human beings as striving toward growth and development rather than merely toward the maintenance of stability (Maslow, 1970). All would agree that one's choices are guided by awareness of the future and the immediate present rather than only by the past. Tageson (1982) emphasized the point that this *actualizing* tendency is more than a biological concept and makes the interesting comment, "It is my conviction that the attribute of consciousness transforms the actualizing tendency in the organism into a directional tendency that has more to do with the notion of the self as a centre of intentionality in a more or less constant search for meaning" (p. 40).

3. The belief in human capacity for self-determination is an important and sometimes controversial focus of humanistic theorists. The ways in which this capacity is developed, fa-

cilitated, or blocked are a key issue. Choice and will are central aspects of human functioning. Individuals are not determined solely by their past or by their environments but are agents in the construction of their world.

4. The fourth shared basic principle is that of person-centeredness. This involves concern and real respect for each person, whether they are subjects of study in research or are engaged in the process of psychotherapy. Each person's subjective experience is of central importance to the humanist, and in the effort to grasp this experience, one is attempting to share the other person's world in a special way that goes beyond the subject–object dichotomy. Being allowed to share another person's world is viewed as a special privilege requiring a special kind of relationship.

The focus of this chapter will be on the emergence and development of the three humanistic approaches to psychotherapy that have been the most influential: the client-centered (person-centered) approach of Carl Rogers, the Gestalt approach of Fritz Perls, and the existential approach. Although there is great variability in the processes engaged in by existential therapists, we will concentrate primarily on the positions shared by Rollo May and Irvin Yalom and, to a lesser extent, on the European existentialists, Binswanger, Boss, and Frankl.

ORIGINS

In examining the historical, geographical, and professional origins of humanistic therapists, it is apparent that, although they emerged from quite different environments, all were directly or indirectly influenced by humanistic philosophers. All were searching for understandings and approaches that would build on the uniquely human capacity for self-reflective consciousness and on the search for meanings, choices, and growth. All were attempting to move beyond what they regarded as the restricted views of human functioning represented in the other two major orientations—psychoanalysis and behavior therapy. Although all humanistic theories explicated views of pathological functioning, the humanistic therapists' primary focus was on understanding ways in which people could be helped to move toward healthy or even ideal functioning.

The Client-Centered Approach

Carl Rogers was born in Illinois in 1902. He began his doctoral studies at Union Theological Seminary in New York, but transferred to Columbia

University Teachers College for graduate training in clinical psychology. His thesis supervisor was Goodwin Watson, who was a well-known expert on group leadership training. Rogers was also indirectly influenced by the ideas of John Dewey through one of his teachers, W. H. Kilpatrick. He received intensive training in psychological assessment, and, through a year's internship at the Institute for Child Guidance, he received training in the psychoanalytic approach. His professional identity was clearly that of a psychologist, strongly imbued with the scientific methods that characterized American psychology. He was president of the American Psychological Association in 1946.

After finishing graduate school, Rogers joined the Child Study Department of a social agency in Rochester. During his 12 years in Rochester he was introduced by social workers to some of the ideas and methods of the psychoanalyst, Otto Rank. Rank's belief in the person's constructive forces, including a will to health, and a belief in the crucial importance of the spontaneous human relationship in psychotherapy influenced and confirmed the views that Rogers had already begun to develop.

During the period when he was on the faculty at Ohio State University (1940–1944), Rogers and his colleagues and students began the practice of studying complete transcripts of audio-recorded therapy interviews in an effort to achieve a fuller understanding of the processes involved. (The practice of recording therapy sessions was almost unheard of in other clinical settings.) Some of the ideas that emerged from this intensive, inductive effort to become aware of and understand some of the essential change processes in psychotherapy were described in his book, *Counseling and Psychotherapy* (Rogers, 1942), which also contained a complete transcript of an actual therapy. (See chapter 19 for further information on this topic.)

After Rogers moved to the University of Chicago in 1945, the intensive listening process continued. Through listening to and discussing their own or each others' therapy sessions, Rogers and his colleagues attempted to identify and reflect on some of the crucial change processes that took place, and how these changes were facilitated by the therapist (Rogers, 1957). The emphasis was usually not on specific content nor on particular insights arrived at, but on process changes in the client that seemed to take place in therapies with successful outcomes. The hypotheses emerging from this experiential understanding were then formulated and tested by means of verification studies conducted by usual scientific methods. Later on at Chicago, there was a strong emphasis on conducting empirical research at the Counseling Center (Rogers & Dymond, 1954). An entire issue of the *Journal of Consulting Psychology* was devoted to research conducted by Rogers' graduate students, including Haigh (1949), Raskin (1949), and Seeman (1949). Rogers' book, *Client-Centered Therapy* (1951), built on the earlier formulations and laid some of the most important foundations for his later work.

There were two indirect but valuable influences on Rogers' thinking. First, he adopted Goldstein's concept of an actualizing tendency in human beings (Goldstein, 1939). Kurt Goldstein was an eminent neuropsychologist at the Institute for Brain Damaged Soldiers in Germany, who had become impressed by the capacity of soldiers with brain injuries to reorganize their own modes of functioning. Goldstein's observations that people reorganized in constructive ways confirmed Rogers' view of the basic human motivation toward growth and wholeness, the actualizing tendency, which became the one central motivational concept in his theoretical system.

A second indirect influence came from the writings of Martin Buber (1957), brought to Rogers' attention by graduate theology students at the University of Chicago. Rogers recognized that the I–Thou relationship, which was viewed by Buber as having a healing effect, was exactly the experience that emerged in especially good therapy hours.

In listing the most important sources of his ideas, Rogers (1980) placed much value on what he had learned from graduate students and colleagues. For instance, Eugene Gendlin, a graduate student and later a colleague, formulated the concept of "experiencing" (Gendlin, 1962), based on the view that, within human beings, there is an ongoing flow of experiencing to which the person can turn, under the right conditions, in order to discover the "felt meanings" of experiences. Rogers felt that the concept of experiencing had influenced his view of therapist empathy as well as a number of other important issues.

In 1957 Rogers moved to the faculty at the University of Wisconsin and began an extensive research project on the processes and effects of client-centered therapy with hospitalized schizophrenic patients (Rogers, Gendlin, Kiesler, & Truax, 1967). In 1964 he moved to California, first to the Western Behavioral Sciences Institute and then to the Center for Studies of the Person. During these years he became increasingly interested in working with groups and with a wide range of issues, including international relations and the prevention of nuclear war. It was also during this period that he decided that client-centered therapy should be renamed "person-centered therapy."

For those interested in a general overview of Rogers' life and ideas, we suggest the chapter by Raskin and Rogers (1989). Rogers' book, On Becoming a Person (1961), is a useful source for getting an "inside feel" for client-centered therapy. Then, after getting a basic background in his thinking, his book A Way of Being (1980), in which he discussed a variety of ideas and turning-points as well as learnings from his own personal and professional life, would be especially meaningful and moving.

The Gestalt Approach

Frederick Perls was born in Germany in 1893. After acquiring medical training, he worked as an assistant to Kurt Goldstein and was strongly influenced by Goldstein's ideas about the organism and the self-actualizing tendency. It was in Germany that he met Laura Perls, who became his wife and collaborator in developing the Gestalt approach to psychotherapy. Laura Perls introduced him to the work of the Gestalt psychologists, Koffka (1935), Kohler (1959), and Wertheimer (1945). She herself had been influenced by the existential writings of Buber and Tillich.

Perls became a psychoanalyst and was especially influenced by his own analyst, Wilhelm Reich. He was also informed by the works of psychoanalysts Karen Horney and Otto Rank. Dissatisfied with psychoanalytic dogmatism, and working within a zeitgeist in Europe that was strongly influenced by phenomenological and existential viewpoints, he began to make revisions of psychoanalytic theory (Perls, 1947). Eventually, in 1951, Perls, Hefferline, and Goodman proposed a new integration among Gestalt, existential, and analytic approaches in the form of a Gestalt therapy, originally called "concentration therapy."

Two additional important influences on Perls's thinking were that of the philosopher Friedlander and the South African statesman and Prime Minister, Jan Smuts. Perls was impressed by Friedlander's (1918) work on the nature of polarities and the importance of a balance between them in human functioning. Perls integrated Smuts's (1926) work on holism with Kurt Lewin's (1951) field theory, leading him to view the person as part of an organism/environment field and to view the mind and body holistically. Zen also has had an important influence on the development of Gestalt therapy, especially in its later years, and it has been referred to as "western Zen," or as a form of existential therapy.

When Perls arrived in the United States after his stay in South Africa, where he had fled as war approached in Europe, he began the active promotion of Gestalt therapy. The New York Institute for Gestalt Therapy was formed in the 1950s, and workshops and study groups were established throughout the country. Perls moved to the west coast in the 1960s and settled for a while at the Esalen Institute in California to establish training workshops. Later he moved to Canada to establish a new institute. Throughout this period many people were trained in the Gestalt approach.

Perls developed many ideas that were subsequently incorporated into general humanistic and eclectic psychotherapy practice. The emphasis on body awareness, direct experience, the importance of encounter, the use of active experimentation, and the use of awareness exercises all became incorporated into the humanistic therapies in the 1960s and 1970s.

As originally practiced by Perls, the Gestalt approach involved some abrasive techniques, including client frustration, when working with clients viewed as manipulative. Since Perls's death in 1970, the Gestalt movement has shifted toward a softer form of therapy, with less use of modes of frustrating clients and more emphasis on the I–Thou dialogue.

The best introduction to Gestalt therapy is the chapter by Yontef and Simkin (1989), followed by Perls's four lectures (Fagan & Shepherd, 1970; Perls, 1969), which can be followed by a reading of *Gestalt Therapy, Excitement and Growth in the Personality* (Perls, Hefferline, & Goodman, 1951). Perls's posthumous work, *The Gestalt Approach and Eyewitness to Therapy* (Perls, 1973), combines a description of the overall approach not provided elsewhere, with transcripts of Perls's practice. *Gestalt Therapy Integrated* (Polster & Polster, 1973) provides an innovative effort to expand the boundaries of the Gestalt approach and is required reading for the serious student who wishes to understand the Gestalt approach.

The Existential Approaches

The existential approaches emerged more or less independently in the 1940s and 1950s in different countries in Europe. There were a number of possible reasons for the spontaneous emergence of this movement. Most existential therapists were psychiatrists with a background in psychoanalysis who felt that the person, as he or she really existed, was being lost in the psychodynamic approaches. Also, European theorists were usually much more aware of the writings of the philosophers Kierkegaard, Nietzsche, Husserl, Sartre, Marcel, Jaspers, and Heidegger than were the North American psychologists and psychiatrists. Moreover, as May and Yalom (1984) have mentioned, this period in Europe was a period of alienation and anxiety, in which there was not only the threat of nuclear war, but awareness of major cultural changes that were taking place in society.

Two of the most influential existential approaches were those of Binswanger (1963) and Boss (1963), who rejected the exclusively biological and mechanistic view of human functioning in Freud's position. Adopting Heidegger's concept of Dasein (existence), they developed an approach that was called *Daseinanalyse*, which emphasized the human capacity for giving meaning to existence. Victor Frankl was another influential European psychiatrist. His existential approach, which he called Logotherapy (1963), has a unique flavor, based to some extent on his own experience at the Nazi death camp at Auschwitz.

Rollo May was largely responsible for introducing existential therapy into the United States (May, Angel, & Ellenberger, 1958). May was trained as a psychoanalyst at the William Alanson White Institute in New York, a neo-Freudian setting in which the views of Sullivan, Fromm, and Horney were incorporated. He practiced as a psychoanalyst and during the period became dissatisfied with some of the methods and underlying assumptions of the psychoanalytic approaches. He began reading about the European existential theories in the early 1950s, and began to focus on what he saw as missing from the Freudian and neo-Freudian positions. As May suggests, the interpersonal world had been incorporated into the views of the neo-Freudians, but the relationship to oneself was still missing in the approaches.

Two other existential therapists in the United States who have written extensively on the theory and practice of existential therapy are Bugental (1967) and Yalom (1981), the latter having provided the first comprehensive volume entitled *Existential Psychotherapy*. Probably the most useful introduction to existential therapy is the chapter by May and Yalom (1989) and the books by May (1977), Yalom (1981), and Bugental (1967).

THE THERAPEUTIC PROCESSES

In this section we would like to convey some flavor of the centrality of the four humanistic principles described in the introduction that guide the actual processes engaged in by humanistic therapists. Although the different approaches implement the principles in different ways, the themes are of central importance in all the humanistic orientations.

1. The phenomenological approach—Discovery-oriented with the client viewed as the expert on his or her own experience. The phenomenological theme in humanistic psychology yields two related but distinctive features of humanistic therapy. First, the emphasis is on the client's process of discovery as opposed to an interpretive focus. In other words, clients are encouraged to identify and symbolize their inner experience for themselves, rather than having the therapist offer symbols to them to help them make sense of their experience. Second, clients are viewed as having privileged access to their unique, inner awareness and are therefore viewed as experts on their own experience; no attempts are made to contradict, oppose, or otherwise shape the content of experience.

Rogers believed that human beings have the "gift of awareness" (Rogers & Skinner, 1956), and if the therapist could provide the appropriate conditions, clients could become aware of their own perceptions of inner and outer reality and thus could increasingly guide their own life's choices in fulfilling directions. The emphasis is on trying to establish optimal conditions for inner exploration, rather than on providing insight, or trying to understand the choices that the client needs to make, or pushing for choice. Empathic reflection of the client's moment-by-moment inner awareness is viewed as the most effective way of enabling clients to discover for themselves the awareness that will motivate and guide their choices.

Viewing clients as experts on their own experience is a central aspect of the client-centered process. The therapist's reflections carry the message of empathic understanding and also the explicit or implicit expectation that the client will correct that reflected understanding and will carry it further. The assumption is that the personal *meaning* of the client's experience is in the experience itself, and under optimal conditions, clients can grasp these meanings for themselves. Thus, the therapist works consistently within the client's frame of reference, reflecting what it is like to *be* the person at that moment and making sure never to assume the position of being more expert than the client about the client's experience. The therapist conveys to clients that they are the best judges of their own reality. This is a very important active ingredient of client-centered therapy because the process provides an experience which is viewed as an antidote to one of the clients' major psychological problems—not trusting their own experience because of learned conditions of worth.

Gestalt therapy is also discovery oriented, with the belief that it is only client discoveries that lead to changes in their view of themselves or the world. In client-centered therapy, with its greater emphasis on following the client's inner track, discovery occurs in the context of self-directed search. In the Gestalt approach however, the therapist both leads and follows. The therapist is, therefore, more directive and influencing, creating experiments in order to help clients discover aspects of their experience, sharing hunches about what may be occurring, and teaching the client about specific interruptive and avoidance processes. Gestalt therapists train clients to become aware both of their experience and of how they interfere with their experience, and the therapists direct them to attend to sensations, nonverbal expressions, and interruptive processes.

In addition, many Gestalt therapists may, at times, confront, frustrate, or challenge blocks or interruptions of experience. Their primary emphasis, however, is on supporting clients in discovering for themselves what it is that they are experiencing and in getting in touch with what they feel and need. The ultimate belief in Gestalt therapy is that clients must discover the truth for themselves from their own internal experience and that truth or insight cannot be provided by the therapist. The therapist does, however, facilitate the process by setting experiments that enable clients to discover their own truths.

In Gestalt therapy, awareness is regarded as the royal road to cure, with awareness knowable only by the client. In this regard, clients are clearly viewed as experts on their own experience. However, a Gestalt therapist makes observations about clients' process, particularly on nonverbal aspects of client expression, and thus, to some degree, the Gestalt therapist views clients as not having full access to, and not being fully expert on, their experience. Although Gestalt therapists emphasize that awareness is curative in itself, they also believe that conflict between aspects of experience can interfere with functioning and that a confrontation between these different aspects of experience, if suitably facilitated, is important in the therapeutic process. In order to achieve conflict resolution, the Gestalt therapist does not always remain nondirective, but may directly encourage or instruct clients to actively express certain emotions or attitudes and may offer opinions or hunches about what the client is experiencing.

The existential position is less clear in its position regarding discovery in the process of therapy. The theoretical base of European existentialists such as Boss (1963) and Binswanger (1963) led them to emphasize that meaning lies in phenomena themselves and that even if the meaning is not seen at first, it can be discovered and brought to light. Thus, their view of the unconscious is that it is potentially accessible to awareness without having to be interpreted from an external agent or vantage point.

In the process of therapy, existentialists use a combination of discovery, interpretation, and confrontation. They challenge and interpret obstacles to choice and action, often confronting and challenging people to turn their wishes into willed action. They confront the blocks, but value clients' finding their own directions and setting their own goals. They clearly see individuals as aware, self-reflective beings and respect consciousness as being at the apex of humanness. Existential therapists do not probe for latent intents, but believe in the centrality of phenomenological understanding. They attempt to avoid making hypotheses or inferences and try to allow phenomena to present themselves on their own terms (Boss, 1963).

In the actual conduct of therapy, the situation is more complicated. On the one hand, existential therapists assume that each person's experience of self and the world is unique, and thus knowledge of any experience, with its own special flavor, must come from the client rather than being imposed by the therapist. It is the client's own goals and choices that are addressed. In another sense, however, existential therapists view the anxiety aroused by awareness of "ultimate concerns" such as death, freedom, isolation, and meaninglessness, as leading to defense mechanisms such as repression, distortion, or avoidance. It is these kinds of "avoidances" that are often directly challenged by the therapist.

The humanistic view of people being able to discover for themselves their own authentic inner experience, endorsed by the three approaches in the manner just described, is often strongly criticized from many perspectives. Critics view the idea that one can know one's own experience and be transparent to oneself as placing too strong a value on each person's inner uniqueness as well as placing too much faith in the validity of a person's self-awareness.

Dynamically oriented therapists believe that awareness reveals only the tip of the iceberg and that much behavior is unconsciously determined, and therefore awareness may need to be interpreted from a frame of reference external to the client. Hermeneuticists, on the other hand, hold that all meaning construction is an interpretive process and that there is, therefore, no essential truth for the client to discover (Sass, 1988).

In response to the unconscious motivation critique, the humanist position does not claim that there is no unconscious processing of information, but subscribes to a view of a cognitive rather than a dynamic unconscious. The key difference is that in a cognitive–affective schematic processing view, the unconscious does not directly motivate behavior, but rather influences perception and construal. Much of whatever is unconscious is simply not currently in awareness and can be made aware by attentional focusing.

With regard to the complex issue of the possibility of knowing oneself, although humanists would not deny the complexity and constructive nature of the creation of meaning, they believe that there *is* an experiential reality for each person and that awareness of this reality can be progressively approximated. Although there may be no single truth that can be attained, there will be many perspectives that would *not* fit the experiential data, and only a few, and perhaps only one, will provide a good fit. We know our world through our bodily felt experience (Gendlin, 1962; Johnson, 1987). Once one accurately symbolizes bodily experience (for example, that one feels tense or afraid or angry), one can construct a variety of meanings from this. But symbolizing one's tension as calmness, one's experience of fear as grief, or one's anger as joy would be inherently inaccurate. People are seen as being able to determine the right paths for themselves from an intensive process of discovery, leading to an inner sense of certitude. Thus, although the person is always constructing the meaning of the experience by a synthesizing process, the elements of the synthesis have an experiential validity, and can be more or less accurately symbolized.

2. The actualizing tendency involving growth, self-determination, and choice. Rogers' belief in a fundamental human motivation toward growth —toward developing autonomy, seeking new experience, and developing one's own potentialities—is central in understanding the process in Rogerian therapy. Rogers, like other humanistic theorists, took a teleological position, viewing human beings as influenced by a vision of the future rather than being directed wholly by the experiences of the past. There is assumed to be a strong motivation toward becoming what one truly can become, but it does not lead Rogerians to push the client to confront the future and make choices. Rather, the therapist's focus is on enabling clients to turn inward, to get in touch with their own *present* organismic experience, and to value it as a trustworthy guide, rather than having their perceptions and feelings screened by their learned criteria of worth. Under these conditions the person can and will make choices that will lead to growth. This conception gives the whole process of therapy a particular flavor. The emphasis is on process rather than on choosing goals, and it is not viewed primarily as a struggle against opposing forces, but as something that can be achieved under the right conditions. The therapeutic conditions of empathy, unconditional prizing, and genuineness are viewed as being sufficient to release and foster the actualizing tendency.

The client-centered therapist is almost never confrontative. The assumption is that the inherent strength of the actualizing tendency, if the person can learn to trust it, will lead in directions that will be growth producing and inherently satisfying for the person. The therapist is very active in fostering inward experiential search, but not in judging what is best for this person.

There is one further process issue related to growth that needs to be discussed, and that is the approach to dealing with conflict in therapy. In the formal statement of his theory of therapy, personality, and interpersonal relationships (1959), Rogers advanced a model in which there was an almost inevitable conflict between the person's inherent tendency to move toward growth, autonomy, and development of his or her full potential and the opposing need to maintain a concept of self, learned from early experience with parents and others. Feeling or behaving in ways inconsistent with one's learned self-concept was assumed to generate anxiety and, thus, to limit the extent to which the person could follow the authentic actualizing tendency. In practice, however, Rogers and other client-centered therapists do not focus on this conflict. The assumption is that in an atmosphere of true empathy and nonjudgmental prizing, clients will be able to let go of their learned conditions of worth and be guided by their own actualizing tendency toward growth and autonomy.

Perls also believed in an actualizing tendency, drawing on Goldstein's (1939) view that the individual's search for ways to maintain and enhance the self is never ending. To the Gestalt therapist, self-actualization becomes possible when people fully identify with themselves as growing, changing organisms and clearly discriminate their feelings and needs. Perls particularly emphasized self-regulation, which is seen as a natural or organismic tendency. Effective self-regulation depends on discriminating feelings and needs by means of sensory awareness. This leads to awareness of intuitive appraisals of either what is good for the person and should be assimilated, or of what is bad and should be rejected. The assumption is that the healthy organism "knows" what is good for it. This organismic wisdom works by a spontaneous emergence of needs to guide action.

Life is the process of a need arising and being satisfied and another need emerging and being satisfied. The figure–background Gestalt formation and destruction process is used to describe the process. A dominant need emerges as figure from a background that claims attention, is satisfied, and fades into the background again, and a compelling new need emerges into the foreground.

Pathology or dysfunction occurs when this need-satisfaction process is interrupted. The cycle is viewed as consisting of four major stages: awareness, excitement, action, and contact. In the cycle, *awareness* of inner or outer stimuli leads to the mobilization of *excitement* which provides an *action* tendency. Finally, action leads to *contact* and need satisfaction. Much of the focus in therapy is on becoming aware of different points at which the cycle is interrupted. Thus the emergence of a clear need can be blocked at the initial sensation stages by dulled sensation and poor awareness of inner or outer stimuli. Therapeutic work, then, involves helping people become more aware of sensation or experience. Blocking at the arousal or excitement stage results from dampening or disavowal of emotional experience. Therapeutic work at this stage focuses on increasing awareness of muscular constriction and clients' other methods of suppressing emotional experience.

At the action stage, need satisfaction is seen as being interrupted by introjected attitudes and values which create a split between wants and 'shoulds' in the personality. Two-chair dialogues are used at this point to resolve the split (Greenberg, 1979). Finally, interruption can occur at the completion stage by the person not experiencing the satisfaction of the need and completion of the cycle. At this stage, awareness is again implemented to help the person become aware of the experience of satisfaction and how one may be preventing it.

Thus, the Gestalt perspective focuses clients' attention on aspects of any situation in which they are involved for which they are responsible and ultimately, the therapists help them to recognize their choice in being involved in the situation. That is, awareness is seen as leading to choice, thus allowing the person to choose how to behave. The emphasis in Gestalt therapy on self-determination and independence led initially to an over-emphasis on self-sufficiency and to an underemphasis on interdependence. More recently, Gestalt therapists have proposed "self-support" as more desirable than "self-sufficiency." If one is self-supportive, one can ask for what one needs and thereby maintain a sense of both autonomy and connectedness.

Existential therapists, although viewing life as purposive and the organism as active in choosing its own destiny, do not explicitly posit a growth tendency. No essence precedes existence; rather, people determine themselves. However, some kind of growth principle can be discerned in the writings of existentialist therapists. Frankl (1963), for example, proposes a "will to meaning," and May and Yalom (1984) suggest that the therapist cannot create engagement or wishing but the desire to engage life is always there.

The existentialists tend to be more future oriented, seeing the person as striving toward and being motivated by goals and ideals. They believe in *possibility* in the sense of potentiality, ability, or capacity. The person exists as a bundle of possibilities for relating to the world, and, at any time, a particular possibility is carried out. In addition, human beings have the capacity for *understanding* that they have possibilities and, therefore, are also aware if they fail to carry them out. Each individual has to choose which possibilities will be carried out and which will not, and the person is viewed as responsible for this choice. In this way, therapy is focused on having people make the choice of which potentialities to carry out.

In understanding how people confront the choices in their lives, conflict is a primary concept for existential therapists. There is an inevitable conflict between the individual and the "givens" of existence, the ultimate concerns such as finiteness, freedom, isolation, and meaninglessness (May, 1977; Yalom, 1981). It is the anxiety generated by the person's awareness of these ultimate concerns that is considered to lead to defense mechanisms which block the person's capacity for making authentic choices. The crucial difference between this conflict model and that of Freud is that in the Freudian model it is repressed instinctual drives that lead to anxiety and thus to defense mechanisms; while for the existentialists, it is the *awareness* of the ultimate concerns that leads to anxiety and defenses (May & Yalom, 1989; Yalom, 1981). Therapy focuses predominantly on dealing with the ultimate concerns.

In the existential approach, freedom is the central issue, with will and choice being the major constituents of freedom. The goal of therapy is to increase persons' freedom to notice where and in what domains they are unfree and then to confront the obstacles to freedom. Therapists work to free people to be engaged, to open up, and be free to relate to whatever happens to them. Rather than asking "why," the existential therapist asks "why not," thus encouraging clients to confront their own blocks and enabling them to turn wishing into willing.

3. Fostering the construction of new meaning. Client-centered therapy, with its focus on the reflection of feelings and inner meanings, engages the client in a process of experiential search which involves attending to, differentiating, and integrating an inner referent in order to construct new meanings. Experiential symbolization, in which one moves from an inner felt referent to symbolizing the experience in words is a key process in client-centered and experiential therapy (Gendlin, 1962, 1984). The process, emphasized by both Rogers and Gendlin, involves the client's explicating the subtle nuances associated with tacit meanings. The clients engage thereby in an experiential search, a type of "inner tasting" process, in order to symbolize accurately their own reactions and feelings.

In the Gestalt process the emphasis is more on intensifying experience or heightening awareness so that a clear emotion and attendant need emerge. There is far less focus in therapy on the work of conceptually symbolizing for oneself the meaning of experience and more emphasis on having an intense experience of what one is talking about. In fact, the Polsters (1973) suggest that meaning is reflexive and that if one has a vivid experience, meaning automatically flows from the experience. Thus, in the Gestalt approach, construction of meaning is viewed as a perceptual awareness process rather than a conceptual process. The world is organized into particular figure–background configurations and the organization of figure in relation to ground provides meaning. Clients, after a vivid experience, are often asked to sit quietly by themselves rather than engage with others or talk about their experience. The solitude is suggested in order to allow clients to absorb the experience and create their own meaning from it, in order not to impose meaning on the client.

In existential therapy, meaning and its creation is a central goal of therapy. The type of meaning pursued is often about more ultimate, even philosophical, concerns about life. Ultimately, it is the meaningfulness of being human that is explored in therapy, and this leads to concerns with universals at the heart of existence, such as time, death, anxiety over mortality, awareness of the future, and guilt at not fulfilling one's possibilities. The human being is, as Sartre put it, condemned to freedom (Sartre, 1943/1956), and each individual has to confront one's own freedom and responsibility. In addition, individuals in therapy need to deal with isolation and the wish to belong and how to find meaning in a meaningless world (Yalom, 1981). In existential therapy, anxiety over ultimate concerns is thus at the center of personality and psychotherapy.

4. Person-centeredness: The therapeutic relationship. The process dimension in therapy that most clearly involves the humanistic principle of person-centeredness is the relationship established between the two participants. The humanistic approaches all dispute the claim that the relationship between the client and the therapist can be reduced to an unconscious repetition of previous attachments. Rather, they propose that a real relationship is developed between the participants and that this real relationship provides a new interpersonal experience for the client.

Rogers always viewed the relationship in therapy as the primary agent of change. Clients' experience of the therapist's genuine and unconditional empathic prizing is viewed as freeing them from the "conditions of worth" that have been assimilated from early experiences with parents and others (Rogers, 1959). Rogers assumed that, in an atmosphere of noncontingent caring, the client can get in touch with and acknowledge feelings and other inner experiences that are organismically experienced, even though they are inconsistent with the learned self-concept. Rogers' view of the therapist's participation in this relationship changed somewhat over the years, and he described therapists as being freer to express some of their own feelings in his later writings. Nevertheless, the emphasis has always been on the belief in the centrality of a relationship that is *real* as opposed to a transference relationship. And there is never an attempt to use confrontation as a therapeutic tool.

The relationship conditions of personal genuineness and empathic prizing enable clients to express and explore their moment-to-moment experience as they describe issues, events, and frustrations in their daily lives. The therapist's empathic reflections of the most poignant feelings and other inner experiences enable the client to explore these inner experiences more deeply and to get in contact with aspects that have never before been fully expressed to others or even to themselves. The therapist's clear, nonjudgmental caring reduces clients' interpersonal anxiety, enabling them to tolerate their own intrapersonal anxiety as they explore more and more deeply. Thus the relationship is not only a primary change agent in itself, but it establishes a climate allowing inner awareness in which clients can engage in the exploratory process of experiential search.

Perls himself did not emphasize the role of the relationship in therapy, although Buber's I–Thou relationship was offered as the model of relating for Gestalt therapy. In Buber's view, the therapist relates with immediacy and is fully present to the other, letting the other in on his or her own inner experience. The genuine dialogue is mutual and nonexploitive with both participants caring about each other's side of the dialogue. Buber (1957) sees the I–Thou relationship as a genuine meeting between two people in which both openly respect the essential humanity of the other. Healing is viewed as occurring in the meeting. Therefore, the relationship is an active change agent in Gestalt therapy. In practice, Perls was more involved in demonstrating the basic Gestalt principles through active interventions than in relating over time to his client's concerns. Thus his practice diverged somewhat from his theory. However, some branches of the Gestalt approach (Yontef, 1969) work predominantly with the I–Thou, here and now, contact between the client and therapist.

True contact is the major principle of relating in the Gestalt approach. Essentially, contact means that the client is fully present and engaged in a congruent fashion in whatever is occurring at the moment. When that contact with the self or therapist is interrupted by the client, the therapist attempts to bring this disengagement to the client's awareness by inquiring about what happened at the point of interruption. Gestalt therapists believe that ultimately it is only in the context of an authentic relationship that the uniqueness of the individual can be truly recognized. So the therapist strives for the genuine contact of a true encounter. How this is done technically is not fully prescribed other than to stress that the therapist needs to be authentic. Authenticity, however, does not mean belaboring clients with self-disclosure or honesty without consideration of their needs or personal readiness.

Existentialists consider that a *real* relationship between client and therapist is a crucial ingredient of therapy. The relationship is difficult to define because it is an essential kind of *being* in the therapy. May has emphasized "presence" on the part of the therapist, who must be fully present and strive for an authentic human encounter with the client.

Psychotherapy, then, is first and foremost a unique form of being together, in which "being-with" the client is an essential ingredient (Craig, 1986; Moustakas, 1986). For May and Yalom it is a very direct, nonformal relationship of equals in which first names are used, and therapists are free to share their own feelings. They view this real, authentic encounter as a change agent in itself. The experience of the relationship is an example of a kind of intimacy from which the client can learn how fulfilling it is to be cared about (Yalom, 1981).

The nature of the authentic relationship is, however, very different from the client-centered relationship. The therapist is often confrontational and sometimes interpretive, but it is important to note that it is not the person's own basic goals that are confronted. These are recognized and respected. It is the blocks and avoidances and other client-perceived obstacles to these goals that are challenged and interpreted. The therapist's emphasis is on whatever stops the person from achieving these goals. Frankl (1963) and other existential therapists, however, sometimes challenge even the client's expressed goals from the position of the expert.

RECENT DECADES

The humanistic approaches have clearly had a substantial impact on the practice of psychotherapy and counseling, as well as related fields such as education and group work. Humanistic approaches have also been influential in less obvious ways, such as the assimilation of the Rogerian conditions of empathy, positive regard, and genuineness into other orientations.

During the past two decades, however, the humanistic psychotherapy approaches have become increasingly separated from mainstream theoretical psychology, especially in North America. The separation from theoretical psychology has been true for the whole humanistic psychology movement. In his article "The Crisis of Humanistic Psychology," Giorgi (1987) vividly described this split and discussed some dilemmas it presents.

There seem to be a number of interrelated causes for the decreasing contact between humanistic theories of therapy and mainstream psychology. One of the more obvious ones has been the overenthusiastic, uncritical adoption of some humanist approaches during the "counter-culture" era of the 1960s and early 1970s. Scholars have turned away from the "faddishness." In *Psychology and Humanism*, Smith (1982) mentioned that the Saybrook conference of 1964—at which the concept of a "third force" in psychology was seriously discussed—was attended by the influential personality psychologists Gordon Allport, Henry Murray, Gardner Murphy, and George Kelly, among others. These pioneers in the psychology of personality, who had been moving toward the third force, later dropped out of the movement, dissatisfied by the direction in which it seemed to be moving.

Humanistic ideals clearly fit well with many of the positive goals of the counterculture movement, such as freedom and individuality. Unfortunately, many of the techniques of the humanist therapies were used indiscriminately in a wide variety of "consciousness raising" contexts as "quick fixes" without firm grounding in humanistic therapy theory and practice. Thus the approaches came to be viewed as unprofessional and even potentially dangerous. Encounter groups, cathartic expression, body work, and the like were often viewed with suspicion.

Another factor that may have played a role in the separation of humanistic psychotherapy from mainstream psychology was the shortage of available academic positions in the 1970s. The few available positions were less likely to be offered to individuals perceived as espousing anti-intellectual or "intuitive" approaches or as less likely to conduct standard empirical research.

During Rogers' years at Ohio State, the University of Chicago, and the University of Wisconsin, courses and internships in client-centered therapy were popular options in graduate psychology programs, but this has not been true in recent years. The Gestalt approach customarily has been taught in freestanding training institutes in the United States and Canada. For instance, in 1982 there were more than 50 Gestalt training institutes in the United States and Canada, but the approach has been poorly represented in universities, with few academic psychologists trained in, or truly knowledgeable about, Gestalt theory. Although there have been a number of books written on different existentialist approaches, there are no established training centers, and, as May and Yalom have mentioned (1984), few existential therapists have received formal training in the approach.

The most striking and potentially serious trend has been the small amount of research in humanistic approaches in recent years. For many years research was an extremely important part of the client-centered tradition. Although Rogers has been viewed as the most "radical" (Tageson, 1982) of the humanistic therapists, he was the least radical in his continuing belief in the need for empirical research on psychotherapy. In fact, in 1956 he received the APA Distinguished Scientific Contribution Award, along with Wolfgang Kohler and Kenneth Spence.

Rogers viewed research as consisting of two very different stages. The first involved intensive listening to taped therapy sessions conducted by himself or by colleagues, trying to get a feel for the "process strands" (Rogers, 1958) that characterized positive change and its facilitation, and then letting hypotheses emerge from this experience. Then the second stage was testing of the hypotheses by the usual positivist methods (Rogers & Dymond, 1954; Rogers, Gendlin, et al., 1967). However, he attributed the weak impact of humanistic theory on mainstream psychology to the lack of significant, humanistically oriented research (Rogers, 1985).

With the exception of the program of studies by Greenberg and his associates on the process of change and the effects of particular Gestalt interventions (Daldrup, Beutler, Engle, & Greenberg, 1988; Greenberg, 1984; Greenberg & Dompierre, 1981; Greenberg & Webster, 1982) and a few studies that showed improved self-actualization and self-concept following Gestalt group experiences (Foulds & Hannigan, 1976), there has been little research on Gestalt approaches.

Within the existential therapy approach, there has been little empirical research. Although research from the Duquesne University group (Giorgi, 1970; Van Kaam, 1966) focused on topics relevant to humanistic psychology as method, there has been little specific application to therapy. One obstacle to research with existential therapy has been the tremendous variability among the different theorists in their manner of conducting therapy, as well as variability even within the different systems. Primary commitment is to "the person" rather than to technique or to research (May & Yalom, 1984).

Intellectual work relevant to the humanistic therapeutic approaches has taken place in Europe in recent years. At the first annual conference on client-centered and experiential therapy, held at Leuven, Belgium, in 1988, there was surprise and excitement among North Americans at the amount of theory development and research occurring in Belgium, Germany, and the Netherlands. Many of the papers presented at the conference have been published in English in a volume edited by Lietaer, Rombauts, and Van Balen (1990). And in his recommendations for the future, Lietaer (1990) stressed the need for more research.

New Developments

One interesting, recent theoretical development evident at this conference is the emergence of two strands within the client-centered approach. One is the more strongly person-centered perspective that considers the Rogerian relationship conditions of empathy, unconditional positive regard, and genuineness, experienced by the client, as the sole change agents (Bozarth, 1990; Brodley, 1990). In the other, more process-oriented view that has been emerging, the centrality of the relationship conditions is still respected, but process-directive components have been added. The therapist's participation is seen as guiding clients toward particular modes of processing in the session in order to facilitate the exploration of their own experience (Greenberg, Rice, Rennie, & Toukmanian, 1991; Rice & Greenberg, 1991). Within the more experiential framework, Gendlin's (1962, 1984) focusing interventions and Rice's (1974, 1984) systematic, evocative, unfolding procedure have each proposed a series of different steps in which the client can engage in the process of discovery and change.

Also, Mahrer (1986), in his version of experiential therapy, proposes certain key steps in which the client needs to engage. Greenberg and his colleagues have proposed and studied a number of process-experiential tasks derived from the gestalt approach, which can be implemented within the framework of a client-centered relationship.

Interestingly, Gestalt therapy is also undergoing a change, one in which the I–Thou relationship is being emphasized more than the use of technique. In addition, a growing interest in self psychology and in the importance of empathy in providing a healing environment has become manifest (Yontef, 1981). The development of a more process-directive aspect within the client-centered framework and a more relational perspective in Gestalt approaches represents an interesting expansion of each tradition and a possible trend toward integration by incorporation and adaptation of the strengths of different humanistic approaches.

May, Yalom, and Bugental remain the most prolific writers in North America on existential approaches. Although no specific new trends appear to be emerging in existential therapy, many of the insights of the existential theorists are being absorbed into integrative practice.

FUTURE DEVELOPMENTS

In looking toward the future of the humanistic therapies, it seems clear that some important developments are already taking place. The anti-intellectual trend seems to have decreased, and clearly with the aging of the academic population, we hope that many more academic openings will be available for younger psychologists interested in theory and research in psychotherapy.

Even more important have been some of the advances in theoretical psychology that seem to fit increasingly well with the basic assumptions and methods of humanistic therapies. The rigid constriction of strict behaviorism has been moderated or replaced by cognitive psychology with its focus on awareness and such human functions as perception, memory, and problem solving. Initially, information processing approaches in experimental psychology appeared equally constricting to the humanist. As Neisser (1976) and others have suggested, the underlying model for these functions was the computer metaphor, in which the person was ignored. Much research involved laboratory studies focusing on separate functions out of context. "Lacking in ecological validity, indifferent to culture, even missing some of the main features of perception and memory as they occur in ordinary life, psychology could become a narrow and uninteresting specialized field" (Neisser, 1976, p. 7). He recommended that we need to study cognitive functions as they occur in the real world, in the context of natural, purposeful activity, which sounds similar to Kierkegaard's lament that ignoring the person as "subject" and viewing him or her only as "object" resulted in losing the real, existing person. Modern constructivist approaches to cognition appear, however, to be far more compatible with the awareness-oriented, humanistic approaches to therapy.

During the past two decades, an approach to understanding human cognitive processes such as perception, memory, and problem solving, occurring in realistic contexts has evolved, resulting in human information-processing models that assign a central role to the constructive functions of mental activity (Craik & Lockhart, 1972; Johnson-Laird, 1988; Mahoney & Gabriel, 1987; Neisser, 1976). This development in psychology, stressing the concept of schema, holds promise for a reuniting of humanistic approaches with mainstream psychology.

A second recent development that is likely to help reintegrate humanistic approaches into mainstream psychology is the focus on emotion, which, until recently, had been sorely neglected in the study of human information processing. In the last decade, a number of schematic and network theories of emotion have been proposed (Bower, 1981; Lang, 1984; Leventhal, 1984), and various attempts at investigating and explaining emotional behavior have appeared (Leventhal & Tomarken, 1986). Drawing on these theoretical developments and on the practice of emotionally focused therapy, Greenberg and Safran (1987) have outlined an integrative model of emotional processing for use in therapy. Emotion is viewed as an action tendency which provides people with biologically adaptive feedback about their responses to situations. When emotion is understood as providing action potentials, it becomes a crucial source of information for therapy. The humanistic therapies focus on awareness of feeling but lack an adequate theory to explain its importance. Developments such as these in emotion theory provide a framework for understanding humanistic therapies and further provide for the possibility of an integration of humanistic approaches back into the mainstream of psychology.

One of the most important areas for both theory and research is the focus on intensive observation of the change processes in the session, followed by descriptive measurement and understanding of these processes (Rice & Greenberg, 1984). These events could become the building blocks for understanding therapeutic change. The process analysis of change points would be one move toward understanding. Another extremely important approach to understanding is the use of "interpersonal process recall" (Elliott, 1986; Rennie, 1990) in order to have the client identify times in the therapy session when something interesting happened and to obtain from the clients' perspective a sense of what these incidents felt like and what seemed to be happening for them.

MOST RECENT DEVELOPMENTS: EVIDENCE-BASED EXPERIENTIAL PSYCHOTHERAPY

In the following, we will bring the reader up to date on recent developments in research, practice, and theory in the experiential–humanistic therapies.

Research Developments

For the first time in 16 years, a review of research on experiential–humanistic therapies appeared in the recent *Handbook of Psychotherapy and Behavior Change* (Bergin & Garfield, 1994). The reappearance of this review in the *Handbook* attested to the accumulation of sufficient research in this area over the past decade to merit such a review. The chapter included a meta-analysis of the effects of experiential psychotherapies that demonstrated the equivalence of experiential approaches to both cognitive–behavioral and psychodynamic approaches. In addition, the review covered research on seven fundamental experiential interventions.

Four of the interventions had been developed within client-centered therapy: (a) systematic evocative unfolding for problematic reactions, in which people are helped to vividly describe problematic situations in order to reevoke their experience for further exploration; (b) focusing on an unclear felt sense, in which people are helped to symbolize bodily felt experience; (c) helping the client to focus on accessing increasingly deeper levels of feeling and felt meaning through posing self-relevant questions that clarify the client's experience; and (d) confrontation. All of these interventions were shown to lead to productive client process, such as increased depth of experiencing, change in vocal quality, and deeper exploration. Two interventions that come from Gestalt therapy, namely two-chair dialogue for resolving conflict and empty-chair dialogue for resolving unfinished business, were also shown to lead to good client process and problem resolution. In addition, a seventh intervention, involving the creation of meaning in emotional crises in which cherished beliefs have been challenged, was shown to be effective.

Investigation of the application of a specific emotionally focused, experiential approach to different populations represents one of the major research developments in the 1990s. Regarding outcome, two major treatment studies have recently demonstrated the effects of this process–experiential therapy (Greenberg, Rice, & Elliott, 1993), one treating clients with major depressive disorder (Greenberg & Watson, in press) and another treating clients needing to resolve unfinished business resulting from childhood maltreatment (Paivio & Greenberg, 1995). An emotionally focused approach to couples therapy (Greenberg & Johnson, 1987) has also repeatedly demonstrated good outcomes (Gordon-Walker, Johnson, Manyon, & Cloutier, in press; Johnson & Greenberg, 1985).

With regard to the relation of process to outcome, Goldman and Greenberg (1995) have recently demonstrated that in the process–experiential treatment of depression, depth of client experiencing—on material that represents core treatment themes—relates positively to outcome. Specifically, they found that increase in depth of experience from early sessions to thematic episodes in later sessions correlated positively with outcome. This supported the hypothesis that increased depth of experiencing is an active ingredient of treatment in experiential therapy. In addition, the fact that an *increase* in depth of experiencing related to outcome refuted the view that depth of experiencing is simply a client capacity with which good clients enter therapy. It appears, rather, that it is an important change process. Although more research is needed, these studies on a process–experiential approach have begun to provide empirical validation for claims of the effectiveness of experiential–humanistic approaches to therapy.

A process experiential approach combines the client-centered relationship of empathy, positive regard, and congruence with active interventions from Gestalt and other experiential approaches (Greenberg et al., 1993). It lays out the basics of an integrative experiential approach to treatment, specifying a number of principles governing both the therapeutic relationship and therapeutic work. The *relational principles* involve the establishment of psychological contact and empathic attunement, the active communication of empathic understanding, positive regard and congruence, and the development of collaboration on the tasks and goals of treatment. The three *work principles* involve the promotion of differential in-session processing (mental operations, such as attending to a bodily felt sense, expressing, or imagining), the promotion of client growth and choice, and the facilitation of the resolution of particular types of emotional problems. This approach combines empathic responding with more active, problem-specific interventions for particular types of problem states. It promotes an approach in which the therapist both follows and leads and in which he or she recognizes particular moment-by-moment client states (process diagnosis) as most suitable for particular types of intervention that will guide clients' processing in an optimal direction.

Developments in Practice

One of the major developments in practice has been the move toward specification of differential treatments for different disorders and problems. A number of books on client-centered therapy have appeared in Europe, mainly in Dutch and German, emphasizing its application to different problems and disorders. For example, Eckert and Bierman-Ratjen (in press) have studied client-centered treatment of borderline clients. In North America, Warner (1997) has focused on working with the fragile self, and Prouty (1994) has written on the experiential treatment of schizophrenic and retarded psychoses. Similarly, Gestalt therapists have begun to look at the type of disturbances of awareness and of psychological contact that occurs in the different personality disorders (Delisle, 1992) and at the importance of the differential application of a variety of aspects of Gestalt therapy to different types of clients. Practice has thus shifted from a "one treatment fits all" approach to the *differential* application of aspects of the different experiential approaches to different disorders (Greenberg, Lietaer, & Watson, in press). Most notable is the development of special methods for working with hallucinations (Prouty, 1994) and with trauma and childhood maltreatment (Elliott, in press; Kepner, 1996; Paivio & Greenberg, 1995).

Developments in Theory

A comprehensive framework for working with emotion has recently been proposed (Greenberg & Paivio, 1997). It encompasses a cumulative, three-phase approach of validating, exploring, and restructuring emotions, in which the former steps are integrated into the latter ones. Within the context of a safe environment, bad feelings are evoked in the session in order to explore them and to access core maladaptive emotion schemes, such as basic insecurity or worthlessness. This is done for one of two therapeutic purposes: either (a) to access clients' biologically based adaptive tendencies, such as when anger at being violated leads to the setting of personal boundaries or (b) to expose core maladaptive schemes to restructuring by the incorporation of new experience (on the basis of more adaptive alternate internal resources), such as when core insecurity is restructured by accessing core pride and mastery motivation.

The focusing approach to experiential therapy continues to develop and has been further elaborated (Gendlin, 1995), as has Mahrer's approach to deepening the experiencing of past scenes (Mahrer, 1995). An existential approach has also recently been articulated that involves stages of presence. In this approach, relational contact is emphasized, evoking the actual experience of what is being discussed, followed by steps of vivifying and confronting resistance and creating meaning (Schneider & May, 1995).

Theoretical developments have also taken place regarding the view of the self and its interpersonal nature, as well as the role of emotion and meaning construction. This is attested by a number of new publications on developments in Gestalt therapy (Kepner, 1995, 1996; Lee & Wheeler, 1996; Nevis, 1992; Wheeler, 1991; Yontef, 1995) emphasizing an interpersonal, field approach, as well as a focus on the body and the role of shame in development and treatment. Client-centered writings have also emphasized the interpersonal aspect of treatment and working more with what is occurring between client and therapist. Bohart (1993), following Gendlin's (1962) original proposal that experiencing is a core change process regardless of therapeutic approach, has suggested that experiencing is a basic ingredient of therapeutic change and is an important construct for furthering psychotherapy integration. He has expanded Gendlin's concept of experiencing beyond the symbolization of internal experience to include the kind of experiencing that results from doing things in the world, or behaving in new ways. He suggested that all therapies engender new experience, when experiencing is defined in this expanded sense.

The continued incorporation into the humanistic approaches of developments in both emotion theory and constructivist theorizing have helped correct a mistaken view of experiential theory as involving a purely biological or genetic blueprint view of human functioning. A more dialectically interactive view of functioning has continued to be elaborated, in which life and experience involve a continuing interaction between biology and culture; each contributes its unique share to the construction of a final synthesis (Bohart, 1995; Gendlin, 1995; Greenberg & Pascual-Leone, 1995; Watson & Greenberg, 1996).

Finally, a resurgence of interest in empathy and empathic attunement as a core element in experiential and self psychological approaches has led to a collection of papers on empathy in psychotherapy (Bohart & Greenberg, 1997). Both Rogers' and Kohut's views are explored and compared, and a new, more differentiated view of empathy emerges. A concept of psychotherapeutic empathy as an experientially based, compassionate understanding of the other, blending both cognitive and affective elements, emerges as quite distinct from empathy as understood from a developmental and social perspective. This view regards empathy as predominantly affective resonance, in which a child has the capacity to feel the same feeling as the other. That is, affective resonance with the other is emphasized over *understanding* the other. It is becoming increasingly apparent that what is meant by empathy in psychotherapy needs to be more clearly specified. An additional point that is emerging about empathy is that it is of central importance in the treatment of more fragile people and processes (Warner, 1997) and with populations having, for instance, borderline and narcissistic personality disorders.

CONCLUSION

Since their emergence during the 1940s, the humanistic psychotherapies have had periods of striking growth and periods of relative neglect and separation from theory and research in psychology. Humanistic insights into psychotherapy and healthy functioning are too important to lose. In the expanding perspectives that are emerging in psychology, attempting to capture more fully the complexities of real human functioning in the world, we are optimistic that humanistic psychotherapy will both contribute to and be enriched by future developments in theory and research.

One of the major emphases that gave birth to the experiential–humanistic view was that people are inherently growth oriented and that therapy involves facilitation of their growth. This view was developed in the 1950s to counteract the prevalent darker, more pathological, and more mechanistic views of human nature. The self was seen rather as an active agent engaged in solving problems-in-living in order to survive and grow optimally. In this historical context, humanistic theories emphasized the importance of therapists' not influencing or controlling clients. Viewing freedom and choice as essential to health, humanistic therapists did not wish to impose their views or their theories on people, nor did they wish to be reinforcing agents. Over the years, however, the noninterpretive, nondirective emphasis has evolved into a view of therapy as genuine contact and as an interpersonal interaction between two human beings. Within this new view, the emphasis has shifted away from a nondirective, noninterpretive stance toward more varied ways of deepening clients' experiencing and of facilitating optimal exploration of issues. Thus, whatever method might help solve a particular problem is now acceptable within the experiential–humanistic framework, provided it is offered in a respectful, nonimposing manner that views clients as the ultimate experts on their own experience. This more flexible style emphasizes the facilitation of deeper emotional exploration as a means of providing new experience and developing new interactions with the therapist.

Reaching toward the end of the century, the humanistic approaches, entering their fifth decade, are becoming more integrative and more complexly differentiated. The four foundational principles of humanistic therapies articulated earlier—commitment to a phenomenological approach, the operation of a growth tendency, self-determination, and respect for the person—are all evolving. First, progress in the phenomenological approach to theorizing has been aided both by the development of rigorous human science research methodologies and by incorporating constructivist theorizing. New research methodologies help observers capture individuals' experience and meanings in a richer descriptive manner (Rennie & Toukmanian, 1992), whereas constructivist perspectives help theorists move beyond purely descriptive theory to deeper explanatory theorizing that promotes an understanding of the underlying processes that lead to the emergence of experience (Greenberg & Pascual-Leone, 1995; Prouty, 1994; Watson & Greenberg, 1996).

Second, the growth tendency has been grounded in the emotion system, and a number of ways in which this system can malfunction have been articulated. Third, the view of human beings as agents that have the capacity for evaluation and choice has been emphasized in a major new philosophical effort at reclaiming these important aspects of humanism (Taylor, 1989, 1992). Finally, the person-centered approach to the relationship has developed from a one-sided view of the provision of relational conditions by the therapist to a truly interpersonal view of therapy in which the client's experience *in*—and *of*—the interaction becomes an important focus for exploration and understanding. No longer is a therapist simply being empathic or creating experiments. Now, the therapist is more fully present, interacting and influencing the interaction.

Thus, the humanistic therapies may be viewed as having forged a new experiential approach that emphasizes the process of working differentially, at different moments, with lived experience in the therapeutic hour in an empathic, validating therapeutic relationship (Gendlin, 1995; Greenberg et al., 1993; Greenberg, Lietaer, & Watson, in press; Mahrer, 1995; Schneider & May, 1995). There appear to be additional encouraging efforts to revive interest in the experiential approaches. The formation of international organizations and international meetings of client-centered and experiential therapy and of Gestalt therapy have taken place in the 1990s. Both groups are eager to promote theory, research, and training in these approaches and to further promote and disseminate what they have to offer (Hutterer & Schmidt, 1996). To this end, new journals of Gestalt therapy and person-centered therapy have been started and a new generation of experientially oriented humanistic therapists are being trained.

REFERENCES

Bergin, A., & Garfield, S. (1994). *Handbook of psychotherapy and behavior change.* New York: Wiley.

Binswanger, L. (1963). *Being in the world* (J. Needleman, Trans.). New York: Basic Books. (Original work published 1951)

Bohart, A. (1993). Experiencing the basis of psychotherapy. *Journal of Psychotherapy Integration, 3*, 51–68.

Bohart, A. (1995). Configuration and constructivism from an experiential perspective. *Journal of Constructivist Psychology, 8*(4), 317–326.

Bohart, A., & Greenberg, L. (1997). *Empathy reconsidered: New directions in psychotherapy.* Washington, DC: American Psychological Association.

Boss, M. (1963). *Psychoanalysis and daseinanalysis* (L. B. Lefebre, Trans.). New York: Basic Books. (Original work published 1957)

Bower, G. H. (1981). Mood and memory. *American Psychologist, 31*, 129–148.

Bozarth, J. D. (1990). The essence of client-centered therapy. In G. Lietaer, J. Rombauts, & R. Van Balen (Eds.), *Client-centered and experiential psychotherapy in the nineties* (pp. 59–64). Leuven, Belgium: Leuven University Press.

Brodley, B. T. (1990). Client-centered therapy and experiential: Two different therapies. In G. Lietaer, J. Rombauts, & R. Van Balen (Eds.), *Client-centered and experiential psychotherapy in the nineties* (pp. 87–108). Leuven, Belgium: Leuven University Press.

Buber, M. (1957). *I and thou.* New York: Charles Scribners Sons.

Bugental, J. F. T. (Ed.). (1967). *Challenges of humanistic psychology.* New York: McGraw-Hill.

Buhler, C. (1967). Human life as a whole as a central subject of humanistic psychology. In J. F. T. Bugental (Ed.), *Challenges of humanistic psychology* (pp. 140–165). New York: McGraw-Hill.

Craig, E. (1986). Sanctuary and presence: An existential view of the therapist's contribution. *The Humanistic Psychologist, 1,* 22–28.

Craik, F. I. M., & Lockhart, R. S. (1972). Levels of processing: A framework for memory research. *Journal of Verbal Learning and Verbal Behavior, 11,* 671–684.

Daldrup, R., Beutler, L., Engle, D., & Greenberg, L. (1988). *Focused expressive psychotherapy.* New York: Guilford.

Delisle, G. (1992). A gestalt perspective of personality disorders. *The British Gestalt Journal, 1,* 42–50.

Eckert, J., & Bierman-Ratjen, E. (in press). Client-centered treatment of borderline disorder. In L. Greenberg, G. Lietaer, & J. Watson (Eds.), *Experiential psychotherapy: Differential intervention.* New York: Guilford Press.

Elliott, R. (1986). Interpersonal process recall (IPR) as a process research method. In L. S. Greenberg & W. M. Pinsof (Eds.), *The psychotherapeutic process* (pp. 503–528). New York: Guilford.

Elliott, R. (in press). Experiential therapy of posttraumatic stress disorder. In L. Greenberg, G. Lietaer, & J. Watson (Eds.), *Experiential psychotherapy: Differential intervention.* New York: Guilford Press.

Fagan, J., & Shepherd, I. L. (Eds.). (1970). *Gestalt therapy now.* Palo Alto, CA: Science and Behaviour Books.

Foulds, M., & Hannigan, M. (1976). Effects of a Gestalt Marathon workshop on measures of self actualization: A replication and follow-up study. *Journal of Consulting Psychology, 23,* 60–65.

Frankl, V. (1963). *Man's search for meaning: An introduction to logotherapy.* New York: Pocket Books.

Friedlander, S. (1918). *Schopferische indifferenz* [Creative indifference]. Munich, Germany: Georg Muller.

Gendlin, E. (1962). *Experiencing and the creation of meaning.* New York: Free Press.

Gendlin, E. (1984). *Focusing* (Rev. ed.). New York: Bantam Books.

Gendlin, E. (1995). *The focusing approach: Experiential psychotherapy.* New York: Guilford Press.

Giorgi, A. (1970). *Psychology as a human science: A phenomenologically based approach.* New York: Harper & Row.

Giorgi, A. (1987). The crisis of humanistic psychology. *The Humanistic Psychologist, 15*, 5–20.

Goldman, R., & Greenberg, L. (1995, June). *Depth of experiencing in the treatment of depression: Relating process to outcome.* Paper presented at the Society for Psychotherapy Research, Vancouver, British Columbia, Canada.

Goldstein, K. (1939). *The organism: A holistic approach derived from pathological data in man.* New York: American Book.

Gordon-Walker, J., Johnson, S., Manyon, I., & Cloutier, P. (in press). On emotionally focused marital intervention with chronically ill children. *Journal of Clinical Psychology.*

Greenberg, L. S. (1979). Resolving splits: Use of the two-chair technique. *Psychotherapy: Theory, Research & Practice, 16*, 316–324.

Greenberg, L. S. (1984). A task-analysis of intrapersonal conflict resolution. In L. N. Rice & L. S. Greenberg (Eds.), *Patterns of change* (pp. 67–123). New York: Guilford.

Greenberg, L. S., & Dompierre, L. (1981). Differential effects of the two-chair dialogue and empathic reflections at a conflict marker. *Journal of Counseling Psychology, 28*, 288–294.

Greenberg, L., & Johnson, S. (1987). *Emotionally focused therapy for couples.* New York: Guilford Press.

Greenberg, L., Lietaer, G., & Watson, J. (in press). *Experiential psychology: Differential intervention.* New York: Guilford Press.

Greenberg, L., & Paivio, S. (1997). *Working with emotion.* New York: Guilford Press.

Greenberg, L., & Pascual-Leone, J. (1995). A dialectical constructivist approach to experiential change. In R. Neimeyer & M. Mahoney (Eds.), *Constructivism in psychotherapy* (pp. 169–191). Washington, DC: American Psychological Association.

Greenberg, L. S., Rice, L. N., & Elliott, R. (1993). *Facilitating emotional change: The moment-by-moment process.* New York: Guilford Press.

Greenberg, L. S., Rice, L. N., Rennie, D. L., & Toukmanian, S. G. (1991). York University psychotherapy research program. In L. E. Beutler & M. Crago (Eds.), *Psychotherapy research: An international review of programmatic studies* (pp. 175–181). Washington, DC: American Psychological Association.

Greenberg, L. S., & Safran, J. D. (1987). *Emotion in psychotherapy.* New York: Guilford.

Greenberg, L., & Watson, J. (in press). Experiential therapy of depression: Differential effects of client centered relationship conditions and active experiential interventions. *Journal of Consulting and Clinical Psychology.*

Greenberg, L. S., & Webster, M. (1982). Resolving decisional conflict by means of two-chair dialogue and empathic reflection at a split in counseling. *Journal of Counseling Psychology, 29*, 468–477.

Haigh, G. (1949). Defensive behavior in client-centered therapy. *Journal of Consulting Psychology, 13*, 181–189.

Heidegger, M. (1962). *Being and time* (J. Macquarrie & E. S. Robinson, Trans.). New York: Harper and Row. (Original work published 1949)

Husserl, E. (1977). *Phenomenological psychology* (J. Scanlon, Trans.). The Hague: Nijhoff. (Original work published 1925)

Hutterer, R., & Schmidt, P. (1996). *Client centered and experiential psychotherapy: A paradigm in motion.* Vienna: Peter Lang.

Jaspers, K. (1963). *General psychopathology.* Chicago: University of Chicago Press.

Johnson, M. (1987). *The body in the mind: The bodily basis of meanings, imagination, and reason.* Chicago: University of Chicago Press.

Johnson, S., & Greenberg, L. (1985). Differential effects of experiential and problem solving interventions in resolving marital conflict. *Journal of Consulting and Clinical Psychology, 53,* 175–184.

Johnson-Laird, P. N. (1988). *The computer and the mind: An introduction to cognitive science.* Cambridge: Harvard University.

Jourard, S. M. (1968) *Disclosing man to himself.* Princeton, NJ: Van Nostrand.

Kepner, J. (1995). *Body process.* San Francisco: Jossey-Bass.

Kepner, J. (1996). *Healing tasks.* San Francisco: Jossey-Bass.

Kierkegaard, S. (1954). *Fear and trembling and the sickness unto death* (W. Lowrie, Trans.). Garden City, NY: Doubleday Anchor. (Original work published 1843)

Koffka, K. (1935). *Principles of Gestalt psychology.* New York: Harcourt, Brace.

Kohler, W. (1959). *Gestalt psychology.* New York: New American Library of World Literature.

Lang, P. J. (1984). The cognitive psychophysiology of emotion: Fear and anxiety. In A. J. Tuma & J. D. Maser (Eds.), *Anxiety and the anxiety disorders* (pp. 130–170). Hillsdale, NJ: Erlbaum.

Lee, R., & Wheeler, G. (1996). *The voice of shame.* San Francisco: Jossey-Bass.

Leventhal, H. (1984). A perceptual-motor theory of emotion. In L. Berkowitz (Ed.), *Advances in experimental social psychology* (pp. 117–182). New York: Academic.

Leventhal, H., & Tomarken, R. (1986). Emotion: Today's problems. *Annual Review of Psychology, 37,* 565–610.

Lewin, K. (1951). *Field theory in social science: Selected theoretical papers.* New York: Harper & Row.

Lietaer, G. (1990). The client-centered approach after the Wisconsin project: A personal view on its evolution. In G. Lietaer, J. Rombauts, & R. Van Balen (Eds.), *Client-centered and experiential psychotherapy in the nineties* (pp. 19–46). Leuven, Belgium: Leuven University Press.

Lietaer, G., Rombauts, J., & Van Balen, R. (Eds.). (1990). *Client-centered and experiential psychotherapy in the nineties.* Leuven, Belgium: Leuven University Press.

Mahoney, M., & Gabriel, T. (1987). Psychotherapy and the cognitive sciences. *Journal of Cognitive Psychotherapy: An International Quarterly, 1,* 39–59.

Mahrer, A. (1986). *Therapeutic experiencing: The process of change.* New York: Morton.

Mahrer, A. (1995). *The complete guide to experiential psychotherapy.* New York: Wiley.

Marcel, S. (1951). *Homo Viator: Introduction to a metaphysic of hope.* Chicago: Henry Regnery.

Maslow, A. H. (1968). *Toward a psychology of being* (2nd ed.). Princeton, NJ: Van Nostrand.

Maslow, A. H. (1970). *Motivation and personality* (Rev. ed.). New York: Harper & Row.

May, R. (Ed.). (1961). *Existential psychology.* New York: Random House.

May, R. (1977). *The meaning of anxiety* (Rev. ed.). New York: Norton.

May, R., Angel, E., & Ellenberger, H. (Eds.). (1958). *Existence: A new dimension in psychiatry and psychology.* New York: Basic Books.

May, R., & Yalom, I. (1984). Existential therapy. In R. J. Corsini (Ed.), *Current psychotherapies* (3rd ed., pp. 354–391). Itaska, IL: Peacock.

May, R., & Yalom, I. (1989). Existential therapy. In R. J. Corsini & D. Wedding (Eds.), *Current psychotherapies* (4th ed., pp. 363–402). Itaska, IL: Peacock.

McWaters, B. (Ed.). (1977). *Humanistic perspective: Current trends in psychology.* Monterey, CA: Brooks/Cole.

Moustakas, C. (1986). Being in, being for, and being with. *The Humanistic Psychologist, 14,* 100–104.

Neisser, U. (1976). *Cognition and reality: Principles and implications of cognitive psychology.* New York: Freeman.

Nevis, E. (1992). *Gestalt therapy: Perspectives and applications.* New York: Gardner Press.

Paivio, S., & Greenberg, L. (1995). Resolving unfinished business: Experiential therapy using empty chair dialogue. *Journal of Consulting & Clinical Psychology, 63*(3), 419–425.

Perls, F. S. (1947). *Ego, hunger, and aggression.* London: Allen & Unwin.

Perls, F. S. (1969). *Gestalt therapy verbatim.* Moab, UT: Real People Press.

Perls, F. S. (1973). *The Gestalt approach and eyewitness to therapy.* New York: Science and Behavior Books.

Perls, F. S., Hefferline, R. F., & Goodman, P. (1951). *Gestalt therapy.* New York: Julian Press.

Polster, E., & Polster, M. (1973). *Gestalt therapy integrated.* New York: Brunner/Mazel.

Prouty, G. (1994). *Theoretical evolutions in person-centered/experiential therapy.* New York: Praeger.

Raskin, N. J. (1949). An analysis of six parallel studies of the therapeutic process. *Journal of Consulting Psychology, 13,* 206–220.

Raskin, N. J., & Rogers, C. R. (1989). Person-centered therapy. In R. J. Corsini

& D. Wedding (Eds.), *Current psychotherapies* (4th ed., pp. 155–194). Itaska, IL: Peacock.

Rennie, D. (1990). Toward a representation of the client's experience of the therapy hour. In G. Lietaer, J. Rombauts, & R. Van Balen (Eds.), *Client-centered and experiential psychotherapy in the nineties* (pp. 152–172). Leuven, Belgium: Leuven University Press.

Rennie, D., & Toukmanian, S. (1992). Explanation in psychotherapy research. In S. Toukmanian & D. Rennie (Eds.), *Psychotherapy process research* (pp. 234–251). Thousand Oaks, CA: Sage.

Rice, L. N. (1974). The evocative function of the therapist. In D. A. Wexler & L. N. Rice (Eds.), *Innovations in client-centered therapy* (pp. 282–302). New York: Wiley.

Rice, L. N. (1984). Client tasks in client-centered therapy. In R. F. Levant & J. M. Shlein (Eds.), *Client-centered therapy and the person-centered approach* (pp. 182–202). New York: Praeger.

Rice, L. N., & Greenberg, L. S. (Eds.). (1984). *Patterns of change: Intensive analysis of psychotherapy process.* New York: Guilford.

Rice, L. N., & Greenberg, L. S. (1991). Two affective change events in client-centered therapy. In J. D. Safran & L. S. Greenberg (Eds.), *Emotion, psychotherapy and change* (pp. 197–226). New York: Guilford.

Rogers, C. R. (1942). *Counseling and psychotherapy.* Boston: Houghton Mifflin.

Rogers, C. R. (1951). *Client-centered therapy.* Boston: Houghton Mifflin.

Rogers, C. R. (1957). The necessary and sufficient conditions for therapeutic personality change. *Journal of Consulting Psychology, 21,* 95–103.

Rogers, C. R. (1958). A process conception of psychotherapy. *American Psychologist, 13,* 142–149.

Rogers, C. R. (1959). A theory of therapy, personality, and interpersonal relationships, as developed in the client-centered framework. In S. Koch (Ed.), *Psychology: A study of science; formulations of the person and the social context* (pp. 184–256). New York: McGraw-Hill.

Rogers, C. R. (1961). *On becoming a person.* Boston: Houghton Mifflin.

Rogers, C. R. (1980). *A way of being.* Boston: Houghton Mifflin.

Rogers, C. R. (1985). Toward a more human science of the person. *Journal of Humanistic Psychology, 25,* 7–24.

Rogers, C. R., & Dymond, R. F. (Eds.). (1954). *Psychotherapy and personality change.* Chicago: University of Chicago Press.

Rogers, C. R., Gendlin, G. T., Kiesler, D. J., & Truax, C. (Eds.). (1967). *The therapeutic relationship and its impact: A study of schizophrenics.* Madison: University of Wisconsin Press.

Rogers, C. R., & Skinner, B. F. (1956). Some issues concerning the control of human behavior. *Science, 124,* 1057–1066.

Sartre, J.-P. (1956). *Being and nothingness.* (H. Barnes, Trans.). New York: Philosophical Library. (Original work published 1943)

Sass, L. A. (1988). Humanism, hermeneutics, and the concept of the human subject. In S. B. Messer, L. A. Sass, & R. L. Wolfolk (Eds.), *Hermeneutics and psychological theory* (pp. 222–271). New Brunswick, NJ: Rutgers University Press.

Schneider, K., & May, R. (1995). *The psychology of existence: An integrative clinical perspective*. New York: McGraw-Hill.

Seeman, J. A. (1949). A study of the process of nondirective therapy. *Journal of Consulting Psychology, 13,* 157–169.

Smith, M. B. (1982). Psychology and humanism. *Journal of Humanistic Psychology, 22,* 44–55.

Smuts, J. (1926). *Holism and evolution.* New York: Macmillan.

Sutich, A. J., & Vich, M. (Eds.). (1969). *Readings in humanistic psychology.* New York: Free Press.

Tageson, W. C. (1982). *Humanistic psychology: A synthesis.* Homewood, IL: Dorsey Press.

Taylor, C. (1989). *Sources of the self.* Cambridge, MA: Harvard University Press.

Taylor, C. (1992). *The ethics of authenticity.* Cambridge, MA: Harvard University Press.

Van Kaam, A. (1966). *Existential foundations of psychology.* Pittsburgh: Duquesne University Press.

Warner, M. S. (1997). Does empathy cure? A theoretical consideration of empathy, processing, and personal narrative. In A. Bohart & L. Greenberg (Eds.), *Empathy reconsidered: New directions in psychotherapy* (pp. 125–140). Washington, DC: American Psychological Association.

Watson, J., & Greenberg, L. (1996). Emotion and cognition in experiential therapy: A dialectical–constructivist position. In H. Rosen & K. Kuelwein (Eds.), *Constructing realities: Meaning making perspectives for psychotherapists* (pp. 264–287). San Francisco: Jossey-Bass.

Wertheimer, M. (1945). *Productive thinking.* New York: Harper & Brothers.

Wheeler, G. (1991). *Gestalt reconsidered.* San Francisco: Jossey-Bass.

Yalom, I. (1981). *Existential psychotherapy.* New York: Basic Books.

Yontef, G. (1969). *A review of the practice of Gestalt therapy.* Los Angeles: Trident Books.

Yontef, G. (1981). The future of Gestalt therapy: A symposium with I. Perls, M. Polster, J. Zinker, & M. V. Miller. *The Gestalt Journal, 4,* 7–11.

Yontef, G. (1995). *Awareness, dialogue and process.* Highland, NY: Gestalt Journal Press.

Yontef, G. M., & Simkin, J. S. (1989). Gestalt therapy. In R. J. Corsini & D. Wedding (Eds.), *Current psychotherapies* (4th ed., pp. 323–361). Itaska, IL: Peacock.

4

THE CONCEPTUAL EVOLUTION OF BEHAVIOR THERAPY

DANIEL B. FISHMAN AND CYRIL M. FRANKS

All major conceptual approaches to psychotherapy—behavior therapy, psychoanalysis, family systems, humanistic therapy, and so forth—are embedded in some broad paradigm that involves a number of dimensions. These include (a) adherence to certain epistemological, philosophy-of-science assumptions; (b) a particular set of theoretical positions; (c) a body of scientific and other data; (d) particular collections of techniques and technologies; (e) specific values and ethical positions; and (f) a particular sociological, political, and historical context (D. B. Fishman, Rotgers, & Franks, 1988; Kuhn, 1962). In this chapter, the focus is on the evolution of behavior therapy in terms of epistemology and theory. However, a full understanding of behavior therapy depends in part on a consideration of the interrelationships among the various components of the overall paradigm, as just defined. Therefore, because we view the development of theory in behavior therapy as a reflection of the philosophical, social, cultural, political, and ethical contexts in which it is embedded rather than as an independent and isolated endeavor, we will devote considerable space to these relationships also.

We view behavior therapy as closely linked with the patterns of thought and values first developed during the seventeenth- and eighteenth-century Age of Enlightenment and later expanded in twentieth-century terms. These include a focus on rationally and scientifically derived, "value-neutral"[1] technology used in the service of promoting individual growth and freedom from irrational authority and arbitrary privilege (see also D. B. Fishman, Rotgers, & Franks, 1988; Woolfolk & Richardson, 1984). In theoretical terms, we view behavior therapy as an approach to the understanding of behavior and therapeutic behavior change that relies in large part on the traditional methodology of behavioral science, with significant links to learning theory, cognitive psychology, and other experimental psychology models. *Behavior* is defined broadly to include both overt actions and observable manifestations of covert affective and cognitively mediated processes. These processes may occur at several levels: psychophysiological, individual, small group, organizational, and community.

In practical terms, we regard behavior therapy as the data-based application of this theoretical approach to generate a technology whose primary goal is cost-effective, constructive behavior change. By *constructive*, we mean behavior change that is endorsed by all concerned and considered ethical. From the point of view of either theory or practice, we view behavior therapy as a major conceptual advance rather than as simply another therapeutic innovation.

The reader will note that, up to this point, we are focusing on the evolution of behavior therapy per se and not using the currently fashionable term *cognitive–behavioral therapy*. We do this in order to communicate our conviction that cognitive–behavioral therapy is best considered within the overall context of behavior therapy of which it is a part rather than as a separate entity (see also Franks, 1987a). Although it is true that the evolution of cognitive–behavioral therapy involved changes in the meta-theoretical foundations of behavior therapy (Baars, 1986; Mahoney, 1988), other developments in behavior therapy have also involved changes at this basic level. In fact, a major theme of this chapter is that such foundational changes have been typical of behavior therapy as it has evolved in response to new philosophical and theoretical models in psychology at large, such as general systems theory (Kanfer & Schefft, 1988) and "social constructionism" (D. B. Fishman, 1988), a philosophical alternative to the logical positivism underlying traditional science. We intend to describe both these types of foundational changes in behavior therapy and those continuities that justify the ongoing use of the term *behavior therapy*.

---

[1]To most behavior therapists, *value-neutral* is a relative term. It refers to a deemphasis on emotionally, subjectively, and socially loaded concepts in favor of those which are "nearer to the empirical data," that is, those that are more observationally based and less inferential and are thus more likely to be agreed upon by different observers.

HISTORY

Learning Theory Beginnings

It was not until the 1950s that behavior therapy as we know it today began to emerge. In another sense, however, behavior therapy has many roots, many origins, and no single starting point. It was during the intellectual and cultural climate of the Enlightenment, that period of European history emphasizing reason and scientific study of the natural world, that the foundations of what today is called behavior therapy emerged. For example, the British empiricists, who spanned the period from 1600 to 1900, emphasized four main principles: (a) that knowledge comes from experience with the world rather than introspective rumination or divine inspiration; (b) that scientific procedures have to be based upon systematic observation rather than opinion, intuition, or authority; (c) that the mind of the child is a blank slate (*tabula rasa*) on which experience writes, so that adult mental life is primarily a recording and unfolding of the previous history of the person concerned; and (d) that consciousness is best viewed in terms of "mental chemistry," in which thoughts can be broken down into basic elements connected through various laws, such as continuity, similarity, contrast, vividness, frequency, and recency, into more complex ideas (Kimble, 1985).

It was similar thinking that led to the conceptualization of behavior therapy in the 1950s as the application of "modern learning theory" to clinical problems (Eysenck, 1959). Nowadays, with the advantage of hindsight, there is a tendency to downplay these early beginnings as simplistic and naive, an oversimplification that disregarded the complexities of life in the real world and summarily dismissed other points of view. Indeed, this was the case. It was not until the mid-1980s that behavior therapists became sufficiently secure to accept the possibility that scientific methodology did not have to be confined to their definition of science and their notions about what constitutes valid data. It took many years for behavior therapists to recognize that the methodology of science could legitimately mean different things to different people, that there is no single and invariant scientific methodology, and that the belief in any form of science or the universality of known scientific principles is ultimately, in itself, no more than a belief.

In any event, psychology emerged as a discipline distinct from philosophy when Wundt established the first formal experimental psychology laboratory at Leipzig in 1879. At that time, psychology was a minor subsection of philosophy, and it was not until the close of the nineteenth century that independent university departments of psychology began to emerge. Soon thereafter, Titchener, one of Wundt's followers, established a similar laboratory at Cornell University and became a dominant figure in American psychology. In the tradition of the British associationists, Titchener developed a stream of psychology called "structuralism," designed to discover the so-called elements of mental chemistry and the principles of association that could be used to explain how such elements combine to form everyday experience. Titchener's methodology, the training of subjects to introspect and report in detail on their conscious experiences, is in direct contrast with the tradition of experimental animal psychology practiced by such individuals as Pavlov and Thorndike. These researchers emphasized objectively observable behavior rather than subjective reports of intrapsychic experiences.

Watson brought this conflict into dramatic focus and used it to develop an alternative system of psychology called "behaviorism." His primary vehicle for launching behaviorism as a movement was a 1913 manifesto in the *Psychological Review*, entitled "Psychology as the Behaviorist Views It":

> Psychology as the behaviorist views it is a purely objective branch of natural science. Its theoretical goal is the prediction and control of behavior. Introspection forms no essential part of its methods, nor is the scientific value of its data dependent upon the readiness with which they lend themselves to interpretation in terms of consciousness. The behaviorist, in his efforts to get a unitary scheme of animal response, recognises no dividing line between man and brute. The behavior of man, with all of its refinement and complexity, forms only a part of the behaviorist's total scheme of investigation. (Watson, 1913, p. 158)

Thus, according to Watson, if psychology were to become a science, as he defined this word, it must become materialistic (as opposed to mentalistic), mechanistic (as opposed to anthropomorphic), deterministic (as opposed to accepting of free will), and objective (as opposed to subjective). For Watson, emotions are exclusively visceral bodily reactions, involving primarily the glands and smooth, or involuntary muscles. Similarly, Watson viewed thinking as "laryngeal habits," that is, tiny movements of the vocal chords. These movements, argued Watson in a series of data-devoid speculations—which, ironically, we would now regard as the antithesis of scientific methodology—are developed from random, unlearned vocalizations. Thus, language is at first overt, and by a process of conditioning, the child acquires words. Because words may serve as a substitute for things and concrete situations, the child is liberated from the environment without making the actual overt movements.

It was during this period that Pavlov demonstrated that dogs could learn to salivate at the ringing of a bell through a process of temporally and spatially contiguous associations between the bell and direct access to food, or even the sight of food. Distrusting absolutism in any form, he deliberately employed the term *conditional* in his writings rather than *conditioned*. His intent was to convey the essentially temporary nature of the connections thus formed, connections that lacked the certainty and regularity of innate reflexes. For Pavlov, as for his distinguished precursor Sechenov, the conditional reflex was a creative, emergent, and highly responsive activity of the organism rather than, as is still the common misbelief, a stereotyped and unchanging process (Franks, 1969).

In Pavlov's first book to be translated into English, the correct English translation, *conditional reflex,* was used. It was in later translations, probably from the German, that the misleading term *conditioned* was introduced. In translating Pavlov into English in what was to become the standard English language text, Gantt—the main spokesman for Pavlov in the English-speaking world at that time—deliberately maintained this inaccuracy in the interest of consistency, a decision that he said he regretted ever since (Gantt, 1966).

Another closely related development was the establishment in 1913 of Thorndike's general principles of human and animal learning. Cats learned to escape from a "puzzle box" to obtain release or bits of food as rewards. Studies such as these led to the formulation of Thorndike's "law of effect":

> Of several responses made to the same situation, those which are accompanied or closely followed by satisfaction of the animal will, other things being equal, be more firmly connected with the situation, so that, when it recurs, they will be more likely to recur; those which are accompanied or closely followed by discomfort to the animal will, other things being equal, have their connections with that situation weakened, so that, when it recurs, they will be less likely to occur. . . . By a satisfying state of affairs is meant one which the animal does nothing to avoid, often doing such things as to attain and preserve it. (Thorndike, 1911, pp. 244–245)

Pavlovian classical or respondent conditioning, based on Aristotelian association by contiguity, and Thorndike's instrumental or operant conditioning, in which the subject is rewarded for making the desired response and punished whenever an undesired response is elicited, became the foundation on which major developments in behavioristic learning theory were based for the next 50 years. It was this movement that dominated American psychology until the cognitive shift of the 1970s and 1980s, a shift that spilled over from psychology at large into the realm of behavior therapy, bringing with it the significant conceptual shift from *behavioristic* to *behavioral* theory. The essence of this shift is that whereas behavioristic theory addresses only directly observable situations and behaviors, behavioral theory deals with thoughts and feelings, as long as they are firmly linked to observable situations and behaviors.[2]

Formation of Behavior Therapy as a Distinct Movement

In the first article devoted exclusively to behavior therapy in the *Annual Review of Psychology*, Krasner (1971) suggested that 15 streams of development within the science of psychology came together during the 1950s and 1960s to form this new approach to behavior change. These streams may be summarized as follows:

1. the concept of behaviorism in experimental psychology;
2. the operant conditioning of Thorndike and Skinner;
3. the development of Wolpe's (1958) systematic desensitization;
4. the emergence of behavior therapy as an experimental science at the University of London Institute of Psychiatry, Maudsley Hospital, under the direction of Eysenck;
5. the application of conditioning and learning concepts to human behavior problems in the United States from the 1920s to the 1950s;
6. the interpretation of psychoanalysis in terms of learning theory (e.g., Dollard & Miller, 1950);
7. the application of Pavlovian principles in explaining and changing both normal and deviant behavior;
8. theoretical concepts and research studies of social role learning and interactionism in social psychology and sociology;
9. research in developmental and child psychology emphasizing vicarious learning and modeling;
10. social influence studies of demand characteristics, experimenter bias, hypnosis, and placebo;
11. an environmentally based social learning model as an alternative to the disease model of human behavior (Bandura, 1969; Ullmann & Krasner, 1965);
12. dissatisfaction with the prevailing psychoanalytically based psychotherapy model, particularly as articulated in Eysenck's (1952) critical empirical study of therapy outcome;
13. the development of the idea of the *clinical psychologist* within the scientist-practitioner model;
14. a movement within psychiatry away from the then orthodox

---

[2]The difference between behavioristic theory and behavioral theory parallels Erwin's (1978) distinction between ideological behaviorism and pragmatic behaviorism, described in the section Epistemological Paradigms.

focus on internal dynamics and pathology toward human interaction and environmental influence; and

15. a Utopian emphasis on the planning of social environments to elicit and maintain the best of human behavior (e.g., Skinner's [1948] *Walden Two*).

As Krasner (1982) pointed out, these streams of development were neither independent nor static, and, as we shall show, new streams of influence are continually emerging.

Behavior therapy in the United States was influenced both by the classical conditioning of Pavlov and Thorndike and by Skinner's instrumental or operant conditioning. The possibility of explaining behavioral abnormalities in conditioning terms was outlined independently by Watson (1924) and Burnham (1924). In 1917, Mateer produced a monograph on the application of conditioning techniques to children. Perhaps the most prophetic publication, however, was that of Dunlap (1932; currently reissued in paperback form [Dunlap, 1972]). The clinical techniques outlined by Dunlap, and even the theoretical formulations to a lesser extent, foreshadowed the armamentarium of the contemporary behavior therapist.

The 1930s saw many attempts to explore the nature of neurosis by inducing so-called neurotic behavior in various animals such as the pig (Liddell, 1958) and the cat (Masserman, 1943), and it must not be forgotten that the pioneering work of Wolpe, to be discussed shortly, arose in large part out of his investigations of neurotic behavior in cats.

Within the universities and in closely related clinical settings, it was the integration of experimental research with clinical procedures, coupled with a general dissatisfaction among many psychologists with prevailing psychodynamic formulations, that led to the development of behavior therapy as a viable intervention strategy. A leader in this effort was Mowrer, who became disenchanted with his original orientation as a psychoanalyst and gradually shifted from a focus on intrapsychic dynamics to the view that a disturbance in interpersonal relationships is often a cause rather than a symptom of neurosis. In conjunction with Mowrer's formulation of two distinct kinds of learning, he and his wife, Mary, developed a now widely accepted treatment for eneuresis on the basis of direct conditioning procedures, known as the bell-and-pad method (Mowrer & Mowrer, 1938).

Other writers of distinction in this context in the early postwar period include Shaw (1948), one of the first to apply systematically the principles of learning based on animal work to psychotherapy; Shaffer (1947), who reviewed the implications of learning theory–based models of behavior for the therapist; and Shoben (1949), who attempted to integrate Mowrer's learning theory approach with the field of mainstream psychotherapy (Krasner, 1982).

Another important influence in the 1940s stemmed from the work of a group of investigators at Yale, notably Dollard and Miller (1950), who attempted to develop a learning theory basis for psychoanalytic formulations. For these individuals, it seemed that psychoanalytic theory formed the ultimate basis for understanding and predicting deviant behavior; consequently, it was hoped that a learning theory formulation was an acceptable translation of psychoanalytic terminology and concepts into learning theory terms for those steeped in stimulus–response (S-R) theory. It was also hoped that this exercise in dictionary construction would facilitate the development and investigation of testable hypotheses in learning theory terms by scientists wedded to the methodology of behavioral science. These could then be retranslated back into the psychoanalytic model where, according to Dollard and Miller, they really belonged.

One notable start of these developments was in the United Kingdom at the Maudsley Hospital, the physical home of the University of London Institute of Psychiatry.[3] At that time, in the United Kingdom as elsewhere, the only available and generally acceptable form of psychotherapy was based on psychoanalytic premises carried out under the leadership of a physician. Psychopharmacology had relatively little to contribute, and the only nonmedical influence of positive significance stemmed from the ministrations of social workers. Psychologists, having little to offer that was both acceptable and distinctive, began to question the utility of spending 3 or 4 undergraduate years studying a body of knowledge that stressed the methodology of the behavioral scientist only to find that graduate training in clinical psychology and its eventual application rested on the goodwill and psychodynamic tutelage of the physician, making little or no use of other than psychodynamic formulations.

Given this set of circumstances, it was understandable that it was a disease model of medical illness that prevailed. Disorders of behavior were regarded as diseases for which an "etiology" had to be found, leading to some form of "treatment." Hence the stress on "diagnosis," "patient," "therapy," and "cure." Psychiatric disturbance remained fundamentally a medical problem in which the nonmedical psychologist was, at best, a useful ancillary worker.

Unfortunately, or perhaps fortunately in the long run, their rigorous training as behavioral scientists soon led psychologists at the Maudsley Hospital to the realization that traditional psychiatric diagnoses were fraught with many problems of reliability, validity, and general utility. To compound matters further, when psychologists examined the limited role that was imposed on them—that of diagnostic testing assistant to the psychiatrist—it became increasingly evident that the traditional psychometric batteries they were expected to administer were themselves of ques-

---

[3]One of the authors of this chapter, Cyril Franks, lived in London during this period and was actively involved in this process.

tionable validity and that new assessment devices would need to be generated.

In any event, dissatisfaction with the role of the clinical psychologist, the lack of viable alternatives, and the perceived deficiencies of psychodynamic therapy served as an impetus for the search for new directions. Many models were considered and discarded, and eventually it became apparent that S-R learning theory—in particular the work of Pavlov—offered the most promise for the testing of theoretically generated predictions and an eventual database for therapeutic intervention. Leaning heavily on empirical verification, the hope was that a rational model of this sort rooted in the discipline of psychology would lead eventually to the development of valid, learning theory–based assessment and intervention strategies. And so it was that the concept of behavior therapy was born in the United Kingdom under the leadership of Eysenck and his associates at the Institute of Psychiatry (Franks, 1987b).

Over the years, Eysenck's many students established Maudsley enclaves and offshoots throughout the world. The first publication of a case based on these principles was Jones' (1956) application of conditioning and learning techniques to the treatment of a psychiatric patient. Those were richly productive times, leading to the publication of probably the first behaviorally based textbook of abnormal psychology in the world (Eysenck, 1960) and one of the first collections of case studies in behavior therapy (Eysenck, 1964); the creation of the first journal devoted exclusively to behavior therapy, *Behaviour Research and Therapy*; and to the invention of a name for this mode of treatment, "behavior therapy." (See Eysenck's [1990] autobiography for a more detailed account of these events.)

At about the same time, a parallel development was proceeding in South Africa under the impetus of a Johannesburg physician dissatisfied with both the theory and clinical usefulness of prevailing psychodynamic concepts. At first in South Africa and later in the United States, Wolpe (1958) used Pavlovian principles to develop his now widely used theory of psychotherapy by reciprocal inhibition and the technique of "systematic desensitization" for the treatment of fears and phobias.

In Wolpe's technique, the patient first learns how to achieve a state of deep muscle relaxation. Then a hierarchy of specific situations and scenes related to the patient's fear is created in terms of intensity of anxiety elicited by the situation. For example, an agoraphobic might establish being near the door of his or her house as mildly anxiety-arousing, walking in the neighborhood as moderately anxiety-arousing, and driving 10 miles from home as extremely anxiety-arousing—with a variety of associated situations filling in points along the hierarchy. Finally, the therapist begins the formal desensitization. The client first relaxes and then imagines the mildest scene on the hierarchy that elicits anxiety. After 5 seconds or so, this experience is followed by a period of terminating the scene image and returning to a state of relaxation, so that the patient starts to learn to associate relaxation rather than anxiety to the previously feared situation. Each scene in the hierarchy is repeated until the patient reports experiencing virtually no anxiety while visualizing it. In this way the patient works his or her way stepwise through the complete hierarchy.

Without doubt, systematic desensitization was the first viable "talk therapy" alternative to traditional psychotherapy. Before the advent of systematic desensitization, conditioning was regarded as a strategy to be applied exclusively to animals, small children, seriously impaired individuals, or perhaps those suffering from some specific and highly focalized disorder. Now, at long last, an alternative to psychodynamic therapy became available, an alternative that could be meaningfully and efficiently applied to the sophisticated patients who came to the psychiatrist's private office for treatment of complex problems. The fact that Wolpe's laborious procedures have been modified many times as a result of subsequent study and the fact that his original theoretical explanation in terms of classical conditioning and Sherringtonian inhibition has long been largely rejected (e.g., Wilson & O'Leary, 1980) in no way detract from the practical significance of these remarkable accomplishments.

The 1950s and 1960s was a pioneering era, an era of ideology and polemics in which behavior therapists strove to present a united front against the common psychodynamic "foe." As behavior therapy began to establish itself in the 1970s as a respected and respectable method of treatment, gradually but progressively, behavior therapists abandoned missionary zeal and began to search for new frontiers within which to extend their approach. These included general outpatient psychotherapy practice, biofeedback, health psychology, community psychology, and the worlds of business, administration, and government. For example, jobs were subjected to careful, systematic analysis, comparing which behaviors were actually rewarded by salary and promotions with which behaviors were most desirable for achieving the goals of the overall organization. By changing incentive systems, work behaviors could then be brought into closer correspondence with organizational objectives (Gilbert, 1978). It was an era of intellectual expansion into concepts, methods, and ways of viewing data beyond those of traditional learning theory. It was also the era of the rise of cognitive–behavioral therapy, in part a reflection of the "cognitive revolution" in psychology as a whole (Baars, 1986). This latter development is very much a part of the contemporary scene in behavior therapy, and more needs to be said about its impact and significance.

One might expect that behavior therapy would have been particularly appreciated in the Soviet Union, with its monolithic emphasis (before the advent of Gorbachev and *glasnost*) on Pavlovian psychology. Yet, with a few notable exceptions (e.g., the use of aversion conditioning for the treatment of alcoholism), until very recently behavior therapy has been virtually nonexistent in the Soviet Union and in what is now Russia.

There appear to be several explanations for this state of affairs (Franks, 1969). First, the profession of clinical psychology, and the necessary training programs to back this discipline up, did not exist in the USSR. Second, psychologists, in common with most Soviet citizens, were not privy to intellectual and professional developments in the West. Third, under the influence of a state-directed Marxism, Western associationism and, hence, behavior therapy were dismissed as "vulgar materialism," attempts to substitute an "inferior" mechanistic materialism for the dialectic alternative stemming from Marxist ideology.

In 1967, the Association for Advancement of Behavior Therapy (AABT) was created in the United States as an organizational home for the growing number of psychologists and other mental health professionals practicing, researching, teaching, or otherwise interested in behavior therapy. Today the AABT, with almost 5,000 members, is the largest behavior therapy association in the world. The other major behavioral organization in the United States is the Association for Behavior Analysis. With several thousand members, this latter group is primarily oriented to the application of Skinner's operant psychology and remains opposed in principle and practice to much of cognitive–behavioral therapy.

Since 1970, the European Association of Behaviour Therapy has organized annual conferences in various European and closely associated countries. Their 10th annual meeting in Jerusalem evolved into the First World Congress in Behaviour Therapy. Since then, behavior therapy has prospered throughout the world, and there are now literally scores of behavior therapy societies in existence and at least 50 journals, most in English, devoted primarily or exclusively to behavior therapy and its many offshoots.

Emergence of Theoretical Submovements

In the 1970s, behavior therapy began to cohere into more or less distinct streams, all sharing a common methodological and learning theory core. At least five are noteworthy (see Wilson & Franks, 1982 for a more extended discussion). *Applied behavior analysis,* the first submovement, describes the application of principles derived from Skinnerian operant conditioning to a wide range of clinical and social problems. For the most part, applied behavior analysts are "radical behaviorists" whose basic assumption is that behavior is exclusively a function of its consequences. There are no intervening variables, mentalistic inferences are disavowed, and intervention procedures are evaluated primarily in terms of single-case experimental designs in which the participant serves as his or her own control. The emphasis is on the manipulation of environmental variables to bring about behavioral change and on the use of laboratory-based principles, such as reinforcement, punishment, extinction, and stimulus control.

The second approach, described by Wilson and Franks (1982) as the *neobehavioristic, mediational S–R model*, invokes primarily the application of classical conditioning and the works of Pavlov, Mowrer, and Wolpe, among others. Intervening variables and hypothetical constructs are acceptable, and publicly unobservable processes, such as the imaginal representation of anxiety-eliciting stimuli in systematic desensitization, are accepted and even encouraged.

Next, *social learning theory*, developed by Bandura and his colleagues, now constitutes, along with cognitive–behavioral therapy, the mainstream of contemporary behavior therapy. In its most advanced form (e.g., Bandura, 1982), social learning theory is interactional, interdisciplinary, and multimodal. Behavior is influenced by stimulus events (primarily through classical conditioning), by external reinforcement (through operant conditioning), and by cognitive mediational processes. Behavior change is brought about largely through observational learning, a process in which people are influenced by observing someone else's behavior. The term *model* is reserved for the exemplar, the person who demonstrates the behavior that the observer views. *Live modeling* occurs when the exemplar is directly seen, whereas *symbolic modeling* takes place when the model is observed indirectly, as in movies, on television, by reading, through an oral description of someone else's behavior, or even by imagining a model's behaviors. Social learning emphasizes reciprocal interactions between the individual behavior and the environment. The individual is considered capable of self-directed behavior change. Bandura's theory of perceived *self-efficacy* is one of the first major attempts to provide a unified theoretical explanation of how behavior therapy and other psychotherapy procedures work. Self-efficacy is the individual's belief or expectation that he or she can master a situation and bring about desired outcomes. It is viewed as a common cognitive mechanism that mediates the effects of all psychological change procedures; that is, these procedures are postulated to be effective because they create and strengthen a client's expectations of personal efficacy.

Staats' (1975) *social behaviorism*, now updated as *paradigmatic behaviorism* (Eifert & Evans, 1990; Staats, 1981, 1988), developed more or less independently of social learning theory. Paradigmatic behaviorism emphasizes the integration of conditioning theory with traditional concepts in personality, clinical, and social psychology. Staats views the principles of reinforcement and contiguity as always present and interacting in the development of personality, with operant conditioning impacting overt behavior patterns and classical conditioning impacting emotional and cognitive response patterns. Staat's concept of "cumulative–hierarchical learning and development" explains how complex combinations of simple behaviors learned by basic conditioning can evolve, over time, into three complex "personality repertoires" of responses: sensory–motor, emotional–motivational, and language–cognitive. Taken together, these ideas provide the conceptual tools for Staats to apply the principles of conditioning to all areas of traditional psychology, including such clinically relevant domains as personality assessment, psychopathology, and psychotherapy.

Finally, *cognitive–behavioral therapy*, a very popular and relatively recent theoretical submovement, derives its main impetus from the so-called cognitive revolution in general psychology. Cognitive–behavioral therapists emphasize cognitive processes and private events as mediators of behavior change. Kendall and Bemis (1983) summarized six basic assumptions within cognitive–behavioral therapy:

1. The human organism responds primarily to cognitive representations of its environments rather than to these environments per se.
2. Most human learning is cognitively mediated.
3. Thoughts, feelings, and behaviors are causally interrelated.
4. Attitudes, expectancies, attributions, and other cognitive activities are central to producing, predicting, and understanding psychopathological behavior and the effects of therapeutic interventions.
5. Cognitive processes can be cast into testable formulations that are easily integrated with behavioral paradigms, and it is possible and desirable to combine cognitive treatment strategies with enactive techniques [such as behavioral rehearsal] and behavioral contingency management.
6. The task of the cognitive–behavioral therapist is to act as diagnostician, educator, and technical consultant, assessing maladaptive cognitive processes and working with the client to design learning experiences that may ameliorate these dysfunctional cognitions and the behavioral and affective patterns with which they correlate.

DEFINITION OF BEHAVIOR THERAPY

Interestingly, the term *behavior therapy* seems to have been introduced more or less independently by three widely separated groups of researchers: (a) by Skinner, Solomon, and Lindsley in the United States in a 1953 status report, to refer to their application of operant conditioning to increase simple social behaviors in severely disturbed, chronically hospitalized psychotic patients; (b) by Lazarus (1958) in South Africa, to refer to Wolpe's application of his "reciprocal inhibition" technique to neurotic patients; and (c) by Eysenck's Maudsley group, to describe their "new look" at clinical intervention, in which behavior therapy is defined simply as the application of modern learning theory to the understanding and treatment of behavioral and behaviorally related disorders (Eysenck, 1959).

With the exception of traditional applied behavior analysis, prevailing behavioral approaches all embrace the use of cognitive mediational concepts, and, to greater or lesser degrees, all emphasize the integration of principles derived from traditional learning theory and conditioning with those stemming from cognitive and social psychology. Moreover, as we will discuss, even some radical behaviorists have recently been actively moving "to bring together the field of cognition with the field of behavioral psychology" (Hayes, 1996, p. 1).

Many authors (e.g., Erwin, 1978; Franks, 1990; Wilson, 1982) point out that it is difficult to articulate a succinct definition of contemporary behavior therapy that does justice to the field. Erwin (1978) noted that most definitions of behavior therapy tend to fall into one of two categories: doctrinal or epistemological. Doctrinal definitions link behavior therapy to doctrines, theory, laws, or principles of learning. Epistemological definitions are more inclined to characterize it in terms of the various ways of studying clinical phenomena. By and large, doctrinal definitions tend to be too narrow and thereby fail to accommodate all of behavior therapy, whereas epistemological definitions tend to be excessively broad and, hence, potentially applicable to many nonbehavioral therapies, thereby confusing the line between behavioral and other therapies.

D. B. Fishman (1988) suggested that this definitional dilemma results from the fact that behavior therapy, like many areas in the social sciences, consists of a series of overlapping domains, as represented in the five circles of Figure 1. The first four circles include

1. therapeutic principles derived from learning theory;
2. therapeutic principles derived from experimental psychology generally;
3. specific therapeutic techniques originated by behaviorally oriented clinicians, such as contingency contracting and systematic desensitization; and
4. ideas and strategies adapted from the general psychotherapy literature, such as the relationship-enhancement methods of Rogerian therapy, therapy process models taken from systems theory (cf. Kanfer & Schefft, 1988), and short-term therapy (e.g., Wells & Giannetti, 1990).

In Figure 1, the partial overlap among the circles is noteworthy. For example, Circle 3 is only partially overlapping Circles 1 and 2. This reflects the fact that some of the accepted techniques in Circle 3, such as contingency contracting, are clearly deducible from the contemporary experimental principles associated with Circles 1 and 2, whereas other accepted

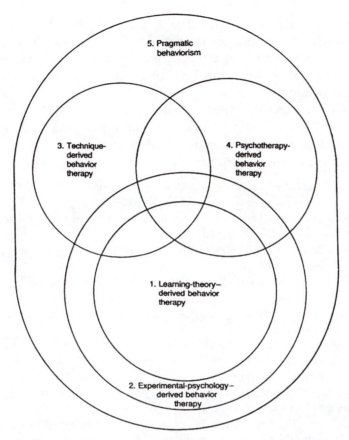

Figure 1. The overlapping domains of the behavioral movement. From
Paradigms in Behavior Therapy: Present and Promise (p. 268) edited by D. B.
Fishman, F. Rotgers, and C. M. Franks, 1988, New York: Springer. Copyright
1988 by Springer Publishing Company. Reprinted with permission.

techniques in Circle 3, such as systematic desensitization, are not (Wilson
& O'Leary, 1980). As another example, Circle 4 overlaps only parts of
Circles 1, 2, and 3. This reflects the fact that, whereas some of the approaches from the psychotherapy literature, such as goal setting and short-
term therapy, are clearly deducible from traditional behavioral techniques
and contemporary experimentally based principles, others, such as Rogerian
relationship enhancement techniques, are not.

Circle 5, which embraces the other four, involves the methodological
principles of behavioral science, such as empiricism, operational definition,
quantification, value-neutrality of theoretical concepts, and experimental
research design. As we will describe, these principles can be framed in
epistemological terms either within the positivist paradigm (traditional experimental science) or within the alternative epistemology of pragmatism
and social constructionism (D. B. Fishman, 1988).

Note that in Erwin's terms, Figure 1 combines both doctrinal definitions (Circles 1–4) with an epistemological definition (Circle 5). By defining behavior therapy in terms of all five circles, Fishman aimed to avoid the problems Erwin pointed out of an exclusively doctrinal or epistemological definition.

Recognizing the difficulty of succinctly defining behavior therapy, O'Leary and Wilson (1987) provided a useful list of nine "common core" assumptions that behavior therapists hold. In our view, these assumptions are beliefs held by the majority of contemporary behavior therapists:

1. Most abnormal behavior is acquired and maintained according to the same principles as normal behavior.
2. Most abnormal behavior can be modified through the application of social learning principles.
3. Assessment is continuous and focuses on the current determinants of behavior.
4. People are best described by what they think, feel, and do in specific life situations. . . .
5. Treatment methods are precisely specified, replicable, and objectively evaluated. . . .
6. Treatment outcome is evaluated in terms of the initial induction of behavior change, its generalization to the real life setting, and its maintenance over time.
7. Treatment strategies are individually tailored to different problems in different individuals. . . .
8. Behavior therapy is broadly applicable to a full range of clinical disorders and educational problems.
9. Behavior therapy is a humanistic approach in which treatment goals and methods are mutually contracted [between client and therapist]. (p. 12)

A METATHEORETICAL FRAMEWORK FOR CHARACTERIZING CONTEMPORARY BEHAVIOR THERAPY

A theory in psychology is a conceptual framework that identifies important dimensions of human experience and behavior and describes relationships among these dimensions. A "metatheory" is a fundamental viewpoint that stands "behind," or logically prior to, the theory. Thus, metatheory consists of those assumptions that are made before the creation, validation, and refinement of a theory.

Table 1 presents an overview of the metatheoretical location of earlier and later versions of behavior therapy, relative to other systems of psychotherapy and applied psychology theory. It thus highlights the underlying assumptional differences among therapy systems. The table is organized as a grid formed by two cross-cutting typologies of metatheoretical assump-

TABLE 1
The Metatheoretical Location of Behavior Therapy Within Applied Psychology

| Dominant theoretical worldview | Epistemological paradigm | | |
| | Logical positivism | Social constructionism | |
	Experimental paradigm	Pragmatic paradigm[a]	Hermeneutic paradigm
Trait	Cattell's psychometrically based theory of personality composed of 16 universal source traits (Cattell, 1966).[b]	Psychometric polling models for predicting voter behavior (e.g., Louis Harris polls).	Freud's theory of oral, anal, and phallic character types (e.g., Freud, 1924).
Interactional	Earlier and later behavior therapy theory.	Later behavior therapy theory only.	[c]
Organismic	General systems theory as applied to living systems (e.g., Miller, 1978).	Program evaluation theory (e.g., Morell, 1979).	Structural family therapy theory (e.g., Minuchin, 1974).
Transactional	[c]	[c]	Humanistic/existential therapy theory (e.g., Rogers, 1961).

[a]In previous writings, this has been called the "Technological Paradigm" (D. B. Fishman, 1988; D. B. Fishman & Neigher, 1987; Neigher & D. B. Fishman, 1985).
[b]Entries in the grid cells are illustrative, not exhaustive.
[c]These cells involve logically incompatible perspectives, and thus they cannot support viable theories (see text).

tions: D. B. Fishman's (1988) "epistemological paradigms" (divided into the "experimental," "pragmatic," and "hermeneutic"); and Altman and Rogoff's (1987) "worldviews" (divided into "trait," "interactional," "organismic," and "transactional"). (A detailed discussion of Table 1 can be found in D. B. Fishman & Franks [1992].)

Epistemological Paradigms

Epistemology is the branch of philosophy that investigates the origins, nature, methods, and limits of human knowledge. An epistemological paradigm sets forth the criteria according to which the relevance and validity of a particular body of knowledge are judged. In other words, philosophically speaking, no knowledge is *given* in any absolute sense. Rather, a variety of possible, coherent epistemological systems are set forth, and the evaluation of a statement's truth or falsity will depend, in part, on the epistemological criteria chosen for the evaluation, and not just on the content of the statement per se (D. B. Fishman, 1988; Gergen, 1982).

Until recently, American psychology was dominated by the episte-mology of conventional natural science, that of logical positivism. In broad terms, logical positivism contends that there is an external world indepen-dent of human experience and that objective, "scientific" knowledge about this world can be obtained through direct sense experience, as interpreted within the framework of theory-embedded, hypothesis-testing laboratory experiments. The data upon which this knowledge is founded consist of discrete, molecular, sensorily based "facts," all of which can eventually be quantified. Knowledge is in the form of a cumulative body of context-free, universal laws about the phenomenon studied. Psychologists who have adopted a positivist perspective generally assume that the universal laws that emerge from "scientific" study will have a form such that they can eventually be applied to help solve significant psychological and social problems in a unique, rationally based manner.

For a variety of philosophical, scientific, cultural, and practical rea-sons, since around 1960 there has been a growing movement in psychology and the other social sciences that rejects positivism as the appropriate epistemology for the field, proposing in its stead "social constructionism" (e.g., D. B. Fishman, 1988; Gergen, 1982, 1985; Krasner & Houts, 1984; Scarr, 1985).

In contrast to logical positivism, social constructionism posits that the reality an individual or group experiences is, to a substantial degree, conceptually constructed rather than sensorily discovered by that group. Objective knowledge about the world is significantly limited because "facts" and "raw data" can be known only within a particular, preempiri-cally established cultural, social, and linguistic context.

As reflected in Table 1, social constructionism has encouraged the growth of two types of nonpositivist epistemological paradigms. The more radical is a hermeneutic paradigm that emphasizes qualitative interpreta-tion; experiential, phenomenological, symbolic meaning; a place for sub-jectivity and intuition; and a historically situated psychology. This model views the goals and proper methods of psychology as similar to those of history, literary criticism, and investigative reporting (Messer, Sass, & Woolfolk, 1988; Packer, 1985).

The alternative approach spawned by social constructionism is that of the technological or pragmatic paradigm (D. B. Fishman, 1988, 1991, 1995a; D. B. Fishman & Neigher, 1987; Polkinghorne, 1992), a hybrid between the experimental and hermeneutic approaches. Like the herme-neutic paradigm, the pragmatic paradigm is based on social constructionism and rejects the theory-based laboratory experiment and the search for gen-eral psychological laws, advocating instead for contextually embedded, case-based knowledge. However, like the experimental paradigm, the prag-matic paradigm values a quantitative, atomistic, observational approach and adapts some of the research methods of the laboratory into "quasi-experimental" and "single-subject" research designs (Barlow & Hersen, 1984). Instead of scientific understanding per se, the pragmatic paradigm values humanistic relevance, adopting action-oriented approaches from engineering and the field of research and development (e.g., Azrin, 1977; D. B. Fishman, 1988; D. B. Fishman & Neigher, 1987; Morell, 1979; Neigher & Fishman, 1985).

As already described and as reflected in Table 1, the origins of the behavior therapy movement are clearly and directly embedded in logical positivism. Watson's original model for behavioristic theory was that of experimental animal psychology, and this model was continued by Hull, Skinner, Tolman, Guthrie, and other learning theory researchers in the so-called Age of Grand Theory (Kimble, 1985). Applying the model of physics and chemistry, these researchers assumed that there are a few basic, universal laws of learning that apply to both animals and humans. In line with this view, these researchers pursued scientific psychology by focusing on publicly observable, circumscribed behaviors such as the food-seeking activities of white mice or pigeons under controlled laboratory conditions. Although these researchers did not deny the existence of the world of consciousness, complex human relationships, and cultural products such as literature and politics, these domains were either overlooked or deliberately excluded because they are highly subjective and not clearly amenable to objective, scientific study in the tradition of logical positivism.

As also shown in Table 1, whereas some groups in later behavior therapy theory have remained within the experimental paradigm (see, e.g., Baars, 1986; Wilson & Franks, 1982), others have moved away from the experimental epistemological paradigm into the pragmatic paradigm (D. B. Fishman, Rotgers, & Franks, 1988).

There are at least three reasons that many behavior theorists have moved from the experimental to the pragmatic paradigm. First, as behavior therapy was beginning in the 1960s, the high point of the experimental paradigm on which behavior therapy was originally based, the Age of Grand Theory, was coming to an unsuccessful end. Its demise derived in large part from the failure of animal-based learning theorists to agree on a single theory and the failure to apply and validate models of learning theory to complex human behavior in rigorous ways (Baars, 1986; Erwin, 1978; Kimble, 1985).

A second possible reason for the breakdown in behavior therapy's commitment to the experimental paradigm came from the experiences of most behavioral practitioners. Like other clinicians, these professionals discovered that they could practice seemingly effectively without having to show a tight link between their practices and the experimental literature (Barlow, Hayes, & Nelson, 1984; Marshall, 1982). A third reason for behavior therapy's movement away from the experimental paradigm, beginning in the 1960s, was the loss of support for logical positivism in the philosophical community (Campbell, 1984; Gergen, 1982; Putnam, 1984).

D. B. Fishman (1988) stated the advantages of locating behavior therapy in the pragmatic paradigm. His position began with Erwin's (1978) critique of traditional "ideological" behaviorism, which claimed that, in principle, only publicly observable behavior is worthy of scientific study. As an alternative, Erwin (1978) introduced the concept of "pragmatic behaviorism":

> [Behavior therapy] treatment should focus primarily on behavior, not because the mind is behavior, but for practical reasons. . . . It may be of some use to learn, for example, that an obese patient has a craving for food, but it is even more useful to learn how many eating responses are engaged in each day and under exactly what conditions. (p. 80)

Building on this view and that of Mahoney (1974), Fishman defined pragmatic behaviorism in terms of a commitment to a variety of methodological principles for the conduct of behavior therapy (Fishman, 1988). These include an emphasis on (a) empiricism; (b) variables that are objective, specific, and concrete; (c) the analysis of problems into smaller parts to be dealt with one at a time; (d) quantification; (e) a view of behavior as a sample (rather than a sign) of personality; (e) functional analysis of the relationship between behavior and the environment; and (f) linkage of all cognitive and affective variables employed to behavioral and environmental referents.

Worldviews

Altman and Rogoff posited four worldviews in psychology that philosophically underlie research and theory. Each is associated with a root metaphor (Pepper, 1942, 1967): the trait view with similarities and differences in the inner qualities of individuals, the interactional view with the machine, the organismic view with the living organism, and the transactional view with the historical event and the purposive act.

Table 1 reflects the fact that behavior therapy, from its origins to its present form, has been primarily embedded in the interactional worldview. This view is in contrast to Freud's theory of psychosexual character types, generally associated with a trait view; to family systems therapy, primarily embedded in the organismic view; and to humanistic therapy, primarily embedded in the transactional view.

Although behavior therapy began as narrowly focused within a "pure," positivist interactional worldview, over time the field has branched out to add to its root interactional view components from the other worldviews. Brief illustrations of the root and its branches follow.

"Pure" Interactional Theories

Perhaps the clearest examples of pure, interactional theory are Watson's behaviorism and the animal-based conditioning research in the Age of Grand Theory. The metatheory behind both of these projects involves a mechanistic, "billiard-ball," linear causal model that focuses on functional links between present environmental stimuli and an organism's responses. This view was carried over into the early development of behavior therapy procedures by Skinner, Solomon, and Lindsley, who applied animal-based operant learning theory to the alleviation of socially unresponsive schizophrenic behavior.

Although cognitive components were present early in behavior therapy's development in the form of "covert conditioning" (Cautela, 1967, 1970), Mahoney (1974) described how this model conformed to the "pure" interactional worldview:

> Thoughts, images, memories, and sensations are described as covert stimuli, covert responses, or covert consequences. The skull becomes a rather crowded Skinner box in which such conventional principles as reinforcement, punishment, and extinction are said to describe the function and patterning of [these covert events]. (p. 61)

Interactional Theories With Trait Components

In 1968, both Mischel and Peterson independently published influential books that linked the interactional thinking of behavior therapy with the emphasis on intrapersonal variables of the trait view. These two authors first criticized the prevalent approach at the time, used by both psychometrically oriented trait theorists and psychoanalytically oriented, personality-dynamics theorists, who assumed that through the use of a limited number of behavioral signs yielded by personality tests (objective tests for trait theorists and projective tests for psychodynamic theorists), one could assign individuals to fixed positions on the assessor's favorite nomothetic trait dimensions. Both Mischel and Peterson argued that, empirically, such a "behavior sign" approach simply had not been shown to be useful or valid, because personality studies found high levels of situational specificity in behavior rather than the cross-situational consistency predicted by the trait approach.

As an alternative to traditional trait and psychodynamic views of personality, Mischel proposed that personality and situation constructs be reconceptualized in terms of social learning theory and cognitive psychology. A recent statement of this approach by Cantor (1990) is illustrative. Cantor did not deny the existence of underlying personality dispositions that persons "have," but she focused her attention on "how these dispositions are cognitively expressed and maintained in social interaction"—

what she called the "doing" side of personality. In this way, Cantor took a middle position between the trait and interaction views by positing cognitively oriented personality constructs such as "schema," "tasks," and "strategies" at the "middle" level of personality inference. For example,

> The shy schematic person . . . is dishearteningly quick to see his or her social faux pas, to retrieve from memory numerous examples of prior mistakes, and to pit the self against an elaborate vision of the outgoing person that he or she is decidedly not like. (Cantor, 1990, pp. 736, 738)

Such schemas are used to interpret life goals for which to strive, which are distilled from the culturally prescribed and biologically based requirements of social life, such as work, play, intimacy, power, and health. Finally, individuals develop various strategies for accomplishing their tasks, with varying degrees of success. For example, although constructive anticipation can create motivation to pursue hard tasks, it can also lead to self-defeating thinking when a person frames a task in unclear and thus frustrating terms (Cantor, 1990).

Interactional Theories With Organismic Components

Because of the importance of the environment in the interactional approach, and because of the social context of much behavior, behavior therapy theorists became interested, early on, in social interaction, social relationships, and the social environment generally. In his 1968 book, Peterson showed how functional analysis could be applied using a similar perspective for solving dysfunction in an individual, a family, and a social system (a state psychiatric hospital). To show the link between individual and group behavior, Peterson (1968) pointed out that "social interaction" (as distinct from the "interactional" worldview)

> refers to a class of social phenomena involving mutuality of stimulation and effect. . . . Explicit behavior by person 1 serves as a stimulus for person 2, who reacts in some way. This either terminates the interchange or leads to a further reaction on the part of person 1, perhaps to an action–reaction chain of indefinite length. . . . [Thus] in his motives and cognitive beliefs, each person takes the other, who has his own motives and beliefs, into account. When relatively stable patterns of [social] interaction develop between two individuals, a relationship has been formed. . . . Groups of people [socially] interacting can be studied as emergent units. A different class of phenomena can be examined, and with this a new order of comprehension may result. (pp. 82–84)

Many later behavior theorists built on this type of reasoning to integrate concepts from family systems therapy (e.g., Gurman & Kniskern, 1981) into cognitive–behavioral therapy with couples (e.g., Birchler &

Spinks, 1980) and families. Robin and Foster's (1989) "behavioral–family systems" model for negotiating parent–adult conflict is an excellent recent example of this approach. These authors viewed the detailed molecular analysis of contingency arrangements from the "pure" interactional, behavioral tradition as providing an excellent starting point for a functional analysis of family members' behavior with each other. This then is combined with organismic elements to address "the circular nature of [social] interaction patterns and the hierarchical structure of families, which overlay contingency arrangements" (Robin & Foster, 1989, p. 7).

Interactional Theories With Transactional Elements

Azrin (1977), Spiegler (1983), D. B. Fishman (1988), and others have conceptualized behavior therapy within a social constructionist, pragmatic metatheory. A major aspect of this perspective is the emphasis on the contextual specificity of behavior. The focus is on developing practical strategies for solving particular problems in particular situations, not on the derivation of empirically confirmed general laws. Fishman pointed out that this perspective leads to a focus on the individual case study, which in turn highlights the fact that each intervention program with a client— be it an individual, group, or organization—consists of a social interactional process over time between the client and the behavior change agent. This process involves a series of sequential, interdependent steps or phases. How such phases link with transactional thinking is outlined in the following section on Kanfer and Schefft's (1988) process model of therapeutic change.

BEHAVIOR THERAPY IN ACTION

In the previous section, we showed how behavior therapy began with a narrow and simplistic theory, limiting itself to a mechanistic, interactionally "pure" worldview. As the field evolved, it has embraced a more comprehensive conceptualization that incorporates a broad spectrum of perspectives and disciplines into its theoretical and clinical framework, including elements from the trait, organismic, and transactional worldviews. These developments are illustrated here through a consideration of three recent models of clinical behavior therapy: Persons' (1989) *case formulation approach*, Barlow's (1993) *packaged therapy for panic disorder*, and Kanfer and Schefft's (1988) *process model of therapeutic change*. All three span the various theoretical submovements and worldviews discussed in previous sections, and they reflect some of the diversity that has evolved under the behavior therapy conceptual umbrella.

Persons' Case Formulation Approach

This model views psychological problems as occurring at two levels. At the "symptomatic" level of "presenting problems" are *overt difficulties*, such as depressed feelings, obsessive–compulsive rituals, anxiety attacks, palpitations and dizziness, procrastination, marital conflict, anger outbursts, thoughts of self-harm, and inability to speak before groups. At a "deeper" level are *underlying psychological mechanisms*[4] that cause the overt difficulties. Persons focused on the mechanisms based on dysfunctional core beliefs, whose origins can be found in the patient's history. (Other possible types of mechanisms are skill deficits and environmental deficiencies.) For example,

> A young accountant who was socially isolated, anxious about his work, and depressed held the belief, "Unless I'm perfect in everything I do, I'll fail." This belief produced his overt difficulties. It led him to avoid social interactions because he feared any blunder in interacting with others would lead to rejection. Similarly, his fear of making a mistake led to anxiety (and paradoxically, to poor performance as a result) at work. His depression resulted from his social isolation and his feelings of incompetence at work. (Persons, 1989, pp. 1–2)

A crucial function of identifying underlying mechanisms is as a guide to planning effective treatment. For example,

> The therapist who hypothesizes that Mrs. Jones' depression is a response to a low level of reinforcement and that Mr. Smith's depression is a response to a constant stream of self-critical statements would work to increase Mrs. Jones' pleasant activities and to decrease Mr. Smith's self-critical statements. (Persons, 1989, p. 13)

As another example, Persons described addressing the problems of two patients who both procrastinated on participating in a regular exercise program. Each was asked to develop an exercise schedule and to bring it to the next therapy session. The intervention was successful for one of the patients, a jogger, and not for the other, an aerobics dancer. Formulation of the jogger's central problems revealed that his procrastination was due to a skill deficit in organizing his life activities: "His failure to jog was due to a chaotic lifestyle in which activities were not scheduled or planned. . . . Use of a schedule addressed his problem and helped him make and follow through on a planned commitment" (Persons, 1989, p.

---

[4]Persons used the term *underlying* to signify that causal psychological factors are constructs that are more inferential and abstract in comparison with the descriptive terms of overt difficulties. However, in using the concept of underlying mechanisms, as a cognitive behaviorist, Persons is committed to clearly and functionally linking underlying variables to behavioral and environmental referents. Also, Persons' underlying mechanisms lack the emphasis on the very early developmental, unconscious processes that permeate the psychoanalytic notion of "underlying personality structure and dynamics."

14). On the other hand, the aerobics dancer's failure to go to class was due to a fear that others would disapprove of how she might look in her leotard: "Because these fears were not addressed by the schedule, the intervention failed" (p. 14).

A third example of the many that Persons provided is that of a 50-year-old bachelor who sought treatment for fears of contamination and for extensive washing rituals dating from early adolescence. He was socially isolated and unemployed, having worked only occasionally over the previous 25 years. However, he stated in the assessment session that he did not want to work on his social and work limitations, only on the contamination fears and washing rituals. However, at the end of this session it emerged that he was ambivalent about giving up his fears and rituals because then he would face the need to go to work and interact with others. Underlying his symptoms, then, appears to be the core belief, "Going out in the world is too dangerous for me."

> This formulation suggests that the fears of work and relationships must be included in treatment if it is to be successful. In fact, the formulation suggests that it may be necessary to treat these fears first. (Persons, 1989, p. 39)

In the Persons model, the therapist develops a case formulation of the patient's problems by systematically exploring and documenting both the patient's overt difficulties and the logically and functionally probable psychological mechanisms that underlie them. Because patients' behavior in therapy is a generalized reflection of their interactional behavior outside the therapy, Persons shows how the case formulation can be a very helpful tool—to both the therapist and the patient—in understanding a patient's interpersonal problems as they are played out in the relationship with the therapist. For example, one of Persons' cases was a young attorney whose frequent rescheduling, coming late to sessions, and bouncing checks to the therapist reflected a generally chaotic and disorganized lifestyle, with events outside therapy such as bouncing other checks, missing work, and running out of gas on the highway. Persons explored his behavioral pattern with him:

> He agreed that he behaved as though he believed, "The rules don't apply to me." This attitude seemed to have originated [as a reaction against] . . . his mother, who was a demanding, rigid person who had insisted that the patient do what the *mother* needed him to do. . . . As a result, if the patient's needs and priorities seemed to him to be at odds with a rule or expectation imposed by another, he simply said to himself, "I don't have time to follow that rule," and he ignored it. (Persons, 1989, p. 163)

As the therapist, Persons set clear contingencies to help the patient to challenge his core belief that the rules didn't apply to him.

> The patient learned that any failure on his part to stick to the rules of the therapy would lead to a discussion of the topic, and this encouraged him to play by the therapist's rules. . . . This event provided an in vivo lesson about the negative consequences of the irrational belief. Over time, the patient's behavior in therapy sessions gradually improved, and his behavior outside sessions improved as well. (Persons, 1989, p. 164)

Persons' emphasis on the causal nature of developmentally based, core beliefs fits into the trait model, with its focus on causal factors within the individual that have formed because of personal history. Persons' model also is clearly embedded in the cognitive–behavioral therapy movement.

Barlow's Packaged Therapy for Panic Disorder

Persons' model proposes that each patient be holistically assessed to develop a list of overt difficulties and a formulation of the psychological mechanisms that functionally appear to underlie these difficulties. This requires expert clinical assessment skills on the part of the behavior therapist. In contrast, Barlow's treatment for panic disorder begins by first administering a battery of questionnaires to determine operationally if the individual falls in the formal psychiatric diagnostic category of panic disorder. If the patient does, the therapist then follows a prepackaged series of intervention procedures to reduce or eliminate the panic reactions.

Panic attacks are discrete, abrupt episodes of intense dread, anxiety, and fear, involving such symptoms as palpitations, sweating, trembling, choking feelings, nausea, dizzying sensations, derealization (feelings of unreality), depersonalization (feelings of being detached from oneself), fear of losing control or going crazy, and fear of dying. Barlow developed his treatment package from a biopsychosocial conceptualization of the cause of panic attacks. According to his model, the initial panic attack is viewed as a misfiring of the fear system, so that a stressful but not truly dangerous stimulus triggers a full-blown, intense physiological "fight or flight" response (the body's way of "priming" for action when confronted by a genuinely life-threatening situation). This response is then interpreted by the patient as catastrophic psychological dysfunction (e.g., losing behavioral control or going crazy) or a medical crisis (e.g., having a heart attack), which in turn increases the patient's level of fear, thus intensifying his or her catastrophic interpretations, and so forth in an ever-increasing cycle of panic.

Following this model, Barlow's program is multifaceted. *Breathing retraining* is employed to deal with a major part of the fight–flight reaction, hyperventilation. Hyperventilatory symptoms—dizziness, palpitations, and so forth—are experienced as very important ingredients of the panic-attack symptoms. Hyperventilation is triggered by overly rapid, shallow breathing in the upper body; it can be avoided by teaching a patient slower, abdominal breathing.

Cognitive restructuring is used to correct a patient's misappraisals of bodily sensations as threatening. Clients are told that errors in thinking occur for everyone when they are anxious, and thus they should be on extra alert for cognitive distortions when they are anxious. Treating thoughts as hypotheses or guesses rather than facts is stressed, and the patient is taught to be an astute observer of his or her habitual self-statements in specific situations.

> Recognition of the thought, "I feel terrible—something bad could happen" is insufficient, nontherapeutic, and may serve to intensify anxiety by virtue of its global and nondirective nature. Instead, recognition of the thought, "I am afraid that if I get too anxious while driving then I'll lose control of the wheel and drive off the side of the road and die" allows for constructive questioning to challenge the series of mis-assumptions. (Barlow, 1993, p. 32)

Interoceptive exposure involves gradually exposing the patient to avoided activities that elicit physical sensations (interoceptive cues) that can cue off fear reactions. Examples are physical exercise, emotional discussions, suspenseful movies, steamy rooms, certain foods, or stimulants. The interoceptive exposure is done both in the therapy session—using situations such as shaking the head from side to side, running in place, holding one's breath, and spinning in a swivel chair—and in the patient's life outside the session, such as exposure to malls, churches, and other crowded places for patients who are agoraphobic.

> The purpose of interoceptive exposure is to repeatedly induce the sensations that are feared and to weaken the fear response through habituating and learning that no actual danger results. In addition, the repeated inductions allow practice in applying the cognitive strategies and breathing strategies. (Barlow, 1993, p. 35)

Barlow's emphasis on interoceptive conditioning connects him with the neobehaviorism movement, whereas his use of cognitive restructuring links him with cognitive–behavioral therapy. In terms of worldviews, Barlow's overall package is more purely interactional than Persons' approach, because Barlow's model emphasizes change through the creation of new kinds of environment–response interactions in the present, such as exposure to previously fear-inducing cues and learning a new way of breathing in stressful situations.

Kanfer and Schefft's Process Model of Therapeutic Change

Kanfer and Schefft's model emphasizes the therapeutic relationship between patient and therapist, and how specific treatment procedures are embedded in that relationship. The process begins at the initial interview. The therapist pays attention to contextual questions surrounding the occurrence of this interview, such as why the patient is coming in *now* (and what this implies about his or her motivation), what expectations the patient has of the therapy and therapist, what cognitive models the patient has for framing the presenting problem and its causes, and whether there is "a possible 'hidden agenda,' such as putting the therapist into the role of a mediator in vocational, legal, familial, or medical problems" (Kanfer & Schefft, 1988, p. 75).

According to this model, the therapist's first objective is to develop a positive, working alliance with the patient, realizing that this alliance will become a very strong motivator for the patient to try out the new ways of behaving, thinking, and feeling that are associated with cognitive–behavioral therapy procedures. The therapist's empathy, warmth, and support are important ingredients in this process. Also to facilitate a positive working relationship, therapists collaboratively develop the goals of therapy with patients, trying as much as possible to help them move to a new way of life that the patients define as more personally satisfying.

Kanfer and Schefft translated cognitive–behavioral principles into six "think rules," which are very much in the spirit of Erwin's (1978) pragmatic behaviorism, discussed above. The therapist models the rules and gradually teaches them to the patient to facilitate eventual self-management. This can include writing the rules on a card and having the patient carry them around as a reminder. The rules include (a) "think behavior," or couching problem situations and their resolutions in terms of actions rather than attributions or reasons (what we do rather than what we are); (b) "think solution," or paying attention to resolving problems rather than focusing on the problems per se; (c) "think positive," or emphasizing patients' strengths and reinforcing the constructive strategies, plans, and actions that patients themselves generate; (d) "think small steps," or setting goals by breaking a task into its component parts and mastering them one at a time; (e) "think flexible," or urging clients to make commitments in therapy "on a tentative, trial-and-error basis," recognizing that "there may be many different paths to reach a goal" (p. 113); and (f) "think future," or focusing on planning strategies for negotiating future challenges and rehearsing future events by role play instead of dwelling on the past.

After the establishment of a therapeutic alliance in Phase 1, there are six other phases in a completed therapy: Phase 2, "developing a commitment for change"; Phase 3, "behavioral analysis"; Phase 4, "negotiating treatment objectives and methods"; Phase 5, "implementing treatment and maintaining motivation"; Phase 6, "monitoring and evaluating progress"; and Phase 7, "maintenance, generalization, and termination of treatment" (Kanfer & Schefft, 1988, pp. 94–95). These phases generally take place in an interdependent, sequential manner, although Kanfer and Schefft emphasized that progress through the phases is not consistently linear. For example, it is not untypical for therapy to return a number of times to the first phase, creating a therapeutic alliance, as later points in the therapy put stresses and strains on the alliance and necessitate a reworking and reinvigorating of the relationship between therapist and patient. Alternatively, the lack of effectiveness of a treatment procedure in Phase 5 might lead the therapist back to reviewing whether the patient is truly motivated for change (Phase 2) or whether the original behavioral analysis of the target problem needs revision (Phase 3).

Kanfer and Schefft's Phase 6, monitoring and evaluating progress, reflects an important theme in behavior therapy. Even though assessment is always the starting point, assessment and intervention are viewed as related, ongoing processes. For example, Kanfer and Schefft (1988) suggested a number of monitoring guidelines, such as the following, that yield ongoing data to continually guide the therapist's conduct of therapy:

1. Check whether the client's rate of progress matches the expectations developed during earlier phases. If not, analyze causes of the discrepancy.
2. Monitor and ensure maintenance of sufficient motivation to carry out the therapeutic program.
3. Review data from previous sessions to demonstrate past gains, to reiterate the principle of "think small steps," or to elicit suggestions on what has worked in the past to produce change. (p. 292)

Kanfer and Schefft's model is a good exemplar of the integration of components from different worldviews. Their Phases 3 and 5 (behavioral analysis and formal implementation of intervention procedures) represent the interactional worldview of traditional behavior therapy. Other phases bring in a relationship focus from the organismic worldview (Phase 1, creating an alliance; Phase 4, collaborative goal setting; and Phase 7, termination). The other two phases represent a contextual focus from the transactional worldview (Phase 2, developing a commitment for change; and Phase 6, monitoring progress and "recycling" through earlier phases when necessary).

In terms of the transactional worldview, D. B. Fishman (1988) conceptualized therapy phases, such as Kanfer and Schefft's, as organized into a decisional flowchart with a variety of feedback loops. Because of the great variety of different patterns created by different choice point decisions, this perspective highlights the idiosyncratic particularities of each case. Kanfer and Schefft (1988) described these particularities in terms consistent with many elements in the transactional worldview:

> The dynamic qualities of all human experiences and the fluidity of social systems and environments suggest that neither therapy plans nor programs for change should be rigid. . . . The everchanging opportunities and limitations that occur as a client progresses along a given path require constant adjustments and appraisal of therapeutic goals. For these reasons, clients are . . . helped to recognize that there may be many different paths to reach a goal and that it is unsound to give up the effort to change if one's specific plan fails. (p. 113)

BEHAVIOR THERAPY IN CONTEMPORARY CONTEXT

For better and sometimes for worse, depending on one's point of view, the evolution of behavior therapy parallels and reflects the prevailing sociopolitical zeitgeist in the United States at large and the professional ethos of practicing behavior therapy professionals in particular. From a variety of recent developments along these lines, we have chosen three major areas to discuss: the impact of "managed care," the cognitive transformation of applied behavior analysis into "contextual" behavior therapy, and the recent resurgence of interest in theoretical and conceptual issues. All offer meaningful perspectives on the overall direction of the field.

Managed Care: A New Ball Game

The major external influence on psychotherapy overall in recent years has been and remains the growing dominance of managed care. In outpatient mental health terms, at the most general level, *managed care* refers to any managed care organization that controls the reimbursement of therapy and thereby intervenes between client and therapist to make rulings about such questions as: Does this client's presenting problem qualify for reimbursed therapy? If so, how many sessions of what type of therapy are appropriate? Within the type of therapy, what particular techniques should be used? And is this clinician an acceptable therapist for this client?

Reactions to managed care by the therapy community are emotional and, in essence, bimodal. Opponents of managed care see it as an attack on the expertise and autonomy of professional therapists and their unrestricted access to clients. A doomsday scenario is envisaged in which therapists are placed in the role of low-paid technicians, allowed only a few restricted, predetermined sessions in which to apply imposed and superficial practice rules to distressed clients whose clinical needs are at best minimized and, at worst, ignored. This view generally predominates among psychodynamic therapists. For example, Fox (1995) associated managed care with the "the rape of psychotherapy," Karon (1995) called managed care "a growing crisis and nightmare," and Messer and Warren (1995) spoke of managed care as providing a new entity, "behavioral health care," and not psychotherapy as it is commonly understood (see also Macchia, 1995; Widmeyer Group, 1994).

In sharp contrast to such a reaction, behavior therapists are more inclined to identify themselves as allies of managed care. These proponents acknowledge that there are many horror stories of how managed care as presently practiced can violate the principles of clinical and community services (e.g., Giles & Marafiote, 1994). At the same time, however, these allies endorse the positive ideals of managed care, acknowledging what Strosahl (1994) aptly termed its "land mines" and "gold mines." In the view of allies, the managed care movement is a rational response by those who pay for services in government and industry to the well-documented skyrocketing health and mental health costs in the 1980s. In light of this, these individuals view managed care more as a vehicle for saving the health service benefit status of psychotherapy than as a weapon of the destruction of psychotherapy (Armenti, 1993; Broskowski, 1995; Cummings, 1995; Strosahl, 1994, 1995). For example, mental health services coverage was in doubt during discussions of President Clinton's proposed national health plans, whereas—at least at the time of this writing—these services are an intrinsic part of the present managed care structure.

Behavior therapists generally become allies of managed care because of the particularly close correspondence between the ideals of managed care (e.g., Broskowski, 1995; Giles, 1993a; Strosahl, 1994, 1996) and the principles of clinical behavior therapy (e.g., Barlow, 1994) and behavioral community psychology (e.g., Glenwick & Jason, 1980; Jeger & Slotnick, 1982). Some examples of this perceived correspondence follow. In each case, the declared managed care goal is provided first.

Cost-efficiency and cost containment. Behavior therapists are committed to brief therapy, cost-effective services, early intervention and prevention, lower cost alternatives to hospitalization, and the active support of other professionals and natural caregivers. Examples of the latter are behavior therapy interventions aimed at training parents to better manage their hyperactive children (Barkley, 1990); training families to cope more effectively with their retarded or chronically disturbed members (Liberman, Cardin, McGill, Falloon, & Evans, 1987; Petronko, Harris, & Korman, 1994); and consulting with primary care physicians about depressed patients (Robinson, 1995).

Provision of high quality services. This goal is in accord with the commitment of behavior therapists to operational definition of treatment goals, procedures, and outcomes in order to carry out objective monitoring and evaluation of the treatment process.

Service effectiveness. Behavior therapists place a high premium on empirical outcome validation of their interventions. Partly as a result, behavior therapy has the best documented track record to date for the effectiveness of their services (see Giles, 1993b for a systematic and thorough review of the relevant literature; see also reviews of this topic by the Clinical Psychology Division of the American Psychological Association [e.g., Chambless et al., 1996]).

Achieving a balance between individual provider freedom and practice guidelines. Sophisticated behavior therapy rests on a tradition of balancing the "art" of therapy against the operationalization of treatment procedures and the monitoring of adherence to them (Goldfried & Davison, 1976; Nezu & Nezu, 1995).

On one hand, behavioral investigators have developed specific, empirically derived treatment manuals that are targeted for individuals with particular, delimited problems, such as depression, phobia, or obsessive–compulsive disorder (Giles, 1993b; Ollendick, 1995). A good example is the work of Barlow (1993) on panic disorder discussed earlier. These "manualized" therapies are sufficiently operationalized and standardized to be administered by less trained therapists with minimal supervision.

On the other hand, these treatment manuals serve only a portion of persons suffering from each condition being addressed (Cummings, 1995, estimated this proportion at around the 30–35% level). Thus, there is a need for an alternative, holistic approach for dealing with the types of clients who typically present in actual practice (see Davison & Lazarus, 1994; Fensterheim, 1995; S. T. Fishman & Lubetkin, 1983; Goldfried & Davison, 1976; Hersen, 1981). In conducting therapy with such clients, Kanfer & Schefft (1988) emphasized the need for a sophisticated, clinical process model. D. B. Fishman (1988, 1995b) and Barlow, Hayes, and Nelson (1984) have proposed a pragmatic, solution-focused case study strategy, including single-case research designs, rather than the customary group research. As discussed earlier, Persons (1989) advocated developing a case formulation of the basic behavioral and cognitive mechanisms that seem to underlie the myriad of presenting, overt problems. And Nezu and Nezu (1995) argued for a model of ongoing and systematic decision making throughout treatment.

In accord with the desire to use cost-efficient and effective services, managed care companies view objective treatment manuals suitable for paraprofessional application as particularly appealing because research in this area can easily be translated into "practice guidelines" that meet predefined levels of cost-effectiveness (Armenti, 1993; Hayes, Follette, Dawes, & Grady, 1995).

Behavior therapy is engaged both in developing manualized therapies and in empirically delineating conditions under which manualized therapies are less effective and the client is better served by an individualized, holistic model (Fishman, Barlow, Giles, & Armenti, 1995). This project is highly congruent with managed care's ultimate goal of maximizing the cost-effectiveness of its services.

Consumer satisfaction. Behavior therapists stress egalitarian relationships between client and therapist, joint goal setting, client strengths, and educating the client in self-management (e.g., Kanfer & Schefft, 1988)—all of which facilitate high client satisfaction with services.

Crisis intervention to prevent more serious psychopathology. Behavior therapists emphasize changing behavior by environmental restructuring, an approach of particular value in crisis intervention. For example, Petronko, Harris, and Korman (1994) discussed the manner in which crises of children with certain types of severe psychopathology, such as autism, can be handled in the home rather than by institutionalization. This approach entails teaching parents child management skills and helping parents to learn how to organize their home milieux so as to reduce the frequency and severity of behavioral crises with their children.

Prevention and early intervention. Behavior therapists advocate first, to train individuals in coping skills to enhance their capacities to handle stress and difficulties on their own; second, to train parents in child management skills to achieve early and natural prevention of mental health problems; and third, to train community "caregivers" such as teachers and police in management skills in order to reduce the development of mental health problems or to achieve early problem identification and to seek professional intervention if indicated.

Planning services for a whole subscriber group. Behavioral community psychologists conduct needs assessments of the populations under scrutiny and then use this information to develop appropriate services.

Developing a collaborative relationship between the managed care agency and the therapist. It is a behavioral community axiom to collaborate with other caregivers and to encourage citizen participation in the planning and evaluation of services.

External accountability. This goal is supported by three behavioral principles: commitment to objectively defined, behavioral measures of outcome and cost-effectiveness; subjecting therapy procedures to controlled, empirical outcome study; and formal planning and program evaluation of services.

Providing "user-friendly," accessible services. Ideally, behavior therapists work in the natural setting to facilitate readily acceptable services and enhanced consumer satisfaction, for example, conducting an initial in-home treatment for agoraphobia and home visits for disturbed families (Petronko et al., 1994).

Encouraging personal consumer responsibility for maintaining a medically healthy lifestyle. One theme in managed care is the desirability of integrating physical health and mental health care (Hersch, 1995). Behavior therapists train clients in self-management skills so they can assume responsibility for self-regulation in areas like proper nutrition, diet, smoking cessation, and stress management (Spiegler & Guevremont, 1992).

Behavior Theory Continues to Evolve

While the managed care movement places pressures on behavior therapy to consolidate its intervention strategies and focus on improving the technological linkages between science and practice (D. B. Fishman, 1988, 1995b; Nezu & Nezu, 1995), the field continues to evolve theoretically. Two examples of this process follow.

The Cognitive Transformation of Applied Behavior Analysis Into Contextual Behavior Therapy

As noted, until recently, applied behavioral analysts disavowed such intervening variables as mentalistic concepts and inferences, emphasizing instead operant conditioning. For example, following Baer, Wolf, and Risley (1968), Mace and Kratochwill (1986) defined the "behavior" in applied behavior analysis as "a physical event produced by an organism that results in observable change in the environment" (p. 154)—thoughts, beliefs, speech acts, interpretations of meaning, and so forth need not apply! Moreover, the "observable change in the environment" is viewed as a physical change that can have reinforcing or punishing properties based on its direct relationship to physical needs. In numerous recent publications, Hayes, Kohlenberg, and their colleagues (e.g., Hayes, Follette, & Follette, 1995; Kohlenberg & Tsai, 1995) have legitimized an equivalent of cognitive psychology—"verbal behavior" and "verbal control"—as appropriate and, in fact, central components of applied behavior analysis. Unlike the *physical* behavior in Mace and Kratochwill's definition, Hayes et al.'s verbal behavior is *symbolic* behavior, whose impact comes from its linguistic meaning and not from its physical effects on the environment per se.

Once verbal behavior—that is, verbal meaning—becomes the focus of behavior analysis, the original, antimentalistic project of radical behaviorists to investigate the functional relationships among directly observable, overt behaviors and their physical antecedents and consequences becomes a cognitive project. The goal of this cognitive project is to study functional relationships among the *meanings* of behavioral antecedents, the *meanings* of the behaviors themselves, and the *meanings* of their consequences. It is no wonder, then, that Hayes (1996), in his platform as candidate for the presidency of AABT, described one of his goals as helping "to bring together the field of cognition with the field of behavioral psychology" (p. 1).

More particularly, Hayes et al. set forth two principles as the determinants of behavior: the traditional "direct contingency principles" drawn from classical and operant conditioning, and "indirect contingency principles," or "rule governance," in which behavior is regulated by verbal formulae. Whereas it was Skinner who first introduced the principle of rule governance in his 1957 *Verbal Behavior,* Hayes et al. have greatly expanded his preliminary theory and tied it to an ambitious program of empirical research (Hayes & Hayes, 1992).

Using the concepts of verbal behavior and rule governance as vehicles for addressing issues of language and meaning allows Hayes et al. to deal with such matters as consciousness, subjective experience, and self. In contrast to the separatist history of applied behavior analysis, which at times viewed itself as an independent discipline separate from "mentalistic" psychology, Kohlenberg's recent work has generated links with cognitive psychology and even psychoanalysis (Kohlenberg & Tsai, 1995) without abandoning behavioral principles. Hayes has done much the same thing for cognitive, Gestalt, and existential psychology (Hayes, Jacobson, Follette, & Dougher, 1994). It is indeed significant that Hayes, Kohlenberg, and many of their colleagues have now become active in the AABT, the mainstream professional society of behavior therapists that now views itself as identified with cognitive–behavioral therapy. The emphasis on meaning has led Hayes to refer to his version of applied behavior analysis as "contextual behavior therapy" (Hayes, Follette, & Follette, 1995).

As an example of this thinking, in an article titled, "I Speak, Therefore I Am," Kohlenberg and Tsai (1995) proposed a model to explain both normal and deviant development of the self. According to the model, the normal individual evolves a concept of the self by first associating self-referential words like *I* and *me* as a general "perspective" vis-à-vis public stimuli (e.g., "I see an apple," "Daddy is tickling me"); that is, words like *I* and *me* first develop under public "stimulus control." As the child grows and experiences fantasies, wishes, and feelings that have no public reference (e.g., "I am angry," and "I imagine meeting the Seven Dwarfs"), words like *I* and *me* come more and more under private stimulus control so that eventually, these words are associated with acts of private experience. This experience may involve perception and contact with clearcut public objects or only imagination and feeling with private objects. Pathologies of the self, such as borderline personality disorder, are then attributed to lack of development of "I" statements associated with private experience (e.g., "I want," "I feel," "I need," and "I believe"), making borderline individuals dependent on others' public cues to know how they feel. This links nicely with more traditional cognitive–behavioral explanations of borderline individuals, such as that of Linehan (1993).

Hayes and Kohlenberg's verbal therapy models rely heavily on the principles of verbal control and rule governance. Kohlenberg's Functional Analytic Therapy or FAP (Kohlenberg & Tsai, 1991, 1995) uses the concept alluded to earlier of helping clients align their self-statements and related self-awareness with their private, subjective experiences. Also, FAP translates the psychoanalytic concepts of transference and countertransference into behavior analytic terms. Thus, "much of what clients complain about in outside relationships have in-session representations with their therapists" (Kohlenberg & Tsai, 1995, p. 644). A major goal of FAP is to elicit these in-session representations, to analyze them functionally and to use this knowledge to develop alternative, more adaptive interpersonal responses.

Hayes' therapy model, Acceptance and Commitment Therapy or ACT (Hayes, 1987, 1994; Hayes, Strosahl, & Wilson, in press), is designed for clients who have not been successful in attempts to modify or eliminate the *content* of unwanted behaviors, thoughts, and feelings. ACT focuses on reinterpreting the problematic psychological phenomena by placing them in a different interpretive *context*, that is, changing the meaning of the original problems to the client. Psychological events that seem uncontrollable and distressing in one context "in another context are no longer the same psychological events.... By establishing a posture of psychological acceptance, events that formerly were taken to be inherently problematic become instead opportunities for growth, interest, or understanding" (Hayes, 1994, p. 13).

This sounds very similar to one of the assumptions of cognitive–behavioral therapy, cited earlier: "The human organism responds primarily to cognitive representations of its environments rather than to these environments per se" (Kendall & Bemis, 1983, p. 565).

Thus, when we respond to the offer of a particular $100 bill, we do not respond to its physical characteristics but to its symbolic value in being able to provide other things and services. Also, the context of the $100 bill is crucial in our response to it. Is it due us as payment for a job? Was it stolen? Is it a bribe? Is it ours because of "luck," such as a lottery winning? Is it a gift from a loved one? The answer to this and many other questions will ultimately determine the meaning of this particular $100 bill to us and, subsequently, our overt behavior in regard to it.

Hayes, Kohlenberg, and their associates have presented innovative theories. Like all theories in behavior therapy, their merit will eventually be judged on two general criteria: (a) Are they translatable into operational terms so that they can be objectively assessed? and (b) Are they as or more demonstrably useful than other approaches in helping clients in behavior therapy reach their goals?

The Renewal of Interest in Theoretical and Conceptual Issues: Behavior Therapy Recalls Its Origins

As we have endeavored to show, behavior therapy has many roots and landmarks. One such landmark is the foundation of the AABT in

1966. At that time, this "advancement" was conceptualized in terms of a commingling, as opposed to a mix, of theory and practice, each preserving its identity with neither designed to stand alone. Empirically validated procedures were viewed as necesary, but not sufficient. The ideal—rarely realized even in those idealistic early days—was a rational theory-driven approach in which some form of learning theory based on S–R would be used to generate testable predictions for eventual translation into empirically validated clinical procedures. Behavior therapy would be unique among all intervention systems! The few practitioners who strayed from this credo felt guilty and strove to return to the "true" path.

This is how it was some three decades ago. The changes that have taken place within the AABT since then are matched, in part, by developments within psychology at large and clinical psychology in particular. Nineteen ninety-six was the 100th anniversary of clinical psychology. When Witmer presented his new "clinical psychology" at the 1896 Fourth Annual Convention of the APA, the reactions were less than positive. As scientists, most APA members considered Witmer's innovation premature and lacking in adequate theoretical foundations. A century later, most APA members are practitioners in some form or another, and few regard themselves as scientists alone—so much so that some scientifically oriented APA members recently formed an organization of their own, the American Psychological Society.

Behavior therapy is comparably divided. The perceived limitations of conditioning and modeling theory led many behavioral clinicians to postulate a cognitive paradigm shift that explicitly mirrored the changes taking place within mainstream psychology. Paralleling this cognitive surge, the behavioral aspects of behavior therapy tend to be mistrusted and deemphasized. There is, at times, a regressive denial of behavior therapy's foundations. All too often, recognition of the need for theory and concept as an essential component of practice seems more a matter of lip service than of genuine belief (Franks, in press).

For all of these reasons, we note with satisfaction a small but potentially significant revival of interest in theory in recent years. At least three major edited texts devoted exclusively to the need for links between behavior theory and behavior research are in print or in press (D. B. Fishman, Rotgers, & Franks, 1988; O'Donahue & Krasner, 1995c; Plaud & Eifert, in press). These cover the spectrum of major theories of relevance to contemporary behavior therapy, with thoughtful contributions by leading theoretically oriented clinicians. Two other texts (Eifert & Evans, 1990; Staats, 1996) likewise alert their readers to the danger that behavior therapy could stagnate if theoretical and conceptual substrates are neglected.

In terms of the substance of theoretical evolution, a positive development is the shift from a simplistic, mechanistic, S–R model to a nonlinear, multicausal but methodologically rigorous perspective. In other words, as already discussed in conjunction with Table 1, there is an incorporation into behavior therapy's traditional interactional worldview of elements from the organismic and transactional perspectives. For example, Goldiamond (1984) recognized the need for both forms of intervention. He used the term *linear* to refer to straightforward, focused interventions in which treatments are defined by the presenting problems and addressed directly towards these areas; and *nonlinear analysis* to refer to the inclusion of broader, indirect interventions initiated by the presenting problems but conceptualized and addressed in terms of behavior-contingency systems rather than more immediate, one-to-one relationships. Similarly, Delprato (1989) offered a nonlinear approach emphasizing the interaction of heredity and environment, evolutionary thinking, life-span developmental psychology, and a retreat from reductionism toward a systems approach that uses field concepts from electromagnetism theory rather than notions from Newtonian mechanics.

In a related vein, there is a revival of interest in Kantor's (1959) neglected "interbehavioral" psychology. For Kantor, psychology's primary subject matter was the holistic and naturalistic coordination of the entire organism, focusing on mutual and simultaneous interactions between organism and environnment. Thus, for Kantor, there never was an artificial and exclusively linear, one-to-one relationship between stimulus and response (see Ruben & Delprato, 1987).

Also, note should be taken of Shapiro's (1995a) Eye Movement Desensitization and Reprocessing (EMDR) as a recent theoretically intriguing development. EMDR involves rapid, rhythmic eye movements during the recollection of a painful traumatic memory, a process purported to reduce the client's anxiety. The eye movements are elicited from the client by instructions to hold the head still and visually track the motion of the therapist's pen or finger. The problem is that EMDR's beginnings in a chance clinical observation led to widespread application without benefit of adequate theoretical formulation, research, and validation—a situation that Shapiro herself acknowledges. A particular problem with the EMDR research to date is the lack of control for patient expectancy and the demand characteristics of the procedure (Blake, Abueg, Woodward, & Keane, 1993). So for the moment, the best that can be said about EMDR is the ancient Scottish verdict, "not proven." However, it should be noted that "not proven" aside, the lure of the basic ingredients of EMDR—"magic bullet" simplicity and clinical claims of striking success with the dramatic problem of trauma-induced anxiety—have in 5 years or so led to the training of 1,200 clinicians who have treated over 10,000 clients (Shapiro, 1995b).

The EMDR phenomenon is emblematic of a major concern of ours: the predominance of professionalism in the field's major association, the AABT, and the relative lack of concern with those conceptual, scholarly, and scientific issues that triggered the formation of this association in the first place. (It is surely no coincidence that there is a striking parallel with current events in the American Psychological Association.) In a field such as behavior therapy, there is a need to balance clinical, methodological, and professional development with conceptual and theoretical development. Much has been written about how to weight these two opposing perspectives (Franks, 1981, 1987a). Future generations of behavior therapists are likely to be influenced both by the training they have received and the role model offered by their older peers. It is for these reasons that the behavior therapy field needs to continue to strive for a proper balance between clinical and conceptual focus.

In sum, with O'Donahue and Krasner (1995a, 1995b), we concur about the importance of theory in the development of behavior therapy. Whether the times are ready for theoretical unification in behavior therapy and the embracing of one encompassing model is a moot point. Staats (1990, 1996) argued persuasively that the time for a comprehensive, thoroughly behavioral theory is now. We would argue that it probably is not but that, regardless, it is essential to emphasize even circumscribed and predictably limited behavioral theory once again. As in 1983, when the question was raised as to whether the coming years would see behavior therapy subsumed under numerous self-contained theories or whether some overarching explanatory model would emerge (Franks & Rosenbaum, 1983), the issue is equally germane in the present moment.

CONCLUSION

Watsonian behaviorism, one of the major theoretical and epistemological sources of behavior therapy, was a radical departure from the mentalistic models of psychology predominant in his time. Behaviorism's power in part came from its contrast with commonsense psychology. In ordinary experience, as reflected in the vocabulary of our language, we typically think of ourselves as being conscious and intentional in our actions and as moving among a variety of subjective emotional states. We also see ourselves as embedded in complex ways in the social institutions in our lives—family, neighborhood, work and school organizations, church, city, country, and so forth.

Watsonian behaviorists rejected subjective inner states, intentionality, and the importance of larger social and cultural forces. Rather, it was argued that people's behavior is determined by focused S–R relationships, and the best models for studying the basic forces in our lives are dogs, cats, and rats. This narrow and exclusionary vision allowed post-Watsonian learning theorists to develop ways of viewing human behavior that maximized objectivity, quantification, operational definition, precision in describing relationships between variables, and the ability to frame psychological questions in clear, linearly causal ways that lend themselves to elegant experimental designs.

Thus, behaviorists deliberately took an exclusionary and focused approach, embracing logical positivism and a "pure" interactional worldview, and this made for the exciting possibility of developing a true science of human behavior. This vision was pursued by Hull, Tolman, Skinner, Guthrie, and the other major figures in the era of grand theories of learning. As this age came to a close at the end of the first half of this century, the first behavior therapy practitioners began to apply seriously and systematically behavioristic or, more often, behavioral concepts and principles to solving human problems in the clinic and hospital rather than in the laboratory. The gradual disillusionment with learning theory as *the* answer in the field of scientific psychology as a whole perhaps allowed many of these early behavior therapists to be somewhat pragmatic rather than completely positivistic in their approach. As behavior therapists gained more and more clinical experience, they realized the value of bringing back into their thinking those elements that behaviorism had originally rejected—consciousness, cognition, inner emotional states, the self, choice and freedom, and individual behavior as interdependently embedded in small groups and organizational and community systems—but always within some kind of explicit, data-oriented, broadly behaviorally based learning theory framework.

In sum, as outlined in Table 1 and the accompanying earlier discussion, behavior theorists have rediscovered "personality" from the trait worldview, "the family as a system" from the organismic worldview, and "psychotherapy process" from the transactional worldview. However, in these rediscoveries, behavior theorists have brought their unique, underlying perspective from the interactional worldview and thereby created new ways to conceptualize, measure, and institute change in these traditional areas of psychotherapy.

Moreover, as pointed out by Pepper (1942), each of these worldviews is only "relatively adequate" from an epistemological perspective. Thus, although each does a credible job in deriving a conceptually coherent and empirically reasonable view of human experience, none of them is completely adequate. Rather, each involves a particular trade-off of adequate and inadequate characteristics, and these different patterns turn out to be mirror images of one another. For example, whereas pure interactional theory maximizes the maintenance of reliability, specifiability, observability, and manipulability, interactional theorists have a difficult time addressing such issues as the nature of human freedom, consciousness, and empathy. Transactional theory has just the opposite pattern of trade-offs. As another example, whereas trait theory can easily create constructs that are subject to psychometrically rigorous measurement, it cannot easily account for dynamic interdependency among systems levels of individual and social behavior. Organismic theory has just the opposite pattern of trade-offs. (For an extended discussion of these issues, see chap. 13 in D. B. Fishman, Rotgers, & Franks, 1988.)

In the 1990s, the principles of behavior therapy are applicable to all types of disorders, individual situations, and settings. Biofeedback, behavioral medicine, and community and environmental psychology are increasingly part of the behavior therapy scene. However, the strength of behavior therapy lies not only in its expansion and demonstration of therapeutic success, but, as previously outlined, in the uniqueness of its conceptual approach. Moreover, appropriately investigated failure can be as valuable as success in behavior therapy's conceptual development (for more extended discussion of these matters, see Barbrack, 1985; Foa & Emmelkamp, 1983; Mays & Franks, 1985).

What all this adds up to is that behavior therapy is building logically and even predictably on its foundation and that there is, indeed, hope for the future. The original emphasis on accountability, rigorous but open-minded thinking, scientific methodology, and learning theory remains much the same but in an evolved form. What has changed is the complexity of the problems addressed, the increased sophistication of the methods with which they are investigated, and the abandonment of an exclusively one-to-one linear approach. The conceptual problem still remains: How can we adopt a multidimensional, interdisciplinary perspective that takes into account data, formulation, and methodologies from disciplines once considered to be largely outside the traditional behavior therapist's bailiwick, while yet retaining the essential unity of behavior therapy (Franks, 1981, 1987b)? How can we take these innovative developments into account and incorporate them into an overall model that still retains the spirit of scientific integrity that brought behavior therapy into being in the first place? In so doing, it must be recognized that behavior therapy is still an emerging and new applied science rather akin in its status and knowledge base to engineering and medicine in the sixteenth and seventeenth centuries. It thus seems far too early to expect either unity or resolution of the issues in the field, and certainly it seems premature to think in terms of any paradigmatic or unifying conceptual integration of behavior therapy.

In our view, then, behavior therapy's continued health, vitality, and viability depends on its ability to cope with two types of challenges—one internal and one external. The external challenge is the need to respond proactively and effectively to changes in the human services delivery system that include limits on health and mental health resources and the subsequent growth of managed care as a response to these limits. We have discussed briefly how behavior therapy as a field is moving beyond the periodic horror stories of managed care to the opportunities presented by the ideals of managed care. Also, we have delineated some of the ways in which these ideals are in close correspondence with the principles and values of clinical behavior therapy and behavioral community psychology.

The internal challenge to behavior therapy is the need to remain rooted in its theoretical and conceptual foundations. It is tempting for behavior therapists to focus on the immediate details and successes of clinical process and empirical outcome findings. However, we believe that it is only by relating these to theory and by keeping theoretical dialogue active and conceptual evolution vital that the future of behavior therapy can be ensured. Recent developments, as described herein, encourage optimism that behavior therapy will continue to rise to this internal challenge.

REFERENCES

Altman, I., & Rogoff, B. (1987). World views in psychology: Trait, interactional, organismic, and transactional perspectives. In D. Stokols & I. Altman (Eds.), *Handbook of environmental psychology* (pp. 7–40). New York: Wiley.

Armenti, N. P. (1993). Managed health care and the behaviorally trained professional. *The Behavior Therapist, 16*, 13–15.

Azrin, N. H. (1977). A strategy for applied research: Learning based but outcome oriented. *American Psychologist, 30*, 469–485.

Baars, B. J. (1986). *The cognitive revolution in psychology.* New York: Guilford Press.

Baer, D. M., Wolf, M. M., & Risley, T. R. (1968). Some current dimensions of applied behavior analysis. *Journal of Applied Behavior Analysis, 1*, 91–97.

Bandura, A. (1969). *Principles of behavior modification.* New York: Holt, Rinehart & Winston.

Bandura, A. (1982). Self-efficacy mechanisms in human agency. *American Psychologist, 37*, 122–147.

Barbrack, C. R. (1985). Negative outcome in behavior therapy. In D. T. Mays & C. M. Franks (Eds.), *Negative outcome in psychotherapy and what to do about it* (pp. 76–105). New York: Springer.

Barkley, R. A. (1990). *Attention deficit hyperactivity disorder: A handbook for diagnosis and treatment.* New York: Guilford Press.

Barlow, D. H. (Ed.). (1993). *Clinical handbook for psychological disorders: A step-by-step treatment manual* (2nd ed.). New York: Guilford Press.

Barlow, D. H. (1994). Psychological interventions in the era of managed competition. *Clinical Psychology: Science and Practice, 1*, 109–122.

Barlow, D. H., Hayes, S. C., & Nelson, R. O. (1984). *The scientist practitioner: Research and accountability in clinical and educational settings.* Elmsford, NY: Pergamon Press.

Barlow, D. H., & Hersen, M. (1984). *Single case experimental designs: Strategies for studying behavioral change* (2nd ed.). Elmsford, NY: Pergamon Press.

Birchler, G. R., & Spinks, S. (1980). Behavioral-systems marital and family therapy: Integration and clinical application. *American Journal of Family Therapy, 8*, 6–28.

Blake, D. D., Abueg, F. R., Woodward, S. H., & Keane, T. M. (1993). Treatment efficacy in posttraumatic stress disorder. In T. R. Giles (Ed.), *Handbook of effective psychotherapy*. New York: Plenum.

Broskowski, A. T. (1995). The evolution of health care: Implications for the training and careers of psychologists. *Professional Psychology: Research and Practice, 26*, 156–162.

Burnham, W. H. (1924). *The normal mind*. New York: Appleton-Century-Crofts.

Campbell, D. T. (1984). Can we be scientific in applied social science? In R. F. Connor, D. G. Altman, & C. Jackson (Eds.), *Evaluation studies review annual* (Vol. 9, pp. 26–48). Beverly Hills, CA: Sage.

Cantor, N. (1990). From thought to behavior: "Having" and "doing" in the study of personality and cognition. *American Psychologist, 45*, 735–750.

Cattell, R. B. (1966). *The scientific analysis of personality*. Chicago: Aldine.

Cautela, J. R. (1967). Covert sensitization. *Psychological Reports, 20*, 459–468.

Cautela, J. R. (1970). Covert reinforcement. *Behavior Therapy, 1*, 33–50.

Chambless, D. L., et al. (1996). An update on empirically validated therapies. *The Clinical Psychologist, 49*, 5–18.

Cummings, N. A. (1995). Impact of managed care on employment and training: A primer for survival. *Professional Psychology: Research and Practice, 25*, 10–15.

Davison, G. C., & Lazarus, A. A. (1994). Clinical innovation and evaluation: Integrating practice with inquiry. *Clinical Psychology: Science and Practice, 1*, 157–168.

Delprato, D. J. (1989). Developmental interactionism: An emerging integrative framework for behavior therapy. *Advances in Behavior Research and Therapy, 9*, 173–205.

Dollard, J., & Miller, N. E. (1950). *Personality and psychotherapy*. New York: McGraw-Hill.

Dunlap, K. (1932). *Habits: Their making and unmaking*. New York: Liveright.

Dunlap, K. (1972). *Habits: Their making and unmaking*. New York: Liveright.

Eifert, G. H., & Evans, I. M. (Eds.). (1990). *Unifying behavior therapy: Contributions of paradigmatic behaviorism*. New York: Springer.

Erwin, E. (1978). *Behavior therapy: Scientific, philosophical, and moral foundations*. Cambridge, England: Cambridge University Press.

Eysenck, H. J. (1952). The effects of psychotherapy: An evaluation. *Journal of Consulting Psychology, 16*, 319–324.

Eysenck, H. J. (1959). Learning theory and behaviour therapy. *Journal of Mental Science, 195*, 61–75.

Eysenck, H. J. (Ed.). (1960). *Handbook of abnormal psychology: An experimental approach.* London: Pitman.

Eysenck, H. J. (Ed.). (1964). *Experiments in behavior therapy: Readings in modern methods of treating mental disorders derived from learning theory.* Elmsford, NY: Pergamon Press.

Eysenck, H. J. (1990). *Rebel with a cause.* London: W. H. Allen.

Fensterheim, H. (1995). More on outcome research: A reply to Warren. *The Behavior Therapist, 18,* 108–109.

Fishman, D. B. (1988). Pragmatic behaviorism: Saving and nurturing the baby. In D. B. Fishman, F. Rotgers, & C. M. Franks (Eds.), *Paradigms in behavior therapy: Present and promise* (pp. 254–293). New York: Springer.

Fishman, D. B. (Ed.). (1991). Epistemological paradigms in evaluation: Implications for practice. *Evaluation and Program Planning, 14,* 351–409.

Fishman, D. B. (1995a). Postmodernism comes to program evaluation II: A review of Denzin and Lincoln's *Handbook of qualitative research. Evaluation and Program Planning, 18,* 301–310.

Fishman, D. B. (1995b, November 18). *Behavioral research and managed care: Developing an Institute to bridge the paradigm gap.* Paper presented at the annual convention of the Association for Advancement of Behavior Therapy, Washington, DC.

Fishman, D. B., Barlow, D. H., Giles, T. R., & Armenti, N. P. (1995, November 18). *Should AABT develop an "Institute of Outcome Research Dissemination" targeted towards managed care organizations?* Panel presented at the annual convention of the Association for Advancement of Behavior Therapy, Washington, DC.

Fishman, D. B., & Franks, C. M. (1992). Evolution and differentiation within behavior therapy: A theoretical and epistemological review. In D. K. Freedheim (Ed.), *History of psychotherapy: A century of change* (pp. 159–196). Washington, DC: American Psychological Association.

Fishman, D. B., & Neigher, W. D. (1987). Technological assessment: Tapping a "third culture" for decision-focused psychological measurement. In D. R. Peterson & D. B. Fishman (Eds.), *Assessment for decision* (pp. 44–76). New Brunswick, NJ: Rutgers University Press.

Fishman, D. B., Rotgers, F., & Franks, C. M. (Eds.). (1988). *Paradigms in behavior therapy: Present and promise.* New York: Springer.

Fishman, S. T., & Lubetkin, B. S. (1983). Office practice of behavior therapy. In M. Hersen (Ed.), *Outpatient behavior therapy: A clinical guide* (pp. 21–41). New York: Grune & Stratton.

Foa, E. B., & Emmelkamp, P. M. G. (1983). *Failures in behavior therapy.* New York: Wiley.

Fox, R. E. (1995). The rape of psychotherapy. *Professional Psychology: Research and Practice, 26,* 147–155.

Franks, C. M. (1969). Behavior therapy and its Pavlovian origins. In C. M. Franks

(Ed.), *Behavior therapy: Appraisal and status* (pp. 1–26). New York: McGraw-Hill.

Franks, C. M. (1990). Behavior therapy: An overview. In C. M. Franks, G. T. Wilson, P. C. Kendall, & J. P. Foreyt (Eds.), *Review of behavior therapy: Theory and practice* (Vol. 12, pp. 1–43). New York: Guilford Press.

Franks, C. M. (1981). 2081: Will we be many or one—or none? *Behavioural Psychotherapy, 9,* 287–290.

Franks, C. M. (1987a). Behavior therapy: An overview. In G. T. Wilson, C. M. Franks, P. C. Kendall, & J. P. Foreyt (Eds.), *Review of behavior therapy: Theory and practice* (Vol. 2, pp. 1–39). New York: Guilford Press.

Franks, C. M. (1987b). Behavior therapy and AABT: Personal recollections, conceptions, and misconceptions. *The Behavior Therapist, 10,* 171–174.

Franks, C. M. (in press). The importance of being theoretical. In J. J. Plaud & G. H. Eifert (Eds.), *From behavior theory to behavior therapy.* Needham Heights, MA: Allyn & Bacon.

Franks, C. M., & Rosenbaum, M. (1983). Behavior therapy: Overview and personal reflections. In M. Rosenbaum, C. M. Franks, & Y. Jaffe (Eds.), *Perspectives on behavior therapy in the eighties* (pp. 3–16). New York: Springer.

Freud, S. (1924). Character and anal eroticism. In S. Freud, *Collected papers: II.* London: Institute of Psychoanalysis and Hogarth Press.

Gantt, W. H. (1966). Conditional or conditioned, reflex or response? *Conditional Reflex, 1,* 69–73.

Gergen, K. J. (1982). *Towards transformation in social knowledge.* New York: Springer-Verlag.

Gergen, K. J. (1985). The social constructionist movement in modern psychology. *American Psychologist, 40,* 266–275.

Gilbert, T. F. (1978). *Human competence: Engineering worthy performance.* New York: McGraw-Hill.

Giles, T. R. (1993a). *Managed mental health care: A guide for practitioners, employers, and hospital administrators.* Needham Heights, MA: Allyn & Bacon.

Giles, T. R. (Ed.). (1993b). *Handbook of effective psychotherapy.* New York: Plenum.

Giles, T. R., & Marafiote, R. A. (1994). Managed care and psychotherapy outcome: Has the pendulum swung too far? *The Behavior Therapist, 17,* 239–244.

Glenwick, D., & Jason, L. (Eds.). (1980). *Behavioral community psychology: Progress and prospects.* New York: Praeger.

Goldfried, M. R., & Davison, G. C. (1976). *Clinical behavior therapy.* New York: Holt, Rinehart & Winston.

Goldiamond, I. (1984). Training parent trainers and ethicists in nonlinear analysis of behavior. In R. F. Dangel & R. A. Polster (Eds.), *Parent training: Foundations of research and practice* (pp. 504–546). New York: Guilford Press.

Gurman, A. S., & Kniskern, D. P. (1981). *Handbook of family therapy.* New York: Brunner/Mazel.

Hayes, S. C. (1987). A contextual approach to therapeutic change. In N. S. Jacobson (Ed.), *Psychotherapists in clinical practice: Cognitive and behavior perspectives* (pp. 327–387). New York: Guilford Press.

Hayes, S. C. (1994). Content, context, and the types of psychological acceptance. In S. C. Hayes, N. S. Jacobson, V. M. Follette, & M. J. Dougher (Eds.), *Acceptance and change: Content and context in psychotherapy* (pp. 13–32). Reno, NV: Context Press.

Hayes, S. C. (1996). *Context Press catalogue: Special AABT election issue.* Reno, NV: Context Press.

Hayes, S. C., Follette, V. M., Dawes, R. M., & Grady, K. (Eds.). (1995). *Scientific standards of psychological practice: Issues and recommendations.* Reno, NV: Context Press.

Hayes, S. C., Follette, W. C., & Follette, V. M. (1995). Behavior therapy: A contextual approach. In A. S. Gurman & S. B. Messer (Eds.), *Essential psychotherapies: Theory and practice* (pp. 128–181). New York: Guilford Press.

Hayes, S. C., & Hayes, L. J. (1992). Verbal relations and the evolution of behavior analysis. *American Psychologist, 47,* 1383–1395.

Hayes, S. C., Jacobson, N. S., Follette, V. M., & Dougher, M. J. (Eds.). (1994). *Acceptance and change: Content and context in psychotherapy.* Reno, NV: Context Press.

Hayes, S. C., Strosahl, K. S., & Wilson, K. G. (in press). *Acceptance and commitment therapy.* New York: Guilford Press.

Hersch, L. (1995). Adapting to health care reform and managed care: Three strategies for survival and growth. *Professional Psychology: Research and Practice, 26,* 16–26.

Hersen, M. (1981). Complex problems require complex solutions. *Behavior Therapy, 12,* 15–29.

Jeger, A. M., & Slotnick, R. S. (Eds.). (1982). *Community mental health and behavioral ecology: A handbook of theory, research, and practice.* New York: Plenum.

Jones, H. S. (1956). The application of conditioning and learning techniques to the treatment of a psychiatric patient. *Journal of Abnormal and Social Psychology, 52,* 414–420.

Kanfer, F. H., & Schefft, B. K. (1988). *Guiding the process of therapeutic change.* Champaign, IL: Research Press.

Kantor, J. R. (1959). *Interbehavioral psychology.* Granville, OH: Principia Press.

Karon, B. P. (1995). Provision of psychotherapy under managed care: A growing crisis and national nightmare. *Professional Psychology: Research and Practice, 25,* 5–9.

Kendall, P. C., & Bemis, K. M. (1983). Thought and action in psychotherapy: The cognitive behavioral approaches. In M. Hersen, A. E. Kazdin, & A. S. Bellak (Eds.), *The clinical psychology handbook* (pp. 565–592). Elmsford, NY: Pergamon Press.

Kimble, G. A. (1985). Conditioning and learning. In S. Koch & D. E. Leary (Eds.), *A century of psychological science* (pp. 284–321). New York: McGraw-Hill.

Kohlenberg, R. J., & Tsai, M. (1991). *Functional analytic psychotherapy: Creating intense and curative therapeutic relationships*. New York: Plenum.

Kohlenberg, R. J., & Tsai, M. (1995). Functional analytic psychotherapy: A behavioral approach to intensive treatment. In W. O'Donohue & L. Krasner (Eds.), *Theories of behavior therapy: Exploring behavior change* (pp. 637–658). Washington, DC: American Psychological Association.

Krasner, L. (1971). Behavior therapy. In P. H. Mussen (Ed.), *Annual Review of Psychology* (Vol. 22, pp. 483–532). Palo Alto, CA: Annual Reviews.

Krasner, L. (1982). Behavior therapy: On roots, contexts, and growth. In G. T. Wilson & C. M. Franks (Eds.), *Contemporary behavior therapy: Conceptual and empirical foundations* (pp. 11–362). New York: Guilford Press.

Krasner, L., & Houts, A. C. (1984). A study of the "value" systems of behavioral scientists. *American Psychologist, 39,* 840–850.

Kuhn, T. S. (1962). *The structure of scientific revolutions*. Chicago: University of Chicago Press.

Lazarus, A. A. (1958). New methods in psychotherapy: A case study. *South African Medical Journal, 32,* 600–664.

Liberman, R., Cardin, V., McGill, C., Falloon, I. I., & Evans, C. (1987). Behavioral family management of schizophrenia: Clinical outcome and costs. *Psychiatric Annals, 17,* 610–619.

Liddell, H. S. (1958). A biological basis for psychopathology. In P. H. Hoch & J. Zubin (Eds.), *Problems of addiction and habituation* (pp. 183–196). New York: Grune & Stratton.

Linehan, M. M. (1993). *Cognitive-behavioral treatment of borderline personality disorder: The dialectics of effective treatment*. New York: Guilford Press.

Macchia, P. (1995). Quality care: Who's kidding whom. *New Jersey Psychologist, 45,* 10.

Mace, F. C., & Kratochwill, T. R. (1986). The individual subject in behavior analysis research. In J. Valsiner (Ed.), *The individual subject and scientific psychology* (pp. 153–180). New York: Plenum.

Mahoney, M. J. (1974). *Cognition and behavior modification*. Cambridge, MA: Ballinger.

Mahoney, M. J. (1988). The cognitive sciences and psychotherapy: Patterns in a developing relationship. In K. S. Dobson (Ed.), *Handbook of cognitive–behavioral therapies* (pp. 357–386). New York: Guilford Press.

Marshall, W. L. (1982). A model of dysfunctional behavior. In A. S. Bellak, M. Hersen, & A. E. Kazdin (Eds.), *International handbook of behavior modification* (pp. 57–76). New York: Plenum.

Masserman, J. M. (1943). *Behavior and neurosis*. Chicago: University of Chicago Press.

Mateer, F. (1917). *Child behavior: A critical and experimental study of young children by the method of conditioned reflexes*. Boston: Badger.

Mays, D. T., & Franks, C. M. (Eds.). (1985). *Negative outcome in psychotherapy and what to do about it*. New York: Springer.

Messer, S. B., Sass, L. A., & Woolfolk, R. L. (Eds.). (1988). *Hermeneutics and psychological theory*. New Brunswick, NJ: Rutgers University Press.

Messer, S., & Warren, S. (1995). *Models of brief psychodynamic therapy: A comparative approach*. New York: Guilford Press.

Miller, J. G. (1978). *Living systems*. New York: McGraw-Hill.

Minuchin, S. (1974). *Families and family therapy*. Cambridge, MA: Harvard University Press.

Mischel, W. (1968). *Personality and assessment*. New York: Wiley.

Morell, J. A. (1979). *Program evaluation in social research*. Elmsford, NY: Pergamon Press.

Mowrer, O. H., & Mowrer, W. M. (1938). Enuresis: A method for its study and treatment. *American Journal of Orthopsychiatry, 8*, 436–459.

Neigher, W. D., & Fishman, D. B. (1985). From science to technology: Reducing problems in mental health evaluation by paradigm shift. In L. Burstein, H. F. Freeman, & P. H. Rossi (Eds.), *Collecting evaluation data: Problems and solutions* (pp. 263–298). Beverly Hills, CA: Sage Publications.

Nezu, C. M., & Nezu, A. M. (1995). Clinical decision making in everyday practice: The science in the art. *Cognitive and Behavioral Practice, 2*, 5–25.

O'Donahue, W., & Krasner, L. (1995a). Theories in behavior therapy: Philosophical and historical contexts. In W. O'Donahue & L. Krasner (Eds.), *Theories of behavior therapy: Exploring behavior change* (pp. 1–22). Washington, DC: American Psychological Association.

O'Donahue, W., & Krasner, L. (1995b). Theories of behavior therapy and scientific progress. In W. O'Donahue & L. Krasner (Eds.), *Theories of behavior therapy: Exploring behavior change* (pp. 695–706). Washington, DC: American Psychological Association.

O'Donahue, W., & Krasner, L. (Eds.). (1995c). *Theories of behavior therapy: Exploring behavior change*. Washington, DC: American Psychological Association.

O'Leary, K. D., & Wilson, G. T. (1987). *Behavior therapy: Application and outcome*. Englewood Cliffs, NJ: Prentice Hall.

Ollendick, T. H. (1995). AABT and empirically validated treatments. *The Behavior Therapist, 18*, 81–82, 89.

Packer, M. J. (1985). Hermeneutic inquiry in the study of human conduct. *American Psychologist, 40*, 1081–1093.

Pepper, S. C. (1942). *World hypotheses: A study in evidence*. Los Angeles: University of California Press.

Pepper, S. C. (1967). *Concept and quality: A world hypothesis*. LaSalle, IL: Open Court.

Persons, J. B. (1989). *Cognitive therapy in practice: A case formulation approach*. New York: Norton.

Peterson, D. R. (1968). *The clinical study of social behavior*. New York: Appleton-Century-Crofts.

Petronko, M. R., Harris, S. L., & Korman, R. J. (1994). Community-based behavioral training approaches for people with mental retardation and mental illness. *Journal of Consulting and Clinical Psychology, 62*, 49–54.

Plaud, J. J., & Eifert, G. H. (Eds.). (in press). *From behavior theory to behavior therapy*. Needham Heights, MA: Allyn & Bacon.

Polkinghorne, D. E. (1992). Postmodern epistemology of practice. In S. Kvale (Ed.), *Psychology and postmodernism*. Thousand Oaks, CA: Sage.

Putnam, H. (1984). After Ayer, after empiricism. *Partisan Review, 51*, 265–275.

Robin, A. L., & Foster, S. L. (1989). *Negotiating parent–adolescent conflict: A behavioral–family systems approach*. New York: Guilford Press.

Robinson, P. (1995). New territory for the behavior therapist . . . Hello, depressed patients in primary care. *The Behavior Therapist, 18*, 149–153.

Rogers, C. (1961). *On becoming a person*. Boston: Houghton Mifflin.

Ruben, D. H., & Delprato, D. J. (Eds.). (1987). *New ideas in therapy: Introduction to an interdisciplinary approach*. Westport, CT: Greenwood Press.

Scarr, S. (1985). Construing psychology: Making facts and fables for our times. *American Psychologist, 40*, 499–512.

Shaffer, L. F. (1947). The problem of psychotherapy. *American Psychologist, 2*, 459–467.

Shapiro, F. (1995a). *Eye movement desensitization and reprocessing: Basic principles, protocols, and procedures*. New York: Guilford Press.

Shapiro, F. (1995b). Time to end the EMDR controversy. *Newsletter of the Disaster and Trauma Special Interest Group of AABT, 4*, 6–11.

Shaw, F. J. (1948). Some postulates concerning psychotherapy. *Journal of Consulting Psychology, 12*, 426–431.

Shoben, E. J., Jr. (1949). Psychotherapy as a problem in learning theory. *Psychological Bulletin, 46*, 366–392.

Skinner, B. F. (1948). *Walden two*. New York: Macmillan.

Skinner, B. F. (1957). *Verbal behavior*. New York: Appleton-Century-Crofts.

Skinner, B. F., Solomon, H. C., & Lindsley, O. R. (1953). *Studies in behavior therapy: Status report I, November 30, 1953*. Unpublished report, Metropolitan State Hospital, Waltham, MA.

Spiegler, M. D. (1983). *Contemporary behavioral therapy*. Palo Alto, CA: Mayfield Publishing.

Spiegler, M. D., & Guevremont, D. C. (1992). *Contemporary behavior therapy* (2nd ed.). Pacific Grove, CA: Brooks/Cole Publishing Company.

Staats, A. W. (1975). *Social behaviorism*. Homewood, IL: Dorsey Press.

Staats, A. W. (1981). Paradigmatic behaviorism, unified theory, unified theory construction, and the zeitgeist of separatism. *American Psychologist, 36*, 240–256.

Staats, A. W. (1988). Paradigmatic behaviorism, unified positivism, and paradigmatic behavior therapy. In D. B. Fishman, F. Rotgers, & C. M. Franks (Eds.), *Paradigms in behavior therapy: Present and promise* (pp. 211–253). New York: Springer.

Staats, A. W. (1990). Paradigmatic behavior therapy: A unified framework for theory, research, and practice. In. G. H. Eifert & I. M. Evans (Eds.), *Unifying behavior therapy: Contributions of paradigmatic behaviorism* (pp. 14–56). New York: Springer.

Staats, A. W. (1996). *Personality and behavior: Psychological behaviorism.* New York: Springer.

Strosahl, K. (1994). Entering the new frontier of managed mental health care: Gold mines and land mines. *Cognitive and Behavioral Practice, 1,* 5–23.

Strosahl, K. (1995). Behavior therapy 2000: A perilous journey. *The Behavior Therapist, 18,* 130–133.

Strosahl, K. (1996). The "gold mine–land mine" themes in generation 2 of health care reform. *The Behavior Therapist, 19,* 52–54.

Thorndike, E. L. (1911). *Animal intelligence.* New York: Macmillan.

Ullmann, L. P., & Krasner, L. (Eds.). (1965). *Case studies in behavior modification.* New York: Holt, Rinehart & Winston.

Watson, J. B. (1913). Psychology as the behaviorist views it. *Psychological Review, 20,* 158–177.

Watson, J. B. (1924). *Behaviorism.* Chicago: The People's Institute.

Wells, R. A., & Giannetti, V. J. (Eds.). (1990). *Handbook of the brief psychotherapies.* New York: Plenum.

Widmeyer Group. (1994, July/August). *American Psychological Association (APA) member focus groups on the health care environment: A summary report* (conducted for the APA Practice Directorate). Washington, DC: American Psychological Association.

Wilson, G. T. (1982). Psychotherapy process and procedure: The behavioral mandate. *Behavior Therapy, 13,* 291–312.

Wilson, G. T., & Franks, C. M. (Eds.). (1982). *Contemporary behavior therapy: Conceptual and empirical foundations.* New York: Guilford Press.

Wilson, G. T., & O'Leary, K. D. (1980). *Principles of behavior therapy.* Englewood Cliffs, NJ: Prentice Hall.

Wolpe, J. (1958). *Psychotherapy by reciprocal inhibition.* Stanford, CA: Stanford University Press.

Woolfolk, R. L., & Richardson, F. C. (1984). Behavior therapy and the ideology of modernity. *American Psychologist, 39,* 777–786.

5

DEVELOPMENT OF FAMILY SYSTEMS THEORY

PHILIP J. GUERIN, JR., AND DAVID R. CHABOT

The family has long been recognized as an important factor in the physical, spiritual, and emotional well-being of its individual members. Research and clinical work on emotional dysfunction in families dates back at least as far as Freud. Thinking about the family in relation to the emotional well-being of its individual members appears to have gone through a series of evolving, yet somewhat repetitive, cycles. In the years when emotional problems were viewed as a by-product of neurological or moral failings within the individual, the family was seen as the victim of its dysfunctional member. As psychological theories moved toward explanations based on deficiencies in nurturing, families came to be viewed as the malignant victimizers.

Today an interesting dichotomy exists. On the one hand, advances in biological psychiatry and neuropsychology have focused on the family as a genetic source of schizophrenia and depression while the family is

This chapter is a revised and expanded version of "Development of Family Systems Theory," by P. J. Guerin, Jr., and D. R. Chabot, 1992, in *History of Psychotherapy: A Century of Change* (pp. 225–260), edited by D. K. Freedheim, Washington, DC: American Psychological Association.

181

simultaneously viewed as being traumatized by the stress of living with the disorder in a family member. On the other hand, self-help movements such as the Adult Children of Alcoholics, in essence, have framed every conceivable malady as a by-product of the victimizing experience of having a parent with a dysfunction such as alcoholism.

From a clinical perspective, the family has long been included in dynamic formulations and treatment planning. Freud's published cases exhibited an interest in and appreciation of family factors. The phobic problems of Little Hans (Freud, 1909/1959) were treated by Freud's coaching of the father, a method not too discrepant from what a modern-day family therapist might use. Alfred Adler's investment in the Child Guidance Movement (1931), with its emphasis on the importance of family in the diagnosis and treatment of emotional problems in children, is another example of focus on the importance of the family. Nathan Ackerman (1937), one of the founders of the modern family therapy movement, demonstrated his interest in the emotional power within the family early in his career, when he studied the impact of the Great Depression on coal miners' families. Minuchin (1987) called attention to the work of child psychiatrist Fred Allen, who interviewed families as part of the clinical evaluations of children at the Philadelphia Child Guidance Clinic as early as 1924.

In the early 1950s, small groups of professionals in the mental health field, working separately and in disparate places, began a movement to make the "family unit" a primary focus of research and clinical intervention. From 1950 to 1990, family psychotherapy has evolved from the research studies of families with a schizophrenic member, and the child psychiatrists' attempts to incorporate family members into the treatment of troubled children and adolescents, to a full-fledged division of the mental health field.

There are many histories of family therapy already in existence. Among those most useful to the student and practitioner are Guerin (1976), Kaslow (1980), Goldenberg and Goldenberg (1985), and Nichols (1984). Each of these is a historical survey of those people whose interactions played a significant part in the development of the family therapy movement. This chapter, in contrast, attempts to focus more on the development of the theory of family psychotherapy than on the oral history of the family therapy movement.

In a paper on comparative approaches to family therapy, Guerin (1979) proposed the first theory-based classification of family therapy. He distinguished between those practitioners who based their clinical methodology on traditional psychoanalytic theory and those who attempted to formulate a systems-based conceptual framework. If this classification were reorganized using the metaphor of the family tree, there would be two major theoretical sources or trunks from which most of what we know as family psychotherapy derived its concepts. One, the communication context trunk was represented in the early 1950s by the Bateson Project. Psychoanalysis, the other major source, has multiple and diverse branches, ranging from technique-oriented, minimal use of the family in support of individual therapy, through group therapy, and on to multigenerational systems therapy. There is a further division within the psychoanalytic trunk into those who became interested in the family via studies of schizophrenia, those whose interest stemmed from working with the families of less severely disturbed children and adolescents, and those who went on to use humanistic psychology as their primary framework. For purposes of using a family tree metaphor to clarify the development of the concepts and clinical methodology of family psychotherapy, the authors of this chapter have tracked the developmental history of four key groups of theorists.

1. The communications trunk began with the Bateson Project, continued with the work of Jackson and Haley, and extended to the brief therapy project of Watzlawick, Weakland, and Fisch. The Ackerman Brief Therapy Project and the work of the Milan Associates also branched from this trunk.
2. The psychoanalytic multigenerational systems trunk included the work of Bowen who developed his theory at the Menninger Clinic, at the National Institute of Mental Health (NIMH), and at Georgetown University; we will describe also the contributions of his major professional descendants. This section of the chapter will also include a view of the work of Wynne, who succeeded Bowen at NIMH, and Nagy and Framo, two other prominent multigenerationalists. All of these clinicians began by studying schizophrenics and moved on to work with a less dysfunctional population.
3. The experiential systems trunk included the work of Whitaker and Satir, both of whom worked independently of one another but shared common humanistic frameworks overlaying primarily psychoanalytic beginnings.
4. The structural family therapy theorists began their work in the child guidance movement. It included the significant contributions of Nathan Ackerman, a child psychiatrist, and continues to the present in the work of Salvadore Minuchin, another child psychiatrist.
5. Behavioral family therapy, which is viewed by the authors as outside family systems theory, is commented on briefly.

COMMUNICATION THEORISTS

Gregory Bateson

The Bateson Project began in California in the early 1950s. Its goal was to demonstrate how the communication patterns in families with a schizophrenic member made logical sense if one understood the rules of the relationship context or culture in which the symptoms were produced.

Gregory Bateson, an anthropologist and student of animal behavior, evolution, ecology, and cybernetics, brought a knowledge and understanding of context, culture, and the structure and function of communications to the work. He was far more interested in the science of communication and in theory building than in therapy. Bateson derived his model for studying communication from the theory of logical types (Whitehead & Russell, 1910). He began his work in psychiatry through a collaboration on the social matrix of psychiatry with Jurgen Ruesh (Ruesh & Bateson, 1951) at the Langley Porter Institute in California.

In 1952, he received a grant from the Rockefeller Foundation to study the nature of communications. The following year, Bateson was joined by Jay Haley, who had just received his MA in Communications from Stanford. Also joining the project at that time was John Weakland, a chemical engineer interested in cultural anthropology. In 1954, Bateson was awarded a grant from the Macy Foundation to study patterns of communication in schizophrenics. It was at this point that Don Jackson, a psychiatrist, joined the project as clinical consultant and supervisor of psychotherapy. Jackson had been supervised as a psychiatric resident by Harry Stack Sullivan and brought with him an understanding of the interpersonal dimension of psychopathology. Bateson, Haley, Weakland, and Jackson then undertook the study of communication in families with a schizophrenic member.

In the early phases of their work, staff members interviewed individual hospitalized patients at the Palo Alto Veterans Hospital. From these interviews and the staff collaboration that followed, the concept of the *double bind* began to emerge. It was based on several preliminary ideas having to do with notions of family homeostasis and multiple, often-contradictory levels of communication in relationships. In certain relationship situations, an overt and explicit meaning of a communication is contradicted by the implicit or "metamessage." Hoffman (1981) cites an excellent example of such a bind when one person in a relationship expresses to the other the command "dominate me." Clearly the person addressed can only dominate by obeying the command, thereby complying—which is the opposite of domination. Hoffman points out that the only way one can respond to such a request is to point out the impossibility, make a joke, or leave the field. However, families often block all attempts to make the implicit explicit, or attempts to clarify contradictory messages even in a joking way, and often, especially in the case of children, it is not possible to leave. When these conditions exist, a potentially malignant context has been established that can foster significant symptomatic behavior.

The six basic characteristics of the double bind may be summarized as follows (Nichols, 1984):

1. Two or more persons are involved in an important relationship.
2. The relationship is a repeated experience.
3. A primary negative injunction is given, such as "do not do or I will punish you."
4. A second injunction is given that conflicts with the first, but at a more abstract level. This injunction is also enforced by a perceived threat. This second injunction is often nonverbal and frequently involves one parent's negating the injunction of the other.
5. A third-level negative injunction exists that prohibits escape from the field while also demanding a response.
6. Once the victim is conditioned to perceive the world in terms of a double bind, the necessity for every condition to be present disappears and almost any part is enough to precipitate panic or rage.

The concept of the double bind (Bateson, Jackson, Haley, & Weakland, 1956), like many ideas before and since, did little to alter the outcome of the treatment of schizophrenia. However, it did mark the beginning formulation of a series of interconnected ideas that form the basis for what is known today as strategic family therapy.

The Bateson group continued to refine the ideas underlying the double bind concept and to obtain a more expansive understanding of communication and the role it plays in family dysfunction. Each of the members of this group went on to make significant further contributions to the field.

Jackson's continued refinement of the double bind concept manifested itself in his work on creating a *therapeutic double bind*. The therapeutic double bind is an intervention wherein the therapist attempts to double bind the patient or family. Whereas the double bind is defined as containing the preceding six characteristics, the *therapeutic* double bind is more loosely constructed. This technique prescribes the symptom and is based on an attempt to turn the natural oppositional forces within the family system onto the pathological process under investigation, thereby neutralizing the pathological forces and eliminating the symptoms.

Nichols (1984) provided an example of Haley's early use of the therapeutic double bind to explain the idea. In this example, Haley recommended hearing voices to a schizophrenic patient. If the patient responds by hearing voices, he is being compliant with the therapist. If he fails to hear voices, he must give up the claim to being crazy. In reality then, the therapeutic double bind was the earliest beginning of what has come to be known as paradoxical injunction.

In *Pragmatics of Human Communications* (Watzlawick, Beavin, & Jackson, 1967), Jackson and his coauthors provide an enriched version of this treatment strategy used with individuals and couples. Hoffman (1981) described two examples of Jackson's work. In one example, a woman with intractable headaches was told her headaches cannot be cured, but that the therapist will direct his attention toward helping her live with her disability. In another case, a couple with a chief complaint of constant arguing and bickering was informed by the therapist that their bickering is a sign of emotional involvement, and, therefore, this apparent continuous conflict only proves how much they love each other. From these two examples, we again see the genesis of the techniques of paradoxical intervention and reframing as practiced in the strategic model of family therapy today.

Jackson founded the Mental Research Institute (MRI) in 1959 and invited Virginia Satir to join him. Although MRI and the Bateson group occupied the same building for three years, there was no formal link between them. MRI had a clinical treatment bent, while the Bateson Project continued its interest in theory. Although the Bateson Project failed to produce a cohesive, comprehensive theory, it did produce a series of interconnected ideas and develop a diverse and multitalented group of clinicians and researchers, many of whom continue to contribute to the field.

At the time of Jackson's death in 1968, he had already published two outstanding books, *Pragmatics of Human Communication*, with Watzlawick and Beavin (Watzlawick et al., 1967) and *The Mirages of Marriage*, with William Lederer (Lederer & Jackson, 1968). As the psychiatrist in the Bateson group, Jackson perhaps felt the most pressure to convert the ideas and observations of the project into clinical methods useful in working with families. His early death in a field dominated by personalities has, to some degree, obscured his contributions.

Jackson shared Bateson's belief that behavior and communication are synonymous. Like Bowen, he borrowed some of his ideas from biology. Jackson's concept of family homeostasis described how families, like other organic systems, resist change, and how, when challenged, these relationship systems strive to maintain the status quo even at considerable emotional cost to one of their members. He was among the first to observe the organizing function that a child's behavioral symptoms provide for camouflaging covert parental conflict.

Thus far we have considered, in a very abbreviated way, some of the ideas of Bateson, the anthropologist, and Jackson, the psychiatrist. Their influence on generations of descendants was strong but often not fully acknowledged or documented. Of the persons who played a part in the Bateson Project, those most directly influential on the clinical behavior of succeeding generations of family therapists have been Haley and Satir. In the remainder of this section, we describe the contributions of Haley and John Weakland who, with his collaborator Richard Fisch, developed one of the first family-based systems of brief therapy. The work of the Ackerman Brief Therapy Group of Hoffman, Papp, and Silverstein and the work of the Milan Associates will also be considered. Satir's work is summarized in the section about the experiential group.

Jay Haley

Jay Haley emerged from his work on the Bateson project with a two-fold conviction that clinical symptoms were a by-product of context and that a power struggle for control was the process behind the behavior patterns in a relationship. A logical consequence of this thinking is the view that a symptom in a person is a strategy for obtaining control within a relationship. The covert nature of the process, its being out of everyone's awareness, and the function it serves for the symptomatic individual and for the family homeostasis, make direct confrontation of the symptom and attempts to make the process explicit fruitless endeavors. Therefore, counterstrategies that bypass or confuse the homeostatic mechanism, creating chaos and allowing for spontaneous reorganization, represent the required clinical methodology. From the beginning of his work, Haley paid close attention to hierarchical structure as it relates to power distribution and advocated therapeutic strategies to defeat entrenched patterns of dysfunctional behavior.

Haley's work with Minuchin and Montalvo helped fashion *structural family therapy*, a method described in detail later in the chapter. Early training videotapes from the structural family therapy project at the Philadelphia Child Guidance Clinic demonstrate clearly Haley's penchant for creating strategies intended to bypass the naturally occurring power struggle between the family and the therapist. Haley believed in exerting influence from an "outsider" position. For example, he formulated intervention plans and supervised their clinical implementation by trainees but did not do clinical work himself.

In the 1970s, Haley left Philadelphia and established his own Family Institute in Washington, DC. From then on his focus shifted away from structural family therapy concepts to the pursuit of a more refined understanding of hierarchy, power, and strategic intervention.

At this time he revealed his affiliation with Milton Erickson, a psychiatrist with a penchant for the creative use of hypnotic techniques that, in some vaguely understood way, seemed to move his patients (mostly individuals) from dysfunction to function. Erickson too "encouraged resistance" as a technique to bypass direct confrontation with symptoms. Haley's derived methods of strategic problem-oriented therapy based on Erickson's methods were presented in his 1976 publication, *Problem-Solving Therapy*. The method came along at a time when long-term psychotherapy was beginning to be viewed by some as inefficient and even abusive to the patient's finances, as well as self-serving for the therapist. By the 1980s, strategic family therapy clearly began to dominate the field of family therapy.

Two predominant characteristics of Haley's methods are his firm belief in the uselessness of direct educational techniques and his corollary commitment never to explain himself but rather to operate covertly upon the processes of power within a relationship. This second concept is perhaps most easily demonstrated with Haley's approach to the concept of triangulation.

Often family therapists will try to deal with triangulation by educating families about how they are caught in the process. Haley rarely ever mentions the concept, but in his training tapes and publications, he frequently operates in a strategic fashion that relies strongly on the concept. For example, in his training tape, "The Boy with the Dog Phobia," he uses the task of the father's buying a dog to confront the father's and son's anxiety about dogs, while simultaneously closing the distance between them. An important side effect of this combined structural and strategic intervention (illustrating the notion of triangulation) is a surfacing of the mother's depression and the covert conflict between the parents.

Since the founding of the Washington Family Institute, Haley's major collaborator has been his wife, Cloé Madanes, who has become a respected clinician and author in her own right. Haley and Madanes have fashioned a clinical method for working strategically with severe marital dysfunction, called ordeal therapy (Haley, 1984). In this method a strategic ordeal is fashioned that provides, on the one hand, a ritual of penance and absolution, and on the other, a bond formed between two people who experience an ordeal together. A classic illustration of this method describes the formation of a strategic ordeal for a couple with a long-term sadomasochistic, physically abusive relationship. They were instructed to shave their heads completely, then to take the hair and bury it in a particular place several hours from their home. As a follow-up they were instructed to make repeated visits on a regular schedule to the burial ground. This strategic ritual represented not only a shared ordeal but also a symbolic burying of their old dysfunctional patterns of relating, thus freeing them to activate the potential of numerous unused, more-functional patterns in the relationship.

Haley has been critical of traditional psychiatric methods and family therapy methods that fail to take into consideration his basic premises about the importance of power and control. In our opinion, there is nothing incompatible in the structural–strategic approach of Haley and the multigenerational system approaches of Bowen and his descendants. One of the places this becomes evident is in the discussion of the systemic therapy of the Milan group which follows.

Milan Associates

The Milan Associates consisted in its early years of four principals (Selvini-Palazoli, Boscolo, Cecchin, and Prata). Maria Selvini-Palazoli, a psychoanalytically trained psychiatrist, began in the late 1960s to treat anorexic children and their families. She moved on to work with schizophrenic families from a systems perspective. The Milan Associates model is an interesting method, with fibers from the work of the Bateson Project, the strategic therapists, Minuchin, Jackson, and Bowen all woven together into a highly creative fabric. Their method stresses the importance of defining the family's rules—an approach similar to that of Jackson in his early work. In addition it pays specific attention to Haley's emphasis on power and control.

The frequency of the sessions—once a month—is often described as making this method "long brief" therapy. This same frequency has been used by Bowen in his work with individuals, families, and multiple family groups since the early 1960s. Bowen, whose methods will be dealt with in detail later in the chapter, has long believed that less frequent sessions were more beneficial to the process of change than once-a-week meetings, which, he felt, fostered dependency between therapist and family and impeded change. Another similarity between the Milan method and Bowen's work has to do with what the Milan group calls "circular questioning." This technique is described as framing every question so as to address differences in perceptions about events and relationships. Any study of Bowen's clinical interviews on videotape demonstrates a very similar technique that Bowen and his descendants have termed the "process question."

Both the Milan model and the work of Bowen emphasize "therapist neutrality," although each approaches the problem from the opposite position. In the Milan model, the therapist tries to remain allied with all family members and thereby attempts to avoid getting caught up in family alliances and coalitions. If opposites are the same, then being allied with all family members is the same as being allied with none of them, which is Bowen's therapeutic stance.

The Milan Associates also include techniques of paradox and counterparadox closely related to the work of Bateson, Jackson, and Weakland on the therapeutic double bind. In this country, the Milan Associates' methods were built upon and modified by Papp, Silverstein, and Hoffman, who worked at the Ackerman Institute and fashioned an American version of the Milan method.

Watzlawick, Weakland, and Fisch

Weakland, one of the original principals in the Bateson Project, collaborated with Jackson on an article that centered on theory, technique, and outcome results of conjoint family therapy used with schizophrenic families (Jackson & Weakland, 1961). In 1967, Watzlawick wrote a book with Beavin and Jackson entitled *Pragmatics of Human Communications*. In this text they explained what they developed—a "calculus" of human communications—that is, a series of principles about communication and metacommunication. They defined disturbed behavior as a communicative reaction to a particular family relationship situation rather than evidence of a disease of the individual mind.

After Jackson's death in 1968, Watzlawick and Weakland were joined by a psychiatrist, Richard Fisch, to form the Brief Therapy Project at the Mental Research Institute. The core of their work became an attempt to define clearly the clinical problem as presented and then carefully link this problem to the repetitive sequences of behavior observable in the relationships surrounding the problem. It was their assumption, derived from the concept of family homeostasis, that these repetitive cycles of relationship behavior, while intended as a solution, end up reinforcing the problem.

For example, in an adolescent-focused family, the problem might be defined as the son's underachieving in school for 10 years. The mother is involved in an intense effort to structure her son's activities and improve his study habits. The more she pressures, the less he does. The strategic therapist, after investigating the "problem" in great detail, suggests the following approach: The mother is told that her interest and caring for her son are admirable, and the only reason it isn't working is that she hasn't done it with quite enough intensity and should increase her efforts. The therapist explains that the reason this is needed is that her son, despite being a fine young man, is somewhat immature for his age and therefore, at present, is unable to assume responsibility for his school performance.

The mother and the son both develop oppositional responses to the intervention. The mother stops pressuring her son, reasoning that she already has too much responsibility and does not have any more time and that he has to grow up some day. The son is incensed that the therapist has labeled him as immature and proceeds to prove him wrong by accepting responsibility for structuring his time better and being less passive about his school performance. With this result, the strategic therapist has completed the work of therapy.

In their book, the three investigators emphasized both the pathological and potentially therapeutic aspects of paradox in human communications and the value of the therapeutic double bind. They demonstrated no interest in triangles or transmission of anxiety, in the son's developmental issues, or in the fact that the mother's father is seriously ill. These factors are not included in the problem definition or in the treatment plan unless presented as a problem by the family to the therapist.

In 1974, Watzlawick, Weakland, and Fisch collaborated on another text that concentrated on "how problems arise, are perpetuated in some instances and resolved in others." It was an outgrowth of the work of the three in MRI's Brief Therapy Center. Problem formation, problem resolution, first-order change, second-order change, and reframing are among the important issues addressed. A summary of the principles of first-order and second-order change reveals the importance of this text.

1. First-order change occurs within a given system which itself remains unchanged. It is a logical, commonsense solution to a problem. If Johnny is failing in school, mother must supervise his school work more closely.
2. Second-order change is applied when first-order change, the logical, commonsense solution, is clearly demonstrated to be at the center of an escalating problem. In other words, use second-order change when first-order change is making the problem worse. The mother's hovering in the previous clinical example is the escalating problem.
3. Second-order change based on reframing and paradox flies in the face of logic and common sense and usually is perceived as weird and unexpected. The second-order change in our example is the defining of mother's escalating behavior as desirable and as required in greater amounts to produce the desired result.
4. The use of second-order change lifts the situation out of the trap created by the self-reflexive, commonsense solution and places it in a different frame. The entrapping, repetitive cycle of mother's pressure and son's responsive passivity is replaced by a new sequence of behaviors which eliminates the symptoms.

Over the first 40 years of the family therapy movement, what began as Bateson's interest in culture, communication, and the mysteries of schizophrenia has become a clinical methodology for dealing with a wide spectrum of psychological disturbances within the individual and in relationships. The clinical methodology rests on a loosely connected set of concepts about the nature and patterns of communication (i.e., the double bind), about family homeostasis as the natural tendency for the perpetuation of dysfunction in relationship systems, and about triangles as structural expressions of the relationship patterns that maintain a dysfunctional equilibrium. These concepts are then linked under two global assumptions that determine the form of the specific clinical methodology to be applied to a particular situation. The first assumption is that individuals or persons in relationships in dysfunction are emotionally caught in a reactive process in such a way that they are unable to free themselves. Increasing efforts to break free only increase friction, frustration, and anxiety; eventually symptoms appear. The second assumption is that in each individual and in each relationship system, there is a naturally occurring oppositional reaction, that is, resistance to attempts at change.

The clinical methodology that arises from these concepts and assumptions is at once simple and complex. The therapist must devise a strategy that neutralizes or bypasses the naturally occurring "resistance" mechanisms. If this task is accomplished, a corrective program may be introduced that has a better chance of being successful. The system will thereby lower friction and tension and alleviate symptoms. Once symptoms have been relieved, the system and its individual members are free to resume their individual and collective developmental pathways.

Interventions traditionally developed in this method are more of an art form than other more linear models. The therapy as an art form aspect of this model is reminiscent of the healing methods of the shaman, a particularly interesting twist when viewed in the light of Bateson's beginnings as an anthropologist.

PSYCHOANALYTIC MULTIGENERATIONAL THEORISTS

The next group of theorists to be considered is implicitly defined by several common features in their work. Each of them maintained a multigenerational focus—that is, their definition of the family unit included a minimum of three generations. In addition, they all began to study family relationships through an interest in schizophrenia and started their work with psychoanalytic theory as their conceptual base. The group can be divided into four subcategories: object relations and multigenerational themes (Nagy and Framo), a group focus (Bell and Wynne), the Bowen group, and the experientialists (Whitaker and Satir). In this section, we will deal with each of them in turn, particularly emphasizing the work of Bowen and his descendants.

Object Relations

As mentioned earlier, Freudian theory has long been influential in understanding the impact of family relationships on the psychological functioning of its individual members. In the early days of family therapy, attempts to formulate a separate theory for "family" were resisted by the core of the psychoanalytic community. Family therapy was viewed as a technique similar to group work which had successfully adapted traditional Freudian theory to its clinical methods. Clinical work with families, from the perspective of the analytic community, was indicated in two situations. One situation was when family members needed education about the ways in which they were potentially defeating the transferential therapy of an individual. The other family situation was one that needed opening up of communications around tension-filled issues within the family. Initially there was considerable skepticism about seeing families because of its possible effects upon the transference, but eventually, a group of therapists still committed to psychoanalytic theory began to experiment with such methods. Those in the analytic community who maintained both the allegiance to analytic theory and an interest in clinical interventions with families moved toward the model of object relations theory as their primary conceptual base.

The theoretical underpinnings of the object relations approach to family therapy rest on the work of Klein and Fairbairn. The Kleinian concept of *good breast/bad breast* refers to infantile ambivalence about the mother derived from the developmental experiences of nurturance and deprivation. Fairbairn developed the idea of the existence of internalized relationship structures. Contained within these proposed structures were partial objects, that is, a portion of the ego and the affect associated with the relationship. The external object was perceived as either all good, all bad, or both, in alternating cycles, which Fairbairn referred to as *splitting*. It was Fairbairn's belief that when the splitting process was not resolved, the individual's ability to objectify relationships was impaired. This concept of splitting has been developed further in the notion of *projective identification*.

Projective identification is defined as a process whereby an individual first projects onto another person certain denied behaviors or characteristics of his or her own personality. Then in the relationship interaction the person behaves in ways that either provoke such behaviors from the other or reacts as if the other possesses these characteristics, which thereby reinforces the projective perception. A simple example from a marital relationship would be when a wife with an internalized judgmental and negative image of herself projects the perception of a harsh, critical, unloving person onto her husband and then behaves in ways that predictably bring forth critical and withholding behaviors on his part.

Family therapists working with these concepts as a theoretical base can track this type of interactional process within the session and interpret the object relation forces that are driving the conflict. These methods closely resemble those used early on in psychoanalytically based family therapy, wherein the existence of naturally occurring "transferences" in the family was hypothesized and interpreted clinically to explain relationship conflict and dysfunction.

Nagy and Framo

Ivan Nagy, a psychiatrist, and James Framo, a psychologist, edited a volume titled *The Intensive Family Therapy of Schizophrenia* (Boszormenyi-Nagy & Framo, 1965) that brought together papers from most of the leading family researchers at that time. Framo adopted Fairbairn's object relations theory as the basis for his work. In his practice, this position led to his inviting significant extended family members into the sessions, especially when dealing with marital conflict. Framo also expended considerable effort in his attempts at integrating his work with that of others whose theoretical stance derived primarily from psychoanalytic theory.

Nagy also maintained his primarily psychoanalytic orientation when he changed from the study of schizophrenia to study the issue of loyalty in families, particularly as it influences coalitions and alliances over multiple generations. This work is described in his book *Invisible Loyalties* written with his colleague Geraldine Spark (Boszormenyi-Nagy & Spark, 1973). In this text Nagy offers the concept of the "family ledger," an invisible ledger of multigenerational accounts of obligations, debts, and events perceived as relationship atrocities. These firmly entrenched emotional wounds require retribution of some kind over the generations. Hoffman (1981) designates forgiveness as the key to therapy. She also draws attention to the aspects of Nagy's method that resemble the reframing techniques of strategic therapy. Hoffman reasons that if a problem's genesis is reframed in terms of old wounds and loyalties, family members have a face-saving mechanism that allows them to give up their present-day conflict.

Group Focus

The family as a naturally occurring group was a logical unit of focus for those who had developed and refined methods of working with artificially formed therapeutic groups. One of the earliest pioneers in the family therapy movement, John Bell (1961) maintained his theoretical group orientation in his work with families (1975). Lyman Wynne, director of the Family Division at NIMH for many years, is another prominent family therapist who uses a group model.

John Bell

Bell began his clinical work with families in the early 1950s. His conceptual framework is based on the work of Bion and the Tavistock Group. His efforts to adapt group therapy principles and techniques to the family unit resulted in his formulation of seven stages in the work of family group therapy (1975).

These seven stages demonstrate clearly Bell's investment in traditional analytic and group theory. They include the "initiation," a feeling-out process between family and therapist in which the goals are defined and the therapeutic contract set. The initiation phase is followed by a period of "testing," in which the rules of the contract formed in the preceding stage are tested and, when necessary, are rewritten to fit more closely the reality of the clinical situation. The third stage is termed the "struggle for power." In this phase individuals and subgroup coalitions maneuver for power and influence within the process of the group. The next two phases consist of "settling on a common task" and working toward "completion of a common task." The working through of the first five stages culminates in the sixth stage, termed "achieving completion." In this stage, having dealt with the power struggles and coalitions, the group is ready to include all members in the task of developing a climate of mutual support as individual and relationship issues are discussed and worked out. This having been accomplished, the family group is ready to separate from the therapist and resume its "natural" developmental life. This seventh and final stage is logically termed "separation." Bell (1975) strongly believes in the importance of maintaining effective boundaries between the therapist and the family group.

Lyman Wynne

Lyman Wynne, who succeeded Murray Bowen as Director of the Family Division at NIMH in 1959, also came to the study of schizophrenia and the family with a psychoanalytic background. In addition, his approach to the family was primarily that of an analytically based group model developed at Tavistock Clinic. In his research on schizophrenic families, he developed two interlocking concepts that were mostly descriptive of the family as a group. These two concepts were "pseudomutuality" and the "rubber fence" phenomenon.

Pseudomutuality was the term used to describe a surface appearance of agreement and attachment among family members, while in reality, the family members were tightly locked into dysfunctional roles that did not permit individuation from the family or truly close relationships within it. Externally, however, particularly in public, the family was unpredictably impenetrable because of its seeming automatic ability to expand and contract in a reflexive fashion. An "outside" person, such as a therapist, seeking to engage family members, might feel a certain ease of entry into the family, only to be bounced out later, as if by a rubber fence, if certain unwritten rules were violated. These concepts describe phenomena present in varying degrees in families throughout the spectrum of dysfunction, but particularly in families with a schizophrenic member. Developed in a research program, the concepts have yet to be integrated into a more diverse and elaborate clinical model of family therapy.

The Bowen Group

Bowenian family systems therapy is a theoretical–clinical model that evolved directly from psychoanalytic principles and practice. It is the most comprehensive model of family systems theory insofar as it consists of a defined number of concepts with a corresponding clinical methodology closely linked with the theory. Murray Bowen, its originator and major contributor, began with an interest in studying the problem of schizophrenia, and brought to his study of the family extensive training in psychoanalysis, including 13 years of personal training analysis.

In the early years of the family therapy movement, many of the pioneers trod lightly in the area of theory. Bowen was the exception to this rule, both in his emphasis on the primary importance of theory and in his belief that his observations and ideas could form the beginning of a new theory of human emotional functioning. He hoped his theory would be viewed as evolving from Freudian theory but as being clearly and distinctly different from it in its systems orientation.

Bowen (1978) believed that the task of the theorist was to find the smallest numbers of congruent concepts that could fit together and serve as a working blueprint for understanding that part of the human experience under observation. He repeatedly warned of the pitfalls of lowest common denominator eclecticism. Bowen dates the beginning of his theory to his clinical work with schizophrenia at the Menninger Clinic from 1946 to 1954. During this time he studied mothers and their schizophrenic offspring who lived together in small cottages on the Menninger campus. From this clinical research he was hoping to gain a better understanding of mother–child symbiosis. Observations from these studies led to the formation of his concept of differentiation. From the Menninger Clinic, Bowen moved to NIMH, where he formed a project to hospitalize and study whole families with a schizophrenic member. It was this project that expanded the concept of mother–child symbiosis to involve fathers and inevitably led to the Bowen concept of triangulation, described later in this section.

In 1959, Bowen left NIMH and went to Georgetown Medical School where he was a professor of psychiatry until his death in the fall of 1990. In his 31 years at Georgetown, Bowen refined his theory by applying it to less dysfunctional populations and by developing a clinical methodology that he could pass on to the psychiatric residents in training at Georgetown. As he developed his method of family psychotherapy, he saw the need for a corresponding method that would assist the psychotherapist in the development of his or her own personal autonomy. For this purpose, Bowen began to research and experiment with the emotional process within his own personal family system. The developing concepts of his theory were presented in two key papers in 1966 and 1976. A documentation of his "research" on his own family of origin was first presented at a national family therapy conference in 1967 and published in 1972.

In these articles, Bowen designates eight concepts as central to his theory: differentiation of self; triangles; nuclear family emotional system; family projection process; emotional cutoff; multigenerational transmission process; sibling position; and societal regression. The concepts of *differentiation* and *triangulation* form the core of Bowen's theoretical contribution.

Differentiation

Bowen's concept of differentiation consists of two component parts: emotional fusion within the dyad and differentiation of the individual. In his observations on mother–child symbiosis, Bowen recorded alternating cycles of closeness and distance within the mother–child dyad. He hypothesized that sequential cycles of separation anxiety and incorporation anxiety were the primary emotional forces driving these seemingly automatic and reactive relationship patterns. The very interdependent nature of the relationship between mother and child limited the potential for autonomous functioning in both of them. Their behaviors were determined by their anxious attachment to each other rather than by their own internal choices. They may be said to be emotionally fused to one another. On a structural level, this fusion denotes a blurring of appropriate personal boundaries.

On a process level, there is a contagious anxiety that entraps both members of the dyad, determining their behavior in relation to one another as well as their individual levels of emotional functioning. Anxiety in either the mother or child produces an automatic reflexive response in the other. These automatic emotional responses and behaviors describe the *fusion* (or lower) level of Bowen's proposed spectrum of emotional functioning.

The opposite profile is of a high functioning individual capable of emotional connection without being determined by the anxiety in an important other person or in the relationship. This differentiated self is capable of behaving in response to his or her own instinct and judgment guided by principles and opinions, even in the presence of considerable anxiety. This profile of autonomy represents differentiation, which is the opposite of fusion and sits at the higher end of Bowen's spectrum of emotional functioning.

Bowen developed a scale of differentiation that ranged from extreme fusion to the opposite, high differentiation, within the person. Higher scores indicated an increasing ability to withstand high levels of anxiety while continuing to be autonomous in life choices, including relationship behavior.

Bowen believed that in dysfunctional families each individual was caught in a reactive emotional process that determined his or her behavior. He further believed that if one individual could, by conscious effort, lower his or her anxiety and reactivity to the surrounding emotional forces, that person could get free of this dysfunctional process. Once even partially free, other potential pathways of behavior would become clear to the individual. These new pathways would be more determined by principles of function than by feelings or by the reactive search for emotional comfort and refuge. If one person in the family could do this, others in the family would be afforded the chance to follow, and the functioning level of the entire relationship system would improve.

Bowen thought that if one individual in a family could get free of the entrapment of the reactive emotional process and begin a potential chain reaction of lowering anxiety throughout the relationship system, this would lead to certain therapeutic consequences. The main one is that a therapist who can remain emotionally free of a family's reactive emotional process can begin the aforementioned desirable chain reaction. How, then, does one train therapists to be capable of such a procedure? In response to this question, Bowen developed his method for training therapists to differentiate a self in their own families of origin. He began by doing it himself in his own family, publishing the results, and then challenging those he trained to follow suit. In a 1972 paper, Bowen spelled out his method in detail. Included in this method were four important steps.

1. *Know the facts about your family relationship system.* Bowen encouraged his trainees to construct comprehensive family diagrams in order to document the structural relationships among members of their family and to gather facts about the timing of important events such as deaths, births, and so forth, which he termed *nodal events.* He also taught the importance of including in the family diagram evidence of physical and emotional dysfunction, relationship conflicts, and emotional cutoffs, which he viewed as indicators of a family's level of emotional functioning.

2. *Become a better observer of your family and learn to control your own emotional reactivity to these people.* Bowen charged therapists-in-training with this central task to be accomplished on planned visits with key members from their family of origin.

3. *Detriangling self from emotional situations.* This part of the method entails developing an ability to stay nonreactive during periods of intense anxiety within one's own family system. To foster this process of "detriangling," Bowen encouraged those in training to visit their families of origin at times of predictably high tension, such as serious illness or imminent death of a key family member. During these visits the goal was to make contact with family members around an anxiety-ridden issue, to remain less emotionally reactive than other family members, and to not choose sides when competing

influences and differences of opinions led to relationship conflict.

4. *Develop person-to-person relationships with as many family members as possible.* This double-barreled axiom was aimed at fostering detriangulation and encouraging the reestablishment of relationship connections where cutoffs or potential cutoffs had previously existed.

From this consideration of the concept of differentiation and its application to the training of therapists, the complexity of the idea becomes obvious. One of the major difficulties in operationalizing the concept is that, by definition, differentiation represents an inborn psychological state inherited at birth from the emotional struggles of previous generations and only changeable to some small measure during an individual's lifetime.

Triangles

Bowen began his working model of the relationship triangle during the NIMH project after including fathers in the study. The interdependence observed in the mother–child dyad also appeared to be present in the relationships involving fathers. Initially, Bowen expressed the idea of an interdependent triad and compared it to a three legged stool, where the removal of one leg destroyed the essence of the stool. Beginning with his observation of the reactive emotional instability of the fusion-laden dyad, Bowen proposed that the transmission of the anxiety in the dyad to involve the most vulnerable other in the relationship system formed a potentially stabilizing but dysfunctional structure called a *triangle*. Considered by many to be the originator of the concept of triangulation, Bowen placed heavy emphasis on the relationship-process part of triangulation and little or none on its structural aspects. He focused instead on the potentially everchanging configurations of relationship triangles. These automatic shifts were driven by the reactive emotional process within the relationship system.

Bowen's method of therapy closely followed his conceptual framework. As a therapist he placed himself in contact with both members of a conflictual dyad and worked to remain emotionally neutral while spelling out the emotional process within the conflictual relationship by using a series of "process questions," such as "What about your wife's criticism upsets you the most?" Theoretically this was meant to induce a corrective emotional experience for the family members in conflict, allowing them to lower their anxiety and seek more functional pathways of relating to each other.

It should be noted that there is a distinction to be made between "triangles" as a relationship *structure*, and "triangulation" as a relationship *process*. A triangle is an abstract way of thinking about a structure in human relationships, and triangulation is the reactive emotional process that goes on within that triangle. In any relationship system, there are any number of potential triangles, and the emotional process of triangulation within the triangle can be either dormant or active in varying degrees at any moment in time.

The clinical description of a triangle is the way the three-way relationship looks at a given moment or the pattern to which it regularly returns after temporary realignments. For example, at the time a couple presents for treatment, the triangle with their son may have become relatively fixed so that the mother and the son are overly close and the father is in the distant, outsider position. This alignment may occasionally shift, so that there are times when either the mother or the son is in the outside position and the father has some closeness with his son or his wife, but then it shifts back to its usual structure.

Triangulation is the emotional process that goes on among the three people who make up the triangle. For example, in the triangle just described, the father might desire a connection with his son and resent his wife's monopoly of the boy's affections; the mother may be angry at the father's distance from her and compensate by substituting closeness with her son. The child, in turn, may resent his father's inattention and criticism and may move toward his mother but, at the same time, be anxious about his overly close relationship with her. As the emotional process of triangulation moves around the triangle, it can produce changes in its structure. For example, the father may try to reduce his loneliness by moving toward his son or his wife, or the son may try to avoid fusion with his mother by distancing toward his peers, causing his parents to draw together in their concern for him.

Thus, triangles can shift their structure at any time for a variety of reasons, and the process of triangulation has the potential for motion at any time. As changes do occur, demands are placed on the individuals and on the system to realign in a way that ensures the emotional comfort of the most powerful person and preserves the stability of the system. As Bowen (1978) pointed out, the most uncomfortable person in the triangle may try to lower his or her anxiety or emotional tension by moving toward a person or thing. If that effort is successful, another person becomes the uncomfortable one and will work to become more comfortable. Bowen's concept of the relationship triangle most clearly differentiated his family systems theory from other theories of human emotional functioning.

Bowen's Descendants

During his 31 years at Georgetown University, Bowen worked on the refinement of his theory and its clinical application with nonpsychotic families. During this time he was instrumental in the training of many psychiatrists. Among the most prominent and influential of these are Philip

Guerin and Thomas Fogarty. Both were trained by Bowen during the 1960s, left Georgetown, and joined the Einstein Family Studies Section in New York where Zwerling and Ferber were assembling a faculty representative of the diversity of thinking and practice in the field of family therapy. While at Einstein, they trained Betty Carter, Monica McGoldrick, Ed Gordon, Eileen Pendagast, and Katherine Guerin. All of them, along with Peggy Papp, joined Guerin and Fogarty in 1973 to form the Center for Family Learning in New Rochelle, New York, the other major research and training facility for Bowenian theory and methods.

The work of Philip Guerin and Fogarty, Carter, McGoldrick, and Michael Kerr (Bowen's closest long-term associate at Georgetown) has been the most extensive and influential in the field at large. Similar to the descendants of the Bateson Group, the interconnections of these individuals is of interest in studying the development of Bowenian theory. Fogarty, Guerin, and Kerr were all psychiatric residents in the Georgetown program. Kerr remained at Georgetown as Bowen's closest associate and his theoretical contributions have been reflective of that close collaboration. Fogarty, although influenced by Bowen, was less wedded to the multigenerational model and most of his contributions to the theory have been confined to the nuclear family and the individual. Guerin adhered more closely to Bowen's emphasis on the importance of family of origin work than Fogarty, but was also influenced by Fogarty and the Einstein faculty, particularly Andrew Ferber and Albert Scheflen. Guerin's most important contributions to family theory are clarifications and elaborations of the concepts of both Bowen and Fogarty, as well as the specific application of the theory to the building of clinical models for the treatment of marital conflict and child- and adolescent-centered families. Carter and McGoldrick were trained by Guerin during his tenure as director of training at Einstein. As third generation descendants, Carter and McGoldrick have contributed to family theory in the areas of the family life cycle, as well as around the issues of ethnicity and feminism.

Fogarty and Guerin

Thomas Fogarty, like Bowen, began his work with a focus on the individual. Unlike Bowen, he paid more attention to the development of structural concepts and their clinical usefulness in therapy. Fogarty's concept of the individual is a highly structural one, which he termed the four-dimensional self, including the lateral dimension, the vertical dimension, the depth dimension, and the dimension of time (Fogarty, 1976a). The lateral dimension represented the interactive part of the individual, where movement toward and away from others is formed and operationalized. It is within this dimension that Fogarty developed his most widely known contribution, the notion of repetitive patterns of pursuit and distance with the corresponding concept of the emotional pursuer and the emotional distancer in the marital relationship.

Closely connected to the lateral dimension was the depth dimension wherein, Fogarty (1984) hypothesized, was stored the residue of an individual's emotions accumulated over time as a by-product of relationship experiences. He proposed a link of significant influence between this depth dimension and the lateral dimension of the individual. Of additional importance in this depth dimension is Fogarty's later focus on the importance of the existential state of emptiness to the process of developing an autonomous self. This intense feeling-level experience is the ultimate experience of the depth dimension.

The vertical dimension contained the occupational and professional potential and actualization of productivity of an individual. The time dimension had to do with the individual's experience of time, the way in times of stress he or she tended to develop future anxiety or ruminate on the failures and misfortunes of the past. In addition, the time dimension contained a person's basic rhythm and was linked to the lateral dimension's pursuit and distance. For example, an emotional pursuer's rhythm was observed to be erratic, varying between high speeds and dead stop, while the emotional distancer was observed to have a much more constant or steady rhythm.

Fogarty's goal in working with this structural model of the individual was to produce a functional emotional balance. The individual should be "centered," that is, in touch with and regulating the appropriate balance among each of the four dimensions of self in his or her life. For example, he or she should not be preoccupied with productivity and irresponsible in personal relationships. Drawing on this concept, Fogarty was the first to describe the relationship dance of emotional pursuit and distance in the marital relationship. This concept, more than any other of Fogarty's, has been incorporated into the work of most practicing family therapists.

Fogarty (1976b) also contributed extensively to the development of the concept of triangulation. Again, unlike Bowen, Fogarty focused on the structural aspect of triangulation especially as it related to the treatment planning. He was perhaps the first to focus on the structural aspects of child-centered triangles with his strategies of altering these structures by moving overinvolved mothers away from, and distant fathers in toward, the symptomatic child. Minuchin, in his structural family therapy, brought together this same type of structural alteration of triangles and combined it with creative strategic movement around the organizing symptom of the child, such as having lunch served in a therapy session with a family in which one of the children has an eating disorder.

Philip Guerin's theoretical contributions also began with the individual. While director of training at Einstein, he formed the first formal training groups for therapists who wished to study themselves in their families of origin. In this work, he focused on the development of the concept of an individual's adaptive level of functioning in order to operationalize the more fixed, innate aspects of differentiation. He drew a distinction between the automatic emotional responses of individuals that emanate from their innate level of differentiation and those more functional responses that can be fashioned over time by conscious effort on the part of individuals within the context of their relationships. The changes brought about by these conscious efforts can be measured by improved functioning in face of significant stress, especially in the categories of productivity, more functional relationship connectedness, and personal well-being. Over long periods of time, these conscious effort changes may become automatic, thereby marking an increase in differentiation. In this way the concept of adaptive level of functioning is consistent with Bowen's concept of differentiation.

Guerin has also contributed an elaboration and further development of Fogarty's emotional pursuer and distancer concept into a paradigm termed "the interactional sequence." This sequence of behavior is central to the clinical methods entailed in his model of marital therapy (Guerin, Fay, Burden, & Kautto, 1987). In that model, as well as in his model for child- and adolescent-centered families, Guerin has proposed a typology of triangles which describes and categorizes the numerous potential triangles in any case of marital discord or child-centered dysfunction. The purpose of the typology is to foster more accurate and teachable (reproducible) methods of intervention.

Carter and McGoldrick's contributions to Bowenian theory have included an expansion of the concept of the genogram and important nodal events into a more developmental perspective. They proposed a "family life cycle" (Carter & McGoldrick, 1980) as a backdrop for understanding development of stress and its role in the production of relationship conflict and symptoms in an individual. In addition, McGoldrick, working with Pearce and Giordano, added the consideration of culture and ethnicity to the view of the "family relationship system." Carter, working with Papp, Silverstein, and Walters, focused on the importance of women's issues in the study of and clinical intervention with families.

In conclusion, it is of interest that Bowen's model consists of the multigenerational family unit as the context in which to study individuals and their relationship conflicts under the siege of intense anxiety. Fogarty and Guerin each focus on the individual, the dyad, and triangles. Kerr focuses on anxiety, and Carter and McGoldrick-Orfanidis on the impact of the contextual aspects of developmental stress, ethnicity, and feminism on the family system.

The Experientialists

Experiential family therapy is characterized by its emphasis on intuition, feelings, unconscious processes, and an atheoretical stance. The two major figures in this branch of the family therapy movement are Carl Whitaker (Whitaker & Keith, 1981) and Virginia Satir (1967). Both of them draw upon quite different epistemologies for their therapies, but they share a common set of experiential assumptions and techniques in their clinical work.

Carl Whitaker

Whitaker's approach to family therapy is pragmatic and atheoretical (to the point of being antitheoretical). He considers theory to be useful only for the beginning therapist. He believes that the real role of theory for the novice therapist is to control his or her anxiety about managing the clinical situation. Whitaker prefers to use the support of a cotherapist and a helpful supervisor to deal with these stresses rather than relying on theory.

The basic goal of therapy for Whitaker is to facilitate individual autonomy and a sense of belonging within the family. The emphasis is on the emotional experience, not conceptual understanding. Above all, the process of therapy is a very personal experience for the therapist.

Existential encounter is believed to be the most important aspect of the psychotherapeutic process for both the therapist and the family. In his own clinical interviews Whitaker's highest stated priority is to "get something out of it for myself." What he does clinically, on a fairly consistent basis, is to seize on a perception of the family's "craziness" and attempt to escalate this state of affairs to the level of the absurd. Hoffman (1981) offers a classical example of this method in her report of an interview in which Whitaker turns to a young man who has recently made a suicide gesture and says to him, "Next time you try that, you should go first class, take someone with you like your therapist." Whitaker explains this maneuver as an attempt at augmenting the pathology of the family until the symptoms disappear. Although Whitaker's contributions to the family therapy movement have been considerable (Whitaker, 1976; Whitaker, Felder, & Warkentin, 1965), his contribution to a theory of family psychotherapy has been minimal.

Virginia Satir

Virginia Satir, like Whitaker, represents a clinical method that is highly personalized, experiential, and immensely popular. Satir began her work with families in Chicago, and in 1959 came to California to join Don Jackson at MRI. There she organized what may be the first formal training program in family therapy. Although she left MRI to work at the Esalen Institute, where she further developed her humanistic experiential approach, much of her conceptual framework is based on the ideas of the Bateson Project, especially in the formulations of Jackson concerning the rules that govern relationships and the forces of family homeostasis. Satir speaks of the family as a "balanced" system and, in her assessment, seeks to determine the price individual family members pay to maintain this balance. She views symptoms as blockages to growth which help to maintain the family status quo. She is more important as a skilled clinician and teacher than as an original theorist. However, her impact on the practices of family therapists was far from minor. Indeed, she may be the most influential of all the people mentioned in this chapter.

Despite the fact that Satir did not primarily concern herself with theory, there are several basic theoretical premises that are contained in her work. First, there is a strong emphasis on individual growth stemming from positive self-esteem. Second, there is an emphasis on communication patterns among family members. Third, she addresses the rules by which the family members interact with one another, and, fourth, she emphasizes the family linkage to society.

These four aspects of family life are viewed as universal needs and forces operating in all families. In Satir's definition of healthy families, the individual member has positive self-esteem and communication is clear, emotionally honest, and direct. The family rules by which the system maintains itself are conducive to individual growth. Thus, family rules are human, flexible, and appropriate to the situation at hand. Fifth, the family does not function as a closed emotional system but is open to larger systems in society and hopeful in its outlook. As a counterpoint, Satir believes that troubled families do not foster positive self-worth; communication patterns are indirect and vague; rules are not flexible but absolute; and the family functions as a closed emotional system in a defensive and negative manner.

Satir stated her goals in family therapy: "We attempt to make three changes in the family system. First, each member of the family should be able to report congruently, completely, and obviously on what he sees and hears, feels and thinks, about himself and others, in the presence of others. Second, each person should be addressed and related to in terms of his uniqueness, so that decisions are made in terms of exploration and negotiation rather than in terms of power. Third, differentness must be openly acknowledged and used for growth" (Satir, 1972, p. 120). While conceptualizing the family by using the above theoretical premises, Satir's technique of therapy involved heavy use of herself in a direct, pragmatic, and supportive way. She described herself both as a "mirror" allowing the family to see how it was functioning and as a "teacher" suggesting ways to grow by offering specifics on how to improve self-esteem and communication patterns.

There is some suggestion that Satir may have overworked the theoretical concepts of self-esteem and communication in her attempts to account for both normal and pathological family functioning. Again, like Whitaker, her highly individual and powerful persona makes reproducibility a problem for descendant generations. On the other hand, the opportunistic view of the potential for growth in families and her dynamic teaching of many other family therapists make her a major personality in the family therapy field.

THE STRUCTURAL FAMILY THERAPY THEORISTS

As mentioned earlier in this chapter, the work of Adler (1931) and others demonstrated the influence of families on troubled children. In this section we will consider the contributions of Ackerman and Minuchin to the theory of family psychotherapy, which came from their work with dysfunctional children and adolescents.

Nathan Ackerman

A man of broad interests, Nathan Ackerman was a prolific writer on a variety of topics. Early in his medical career he published on the psychological aspects of hypertension and on the impact of the economic depression of the 1930s on coal miners' families. A psychoanalyst, he maintained his commitment to psychoanalytic thought and practice. Ackerman's belief in the primacy of analytic theory resulted in his not developing a conceptual model for the clinical work he did with families. His clinical artistry was tied to his ability to utilize psychodynamic concepts in clinical work with families.

A study of his clinical interviews on film suggests three themes in his work, consistent with his use of analytic theory: nurturance and dependency, control and anger, sexuality and aggression. These themes can be viewed as corresponding to the different stages of psychosexual development of the individual: oral, anal, and phallic. Operationalizing the oral theme, Ackerman would challenge family members on their excessive need to be fed, on their "sucking" behavior, and on their desire to be a baby. He would provoke them into expressing their anger and would openly discuss their unconscious oedipal strivings. As a clinician in a family session he quickly took charge and made contact with each family member after playfully teasing the children, flirting with the women, and challenging the men in a fairly aggressive style. He was an activist, stirring up emotion by a process he called "tickling the defenses." He believed it was healthy to let emotions out, especially to express anger openly.

Today, Nathan Ackerman's contribution to family psychiatry is experienced by many as remote, in much the same way most people experience the process in their own extended families—interesting, but irrelevant to the present.

As remote as Ackerman's contribution may seem to some, it remains relevant to the major issues in family therapy. A disciplined clinical investigator with a broad perspective, he was sensitive to the impact of the social context on families far earlier than most. His study of the families of coal miners enduring the lingering depression of the late 1930s remains a model for studying the impact of social context on the internal dynamics of the family. It raises questions still pertinent today, such as what constitutes a functional adaptation versus a maladaptation? What are the premorbid or pre-event characteristics of those who adapt well as opposed to those families who are thrown into chaos and fragmentation?

A current issue in the field of family therapy to which Ackerman contributed is the need for a typology of families. The advent of the *Diagnostic and Statistical Manual III* and the federal government's push for evaluation of clinical results are two factors that have reawakened interest in this area. In Ackerman's 1958 book *The Psychodynamics of Family Life* he presented a preliminary typology of families. The categories included were: disturbance of marital pairs; disturbance of parental pairs; disturbance of childhood; disturbance of adolescence; and psychosomatic families. A clinical typology, even one that is symptom-focused as is this one, is essential to the development of corresponding clinical methodologies, which can then be evaluated.

Hoffman (1981) offers an interesting thesis concerning the connection between Ackerman and Minuchin. She sees Ackerman as basically a structuralist in his approach to dysfunctional families. In her analysis of a transcript of one of Ackerman's cases she draws some fascinating parallels between the clinical work of the two men. Indeed, it is interesting to note that Ackerman had been Minuchin's supervisor in the latter's psychiatric training.

Salvador Minuchin

Salvador Minuchin, a child psychiatrist and psychoanalyst, began to do family therapy at the Wiltwyck School for Boys in New York in the late 1950s, in which he included the parents and siblings of the identified patients in family sessions. The staff of the Wiltwyck Project, begun in 1962, included E. H. (Dick) Auerswald, Richard Rabkin, Bernice Rossman, and Braulio Montalvo. Auerswald, who was strongly influenced by Bateson's "ecological system" ideas, brought these ideas to the Wiltwyck project. Rabkin (1970), also a psychiatrist, brought a certain irreverence for traditional theories and methods, best documented in his text *Inner and Outer Space* and in an essay entitled "Is the Unconscious Necessary?"

The Wiltwyck Project was an important experience for Minuchin, greatly enriching his developing models of family therapy. The Wiltwyck experience was followed by his tenure as Director of the Philadelphia Child Guidance Clinic to which he brought along Montalvo and Rossman, and also attracted Jay Haley, Lynn Hoffman, Peggy Papp, and Carl Whitaker.

When all of the major early contributions to family therapy are considered, Minuchin stands out for his openness to the ideas and work of others. This is perhaps best demonstrated by his 1962 tour of family therapy centers throughout the country to observe and learn what others were doing with symptomatic families.

As a practicing clinician, Minuchin's training videotapes show him to be a flamboyant and skilled operator of relationship systems, and at times outrageous, in the tradition of Ackerman and Whitaker. Minuchin differs from Ackerman and Whitaker in his conceptual framework, however, just as they differ from each other. Ackerman remained wedded to psychoanalytic theory, while Whitaker maintained the antitheoretical position that theory can be a rationalization for certain behaviors and a method for avoiding the emotional experience of the moment. Although analytically trained, Minuchin formed his model based on the family as a relationship system. This model rests heavily on the notion that most symptoms, whether they present as a dysfunction in an individual (such as anorexia) or as a conflict in a relationship, are a by-product of structural failings within the family organization.

The conceptual model begins with the notion that the family is normally determined by structure, function, boundaries between subsystems, and degrees of functional attachment among individuals. The family, as defined by Minuchin, is the nuclear family or household. Minuchin would include the grandparental generation into his observational lens only when the grandparent was a part of the household. His description of the family system as a whole relates to the degree to which a family structure demonstrates appropriate boundaries. Those families with dysfunctional structures are grouped into two categories. "Enmeshed" is the term used for those families characterized by overly permeable or absent boundaries, and the term "disengaged" is used for families with rigid boundaries between individuals that do not allow enough flexibility of response or sufficient relationship attachment. The "structure" of structural family therapy can be best understood by a consideration of the concept of boundaries and triangles or "conflict detouring triads" as triangles have at times been termed within this model.

Minuchin's concept of boundaries calls for clearly demonstrated "membranes" among the various subsystems within the family organization. The family monitor or gatekeeper, so designated by appropriate function and position of power, decides what member or members of the family may pass through these membranes and when they may do so. For example, the father might be designated as the gatekeeper of the membrane or boundary surrounding the marital relationship, and the oldest sibling might be viewed as the appropriate gatekeeper for the sibling subsystem. Developmental issues are also a part of these boundary decisions. This is most clearly evident in the therapeutic importance given to establishing and maintaining the privacy of an adolescent's room.

The structural therapist maps out weaknesses in the boundaries of family organization and plans direct interventions as remedies to this problem. For example, in a child-centered family in which the parents expend most of their time and emotional energy on the kids, the structural therapist, very early in the therapy, might suggest that the parents retire to their room by 9:30 p.m. three evenings a week, keeping the door closed until at least 11:30 p.m. and that once a month they go away by themselves. In a similar way, an adolescent might be given permission to close the door of her bedroom for two hours every evening. These interventions make explicit therapist-perceived boundary problems and allow the relationship and individual process linked to them to surface.

In his classic text, *Families and Family Therapy* (1974), Minuchin relies heavily on the construct of relationship triangles both to track the pathological relationship process in the family and to provide the rationale for various structural interventions. In a later text, *Psychosomatic Families* (Minuchin, Rosman, & Baker, 1978), based on his work with the families of children suffering from either asthma, diabetes, or anorexia, Minuchin proposed a typology of triangles in these families. In this typology he has designated two types of what he terms "conflict detouring triads: detouring attacking or detouring supportive."

In the detouring attacking triads, the parents are joined together in agreement over what is wrong with their child's behavior. Both parents are angry with the child and they take turns in criticizing the behavior. However, the fact that each of them usually has a different idea of how to fix the problem may drive them into conflict with each other. In the "detouring supportive" structure both parents join together in mutual concern over a child with emotional or psychosomatic problems. Rather than attacking their child, they are almost overly concerned and supportive in their efforts to alleviate the situation for him.

It is evident in Minuchin's case reports that there is a consistent application of principles based on a theory of family structure and organization. These principles include

(a) The importance of the therapist relating to the power distribution within the family system and the hierarchical structure of that system. For example, his first move in a therapy session is often to connect with the father as the gatekeeper to the family system. At times he will even ask explicit permission of the father to talk to the other family members present in the room.

(b) An assessment of the generational boundaries and the dysfunctional structure of the intergenerational triangles. This is demonstrated by the way Minuchin fashions his interventions around boundary problems and around alterations in the structure of a central symptomatic triangle.

Minuchin's model was a major breakthrough in the history of family therapy. His video training tapes demonstrated the systemic aspects of clinical problems formerly thought of as residing within the individual. In addition, these same tapes demonstrated relief of the symptoms over time. The impact of Minuchin's model was to turn the attention of the mental health movement toward the developing field of family therapy. One of the most admirable aspects of Minuchin's work has been the ability to make his conceptual ideas and clinical methodologies effective with an underprivileged population.

COMMENT ON BEHAVIORAL FAMILY THERAPY

Behavioral therapists have a long history of applying their behavioral principles to a variety of problems that occur within the family. However, the major part of this work has occurred outside the mainstream of the family systems therapy movement. Family system therapists, for the most part, left the established theoretical groups with which they were originally associated to form their own informal, and later formal, organizations. These organizations were committed to the development of new theoretical formulations of family functioning. On the other hand, behavioral family therapists tended to maintain their identification with organizations wedded to established behavioral theory. This was mostly due to their commitment to established behavioral theory.

However, there have been some noteworthy efforts by behaviorists to deal more fully with the problems of the family system. Jacobson and Margolin (1979) in their marital therapy work have developed a view of reinforcement that is both circular and reciprocal. An example is the following: A wife asks her husband for more time together, the husband is not so inclined and does not respond. The wife begins to become angry and demanding, and the husband says, "There is no way I'm going to spend time with you when you act like such a shrew." This only serves to increase the wife's anger and behavioral tirade. Finally, in exhaustion the husband gives in, saying, "Okay—if you just stop we will go out somewhere to eat."

In this sequence the wife has been reinforced for throwing the tirade and the husband has been reinforced for giving in to the wife's negative behavior by her stopping her tirade after he agrees to go out. In their model each marital partner's behavior is both being affected by and influencing the other. Thus, this model maintains the centrality of behavior modification by intervening to alter the reinforcement contingencies, while at the same time attempting to deal with a relationship focus by focusing on how both spouses participate in the process of reinforcement.

Gordon and Davidson (1981) in their work with behavioral parent training acknowledge the importance of a broad-based model of assessment. This broad-based model includes factors in the family system which may potentially interfere with behavioral parent training such as marital conflict. They even go so far as to state, "In certain situations, successful treatment of these other family difficulties may obviate the need for any further treatment (of the child)" (p. 521). The "broad-based model" of assessment extends the potential focus of treatment to other areas of the family system. However, the theory used to conceptualize and treat the problems of the child remains embedded in individual behavioral psychology.

Stuart (1980) in his behavioral marital therapy makes a point of including some efforts to improve the general communication skills of the couple. The attempt to improve communication skill is over and beyond his attempts to modify specific behaviors in the relationship. Liberman (1972) acknowledges the importance of the therapeutic relationship over and above the specific behavioral techniques: "Without the positive therapeutic alliance between the therapist and those he is helping, there can be little or no successful intervention" (p. 332).

Thus, as behavior therapists attempt to deal with the complex problems of families, they are not only modifying their procedures but are attempting to incorporate systems principles. To date, however, a real difference continues to exist between the underlying theory of behavioral family therapy and family systems therapy.

SUMMARY OF THE YEARS 1950–1990

Due to restrictions of length, the significant contributions of a number of prominent family therapists have not been included in this chapter. We have attempted to present the work of those investigators who have been most focused on the development of a conceptual framework for family psychotherapy. Forty years into its life-cycle, the family therapy movement has not yet developed a single comprehensive integrated theory. Three major models have been developed and emphasized in this chapter: the strategic, the multigenerational (Bowen), and the structural (Minuchin) approaches. Each of these models has its strengths as well as its weaknesses. The strategic model, although it clearly demonstrates the power of context and *the magic* of paradox and reframing, fails to offer a consideration of the internal developmental struggles of the individual. Therefore, it overvalues context in much the same way that a theory of the individual undervalues it.

The multigenerational models of Bowen and his descendants represent the most consistent effort at developing a broad-based theory of family psychotherapy, including their attention to the development of individual autonomy. However, Bowenian models become somewhat murky in attempts to define and describe differentiation and triangulation. In addition, their clinical techniques can become overly ritualized and constricted.

The structural model of Minuchin is the clearest and most easily understood among the three models. However, it is much more a model for doing therapy than an attempt at developing a comprehensive theory of family psychotherapy. In addition, although it is eminently teachable and reproducible, it is almost entirely a method for working with child-focused families. It offers little assistance for working with the problems of relationship conflict between adults and/or working with an individual.

One of the most important questions for the future of the family therapy movement is what will happen as the old guard of pioneers moves on and a new generation steps forward. How much of an attempt will be made to elaborate further some or all of the concepts developed in the first 40 years? If family theory is to continue to develop as the conceptual basis of a comprehensive model for understanding the individual's emotional functioning in relationship context, several eventualities must occur. There must be a sophistication and refinement of the characteristics of functional compared with dysfunctional relationship systems, a systemic model of the individual including a continuum linking his or her "inner and outer space," and a model for tracking dyadic interaction and triangle formation. The goal of these refined family concepts and models would be the development of an integrated system of interventions that would enhance the ability of a therapist to steer relationship process toward better functioning both for individuals and for the family systems as a whole. If this is not forthcoming, family psychotherapy may become more like group therapy —a clinical modality to be used at specific times in response to specific clinical indications in conjunction with, or in lieu of, traditional psychodynamically based individual therapy.

MOST RECENT DEVELOPMENTS

In the 1990s, family therapy has continued to move away from the development and refinement of a formal comprehensive theory and has moved toward the formulation of a more broad-based, eclectic, symptom-oriented approach. Previously, we have mentioned how the cultural demands of the 1980s insisted upon less complicated explanations of psychiatric symptoms and less labor-intensive, shorter-term methods of intervention. In the 1990s, this trend joined the revolution in medical and psychological services with the forces backing managed care. This combination of forces at times appears to threaten the very existence of psychotherapy as we have known it. It also provides a pervasive climate that makes debates on the validity of theoretical positions fade to the background.

Marriage and family therapists as a group have been recognized more for the development of creative models of intervention than for rigorous research, clearly documented treatment protocols, or outcome studies. However, this is changing, as demonstrated by an entire issue of the *Journal of Marital and Family Therapy* (Sprenkle, 1995) devoted to outcome studies. Of particular interest is a study by McFarlane (1994) evaluating the importance of family psychoeducation and the support of multiple family groups, which were found to be more effective than family therapy with individual families alone or psychopharmacotherapy alone.

"Uncovering" Versus "Containment" Models

For decades, models that did not foster the uncovering of underlying pathology and traumatic experiences were undervalued, while those that fostered an intensive search for affect-block and metaphorical meaning were deemed the desired pathway to optimal emotional functioning and creative expression. Today, with the demand for brief treatment and symptom relief, containment becomes an essential ingredient of most treatment protocols; as in general medical practice, symptom relief is increasingly the focus of intervention, whereas attempts to consider in depth the underlying pathophysiological mechanisms recede in the face of heavy clinical caseloads.

In recent years, general medicine has given considerable effort to shifting its focus away from pathology and toward a proactive quest for programs that foster wellness and health education in the service of prevention. Psychiatry has not been without its efforts in these areas. Schizophrenia and depression, for example, have been impacted by a combination of drug therapy and psychoeducation. However, in psychiatry—and in family psychiatry in particular—there are at least two significant problems that arise from these methods. The first is that although family psychoeducation for serious mental illness points to the biological component of these disorders, helping to alleviate inappropriate family guilt, these new methods do not address the family system and other environmental factors that may be triggering or maintaining the symptoms. A potentially negative effect from this family psychoeducation model may be the absence of even an attempt to raise the functioning level of the surrounding relationship system. In theory at least, failure to address system factors will increase morbidity in the symptomatic individual over time and increase the potential for symptomatic development in other vulnerable family members. Decades of clinical observation give this concern some credibility, but only appropriate validation through research will document its importance.

The Changing of the Guard

In the past few years, the "family systems movement," which had been the driving force in family psychiatry, has suffered a loss of momentum and a fragmentation of purpose. Developmentally, these phenomena were predictable, given the passing of the movement's pioneers. Jackson, Ackerman, Satir, Bowen, and Whitaker are all deceased; Haley and Minuchin are retired. The schools of family therapy that represented their work continue their efforts in somewhat less dramatic form than was seen earlier in their history.

In the presence of this vacuum, newer forces are beginning to take the theory and practice of family psychotherapy in divergent directions. Senior clinicians in the field, with the possible exception of Bowenians, have focused more and more on the development of an integrated, eclectic version of family therapy that borrows from each of the aforementioned schools. Thus, some therapists working with individuals may borrow Bowenian concepts of differentiation, fusion, or multigenerational transmission process, and they may also use the experiential–humanistic concepts of communication clarity and symbolic representations from inner to outer reality. Those family therapists who remain inclined toward a psychodynamic orientation borrow the concepts of attachment, introjects, projective identification, roles, interlocking pathology, and family themes and loyalties from object relations theory and the work of Ivan Nagy. More eclectic models borrow concepts and techniques more randomly and have an expanded definition of what constitutes a "family," and put considerable effort into expanding the concept of "normality."

In the midst of these developments, there still have been some efforts at defining sets of theoretical assumptions linked to a particular clinical methodology. Selekman (1993), for instance, listed seven assumptions that family therapists make as a basis for their interventions in solution-oriented therapy:

1. *Resistance is not a useful concept.* Clients want change, and the therapist should join with the family in its efforts at change.
2. *Change is inevitable.* The problem is to be viewed optimistically, and the therapy emphasizes possible solutions to the problems.
3. *Only a small change is necessary.* Therapy should proceed in a fashion that links one small change to another.
4. *Clients have the strengths and resources to change.* Therapy emphasizes a health perspective.

5. *Problems are unsuccessful attempts to resolve difficulties.* Families need new consultation to get unstuck from old attempts at problem solving.
6. *You don't need to know a great deal about the problem in order to solve it.* Understanding why the problem initially began is not necessary to finding a solution to the current problem.
7. *Multiple perspectives.* There is no one way to view the problem. There is no one solution to the problem.

We agree with others who have indicated that the field of family therapy in recent times has been preoccupied with organization, expansion, and integration rather than direct development of established or new theoretical concepts. Goldenberg and Goldenberg (1996) in the latest edition of their textbook proposed that the 1990s are a time of integration and eclecticism. Periods marked by efforts at integration and eclecticism have tended to focus more on the application of concepts to diverse models of clinical care rather than on further development and refinement of basic theoretical positions. The formation of the family division of the American Psychological Association is an excellent demonstration of this point. Formed in 1984, the first 11 years of its work culminated in the publication of the volume *Integrating Family Therapy: Handbook of Family Psychotherapy and Systems Theory* (Mikesell, Lusterman, & McDaniel, 1995). This text vividly demonstrates the movement of family systems and family therapy away from the specialized schools and into a division of the general field of psychology.

Although in some ways the work of this group of psychologists has been consistent in assumption and principle with the Bowen, Haley, and Minuchin approaches of the past, its theoretical position has a much broader base than did the position of the original family therapists. General systems theory is proposed as its basic underpinning. Mikesell et al. (1995) defined their perspective as a shift in thinking designed to "move beyond the reductionistic and mechanistic tradition in science that focused on cause and effect equation" (p. xiv). They went further than Goolishan and Anderson when defining their model of systems therapy as "a comprehensive set of interventions for treating the family, including individuals, couples, nuclear families, families of origin, medical systems, and other larger contexts" (p. xv). Of special note is their assumption that work with individuals as well as couples and families is carried out from a systems perspective. This notion is certainly not a new one. Bowenians and Eriksonians have used their brand of systems on individuals for many years.

Their text also attempted to address issues of language and technique, gender and ethnicity, life cycle development, and variations of traditional and nontraditional family structure, as well as problems of research and assessment. They combined a consideration of these issues with clinical application of their approaches to therapy with couples, individuals, and larger organizational systems. Their text may well mark a major developmental shift in the field of family therapy, systems theory, and systems therapy much in the way Boszormenyi-Nagy and Framo's (1965) edited volume *Intensive Family Therapy* did more than 30 years ago.

Research Contributions

As evidenced by these developments, family therapy has moved into the graduate schools of major universities, thereby usurping to some degree what had been the educational territory of free-standing family institutes. As the graduate school faculties took more interest in the family perspective, a corresponding increase in research took place, which in turn fostered the beginnings of outcome studies in the field of family therapy.

These research efforts are now beginning to make an important contribution both to the validation of established core systems theory concepts and to the introduction of new concepts. Most theories that are born from clinical observation and practice and that become accepted as clinically useful eventually receive more formal research evaluation. Some modification and understanding of core concepts have come about as a result of this increase in formal research efforts. For example, research with Olson's concept of cohesion has indicated that families at different developmental points need different levels of cohesion (even to the level of enmeshment) to be functional at different times in their life cycle. In somewhat related fashion, Anderson and Sabatelli (1992) have found good results with their scale of differentiation that is defined as interpersonal only and not combined with the intrapsychic as defined by Bowen. Research with Minuchin's concept of family structure (hierarchy) has offered mixed results. Unfortunately, the clinical and economic pressures noted earlier have discouraged further research examining the validity of key theoretical concepts, and contemporary research has become more exclusively concerned with assessing outcome. Although important, these studies have been concerned with the question of symptom removal in response to a particular method of therapy rather than with finding a way of also measuring the interventional impact on the level of functioning of the family as a unit. These approaches do not help us to test the validity of a fundamental theoretical tenet of family systems, namely that symptoms in an individual or dyadic relationship are in some way related to family pathology.

That is to say, if outcome studies tell us only whether a symptom was removed but do not tell us how a family's functioning was improved, no stockpiling of evidence occurs to support the hypothesized relationship between family dysfunction and individual or relationship symptoms. This overemphasis on specific behavioral outcome seems to be echoing a distinction made by Hazelrigg, Cooper, and Borduin (1987) between "pragmatic" therapies that are "principally concerned with behavioral outcomes" and "aesthetic" therapies that "arise from phenomenological, psychodynamic, existential, and systems perspective." Today's climate seems to favor pragmatic therapies to the detriment of theoretical development. Although family therapy should not be theory driven only, the contribution that could be made by good research remains underdeveloped. The outcome studies potentially represent only the first wave of research in a field that has long avoided putting itself to the test.

Research on Normal Family Functioning

Closely linked to the increased attention being paid to outcome studies is a predictable corresponding interest in normalcy. In other words, just what is considered a functional family? For some time now, there have been a number of programmatic efforts in family research that have used proposed models of family functioning to direct their research efforts. Although the original concepts in these models have been both theoretically and empirically determined, the amount of empirical data generated from these models is helpful in further conceptualizing family systems. Three of the more developed research models of family functioning are (a) Olson's Circumplex Model (Olson, Russell, & Sprenkle, 1989), (b) Beavers' Systems Model (Beavers & Hampson, 1990), and (c) The McMaster Model (Epstein, Bishop, Ryan, Miller, & Keitner, 1993).

Olson's Circumplex Model involves two orthogonal dimensions of family functioning: cohesion (emotional bonding of the family members to one another) and adaptability (ability to permit change in rules, roles, and power structure). **Beavers' Systems Model** involves five dimensions: (a) structure of the family, (b) mythology (congruence of family's self-concept with reality), (c) goal-directed negotiations, (d) autonomy, and (e) affect. The **McMaster Model** measures family functioning in six areas: (a) family problem solving, (b) family communication, (c) family roles, (d) affective responsiveness, (e) affective involvement, and (f) behavioral control. These six dimensions of functioning are assessed in three areas: (a) basic task area (daily living), (b) developmental task area (changes over time), and (c) hazardous task area (crisis).

When comparing the dimensions of these models to the theoretical concepts developed by the charismatic pioneers in family therapy mentioned earlier in this chapter, one can see many basic similarities. The original concepts of fusion, differentiation, communication, structure, roles, and affect continue to be well represented. However, it is important to note that although these models may use family concepts, they may not apply these concepts in a systemic manner. That is, they may not employ nonlinear causality.

In addition to these contextual developments in the fields of psychiatry and psychology in general and family therapy in particular, it is important to consider those clinical models that have risen to prominence over the past 3 to 5 years. Nichols and Schwartz (1994), in the third edition of their text *Family Concepts and Methods*, highlighted what they have called the "emergent models" of the 1990s. Their list includes five models: (a) the solution-focused model, (b) the collaborative–conversational model, (c) the deconstruction model, (d) the internal family systems model, and (e) the psychoeducational and family therapy models. Nichols and Schwartz have credited Steve de Shazer, William O'Hanlon, and Michelle Weiner-Davis for the **solution-focused model**. Tracing its roots to the "soil of strategic therapy," Nichols and Schwartz saw this method as having evolved from the influence of the Palo Alto group's Brief Therapy Project at the Mental Research Institute (MRI). The model focuses on behavior and combines reframing and process questions with shifting perception from the negative to the positive. In some ways, it may represent family therapy's version of cognitive therapy insofar as the therapeutic process aims to remove the anxiety-driven distortions of perception and to shift the perception of the problem from a negative framing to a positive proactive perspective, thereby providing the necessary conditions for functional change.

The **collaborative–conversational model** was developed by Harlene Anderson and the late Henry Goolishan and their followers. The commonality between this perspective and the previously described solution-focused approach is a belief in the power of the "narrative metaphor"; their differences lie in the ways they make use of language. The solution-focused therapists use a relatively standardized set of techniques and attempt to manipulate language to act on the family in the service of change. The collaborative–conversational model leaves the language and the process flow more to the family. In a way, this method is reminiscent of the 1970s, when Carl Whitaker and Andrew Ferber challenged therapists to abandon "dummy-expert" models of therapy and develop more collaborative models in which family and therapist come together in a joint effort at healing. The collaborative–conversational model revives this challenge and attempts to get therapist and family into an "egalitarian partnership" by the use of "empathetic conversation." As a group, they downplay the development of "techniques." This can be problematic for others when they try to improve the reproducibility of the method. However, this group of clinicians, who are in many ways like the experientialists of old, appear to believe that if the therapist embraces the core concept and believes that what happens in the interactional space of the therapeutic and family relationships is what counts, then empathy, listening, and validation will lead the way to the desired change.

In the early days of family therapy, a polarity was supposed to exist between the "lone wolf," cognitive, theory-based Bowenians and the "all together now" experientialists led by Whitaker, Ferber, and their colleagues. The collaborative–conversational clinicians offer their own version of this polarity between the mechanics of the structural–strategic–oriented approaches and their own methods.

The **deconstruction model** is credited to Michael White (White & Epston, 1990), an Australian family therapist. In his clinical work, White has appeared uninterested in what causes peoples' problems. Rather, he has focused on the effect these problems have on individuals and their families and how the therapist can empower them to overcome "the oppression" of their "negative lives." In doing this work, White has used two main techniques. The first technique is the development of a new narrative story in which the therapist helps the family members fashion a more functional and more hopeful story line for their lives. The second technique centers on the externalization of the problem outside of the individual and the family in a way that makes the *problem* the external common enemy. In this way, the family as a group can join forces and become empowered to change. Again, this approach uses concepts and techniques that are reminiscent of cognitive therapy and group therapy in combination with the narrative techniques employed by Twelve-Step programs, especially Alcoholics Anonymous.

A focus on the individual as well as on the relationship system is highlighted by Richard Schwartz's (1995) development of an **internal family systems (IFS) model**. This model creates a map of intrapsychic space occupied by subpersonalities that relate to each other and continue to behave in many of the same ways as the component parts of a family system. For example, at times the subpersonalities form dysfunctional coalitions that can paralyze functional movement in the individual, just as family members align with each other and perpetuate dysfunction in individual members of the family and in the family systems at large.

The fifth emergent model is the **psychoeducational approach** to the treatment of emotional dysfunction. The history of this method goes back at least to the early 1970s. At that time, the Center for Family Learning (CFL), funded by a federal grant from the National Institute of Alcohol and Alcohol Abuse, conducted multiple family groups for family members at risk for abusing alcohol. Philip Guerin, Eileen Pendagast, and Randy Sherman, beginning with the family sculpting work of Peggy Papp, created a psychoeducational model called Family Systems Training (FST), using a classroom format with families from the community. FST taught families the principles of family systems theory and how families function emotionally. This program targeted families with a history of alcohol abuse. In the same period, at Albert Einstein College of Medicine, Christian Beels, Jane Ferber, and William McFarlane were formulating a psychoeducation multifamily group approach for schizophrenics and their families.

The difference between these efforts was that the CFL program was a primary prevention model that attempted to teach family systems principles to those families at risk for alcohol abuse as determined by cultural background and family history. The Einstein program, on the other hand, was a tertiary prevention program created to teach families with a schizophrenic member about the phenomenon of schizophrenia. It aimed to help them cope with the emotional fallout of the disease and to relieve them of misplaced guilt that they had caused the schizophrenia in their family member. In addition, it attempted to educate the family members in very specific ways about how to relate to the schizophrenic member in order to promote better functioning in that person and prevent the exacerbation of symptoms that would require rehospitalization. This latter model is consistent with methods that took hold in the early 1980s and have continued to develop from that time in various centers throughout the country. Of special note is the work of Carol Anderson at the University of Pittsburgh and that of Michael Goldstein at UCLA. William McFarlane, a member of the original Einstein group and now at Maine Medical Center, has demonstrated the effectiveness of this model with his previously mentioned outcome study. It showed that multiple family psychoeducation groups for schizophrenics and their families are more effective than medication alone in preventing rehospitalization and more effective than a combination treatment of medication and family sessions with their individual families.

We believe that all theory, whether relying on the elaboration of the "subjective" or the refinement of the "objective," represents a series of abstractions brought to bear on a naturally occurring process. The differences between the traditional objectivists and the postmodern constructivists or subjectivists lie in their basic assumptions and corresponding clinical methods. Nonetheless, they are still describing the same phenomenon. Years of clinical experience in psychiatry and psychology have taught us the importance of matching clinical intervention to the patient, that is, choosing a treatment based on how well it fits the patient's problem and the patient's ability to make use of it. In a similar way, a theory or clinical paradigm should match the philosophical beliefs of a particular professional and the therapist's natural clinical talents. In this way, the integration between the human instrument of the clinician and his or her conceptual base and clinical methodology is possible. It does not matter whether a clinician is subjective, objective, or somewhere in between in philosophical orientation. What matters is the clinical results obtained by the model in use.

For example, the early pioneers believed schizophrenia to be a psychosocial phenomenon. Jay Haley, a participant in the formulation of the concept of the "double bind," continues to hold steadfastly to this perspective. Murray Bowen would certainly continue to view schizophrenia as "more psychological than biological." Today, however, the dominant clinical view of schizophrenia defines it as a biological abnormality with its origins most likely rooted in the dopamine receptors of the neurosynapse. Psychopharmacological intervention coupled with psychoeducation done in multiple family groups is the treatment of choice. Family members are seen as the victims of "fallout" from schizophrenia rather than as the perpetuators of psychological pathology.

From our view, the question arises: Does one of these perspectives have to be right and the other wrong? Perhaps in the future we will reach a point where direct measurement of the impact of transgenerational stress on the neurosynapse will be possible. This could lead to an ability to measure how much developmental and situational stress, with its corresponding effect on relationships, is necessary to bring about the changes at the neurosynapse that result in the clinical expression of a genetic vulnerability. The purpose of considering this futuristic scenario is to reflect for a moment on the importance of continuing to work from multiple perspectives. Such effort keeps the evolutionary wheel of creative theoretical abstraction and the integration of multiple methods of clinical intervention turning.

In addition to the current multiple family groups used in the treatment of schizophrenia, work with children and their families continues to be refined. Many years ago, the frustration of therapists in child guidance clinics at the "undoing" of their work with the child by the child's family was another primary driving force in the development of family systems therapy. Creative work continues on this staple of family therapy, the child-centered family. Of note is Ellen Wachtel's (1994) attempt to devise an integrated model for working with children and their families. Her theoretical position was based both in psychodynamic theory and family systems theory, with attention as well to the concrete behavioral aspects of the child's difficulties. She has placed great emphasis on treating the multifaceted family system while not losing perspective on the particular needs and characteristics of the individual child. Focus on the importance of keeping the child's internal developmental struggle as part of the model is not surprising, given the author's dual background in family therapy and psychodynamic approaches and her earlier work with her husband Paul Wachtel on a psychodynamic view of the individual adult from a family perspective (Wachtel & Wachtel, 1986).

CONCLUSION

This chapter has attempted to trace the chaotic evolution of family systems theory, which began with a singular focus in psychodynamic theory and has since traveled many divergent pathways in 40 years of development. It is in this very diversity that the strength of family systems theory resides. In a way almost reflective of paradox, family systems theory—noted for its diversity and fragmentation—offers perhaps the most effective organizing matrix for the field of psychiatry in general and psychotherapy in particular in that it attempts to integrate newer developments from multiple perspectives.

The basic multigenerational genogram, which many family therapists of differing theoretical perspectives are already creating as the first step in approaching a family, provides the hierarchy and the structure through which relationship process in the present and over time can be studied. Structural and strategic interventions and techniques are easily introduced on the basis of the view of the family thereby achieved. Narrative stories that find and develop a family's strength can join psychodynamic and cognitive–behavioral techniques and psychopharmacological intervention on an individual level. Family systems theory allows for an integration of all of these conceptualizations, techniques, and interventions to be brought to bear in varying ways to do battle with schizophrenia, anxiety, depression, and disorders of children and adolescents, as well as the multiple types of relationship conflict that present themselves clinically in a variety of forms.

It is our hope that these recent developments will bring family systems theory more into the mainstream and foster research, concept validation, and outcome studies. It is our hope that this can happen without stifling the creative forces from the past and that it will continue to feed the future development of the family therapy perspective.

REFERENCES

Ackerman, N. (1937). The family as a social and emotional unit. *Bulletin of the Kansas Mental Hygiene Society.*

Ackerman, N. (1958). *The psychodynamics of family life.* New York: Basic Books.

Adler, A. (1931). *Guiding the child.* New York: Greenberg.

Anderson, S. A., & Sabatelli, R. M. (1992). The differentiation in the Family System Scale: DIFS. *American Journal of Family Therapy, 20*(1), 77–89.

Bateson, G., Jackson, D., Haley, J., & Weakland, J. (1956). Toward a theory of schizophrenia. *Behavioral Science, 1*, 251–264.

Beavers, W. R., & Hampson, R. B. (1990). *Successful families: Assessment and intervention.* New York: Norton.

Bell, J. E. (1961). *Family group therapy* (Public Health Monograph No. 64). Washington, DC: U.S. Government Printing Office.

Bell, J. E. (1975). *Family therapy.* New York: Jason Aronson.

Boszormenyi-Nagy, I., & Framo, J. (Eds.). (1965). *Intensive family therapy: Theoretical and practical aspects.* New York: Harper & Row.

Boszormenyi-Nagy, I., & Spark, G. (1973). *Invisible loyalties: Reciprocity in intergenerational family therapy.* New York: Harper & Row.

Bowen, M. (1966). The use of family theory in clinical practice. *Comprehensive Psychiatry, 7*, 345–374.

Bowen, M. (1972). On the differentiation of self. In J. Framo (Ed.), *Family interaction: A dialogue between family researchers and family therapists* (pp. 111–173). New York: Springer.

Bowen, M. (1976). Theory in the practice of psychotherapy. In P. Guerin (Ed.), *Family therapy: Theory and practice* (pp. 42–90). New York: Gardner Press.

Bowen, M. (1978). *Family therapy in clinical practice.* New York: Aronson.

Carter, E. A., & McGoldrick, M. (1980). *The family life cycle: A framework for family therapy.* New York: Gardner Press.

Epstein, N. B., Bishop, D., Ryan, C., Miller, I., & Keitner, G. (1993). The McMaster Model: View of healthy family functioning. In F. Walsh (Ed.), *Normal family processes* (2nd ed., pp. 138–160). New York: Guilford Press.

Fogarty, T. F. (1976a). Systems concepts and the dimensions of self. In P. J. Guerin (Ed.), *Family therapy: Theory and practice* (pp. 144–153). New York: Gardner Press.

Fogarty, T. F. (1976b). Marital crisis. In P. J. Guerin (Ed.), *Family therapy: Theory and practice.* New York: Gardner Press.

Fogarty, T. F. (1984). The individual and the family. In E. Pendagast (Ed.), *Compendium II: The best of the family (1978–1983)* (pp. 71–77). New Rochelle, NY: Center for Family Learning.

Freud, S. (1959). Analysis of a phobia in a five-year-old boy. *Collected papers, Vol. III.* New York: Basic Books. (Original work published 1909)

Goldenberg, I., & Goldenberg, H. (1985). *Family therapy: An overview* (rev. ed.). Monterey, CA: Brooks/Cole.

Goldenberg, I., & Goldenberg, H. (1996). *Family therapy: An overview* (4th ed.). Pacific Grove, CA: Brooks/Cole.

Gordon, S., & Davidson, N. (1981). Behavioral parent training. In A. Gurman and D. Kniskern (Eds.), *Handbook of family therapy* (pp. 517–555). New York: Brunner/Mazel.

Guerin, P. (1976). Family therapy: The first twenty-five years. In P. Guerin (Ed.), *Family therapy: Theory and practice* (pp. 2–23). New York: Gardner Press.

Guerin, P. (1979). System, system, who's got the system? In E. Pendagast (Ed.), *Compendium I: The best of the family, 1973–1978* (pp. 9–16). New Rochelle, NY: Center for Family Learning.

Guerin, P., Fay, L., Burden, S., & Kautto, J. (1987). *The evaluation and treatment of marital conflict: A four stage approach.* New York: Basic Books.

Haley, J. (1976). *Problem solving therapy.* San Francisco: Jossey-Bass.

Haley, J. (1984). *Ordeal therapy.* San Francisco: Jossey-Bass.

Hazelrigg, M. D., Cooper, H. M., & Borduin, C. M. (1987). Evaluating the effectiveness of family therapies: An integrative review and analysis. *Psychological Bulletin, 101*, 428–442.

Hoffman, L. (1981). *Foundations of family therapy.* New York: Basic Books.

Jackson, D. D., & Weakland, J. H. (1961). Conjoint family therapy. *Psychiatry*, *24*, 30–45.

Jacobson, N., & Margolin, G. (1979). *Marital therapy: Strategies based on social learning and behavioral exchange principles.* New York: Brunner/Mazel.

Kaslow, F. (1980). History of family therapy in the United States. *Marriage and Family Review*, *3*, 77–111.

Lederer, W., & Jackson, D. (1968). *The mirages of marriage.* New York: Norton.

Liberman, R. P. (1972). Behavioral approaches to family and couple therapy. In C. J. Sager and H. S. Kaplan (Eds.), *Progress in group and family therapy* (pp. 329–345). New York: Brunner/Mazel.

McFarlane, W. R. (1994). Multiple-family groups and psychoeducation in the treatment of schizophrenia. In A. B. Hatfield (Ed.), *Family interventions in mental illness* (pp. 13–22). San Francisco: Jossey-Bass.

Mikesell, R. H., Lusterman, D.-D., & McDaniel, S. H. (1995). *Integrating family therapy: Handbook of family psychology and systems theory.* Washington, DC: American Psychological Association.

Minuchin, S. (1974). *Families and family therapy.* Cambridge, MA: Harvard University Press.

Minuchin, S. (1987). My Many Voices. In J. Zeig (Ed.), *The evolution of psychotherapy* (pp. 5–14). New York: Brunner/Mazel.

Minuchin, S., Rosman, B., & Baker, L. (1978). *Psychosomatic families: Anorexia nervosa in context.* Cambridge, MA: Harvard University Press.

Nichols, M. (1984). *Family therapy: Concepts and methods.* New York: Gardner Press.

Nichols, M. P., & Schwartz, R. C. (1994). *Family therapy: Concepts and methods* (3rd ed.). Needham Heights, MA: Allyn & Bacon.

Olson, D. H., Russell, C. S., & Sprenkle, D. H. (Eds.). (1989). *Circumplex model: Systemic assessment and treatment of families.* New York: Haworth Press.

Rabkin, R. (1970). *Inner and outer space.* New York: Norton.

Ruesh, J., and Bateson, G. (Eds.). (1951). *Communication: The social matrix of psychiatry.* New York: Norton.

Satir, V. (1967). *Conjoint family therapy.* Palo Alto: Science and Behavior Books.

Satir, V. (1972). *Peoplemaking.* Palo Alto: Science and Behavior Books.

Schwartz, R. C. (1995). *Internal family systems therapy.* New York: Guilford Press.

Selekman, M. D. (1993). Solution-oriented brief therapy with difficult adolescents. In S. Friedman (Ed.), *The new language of change: Constructive collaboration in psychotherapy* (pp. 138–157). New York: Guilford Press.

Sprenkle, D. (Ed.). (1995). *Journal of Marital and Family Therapy*, *21*(4).

Stuart, R. (1980). *Helping couples change.* New York: Guilford Press.

Wachtel, E. F. (1994). *Treating troubled children and their families.* New York: Guilford Press.

Wachtel, E. F., & Wachtel, P. L. (1986). *Family dynamics and individual psychotherapy*. New York: Guilford Press.

Watzlawick, P., Beavin, J., & Jackson, D. (1967). *Pragmatics of human communication*. New York: Norton.

Watzlawick, P., Weakland, J., & Fisch, R. (1974). *Change: Principles of problem formation and problem resolution*. New York: Norton.

Whitaker, C. (1976). The hindrance of theory in clinical work. In P. J. Guerin (Ed.), *Family therapy: Theory and practice*. New York: Gardner Press.

Whitaker, C., Felder, R., & Warkentin, J. (1965). Countertransference in the family treatment of schizophrenia. In I. Boszormenyi-Nagy and J. Framo (Eds.), *Intensive family therapy* (pp. 323–342). New York: Harper & Row.

Whitaker, C., & Keith, D. (1981). Symbolic experiential family therapy. In A. Gurman and D. Kniskern (Eds.), *Handbook of family therapy* (pp. 187–225). New York: Brunner/Mazel.

White, M., & Epston, D. (1990). *Narrative means to therapeutic ends*. New York: Norton.

Whitehead, A. N., & Russell, B. (1910). *Principia Mathematica*. Cambridge, England: Cambridge University Press.

6

INTEGRATIVE THEORIES OF THERAPY

HAL ARKOWITZ

There are many contradictions in the field of psychotherapy. On the one hand, a large number of psychotherapists have a strong commitment to a particular psychotherapy approach. On the other hand, there is little evidence that any of the over 400 different psychotherapy approaches (Karasu, 1986) is more effective than another (e.g., Beckham, 1990; Elkin et al., 1989; Lambert, Shapiro, & Bergin, 1986; Sloane, Staples, Cristol, Yorkston, & Whipple, 1975; Smith, Glass, & Miller, 1980; Stiles, Shapiro, & Elliott, 1986).

Another contradiction exists as well. On the one hand, societies, institutes, centers, and journals devoted to particular therapy approaches dominate the field of psychotherapy. On the other hand, the majority of practicing therapists do not identify themselves as adhering to one particular approach, but instead refer to themselves as "eclectic" or "integrative" (Garfield & Kurtz, 1976; Norcross & Prochaska, 1983, 1988).

In part, the emergence of the field of *psychotherapy integration* has been

This chapter is a revised and expanded version of "Integrative Theories of Therapy," by H. Arkowitz, 1992, in *History of Psychotherapy: A Century of Change* (pp. 261–303), edited by D. K. Freedheim, Washington, DC: American Psychological Association.

I would like to express my appreciation to Stanley Messer and Paul Wachtel for their helpful comments on an earlier draft of this chapter.

a response to these contradictions. Psychotherapy integration has had a long history, but it was not until the late 1970s that it crystallized into a strong and coherent force on the psychotherapy scene. It is characterized by a dissatisfaction with single-school approaches and a concomitant desire to look across and beyond school boundaries to see what can be learned from other ways of thinking about psychotherapy and change.

Other chapters in this book document the evolution of the major schools of psychotherapy. Proponents of each school share certain fundamental assumptions about human nature, psychopathology, psychotherapy, and change. Along with the growth of each of these approaches, another development was occurring, albeit more quietly and steadily. Over the past 60 years, a number of writers have attempted to examine various ways to cross school boundaries, integrate theories and techniques from two or more approaches, or suggest factors that the different therapies have in common. Often, they were not aware of the work of others who proposed somewhat different integrations nor aware that they were part of a growing movement in which integration was the defining theme.

Beginning around 1980, interest in psychotherapy integration grew dramatically. In this chapter, I will discuss what psychotherapy integration is, the historical context from which it emerged, and the factors that shaped its development. Further, I will consider what impact integrative thinking has already had on the field of psychotherapy, as well as some of the potentials it holds for the future.

WHAT IS PSYCHOTHERAPY INTEGRATION?

In some respects, it is easier to define what psychotherapy integration *is not* rather than what it *is*. Psychotherapy integration is not an adherence to one particular approach to psychotherapy. In the single-school approach, the therapist believes in the theory on which the approach is based, uses the techniques and strategies associated with it, and may conduct research on hypotheses derived from that theory.

Psychotherapy integration includes various attempts to look beyond the confines of single-school approaches in order to see what can be learned from other perspectives. It is characterized by an openness to various ways of integrating diverse theories and techniques.

This description may sound suspiciously like what has been called "eclecticism." The term eclecticism has been used to denote a largely pragmatic approach in which the therapist uses whatever techniques he or she believes are likely to be effective, with little or no underlying theory to guide these choices. By contrast, the integrative approaches of today all attempt to build some coherent framework for understanding or predicting change and for determining the choices of therapy procedures.

Presently, there are three main directions that characterize the field of psychotherapy integration (Arkowitz, 1989). They are (1) theoretical integration; (2) common factors; and (3) technical eclecticism. All are guided by the general assumption that we have much to learn by looking beyond the boundaries of single approaches. However, they do so in rather different ways. In *theoretical integration*, two or more therapies are integrated in the hope that the result will be better than the individual therapies on which they were based. As the name implies, there is an emphasis on integrating the underlying theories of psychotherapy (what London, 1986, has so eloquently labelled "theory smushing") along with the integration of therapy techniques from each (what London has called "technique melding"). The various proposals to integrate psychoanalytic and behavioral approaches best illustrate this direction, most notably the work of Paul Wachtel (1977, 1987). Other writers have focused on different integrations (e.g., Appelbaum, 1976; Feldman & Pinsof, 1982; Greenberg & Safran, 1987; Gurman, 1981; Lebow, 1984; Segraves, 1982; Thoresen, 1973; Wachtel & Wachtel, 1986; and Wandersman, Poppen, & Ricks, 1976).

The *common factors* approach attempts to look across different therapies to search for elements that they may share in common. This view is based on the belief that these factors may be at least as important in accounting for therapy outcome as the unique factors that differentiate among them. The common factors identified may then become the basis for more parsimonious theory and technique. Frank (1961, 1982) and Goldfried (1980, 1991) have been among the most important contributors to this approach.

Technical eclecticism is considerably less theoretical than either theoretical integration or the common factors approach. Technical eclectics seek to improve our ability to select the best treatment for the person and problem. This search is guided primarily by data on what has worked best for others in the past with similar problems and similar characteristics. In contrast to theoretical integration and common factors, technical eclecticism pays significantly less attention to why these techniques work and instead focuses on predicting for whom they will work. The foundation for technical eclecticism is primarily actuarial rather than theoretical. The work of Beutler (1983), Beutler and Clarkin (1990), and Lazarus (1976, 1981) are illustrations of this form of integration.

PSYCHOTHERAPY INTEGRATION: A HISTORY OF IDEAS

In this section, I will trace the history of each of these three trends in psychotherapy integration. The review focuses on selected proposals exemplifying each integrative direction. These are presented in sufficient detail to give the reader a sense of the ideas involved. More comprehensive histories of the entire field of psychotherapy integration can be found in Goldfried & Newman (1986) and of theoretical integration in Arkowitz (1984).

Theoretical Integration

Early History

The history of theoretical integration is largely the history of attempts to combine psychoanalytic and behavioral approaches to psychotherapy. Several early writers attempted to demonstrate that concepts from psychoanalysis could be translated into the language of learning theory (e.g., French, 1933; Kubie, 1934; Sears, 1944; Shoben, 1949). With these notable exceptions, the 1930s and 1940s were mainly characterized by growth and development within psychoanalytic and behavioral approaches respectively, with relatively few attempts to relate them.

A significant event in the history of theoretical integration occurred in 1950 with the publication of Dollard and Miller's book, *Personality and Psychotherapy: An Analysis in Terms of Learning, Thinking, and Culture*. This book went far beyond its usual description as a simple attempt to translate psychoanalytic concepts into behavioral language. In fact, it was far more than that. It was an attempt to synthesize and integrate ideas about neurosis and psychotherapy from these two perspectives in order to provide a unifying theory for the field. In the opening, Dollard and Miller wrote:

> The ultimate goal is to combine the vitality of psychoanalysis, the rigor of the natural science laboratory, and the facts of culture. We believe that a psychology of this kind should occupy a fundamental position in the social sciences and humanities—making it unnecessary for each of them to invent its own special assumptions about human nature and personality. (p. 3)

What they achieved was no less than an integrative theory of neurotic behavior based on anxiety and conflict and new suggestions for psychotherapy that grew out of their integration. It is true that some of their work is an attempt to translate the concepts of psychoanalysis into the language of learning theory (e.g., they attempted to explain the pleasure principle in terms of reinforcement and repression in terms of the inhibition of cue-producing responses that mediate thinking). However, they also presented a rather sophisticated formulation of the dynamics of conflict and anxiety in neurosis, drawing from concepts in both learning theory and psychoanalysis. They also suggested procedures for overcoming repression and proposed the use of modeling, self-control strategies, and homework assignments in therapy. Many of these techniques have since been "rediscovered" and are now a basic part of several modern-day therapies.

Although their theory of anxiety and conflict caught the attention of researchers in learning (see review by Heilizer, 1977), their integration did not have very much direct influence on the field of psychotherapy. Its influence has been more indirect, serving as a reminder of the possibility and potentials of integration during times when integrative thinking was not a part of the zeitgeist. Now that psychotherapy integration is more established as a field, perhaps their work will be rediscovered as it deserves to be.

The work of Dollard and Miller still stands as one of the most comprehensive and ambitious attempts to integrate these two seemingly diverse approaches. However, the time was not right for this integration, in part because of the nature of the behavioral approach of the time. There was a considerable body of learning theory and learning research, but there was not yet much of a behavior *therapy* with which to integrate psychoanalytic therapy. Thus, Dollard and Miller were only able to attempt to integrate what was there—a learning *theory* with a psychoanalytic theory *and* therapy.

Behavior therapy emerged during the 20 years following the publication of Dollard and Miller's book. This period was one in which behavior therapists offered definitions of their approach that emphasized its differences from psychoanalytic theory and therapy (e.g., Eysenck, 1960; Wolpe & Rachman, 1960). The strident tone of many of these papers probably contributed to an antagonism between the two approaches that may have discouraged any further attempts at integration during this time. Of those who did raise the possibility of integration, most answered in the negative. The title of a paper by Levis (1970), a behavior therapist, illustrates this: "Integration of Behavior Therapy and Dynamic Psychiatry: A Marriage With a High Probability of Ending in Divorce."

Through much of the 1960s and early 1970s, behavior therapists were actively defining and expanding the scope of behavior theory and therapy. Again, the time was not right for behavior therapists to consider an integration with the very approach they sought to replace.

Another factor contributing to the relative lack of interest in integration during this period was that early behavior therapy was distinctly noncognitive, if not anticognitive (e.g., Wolpe, 1958). This made any potential links to the highly cognitive psychoanalytic approach even more difficult.

Despite these constraints, there remained a small but steady stream of writers from both sides who continued to explore a behavioral-psychodynamic integration. From the analytic side, Franz Alexander (1963) wrote that much of what happens in psychotherapy could best be understood in terms of learning theory, especially the principles of reward and punishment. Weitzman (1967) took an important step toward integration when he presented a cognitive and psychoanalytic interpretation of systematic desensitization, pointing the way not only to convergences but also to how psychoanalytic free association and imaginal desensitization might be integrated into a unified clinical approach. He argued that "dynamically rich material," typically ignored by behavior therapists, was produced and could be utilized during the course of systematic desensitization. Weitzman's proposal was one of the first that pointed to integration at the level of therapy techniques.

During this time, some behavior therapists also expressed interest in integration (e.g., London, 1964; Marks & Gelder, 1966), but others like Bandura (1969) remained highly critical of psychoanalytic approaches and showed no interest in integration. London (1964) characterized most existing therapies as oriented primarily toward either insight or action. He argued that action therapies were more successful in the treatment of symptoms but that they mostly ignored thinking as a means of controlling human behavior. He suggested that a system that attempts to integrate insight and action might be more effective for a wider variety of problems than one emphasizing only one of these approaches. London's book was widely cited and was one of the earliest and most eloquent statements calling for a broad integration between very different therapy approaches. The second edition of his book (London, 1986) also remains influential in the field.

The end of the 1960s was marked by the appearance of a unique paper reflecting the observations of several prominent psychoanalytically oriented therapists (Klein, Dittman, Parloff, & Gill, 1969), who reported their conclusions after a week of observing the clinical work of prominent behavior therapists. The authors suggested that the relationship in behavior therapy and the general clinical skills of the behavior therapist were important factors that were ignored in the writings on behavior therapy. Although they did not advocate an integration, they did argue against the development of behavior therapy as a "closed system of treatment" and thought that behavioral approaches did have a contribution to make in psychotherapy.

Increasing Interest in the 1970s

In the 1970s, interest in a behavioral–psychoanalytic integration showed signs of acceleration, increasing specificity, and greater comprehensiveness. In 1972, Feather and Rhoads (1972a, 1972b; Rhoads & Feather, 1972) published a series of papers describing their "psychodynamic behavior therapy." In one illustration of their approach, systematic desensitization was applied to hypothesized underlying psychodynamic themes and fantasies. A summary of these and other related clinical integrations is available in Rhoads (1984). Birk (1970) and Birk and Brinkley-Birk (1974) also presented several clinical illustrations demonstrating how insight-oriented therapies might enhance behavior change and how behavior change could, in turn, facilitate cognitive changes. All of these papers were important in illustrating the clinical feasibility of the integration of behavioral and psychoanalytic techniques. The case illustrations and under-lying rationales were also important in facilitating the later emergence of more specific proposals for a psychodynamic–behavioral integration. The appearance of this work and others (e.g., N. E. Murray, 1976; Silverman, 1974; P. L. Wachtel, 1975, 1977) pointed to a noticeable increase in the interest in psychodynamic–behavioral integration during this period.

Some important trends in both psychoanalytic and behavioral ther-apies during the 1970s may have contributed to the increased interest in integration. Messer (1986) pointed out that a number of changes in psy-choanalytic theory and therapy were occurring during this time that made an integration with behavior therapy more feasible. These included a greater emphasis on goal-setting and treatment focus (e.g., Malan, 1976); greater attention to the actual effects of events on people's lives (Shengold, 1979); more attention to people's adaptive efforts to deal with those events (Blanck & Blanck, 1976; Langs, 1976); and greater emphasis on patient responsibility for their feelings and actions (e.g., Appelbaum, 1982; Schafer, 1983).

Important trends in behavior therapy during this time also allowed more room for the possibility of integration. By this time, behavior therapy had firmly established its identity and made a significant impact on the field of psychotherapy. There was now an expanded social learning theory (Bandura, 1969, 1977; Mischel, 1973) and a body of behavior therapy techniques to consider for integration with psychoanalytic approaches. During this time, behavior therapy was beginning to incorporate cognitive mediating constructs (e.g., Bandura, 1969) and even cognitively oriented techniques (Mahoney, 1974; Meichenbaum, 1977). Thus, as behavior ther-apy became somewhat more cognitive, there was an even greater potential for exploring integration with psychoanalytic therapies that so strongly emphasized the exploration of mental content (Gill, 1984).

Wachtel's Proposal for Psychodynamic–Behavioral Integration

In 1977, P. L. Wachtel published his book *Psychoanalysis and Behavior Therapy: Toward an Integration*. It remains the most comprehensive and successful attempt to integrate behavioral and psychodynamic approaches and one of the most influential books in the entire field of psychotherapy integration. Wachtel did his graduate work at Yale when both Dollard and Miller were on the faculty. In fact, Dollard was one of his first therapy supervisors. Wachtel (1987) notes that he was quite impressed with their attempt to build a theoretical bridge between the concepts of psychoanal-ysis and learning theory.

Wachtel (1977) noted that any attempt to integrate behavioral and psychoanalytic approaches needs to appreciate the diversity within both and must be specific about the components of such an integration. Which behavior therapy and which psychoanalytic therapy shall be integrated? Some may be more compatible than others. For example, orthodox Freudian psychoanalysis and operant behavioral therapies are probably so incompatible that an integration between the two is unlikely. By contrast, Wachtel pursued an integration that incorporated a behavior therapy emphasizing anxiety reduction and changes in interpersonal behavior with interpersonal psychoanalytic approaches (e.g., those of Erikson, Horney, and Sullivan) that emphasized the current interpersonal context of the individual and encouraged greater therapist activity than many other psychoanalytic approaches.

Wachtel's goal was to build a framework that could incorporate selected elements of interpersonal psychodynamic approaches and behavioral approaches. It is important to note that his goal was not a fixed superordinate theory (or therapy) that would be a hybrid of two sub-approaches. Instead, Wachtel sought to include what he believed were some of the virtues of both in an evolving framework that could incorporate elements of each in a logical and internally consistent way, benefiting from what he saw as their complementary strengths (Wachtel, 1984). This framework, which might change with further developments in each field, could show how concepts from each of the therapies interacted with each other in ways that might suggest new theory for understanding the causes of psychopathology and new clinical strategies for change. From the psychodynamic perspective, he emphasized unconscious processes and conflict and the importance of meanings and fantasies that influenced our interactions with the world. From the behavioral side, the elements included the use of active-intervention techniques, a concern with the environmental context of behavior, a focus on the patient's goals in therapy, and a respect for empirical evidence (P. L. Wachtel, 1977, 1987).

In understanding the origins of psychopathology, Wachtel paid considerable attention to the importance of early experience. He adopted the psychoanalytic view that ways of feeling, acting, and behaving that reflect unresolved conflicts will persist into our later life, continuing to influence us even outside of our awareness. Had he stopped here, he would have remained a primarily psychodynamic theorist. However, based on learning and interpersonal orientations, he also saw the importance of present interpersonal influences. He wrote:

> Thus, from this perspective, the early pattern persists, not in spite of changing conditions but because the person's pattern of experiencing and interacting with others tends continually to recreate the old conditions again and again. (Wachtel, 1977, pp. 52–53)

In this view, our past experiences skew our present environment and often lead us to create the very conditions that perpetuate our problems in a kind of vicious circle. For example, the people we choose and the relationships we form may confirm the dysfunctional views that we carry forward from our past and that are at the heart of many of our problems. Wachtel later called this approach "cyclical psychodynamics" (1987). The view of causality in this theory is circular and reciprocal, rather than the linear causal views of behavioral and psychoanalytic theories.

Wachtel also explored the implications of this integration for the practice of psychotherapy. It follows from cyclical psychodynamic theory that intervening into the factors currently maintaining the problem will be an important aid to change. In addition, active behavioral interventions may also serve as a source of new insights (P. L. Wachtel, 1975), and insights can promote changes in behavior (P. L. Wachtel, 1982), with the two working synergistically. In some respects, the most important achievement of Wachtel's book for psychotherapy integration was his demonstration that an integrative framework was possible. The challenge of psychotherapy integration was now a comprehensive and concrete proposal. This allowed the debate about the merits of integration to move beyond broad polemics and to focus on substantive issues. In this sense, Wachtel's work served as a catalyst to the entire field of psychotherapy integration, as well as constituting a significant achievement in its own right.

The achievement and challenge of Wachtel's integration was acknowledged by the contributors to a book edited by Arkowitz and Messer (1984) entitled *Psychoanalytic Therapy and Behavior Therapy: Is Integration Possible?* In it, prominent representatives of behavioral, psychodynamic, and integrative points of view addressed the possibilities and problems of a psychodynamic–behavioral integration. While the contributors raised many provocative issues, the most basic ones that cut across the chapters concerned questions about the *units* and *forms* of an integration.

Schacht (1984) suggested that different writers have often referred to theoretical integration at different levels or units of analysis. For example, integrations have been addressed to theories, techniques, assumptions about human nature, methods of verification, or combinations of these. Schacht suggested that some of the conflict and confusion that characterized previous discussions may have resulted from ambiguity about the units and levels that were being discussed.

Gill (1984) distinguished among psychodynamic therapy, psychoanalytic therapy, and psychoanalysis, and he characterized them as having increasing emphases on examination of mental processes and analysis of the transference. He acknowledged "that psychodynamic and behavioral theories of intervention can be combined is no longer in question. They can be and are being combined" (1984, p. 180). However, he suggested that integration becomes less possible and less desirable as we move toward psychoanalytic therapy and psychoanalysis because the techniques and approaches necessary for exploration and analysis of the transference are antithetical to the active intervention techniques of behavior therapy. Thus, the issue of the form of psychoanalytic therapy or the units to be integrated was relevant for Gill as well.

Franks (1984) also believed that some kind of integration at the clinical level was possible, although he believed that it would not advance practice in any significant ways. His strongest conclusion was that an integration at the conceptual or theoretical level was neither possible nor desirable. He argued that the two approaches differed in basic ways involving what constitutes acceptable evidence, the methods of verification, the goals of change, and how outcome should be evaluated.

Other contributors also concluded that some form of integration between psychoanalytic and behavioral approaches was possible, but they questioned whether it was desirable (e.g., Kazdin, 1984; Mahoney, 1984). Still others presented further critiques or proposals for integration (Mahoney, 1974; Mendelsohn & Silverman, 1984; Rhoads, 1984).

Messer and Winokur (1984) discussed the underlying views of human nature in the two approaches. They characterized the behavioral approach as oriented toward the external world of reality, in which conflict resulted from situations in which people found themselves, and that conflict could be eliminated by action. By contrast, they characterized psychoanalytic views as incorporating the inevitability and centrality of internal conflict, the limits that an individual's early history places on the extent of possible change, and emphasis on contradiction and ambiguity in the process of therapy. They pointed to how these different visions are important not only at an abstract philosophical level but also at a more concrete clinical level where they may determine how we act at various choice points in therapy (Messer, 1986). Nonetheless, Messer and Winokur did not entirely rule out the possibility of some form of integration. In later work by Messer (Lazarus & Messer, 1991), he seems to have moved cautiously toward what he has called assimilative integration in which "techniques and concepts from one therapy do indeed find their way into another and get incorporated within its slowly evolving theory and mode of practice" (p. 153).

Contributors also raised questions about the forms or models integration may take. Schacht (1984) saw the most elementary one as a simple *translation* of concepts. In a *complementary model*, each approach is seen as appropriate for dealing with different problems in the same patient (e.g., systematic desensitization for a phobia and psychoanalytic therapy for identity problems). A third model is a *synergistic* one in which the two therapies may be applied to the same problem and are expected to interact in the patient to produce clinical results superior to what might be obtained by either therapy alone. The techniques of each therapy remain unchanged, but the locus of their integration lies in their effects on the patient. In the *emergent* model, the different therapies merge to produce a novel hybrid approach with new characteristics not contained by either therapy alone. This is exemplified by Feather and Rhoads' (1972a, 1972b) psychodynamic behavior therapy involving the application of desensitization to inferred underlying fantasies and conflicts. Finally, according to Schacht, the most challenging level is *theoretical integration* in which there is an integration of theories and metapsychologies, with the hope for an emergent model of human behavior. Wachtel's work best illustrates this approach.

In his chapter, Wachtel (1984) addressed criticisms of integration. He made the point that many of the arguments have focused on how psychoanalytic and behavioral approaches are different. However, he argued that it is precisely because of these differences that integration was proposed in the first place. The goal of the integration was to incorporate some of the different strengths and contributions of each. By carefully selecting which elements of each theory to incorporate and by creating a new framework to fit them together, he argued, a coherent synthesis can be achieved even if, taken as a whole, the two separate theories are quite different.

Recent Developments

The debate about integration was now dealing with important and substantive issues in psychotherapy theory and practice. Interest in a psychodynamic–behavioral integration has continued to grow and remains a strong force in psychotherapy integration. Published in the 1980s were three books that reprinted classic papers relating to theoretical integration (Marmor & Woods, 1980; Goldfried, 1982a; Wachtel, 1987). It seemed that there was interest in reading and rereading earlier contributions, now that they could be understood in the context of a growing body of thought on psychotherapy integration. A number of books and papers appeared during the 1980s that continued to develop clinical strategies and debate issues relating to psychodynamic–behavioral integration (Arkowitz, 1985, 1989; Beutler, 1989; Fensterheim, 1983; Fitzpatrick & Weber, 1989; Lazarus & Messer, 1988, 1991; Papajohn, 1982; Rhoads, 1984; Segraves, 1982; Wachtel, 1977, 1987, 1991; Wachtel & Wachtel, 1986; Wolfe, 1989).

The spirit of lively debate has also continued with the appearance of several series of articles in different journals reflecting the controversy that theoretical integration had sparked, as well as psychotherapy integration more broadly. These appeared in clinical psychology, counseling, and psychiatry journals, both within and outside of the United States. The journals included *Behavior Therapy* (Garfield, 1982; Goldfried, 1982b; Kendall, 1982; Wachtel, 1982); the *British Journal of Clinical Psychology* (Davis, 1983; Messer, 1983; E. J. Murray, 1983; Wachtel, 1983; Yates, 1983); the *British Journal of Guidance and Counselling* (Beitman, 1989; Dryden & Norcross, 1989; Lazarus, 1989; Messer, 1989; Norcross & Grencavage, 1989); and *Psychiatric Annals* (Babcock, 1988; Birk, 1988; London & Palmer, 1988; Powell, 1988; Rhoads, 1988). In addition, a major article on psychotherapy integration appeared in the *American Journal of Psychiatry* (Beitman, Goldfried, & Norcross, 1989). The National Institute of Mental Health sponsored a workshop on research in psychotherapy integration (Wolfe & Goldfried, 1988) in which theoretical integration was extensively discussed. In addition, theoretical integration was reviewed prominently in the recent *Annual Review of Psychology* chapter on individual psychotherapy (Goldfried, Greenberg, & Marmar, 1990).

There has also been some interest in theoretical integration other than the psychodynamic–behavioral. Some papers have discussed the possibility of an integration between humanistic and behavioral therapies (e.g., Thoresen, 1973; Wandersman et al., 1976). In addition, a number of writers from the family therapy area have been exploring various clinical and theoretical integrations between family/systems therapies and others (e.g., Feldman & Pinsof, 1982; Gurman, 1981; Lebow, 1984; Pinsof, 1983; Segraves, 1982; Wachtel & Wachtel, 1986). There has also been a small but growing literature on incorporating interpersonal factors into an integrative model (e.g., Andrews, 1991a, 1991b; Safran & Segal, 1990).

New Directions in Theoretical Integration

Clearly, theoretical integration is having an impact on thinking and practice in the field of psychotherapy. Yet, there is a potential contradiction to the integration of two or more approaches to psychotherapy: The integration of today may become the single-school approach of tomorrow. Such a scenario suggests visions of Institutes for Integrative Psychotherapy and certification of integrative therapists. Is this what theoretical integration is about? I believe not. Such a path takes us full circle back to where we started.

It is important to keep Wachtel's original vision in mind. He sought an "evolving framework" for integration rather than a fixed integration of one approach with another. What does the concept of an evolving framework imply? This question may hold the key to one of the most important new directions for psychodynamic–behavioral integration and theoretical integration more broadly. I believe that we may be moving toward what Schwartz (1991) and others have described as an "open system" model that not only consists of the interaction of its existing components, but also allows for new elements to be introduced and old ones to exit. There is some internal cohesiveness to the system—not all elements can enter readily into it. Some elements fit more readily into the existing system than others. Other elements either are unable to enter into the system or must change in order to do so. In addition, a change in one element of the system potentially changes the entire system.

For example, a psychodynamic–behavioral integration may be an overall framework that encourages attempts to introduce a number of different elements from an evolving behavior therapy and to introduce them at different times, to see how they interact with elements that are also introduced from an evolving body of psychodynamic theory and therapy. Different elements can be introduced and different resulting systems can be explored. This view of integration is quite different from a fixed synthesis of two static entities. The open system framework is one which can generate different models at different times that may lead to new theories, new variations of clinical therapy, and new research.

There has been a trend in recent theory in psychotherapy toward a framework even broader than a psychodynamic–behavioral one which seeks to integrate cognitive, affective, behavioral, and interpersonal aspects of human functioning (e.g., Andrews, 1991b; Beckham, 1990; Goldfried & Safran, 1986; Greenberg & Safran, 1987, 1989; Horowitz, 1988, 1991a; Safran & Segal, 1990; Schwartz, 1991). Some are even questioning a sharp distinction among these response systems, suggesting that such a distinction may be artificial (e.g., Schwartz, 1984, 1991). A recent paper by Beckham illustrates this trend. After reviewing the outcome research on depression, Beckham (1990) suggested that:

> Depression may be viewed as a homeostatic system to the extent that it involves many different components of a patient's life and consists of feedback loops of reciprocal maintaining processes between those components. According to this model the effect of a psychotherapy in altering one element of the depressive homeostasis quickly spreads to other elements in the depressive system. (Beckham, 1990, p. 211)

He further suggested that the elements in this homeostasis are cognitive, affective, interpersonal, and biological. Further, Beckham argued that different therapies for depression may be equally effective because they all disturb this homeostatic balance by intervening through one part of the system (cognitive, affective, interpersonal or behavioral, or biological). Others have also presented integrative systems proposals as a basis for theoretical integration (e.g., Schwartz, 1984, 1991).

This broader systemic framework for psychotherapy integration parallels the interest in similar views in other areas of psychology (e.g., Izard, Kagan, & Zajonc, 1983; Schwartz, 1984). This type of theory holds a great deal of promise for a more comprehensive framework for theoretical integration.

Evaluation of Theoretical Integration

It is clear that a great deal of work in theoretical integration has already been done, but much work remains. Theoretical integration has led us to question and challenge the assumptions of the single-school approach. It has presented the field with new proposals for theory and practice. However, it has not yet led to any new research. Well-controlled outcome studies of integrative therapies have not yet been conducted so we do not yet know if their promise of greater effectiveness is real. Further, the new theory development has not been accompanied by experiments to test hypotheses about psychopathology and change derived from these theories. Part of the problem is that integrative theories have not yet led to clear hypotheses that are identifiably different from those derived from the separate theories that entered into the integration. More recent integrative proposals dealing with the interactions among cognition, affect, and behavior hold considerable promise for new hypotheses and new research because of the close connections that these views have to basic research, theory, and measurement in other areas of psychology.

At the level of practice, a large number of therapists identify themselves as practicing some type of theoretical integration (Norcross & Prochaska, 1982). However, this endorsement probably does not convey much specific information about their practice. The term *theoretical integration* suggests an overall framework rather than the endorsement of a specific integrative theory and specific therapy techniques.

Common Factors

The common factors approach has been a search for the basic ingredients that different therapies may share. Whereas theoretical integration emphasizes the integration of *differences*, the common factors approach seeks to abstract *similarities* across different therapies.[1] These similarities may be at the level of theory or clinical practice. Those persons interested in common factors believe that apparent differences in theoretical constructs or clinical techniques are more superficial than real and may mask some basic underlying similarities. Implicit in the common factors approach has been the promise that identification of common factors can help us build not only better theories of change but more effective therapies as well.

One of the guiding themes in the search for common factors is the view that all reasonable therapies are equally effective. Until around 1970, this was simply an unconfirmed belief. After this time, a large number of well-controlled comparative outcome studies appeared whose results were also consistent with this conclusion (see Beckham, 1990; Elkin et al., 1989; Lambert, 1986; Lambert et al., 1986; Sloane et al., 1975; Smith et al., 1980; Stiles et al., 1986).

How can the identification of what is already there create something better than what we started with? The concept of bootstrapping may be

---

[1]It should be noted that theoretical integration *does* seek commonalities among different approaches to some degree. Without such common ground, theoretical integration would be impossible. However, the strongest emphasis in theoretical integration is in integrating different components from different approaches into a unified framework.

useful here. The dictionary defines *bootstrapping* as a procedure that creates something better without external aid. In statistical terms, bootstrapping tries to improve our ability to predict by reducing the bias and measurement error that are associated with each of the individual predictors (see example by Dawes, 1971). In the case of psychotherapy integration, those individual predictors are the different therapies. The bias and measurement errors relate to those sources of error uniquely associated with each therapy which may obscure the "true" factors that may be the causal agents for change in all therapies.

Crucial to the bootstrapping process is the relation of the identified factors to some important criterion. One goal of the common factors approach is to discover the profile of factors *that are most strongly associated with positive therapeutic outcome*. Once identified, such factors may be used as starting points for the development of improved theories and therapies. It is even conceivable that such bootstrapping can yield a weighting of different factors for different clinical problems.

Early History

In many ways, the history of the common factors approach parallels that of theoretical integration. Early proposals appeared as far back as the 1930s. During the next 40 years, occasional and isolated publications on the topic appeared. There was a rapid growth in the number of publications in the late 1970s and thereafter.

One of the earliest papers on common factors was by Rosenzweig (1936). In it, he pointed to several factors that he believed might account for the effectiveness of different therapies. These included the therapist's ability to inspire hope, the importance of providing the patient with alternative and more plausible ways of viewing the self and the world. Alexander and French (1946) coined the term "corrective emotional experience" for what they believed was a central process of change in psychotherapy. They wrote:

> In all forms of etiological psychotherapy, the basic therapeutic principle is the same: To re-expose the patient, under more favorable circumstances, to emotional situations which he could not handle in the past. The patient, in order to be helped, must undergo a corrective emotional experience suitable to repair the traumatic influence of previous experiences. (p. 66)

The corrective emotional experience involves a relationship different from ones expected or experienced in the past. This basic concept has remained a central one in more recent formulations (e.g., Arkowitz & Hannah, 1989; Brady et al., 1980; Frank, 1961, 1982; Strupp, 1973).

Results from a series of studies by Fiedler (1950a, 1950b) also focused on the relationship as a source of common factors in psychotherapy and provide a fascinating, although indirect, examination of some of these factors. Fiedler asked therapists of different experience levels and orientations to describe what they considered to be the components of the ideal therapeutic relationship. He found that expert therapists of different schools agreed more with each other than they did with novices from their own school. In a companion study using ratings of actual therapy sessions, Fiedler found a similar pattern of findings using actual ratings of the therapy sessions. The experts from different schools were more similar to each other than to novices within their own school in the characteristics of the relationship they actually developed with their clients. Although Fiedler did not examine the outcome of these therapies, his results provide some indirect support for the common factors notion by suggesting that experience may shape therapists to behave in some basically similar ways, at least with respect to the type of relationship they establish.

Certainly, one of the most influential early writings on common factors was a book by Jerome Frank (1961) titled *Persuasion and Healing*. Frank argued that psychotherapy was an influencing process and that we may learn about what accounts for change by looking at other influencing processes. He examined basic similarities among psychotherapy, placebo effects in medicine, brainwashing, and faith-healing in our own culture and in others. Based upon his review, he suggested that some of the basic ingredients in all psychotherapies include arousing hope, causing emotional arousal, encouraging changed activity outside of the session, and encouraging new ways of understanding oneself and one's problems through interpretations and corrective emotional experiences.

In a book with a title as provocative as its content, Schofield (1964) raised the issue as *Psychotherapy: The Purchase of Friendship*. He discussed a number of possible common factors in different psychotherapies but stressed the importance of relationship factors. He suggested that therapists, as representatives of their culture, provide to their patients "acceptance in our culture in this time" (1964, p. 109), and in this sense they provide a very special, perhaps ideal, form of friendship.

Carl Rogers (1951, 1957) indirectly contributed to the common factors theme by proposing that therapy was effective not because of specific techniques but because it provided a particular type of human relationship in which change could occur. Truax and his associates (e.g., Truax & Mitchell, 1971) elaborated on some of these ideas and pointed to the importance of warmth, empathy, and unconditional positive regard in the outcome of therapy.

In 1966, an unusual book by Goldstein, Heller, and Sechrest (1966) appeared. These authors conceptualized psychotherapy as a persuasion process and looked to the social psychological literature on attitude change and persuasion to see what can be learned of benefit to psychotherapy. They reviewed literature from social psychology on such topics as the attractiveness, credibility, and status of the persuader; the distance between the two positions; and expectancies. Their fascinating journey from psychotherapy to social psychology led them to make concrete suggestions about ways to increase the amount of attitude change in psychotherapy. Their book was one of the earliest attempts to conceptualize psychotherapy as an influence and persuasion process and to draw on social psychology for concepts and ideas for techniques. Perhaps because these authors, as well as Frank, saw psychotherapy as a process of persuasion, they clashed with the trends in psychotherapy of that time that were antithetical to the idea of direct influence and active intervention.

The 1960s and 1970s yielded several other discussions of common factors (e.g., Garfield, 1973; Goldstein, 1962; Hobbs, 1962), but overall, there was little published on the topic. Raimy (1975) suggested that all forms of psychotherapy were directed toward changing misconceptions about the self by presenting the person with evidence to challenge these misperceptions. He suggested that therapies differed only on the methods used to present this challenging evidence. Raimy pointed to the importance of changing beliefs and schemas in virtually all psychotherapies. This emphasis on changing schemas was at the heart of Beck's cognitive therapy and has also received attention in the later common factors literature (Arkowitz & Hannah, 1989; Goldfried & Robins, 1983).

Jerome Frank (1961, 1973, 1974, 1982) continued to modify and develop his common factors model and has more recently focused on the restoration of morale as a significant common factor. Frank hypothesized that all therapies address a common problem—a "demoralization," consisting of a loss of self-esteem and subjective feelings of incompetence, alienation, hopelessness, and helplessness. He suggested that all therapies may be equally effective in restoring morale, despite the different ways in which they do so. He has also further articulated his earlier work and suggested the following as therapeutic components shared by different psychotherapies: An emotionally charged confiding relationship with a helping person; a healing setting; a rational conceptual scheme or myth to explain symptoms; and a ritual to help resolve symptoms (Frank, 1982).

Some of the central themes of common factors thinking were already apparent during this time. There was a strong emphasis on the commonalities in the therapy *relationship* and various attempts to conceptualize these relationship factors. Many proposals also included corrective emotional experiences in therapy and the disconfirmation of dysfunctional expectancies, the arousal of hope and positive expectancies, changes in self-perceptions, persuasion and attitude change, and restoration of morale.

From the time of Rosenzweig's paper (1936) until about 1980, there was a slow but steady progression of thought regarding common factors. Nonetheless, this kind of thinking did not exert any significant impact on psychotherapy until the late 1970s. Many of the reasons for this paralleled those affecting theoretical integration, discussed earlier. For the most part, the therapies were too busy defining themselves and their differences to seek commonalities that might threaten their distinct identities.

Recent Developments

Since 1980, there has been a sharp increase in interest in a common factors approach, with more books and papers published during these years than perhaps all previous years combined (e.g., Arkowitz & Hannah, 1989; Beutler, 1983; Brady et al., 1980; Cornsweet, 1983; Garfield, 1980; Goldfried, 1980, 1982a; Grencavage & Norcross, 1990; Haaga, 1986; Jones, Cumming, & Horowitz, 1988; Karasu, 1986; Lambert, 1986; Orlinsky & Howard, 1987; Prochaska, 1984). The proposals became more specific and there was more discussion about the locus of the common factors (e.g., in patient, in therapist, in relationship, in techniques, etc.). During the 1980s, a considerable amount of therapy outcome research appeared consistent with a common factors argument; finally, and perhaps, most important, empirical studies growing out of a common factors perspective began to appear (e.g., Goldfried, 1991). Such studies attempted to measure common factors, test hypotheses about them, and determine the correlations of different possible common factors with therapy outcome.

The 1980s opened with two papers significant to the common factors approach. In a study by Brady et al. (1980), prominent therapists from a variety of orientations responded to a series of questions regarding the effective ingredients in psychotherapy. There was consensus that *providing the patient with new experiences*, both inside and outside of therapy, was a central ingredient of all psychotherapies. These new experiences were considered important because they lead to changes in the ways people think about themselves. While there were differences in how such experiences should be provided and their precise role in the change process, all agreed on the centrality of such experiences. This emphasis on new experiences was consistent with earlier proposals involving the corrective emotional experience. However, "new experiences" is only a very general description, and how these new experiences may be provided and how they facilitate change are themes that remained to be developed more precisely in common factors models.

In another significant paper, Goldfried (1980) raised the issue of the level of abstraction that might be most useful from which to derive common factors. He suggested that we search for commonalities at an intermediary level of abstraction, between broad theories and specific techniques. He called this the level of "clinical strategies" or change principles that guide our efforts during therapy. He suggested two strategies that are important in all psychotherapies. One is having the patient engage in new, corrective experiences. The second was providing feedback, a process in which the therapist's interventions help patients increase their awareness of thoughts, feelings, and actions.

Goldfried focused his subsequent efforts on feedback and has developed an extensive coding system for measuring different aspects of feedback. He has completed several preliminary but provocative studies using this coding system (Goldfried, 1991). His work points to the importance of *both* common and unique factors in different approaches to therapy.

In one study, Goldfried (1991) found that both cognitive–behavioral therapists and psychodynamic–interpersonal therapists tended to focus more on feedback about interpersonal themes than on feedback about intrapersonal themes, despite theoretical differences that might lead one to think otherwise. Some differences between the two did emerge. Cognitive–behavioral therapists focused more on patients' actions, whereas psychodynamic–interpersonal therapists focused more on emotions and expectations. One particularly provocative finding was that, although the two therapies did not differ in their emphasis on interpersonal feedback, this type of feedback was associated with outcome more strongly in the psychodynamic than in the cognitive–behavioral therapy. In addition, feedback relating to "transference" themes had a stronger relation to outcome for psychodynamic therapy than for cognitive therapy. Thus, the same strategy may have a different impact in the context of different patients, therapies, and therapy relationships. This suggests the possibility that our conceptualization of common factors may be too unitary and simplistic and that we may need to examine contextual factors as well (cf. Jones et al., 1988). Although many of Goldfried's results are still preliminary, his work stands as an excellent illustration of how psychotherapy integration can lead to new research directions on clinically interesting questions. His focus has been to search for common factors starting with what therapists actually do in therapy, rather than on what they say they do. Further, his findings point to the importance of both common and unique factors in therapy outcome.

In another proposal, Prochaska and his associates (Prochaska, 1984; Prochaska & DiClemente, 1986; Prochaska, Rossi, & Wilcox, 1991) focused on commonalities in the process of change across different problems and different methods of change. Prochaska pointed to stages of change (e.g., precontemplation, contemplation, action, and maintenance), levels of change (e.g., symptoms, maladaptive cognitions, current interpersonal conflicts, family/systems conflicts; intrapersonal conflicts), and change processes (e.g., consciousness raising, stimulus control, self-reevaluation, environmental reevaluation). Prochaska and his associates have demonstrated that it is possible to measure these stages, levels, and processes and have published several studies that have demonstrated interesting interactions among them in people trying to change (Prochaska, 1984; Prochaska & DiClemente, 1986; Prochaska et al., 1991).

A number of other interesting proposals and discussions of common factors have appeared in recent years (e.g., Arkowitz & Hannah, 1989; Beitman, 1987; Beutler, 1983; Kilbourne & Richardson, 1988; Orlinsky & Howard, 1987; Wills, 1982). In a recent paper, Grencavage and Norcross (1990) took the unique approach of looking for the commonalities among common factors suggested in the writings of different psychotherapists. They grouped the various suggestions into categories and presented the most frequent ones within each. Under *client characteristics*, they found that positive expectations, hope, or faith were by far the most frequent. For *therapist qualities*, they found a general category of positive descriptors, followed by cultivation of hope and positive expectancies, as well as factors relating to warmth, positive regard, and empathic understanding. The largest number of different factors related to *change processes*. These included catharsis, acquisition and practice of new behaviors, provision of rationale, fostering insight or awareness, and emotional and interpersonal learning. *Treatment structures* that were frequently suggested included use of techniques and rituals, focus on inner world and exploration of emotional issues, adherence to theory, and a healing setting. Under *relationship elements*, there was a general factor endorsed by a majority of the writers that they described as the development of the alliance or relationship. In addition to trying to extract what common wisdom there may be among those proposing common factors, this paper also draws our attention to possible loci of the various common factors. Clearly, they are all interrelated (e.g., the relationship and change processes), but there are still questions to be answered about the best places to look for the most potent common factors.

The accelerating interest in common factors in the 1980s was largely sparked by the well-controlled therapy outcome studies that began to appear which suggested a lack of differential outcome among different therapies. In addition, reviews by Beutler, Mohr, Grawe, Engle, and MacDonald (1991) and by Lambert (1989) suggested that techniques accounted for less than 15 percent of the outcome variance in psychotherapy. This conclusion provided a further impetus to look toward common factors and away from the technique factors uniquely associated with the different therapies.

Evaluation of the Common Factors Approach

The common factors approach has led to some fascinating speculations about factors that may cut across therapies, to promising beginnings of the measurement of common factors, to studies looking at the association of common factors with therapy outcome, and to formulations that have potential for new lines of research and hypothesis testing. However, the impact of the common factors approach on clinical practice has been relatively minor thus far. Because we have not yet been able to confidently identify what the potent factors really are, we are unable to modify our practice accordingly.

An important requirement for the common factors bootstrapping strategy is the demonstration that the factor is correlated with therapy outcome. Some beginnings have been made in this direction (e.g., Goldfried, 1991), but reviews of other studies in this area have yielded only low to moderate correlations of process and outcome variables (Orlinsky & Howard, 1986).

Even if we do demonstrate a strong correlation between a factor and therapy outcome, we are still left with many questions about causality. For example, the arousal of hope and positive expectancies has been frequently referred to as an important commonality across therapies. Several studies have demonstrated correlations between this variable and therapy outcome (see review by Orlinsky & Howard, 1986). Does this suggest that hope causes positive outcome? It is just as plausible that as positive outcomes begin to occur, hope is aroused. Further, a third factor such as a supportive relationship may increase both hope and positive outcome. Essentially, we are generating correlational data to try to answer questions about causal factors, and so our conclusions are limited at best. Perhaps correlational research relating process and outcome might benefit from statistical procedures involving causal modeling (e.g., James, Mulaick, & Brett, 1982). These procedures allow the investigator to rule out alternative explanations to a greater degree than do simple correlational techniques. In addition, as research on common factors moves toward true experimental designs and the manipulation of variables, problems of interpretation of causality will diminish.

Determining the *type* and *level* of common factors is another challenge facing this area. What common factors shall we examine? We can search for commonalities in therapist characteristics, patient characteristics and processes, setting characteristics, change processes, relationship processes, clinical techniques, and theories of change. Further, not every commonality is necessarily important. There are many similarities among the different therapies. For example, most psychotherapies involve two or more people in seated positions who make eye contact. Nonetheless, few would suggest that these are crucial change elements in psychotherapy. Thus, simply identifying a factor common across therapies is only a first step to finding out the contribution of that factor to the change process. In addition, as Goldfried (1980) has pointed out, we can seek commonalities at many levels. A strategy that can help us determine what the important factors might be is still lacking, as are methods to determine which are the most important factors. Perhaps part of the answer lies in better theories, along with true experimental designs or causal modeling procedures to test out hypotheses from these theories.

The *degree of specificity* of the proposed common factors has also been a problem in the past. I have serious questions about the merits of discussing the therapy relationship as a common factor without attempting to define what *specific aspects* of the relationship may be important in creating change. Greater specificity also permits measurement and research to examine the role of the identified relationship factors.

In addition to trying to specify and measure the factors that are important in the therapy relationship, it may also be helpful to look at *other* relationships that involve helping, influence, or change (Higginbotham, West, & Forsyth, 1988; Wills, 1982). In this regard, recent work on social support (e.g., Brown & Harris, 1978; Cohen & Syme, 1985) suggests that it may be a useful construct for thinking about common factors. The relative effectiveness of control conditions in psychotherapy research that consist mostly of support and positive expectancies (e.g., Elkin et al., 1989) point to the potential importance of social support as a common factor.

We may also need to look at interactions of particular common factors with particular forms of psychopathology. For example, it may not be a coincidence that the "control group" therapies involving social support have been shown to be almost equivalent to other therapies for treating depression, given the association of low social support and depression (e.g., Brown & Harris, 1978).

Another issue that needs to be considered in common factors is the unidimensional and linear view of causality inherent in most common factors proposals. Most of the proposals reviewed suggest that a certain number of specified factors are important. They do not suggest that the factors may relate to one another and to other contextual variables (e.g., Goldfried, 1991) or that the factors may change over the course of therapy. We need to think more in terms of multivariate and interactive relationships among common factors to explain changes in therapy as well as possible changes in the role of particular common factors over the course of therapy.

Finally, the reader of the common factors literature may come away from it with the impression that advocates of this position are arguing for common *versus* unique factors in determining therapy outcome. While most discussions of common factors either ignore or minimize factors that differentiate among different therapies, I believe that it is a mistake to do so. The issue can be more productively posed as common *and* unique factors and the contributions that both may make to the therapy process. Studies like those of Goldfried (1991) and of Jones et al. (1988) provide support for both common and unique factors.

Finally, the main foundation for the search for common factors has been the lack of differential outcome in many studies comparing the effectiveness of different therapies. This type of finding is by no means uniform, and Stiles et al. (1986) have discussed a number of possible interpretations, only one of which is compatible with a common factors point of view. One particularly plausible explanation of this finding is that the lack of group differences obscures the important *variability* in outcome for different people in the different therapies. This line of thinking suggests that we ought to try to identify individual differences in response to therapy and use these as the basis for building a conceptual framework. It is exactly this strategy that is adopted by those interested in the third main direction in psychotherapy integration—technical eclecticism.

Technical Eclecticism

Background and Early History

Eclecticism is a strategy of selecting whatever seems best from a variety of alternatives. Eclectic psychotherapists choose from among available therapy techniques on the basis of what they think will work best for the particular person and problem. Different techniques from different therapies may be applied to the same person, or a certain technique may be used with different patients and problems.

In eclecticism, the basis for treatment selection is more actuarial than theoretical. The main criterion used by eclectic therapists when selecting treatments is what has worked best for similar people with similar problems in the past. Theory is not viewed as a particularly important basis for treatment selection. This relative deemphasis on theory distinguishes eclecticism from both theoretical integration and the common factors approach.

An eclectic approach was not really feasible until the 1970s. Prior to that time, the field of psychotherapy was, to a large extent, dominated by monolithic psychoanalytic and client-centered approaches that were being applied to all people and all problems. In none of these therapies were there many specific or clearly described techniques from which therapists could choose to form an eclectic approach.

Prior to the 1980s, there was little interest in eclecticism in the published literature on psychotherapy. Nonetheless, various surveys since the early 1960s demonstrated that a large percentage of practicing therapists endorsed some form of eclecticism to describe their approach (e.g., Garfield & Kurtz, 1976; Kelly, 1961; Norcross & Prochaska, 1983). This suggests that the realities of practice were leading practicing clinicians toward some form of eclecticism and that psychotherapy theories were not reflecting this fact. Nonetheless, prior to 1980, eclecticism was often little more than an idiosyncratic mixture of techniques selected on no clearly discernible conceptual basis. There was little information about how therapists practiced and how techniques were selected and combined. This chaotic situation led Eysenck (1970) to describe eclecticism as "a mish-mash of theories, a hugger-mugger of procedures, a gallimaufry of therapies" (p. 145). Eysenck strongly criticized eclectics for lacking an acceptable rationale and empirical evaluation of their approach.

Since 1980, a number of books and articles have appeared that presented more systematic bases for eclecticism and included debates on the merits of such an approach (e.g., Beutler, 1979, 1983; Beutler & Clarkin, 1990; Frances, Clarkin, & Perry, 1984; Garfield, 1980, 1986; Lazarus, 1986; Norcross, 1986). In this period we also saw the appearance of the *International Journal of Eclectic Psychotherapy*, which was later changed to the *Journal of Integrative and Eclectic Psychotherapy*. A *Handbook of Eclectic Psychotherapy* (Norcross, 1986) was also published. This book brought together the major contributors to eclecticism and included chapters on a wide variety of eclectic approaches. Why was there now so much interest in eclecticism in the literature? Part of the answer may have to do with developments in behavior therapy.

In 1969, Gordon Paul posed a question for behavior therapy that was to later guide psychotherapy research more generally. Paul asked: "What treatment, by whom, is most effective for this individual with that specific problem, under which set of circumstances, and how does it come about?" (Paul, 1969, p. 44). This question directed the attention of therapists and researchers to the many variables that could possibly influence the outcome of psychotherapy. It also pointed to the possibility of maximizing treatment outcome by an optimal selection and matching of particular therapies with particular people and problems. Paul's question became the cornerstone of later eclectic approaches to psychotherapy.

As noted earlier, in the 1960s and 1970s behavior therapy made its greatest impact on psychotherapy. In many respects, behavior therapy can be viewed as a form of limited eclecticism. It is characterized by a diversity of behavioral techniques from which to choose, with an emphasis on selecting the best techniques for the particular problem based on probable efficacy. It may be that the success of the eclecticism of behavior therapy stimulated interest in broader eclectic proposals that drew from a wider range of therapies. Consistent with this point of view, it is probably not purely coincidental that one of the earliest and most important eclectic proposals was developed by a leading figure in behavior therapy, Arnold Lazarus.

The Technical Eclecticism of Arnold Lazarus

The concept of *technical eclecticism* was introduced by Lazarus in 1967. In this and subsequent publications, Lazarus (1967, 1971, 1973, 1976, 1981, 1986; Lazarus & Messer, 1988, 1991) broadened the potential base of eclecticism from behavior therapy to techniques associated with other therapy systems. Lazarus (1971) argued that clinicians can use techniques from different therapy systems without necessarily accepting the theoretical bases associated with them.

Lazarus referred to his eclectic approach as "multimodal behavior therapy" (Lazarus, 1973, 1976) and later as "multimodal therapy" (Lazarus, ·

1981, 1986). He demonstrated the importance of assessment and intervention in the various modalities that characterize human functioning including behavior, affect, sensation, imagery, cognition, interpersonal relationships, and biology. Consistent with other modern eclectics, Lazarus emphasizes treatment specificity, the matching of techniques to persons and problems and the selecting of treatments based on empirical evidence of their effectiveness.

Despite his deemphasis on theory, Lazarus (1986) acknowledged that every practitioner uses at least some theory to guide their choices. Multimodal therapy, Lazarus (1986) asserted, rests primarily on the theoretical foundation of social learning theory, drawing also from general systems theory and communications theory. Indeed, the techniques that Lazarus (1986) lists as part of multimodal therapy draw most heavily from behavioral and cognitive therapies, and minimally, if at all, from psychodynamic and other therapies. This is surprising given Lazarus' criterion of empirical data for selecting therapies and the accumulating evidence of the effectiveness of such approaches (e.g., Sloane et al., 1975; Smith et al., 1980; Steuer et al., 1984). Lazarus' eclectic approach appears to fall somewhere between a broadened version of behavior therapy and an eclectic strategy that can choose from among *any* therapy system if there is empirical data to support that choice. Beutler's (1983, 1986) systematic eclecticism is closer to a comprehensive and empirical eclecticism, and it is to this approach that we turn next.

Beutler's Systematic Eclectic Psychotherapy

Beutler's systematic eclectic psychotherapy shares several features with Lazarus' technical eclecticism: an emphasis on treatment specificity and the matching of technique to person and problem; an emphasis on empirical data to determine choice of therapy; and a relative deemphasis on the role of theory to guide the choice of therapy (Beutler, 1983, 1986). Unlike Lazarus' technical eclecticism, Beutler's approach draws from the entire range of psychotherapy approaches.

Beutler, Mohr, et al. (1991) have argued that there are data to suggest that most of the variance in outcome in psychotherapy is due to variables other than specific techniques. Systematic eclecticism concentrates on the matching of a broad array of patient variables, treatment variables, and patient–treatment interactions that are most likely to maximize therapy outcome. Instead of focusing primarily on the match between problem and technique, Beutler also includes such variables as therapist characteristics (e.g., experience, attitudes, beliefs), patient characteristics (e.g., symptom complexity, coping style and resistance to influence), technique variables, and interactions among these variables. According to Beutler, it is only within this broad context that we should seek the best match between problems and techniques.

As Beutler, Mohr, et al. (1991) correctly point out, the number of potential variables to be considered in such a matrix are limitless. Further, there is little to guide us in the selection of variables that might be most productive or relevant. It is here that Beutler turns to theory to help guide these choices.

Beutler (1986) suggests that a *functional* theory must be developed that encourages and dictates the utilization of these approaches. Such a functional approach would be highly actuarial in nature, emphasizing what has worked best in the past in similar matches among variables. In addition, Beutler bases his work on social psychological theories of persuasion and influence to understand some of the possible interactions of patient and treatment characteristics.

In a recent extension of the systematic eclectic approach, Beutler and Clarkin (1990) tried to empirically identify the patient qualities that hold most promise for enhancing the fit between specific patients and treatments. These dimensions included level of motivating distress, problem severity, coping style, and the propensity to resist interpersonal influence. Beutler (1989) found that the mean amount of outcome variance accounted for by such variables was substantially higher than the amount of variance that could be accounted for by techniques alone. Beutler, Mohr, et al. (1991) reviewed research on patient coping style and reactance levels as predictors of different rates of response to different procedures and have presented some preliminary data from prospective studies in which some of these variables were used to predict therapy outcome. Thus, Beutler's systematic eclecticism continues to evolve and has begun to stimulate empirical research as well.

Evaluation and Current Status of Technical Eclecticism

Clearly, recent versions of eclecticism are less vulnerable to critics like Eysenck who see them as unsystematic approaches with little or no associated conceptual foundations or research. In fact, proposals like those of Lazarus and Beutler strive for coherent frameworks for organizing and selecting treatments. Each also looks to empirical research to help guide the choice of technique.

Beutler's systematic eclecticism comes closest to an actuarial approach that can sample the whole range of therapies based on evidence for the effectiveness of the techniques. In addition, Beutler includes the many variables that need to be taken into account beyond those associated with technique and problem.

At the very heart of modern eclecticism is an actuarial approach that uses data from past cases to predict what will work best for new cases. This actuarial approach requires a search for relations among variables, rather than for an overall theory to fit to these data. The hypothetical matrix that such an approach might generate shows promise for guiding clinicians in choosing the best therapy for the person and problem. This is the promise of eclecticism. However, the actuarial strategy is also the Achilles heel of eclecticism.

One problem is the enormous number of possible variables that may correlate with the enormous number of outcome measures. How can we organize such an incredible number of variables to permit the kinds of predictions that eclecticism seeks? Orlinsky and Howard (1986) reviewed over 1,100 studies over a 35-year period relating process variables to outcome measures. There were almost as many specific variables as there were different studies, and the magnitudes of many of the significant correlations were often disappointingly small. Without some theory to guide our search for relevant variables, we run the risk of generating another 1,100 correlational studies that tell us little. As Arkowitz (1989) has pointed out, eclecticism may need more theory to help select and order the variables and to generate hypotheses about what causes change.

The variables in this hypothetical matrix are also not independent of one another. Technical eclectics are not simply searching for correlations between two events, but for multivariate interactions among a wide array of intercorrelated variables. If the number of variables is limitless, the number of interactions among them is also limitless. In simple terms, the task seems overwhelming unless we have some coherent framework to guide the selection of relevant variables and to help in understanding the interactions among variables. It is here that theory is helpful, and perhaps even essential.

There is yet another problem. The actuarial matrix sought by eclectics is basically a correlation matrix of process variables and outcome variables with different types of people and problems. Even if we were able to meaningfully organize such a matrix of variables, our hypothetical actuarial table does not help us to identify those truly causal factors that, if employed, would influence the outcome of psychotherapy. Again, it appears that some greater theoretical structure is needed.

The empiricism of eclecticism and the theory of common factors and theoretical integration may be complementary rather than antagonistic approaches to the same goals. Eclecticism emphasizes the collection of data on relationships among variables with minimal theory to guide that undertaking. More theoretically oriented integration approaches emphasize theories but have been weak in data. The data of eclecticism should form the basis for the theories of psychotherapy integration, just as the theories of psychotherapy integration may serve to guide the search for data of the eclectics. All of the psychotherapy integration approaches share similar goals. They do differ, however, on the level and type of theory that are considered to be most helpful at this stage in the development of the field.

WHY INTEGRATION NOW?

To some extent, different factors have influenced the development of each of the three approaches to psychotherapy integration. However, there have also been some important influences that they have shared. For example, the temporal fluctuations in interest in each of the three approaches (as indexed by the number of publications) is rather similar. There was little interest in integration before 1970, a growing interest during the 1970s, and a rapidly accelerating interest from 1980 up to the present. What factors could have accounted for this pattern?

First, psychotherapy integration has, in part, been a response to *the improved quality of psychotherapy outcome research* during this period, and to the lack of strong evidence to support differential outcomes among existing therapies. Prior to the late 1970s, there were very few well-designed studies on the outcome of psychotherapy. Since then, the number of such studies has increased dramatically (e.g., see review by Lambert et al., 1986), and meta-analytic procedures (e.g., Smith et al., 1980) have provided more objective ways to summarize and compare the results of different studies. These studies have revealed surprisingly few significant differences in outcome among different therapies. Although we do need to be cautious in accepting the null hypothesis and to remember that there are many possible interpretations of such findings (e.g., Stiles et al., 1986), they very likely served as a catalyst for many who began to consider integrative interpretations of these results.

Another likely contributing factor was *the increase in the number of specific therapies* that became available. Paralleling the growth of interest in psychotherapy integration has been a sharp increase in the number of different therapies (Karasu, 1986) and in the number of variations within each of the major psychotherapies. This increasing diversity had two effects. One was to make available a greater range of theories and techniques, from which an integration could be crafted. Another was to alert therapists to the almost infinite number of variations in technique. The latter may have discouraged the search for further variations and encouraged therapists to seek more creative ways to utilize existing therapies.

Along with the growing number of therapies was a trend toward *more specific and operational descriptions of psychotherapy techniques and strategies.* Prior to 1970, there were few specific, operational descriptions of techniques and strategies in psychotherapy. From the late 1970s on, a number of specific treatment manuals appeared (e.g., Beck, Rush, Shaw, & Emery, 1979; Luborsky, 1984; Strupp & Binder, 1984), often growing out of research on the different therapies. Luborsky and DeRubeis (1984) referred to this sharply increasing emphasis on manuals as a "small revolution." The availability of more clearly described therapy procedures permitted more accurate comparisons and contrasts among them, providing further impetus for various approaches to psychotherapy integration.

Increasing interest in short-term psychotherapies during the past 20 years (e.g., see Budman, 1981) also contributed to the growing interest in integration. An interest in short-term therapies was accompanied by the development of more problem-focused therapies. Emphasis on a problem focus in different therapies (although there were still differences in how to define "problem") may have created a greater awareness of commonalities among therapies.

The success and popularity of cognitive therapy, which emerged during the 1970s, may also have contributed to the interest in integration. Some have suggested that cognitive therapy can be thought of as an integrative therapy (e.g., Alford & Norcross, 1991; Beck, 1991) that combines behavioral techniques with cognitive techniques and theory. The popularity of this therapy, as well as the evidence for its effectiveness (see Freeman, Simon, Beutler, & Arkowitz, 1989) may have served as an impetus to examine other types of integration.

London and Palmer (1988) have suggested that the trend toward *increasing interactions among professionals of different therapy orientations in specialized clinics for the treatment of specific disorders* may also have affected the development of psychotherapy integration. After the 1970s, there was a movement toward specialized clinics for a variety of problems including sexual dysfunctions, agoraphobia, obsessive-compulsive disorders, depression, and eating disorders, to name just a few. These clinics were often staffed by professionals of different therapy orientations, who placed greater emphasis on their expertise about the clinical problem than on their theoretical orientation per se. This diversity stood in contrast to the earlier emphasis on institutes devoted to specific therapies. At the very least, the exposure to other theories and therapies in such clinics may have stimulated some to consider other orientations more seriously.

The development of a professional network has been both a consequence and cause of the interest in psychotherapy integration. Earlier, I noted that most writers on psychotherapy integration before 1970 tended to be unaware of the work of others who had also published on integration. In fact, the term *psychotherapy integration* was not even used to describe these efforts until the 1980s. The strands for psychotherapy integration were there, but they did not yet form a connected and unified body of thought. In 1983, the Society for the Exploration of Psychotherapy Integration (SEPI) was formed (see description by Goldfried and Newman, 1986) to bring together those who were interested in various forms of rapprochement among the psychotherapies. Even at the outset, many professionals from a variety of orientations and backgrounds supported this group. The organization has brought together those interested in integration through a newsletter and annual conferences. In addition, the *Journal of Psychotherapy Integration* appeared in 1991, sponsored by SEPI.

The emphasis of SEPI has been on the *exploration* of integration, rather than on formalizing or promoting any particular forms of integration. The growth and success of this organization is a consequence of the growing interest in psychotherapy integration. It has also been a catalyst for this interest, because it helped to define the field and is providing avenues of communication for developing a coherent body of thought about psychotherapy and change.

PSYCHOTHERAPY INTEGRATION: CONTRIBUTIONS, PROBLEMS, AND PROMISES

After reviewing the history and current status of the three main directions in psychotherapy integration, I will examine the contributions that integrative thinking has made to the field of psychotherapy, as well as some of its problems and promises. At present, psychotherapy integration has probably had its strongest impact in desegregating the field of psychotherapy, rather than in truly integrating it. Integrative perspectives have been catalytic in the search for new ways of thinking about and doing psychotherapy that go beyond the confines of single-school approaches. Practitioners and researchers are examining what other theories and therapies have to offer. These perspectives have also encouraged new ways of thinking about psychotherapy and change. Further, this has been accomplished without institutionalizing any one way as "the" way. Integration is still an open field in which different ways of thinking and acting are being proposed, explored, and debated. This exploration has already been a healthy challenge to more established ways of thinking about psychotherapy.

Integrative perspectives have already opened up several new avenues for theory, research, and practice in psychotherapy. One type of theoretical integration suggests new ways of thinking about therapy by integrating existing theories. Another type of theoretical integration, based on systemic interactions among affect, behavior, cognition, and social factors has also begun to stimulate new thinking in the field. Both theoretical integration and common factors approaches have begun to suggest new research questions and strategies for therapy. Finally, technical eclecticism has been a stimulus for research in psychotherapy in its search for data on optimal matching strategies to improve therapy outcome. There have also been a number of integrative clinical proposals that suggested new therapy strategies. The achievements of integration have already been noteworthy.

There are a number of problems facing the field as well. In part, this may be due to its relatively early stage of development. At a clinical level, there have been several new suggestions for clinical strategies based on psychotherapy integration. However, these have been relatively few. I believe that we are not yet sure what integrative therapies look like. They are probably not fixed hybrids. They may grow out of general strategies or frameworks, but they remain elusive. Several promising starts have been made in clinical proposals for integrative therapies, but it is clear that much more work needs to be done in the area of integrative therapies, as well as in integrative theory and research.

There are also problems with theories of psychotherapy integration (both theoretical integration and common factors). Such theories are more like general perspectives than formal theories. It is often difficult to derive testable hypotheses from them that allow us to accept or reject their ideas. They may be good general ideas, but they are still far from good theory. In addition, those proposals that call for an integration of two existing therapy theories have yet to demonstrate that they can lead to predictions other than those generated by each theory separately. The relative lack of good theory in psychotherapy integration may be one of the reasons that it has been so hard to generate very much new research as yet.

While psychotherapy integration has stimulated some research, the number of empirical studies that have derived directly from this way of thinking has been disappointingly low. Even technical eclecticism, with its empirical emphasis, has not yet generated new hypotheses. The data of technical eclecticism are largely the data of single-school approaches. Perhaps the problems with integration theories discussed earlier have limited research attempts or perhaps it is partially a matter of time until more people initiate research programs in the area.

I believe that the single biggest challenge facing the field of psychotherapy integration is to find ways to generate and test hypotheses from these new points of view. Without such data, integrative theories will either become extinct or become a part of a large body of unsubstantiated clinical lore. In this chapter, I have reviewed several promising research programs that have grown out of integrative thinking. However, we need more. The NIMH workshop on research on psychotherapy integration (Wolfe and Goldfried, 1988) generated specific suggestions for research in the area. It is time to take those recommendations seriously in order to create a stronger empirical foundation for psychotherapy integration.

If we can overcome some of the problems discussed above, psychotherapy integration can be a strong factor in encouraging the development of new ways to think about psychotherapy, new strategies for the conduct of therapy, and new theories and research to advance our knowledge about psychotherapy and change. Further, by expanding our scope beyond theories of psychotherapy and by looking toward areas of theory and research in other areas of psychology (e.g., cognitive sciences, social psychology, health psychology, psychobiology), psychotherapy integration promises to bring psychotherapy back to the field of psychology from which it has become somewhat isolated.

PSYCHOTHERAPY INTEGRATION COMES OF AGE: RECENT DEVELOPMENTS

In the relatively few years since the material in the earlier part of this chapter appeared in print, there has been a rapidly growing interest in psychotherapy integration. For example, psychotherapy integration was highlighted as an important trend in Bergin and Garfield's (1994) influential *Handbook of Psychotherapy and Behavior Change*. Most major texts in abnormal psychology now discuss psychotherapy integration (e.g., Alloy, Acocella, & Bootzin, 1996; Davison & Neale, 1996; Wilson, Nathan, O'Leary, & Clark, 1996). In addition to the appearance of the *Journal of Psychotherapy Integration* in 1991, interest in psychotherapy integration can be gauged by the number of books,[2] handbooks (Norcross & Goldfried, 1992; Stricker & Gold, 1993), special journal issues (Alford, 1995; Arkowitz, 1996a; Safran & Muran, 1995a), and book chapters and journal articles that have been devoted to integrative themes. International interest in psychotherapy integration has also grown at a dramatic rate.

Theoretical Integration, Common Factors, and Technical Eclecticism

Earlier in this chapter, I discussed three main areas of psychotherapy integration (theoretical integration, common factors, and technical eclecticism). Although these categories still have some heuristic value, it is a testament to the growth of the field that they are less able to capture some of the more recent developments. Some contributions reflect more than one category, whereas others reflect rather new directions entirely. I will begin this update with a discussion of how these distinctions have become blurred and why they no longer adequately cover more recent developments in the field. In the remainder of the chapter, I will highlight some of these developments in an attempt to give the reader a sense of the activity and excitement of recent years.

Since 1991, it has become clearer to me that theoretical integration is not so integrative, common factors are not so common, and systematic eclecticism is not so eclectic.

---

[2]For example, Caspar, 1995; Garfield, 1995; Goldfried, 1995; Greenberg, Rice, & Elliott, 1993; Hayes, Jacobson, Follette, & Dougher, 1994; Held, 1995; Horowitz, 1991b; Kleinke, 1994; Kohlenberg & Tsai, 1991; Linehan, 1993a, 1993b; Omer, 1994; Pinsof, 1995; Prochaska & Norcross, 1994; Prochaska, Norcross, & DiClemente, 1994; Robertson, 1995; Ryle, 1995; Sponsel, 1995; P. L. Wachtel, 1993; Walborn, 1996.

Theoretical Integration Is Not So Integrative

My earlier discussion of theoretical integration suggested that therapists integrate the theories and techniques of different approaches into a unified whole. One implication of this idea is that the integration draws about equally from the component approaches. Yet it has become clear to me that this is rarely the case. Although P. L. Wachtel's (1977) integration came closest to this balance, even his psychoanalytic–behavioral integration was primarily based in one approach (interpersonal psychoanalytic) into which the ideas and strategies of others (cognitive–behavioral and systemic) were assimilated. Gold and P. L. Wachtel (1993) wrote of this approach that it

> is based upon a theory of personality and psychopathology which is rooted in the tradition and concepts of psychodynamic theory, but takes it in new directions. The cyclical approach to psychodynamics allows concepts from behavioral, cognitive, and systems approaches to be included in a contextually oriented dynamic theory and therapy. (p. 59)

Messer (1992) introduced the concept of "assimilative integration" as one that "favors a strong grounding in any one system of psychotherapy, but with a willingness to incorporate or assimilate in a considered fashion, perspectives or practices from other schools" (p. 150). This way of describing integration better captures what integrative therapists actually do than does the concept of theoretical integration. For example, Linehan (1993a) assimilated concepts from Zen thinking into a cognitive–behavioral framework, and Stricker and Gold (1996) assimilated strategies from cognitive–behavioral and experiential therapies into their essentially psychoanalytic base. Most integrative therapists seem to work best from the perspective of a single basic approach, but they broaden that approach by assimilating other ideas and techniques into it.

Messer (1992) wrote that "when incorporating elements of other therapies into one's own, a procedure takes its meaning not only from its point of origin, but even more so from the structure of the therapy into which it is imported" (p. 151). As an example, he suggested that when Arnold Lazarus imports a two-chair Gestalt procedure into his social learning approach, he uses it differently and to achieve different goals than would a Gestalt therapist using the same technique. According to Messer (Lazarus & Messer, 1991), the assimilated technique is changed by the context into which it is assimilated. I would add a related point: As we assimilate clinical strategies and clinical theories from one approach into another, we may find accommodations in our fundamental approach so that it, too, is changed in both theory and practice by the imported material. Such accommodation may be minimal when assimilating an isolated technique (as in the two-chair example) or may be more profound as in the case of Wachtel's assimilation of basic cognitive–behavioral concepts and strategies into his interpersonal psychoanalytic base. Undoubtedly, we will hear more about the concept of assimilative integration in the future, and possibly about accommodation as well.

Common Factors Are Not So Common[3]

Most of the proposals for common factors do not limit their focus in any way to particular subsets of people, problems, or therapies. Instead, they are proposed as rather general factors that are assumed to cut broadly across all patients and all therapies. This is true of all of the common factors models, including Alexander and French's (1946) "corrective emotional experience," Frank's (1985) ideas about restoring morale through myths and rituals, and more recent discussions of alliance and relationship factors (Horvath & Luborsky, 1993). Although such uniformity is possible, it is also possible that we are once again perpetuating what Kiesler (1966) called the "uniformity myth" in psychotherapy, in which broad generalities mask a complexity of specific interrelationships. Perhaps some factors are common across some techniques and not others, across some people and not others, and across some problems and not others.

As one example of this possible specificity, I have proposed that the provision of social support to depressed people may be a common factor in the treatment of depression (Arkowitz, 1992a). This was based on data showing that depressed people are lower in social support than others and that lack of social support in the nondepressed state predicts subsequent episodes of depression. These results, combined with the equivalent outcomes of different types of therapy for depression and with the apparent power of so-called placebos in the treatment of depression (Elkin et al., 1989), make a plausible case for lack of social support as a cause of depression and the provision of social support as a possible common factor in different treatments of depression. Is the provision of support equally important for patients with obsessive–compulsive disorder, anorexia, specific phobia, and antisocial personality disorder? Perhaps. But it seems just as likely that social support plays a *selective* role, applying to some disorders and not to others.

I believe that we need to be more precise about our common factors proposals, specifying those instances in which we think they are universally applicable and those in which they are not. We need to avoid further perpetuation of uniformity myths in common factors thinking. Common factors may indeed be less common than we thought.

---

[3]This phrase was used earlier by Weinberger (1995) in a somewhat different context.

Technical Eclecticism Is Not So Eclectic

Earlier in this chapter, technical and systematic eclecticism were characterized as more actuarial than theoretical. That was and is true. A totally atheoretical eclecticism, however, is neither feasible nor desirable. Therapists need to operate from some base of theory in order to guide their practice, and that seems to be the case even for technical eclectics. In describing their systematic eclectic therapy, Beutler and Consoli (1992) stated that this approach is loosely based on a social-persuasion theoretical model that emphasizes interpersonal relationships. Lazarus (1992) described his technically eclectic Multimodal Therapy as rooted in a social and cognitive learning theory. In fact, because of the presence of such theoretical underpinnings, Stricker (1994) suggested that the approaches of Beutler and Lazarus might be better characterized as assimilative integration. Stricker (1994) described truly atheoretical eclecticism as "an undisciplined grab bag of techniques to be used in a near random manner as the mood strikes the therapist" (p. 6).

In 1991, it appeared that psychotherapy integration was more of a "promissory note," holding the potential for substantive contributions to research and practice but still falling somewhat short of this goal. In what follows, I believe that the reader will see that much of this potential has now been realized.

I will begin with an update of work in the three categories discussed earlier, although I will use the term *theoretical–assimilative integration* instead of *theoretical integration*. The remainder of this update will reflect somewhat unsystematic and arbitrary groupings of work that has appeared during the past years. The field of psychotherapy integration has progressed so rapidly in so few years that another major review is already necessary, although space limitations preclude such a review here. Following, I will highlight some of the main trends in the past few years.

Recent Developments in Theoretical–Assimilative Integration, Common Factors, and Technical Eclecticism

Theoretical–Assimilative Integration

P. L. Wachtel has continued to develop and elaborate his views on theoretical–assimilative integration (Gold & P. L. Wachtel, 1993; P. L. Wachtel, 1991, 1993, 1994, 1997; P. L. Wachtel & McKinney, 1992). His recent writing has reflected a continuing interest in the assimilation of cognitive–behavioral and systems approaches into an interpersonal psychoanalytic framework and in the role of "vicious cycles" in the perpetuation of psychopathology (P. L. Wachtel, 1994). In this context, he (Wachtel, 1993) discussed therapeutic communication, demonstrating how some types of communication are effective, whereas others addressing the same content are not.

In an especially provocative article, Wachtel (1991) attempted to describe the nature of integrative therapy in practice. This article was partially a response to supervisees' questions about when to shift from one approach (e.g., psychoanalytic) to another (e.g., cognitive–behavioral or systems). He responded by suggesting that the question relates more to eclecticism and selecting treatment alternatives than it does to integration. He illustrated a "seamless" integration by two case examples. This therapy is strongly influenced by psychoanalytic, cognitive–behavioral, and systems thinking, but cannot be recognized clearly as any of these. The "seams" between the approaches disappear in this type of integration, and what occurs is an emergent form of integration (Schacht, 1984).

There have been several other contributions relating to psychoanalytic and cognitive–behavioral integrations. Ryle (1990) described his cognitive–analytic therapy as consisting of "the application of psychoanalytic understanding and of some psychoanalytic techniques within a framework, and with additional treatment methods derived from cognitive psychology and psychotherapy" (p. vii). Ryle (1978) has long advocated the use of a "common language" for psychotherapy as a way of clarifying similarities and differences across therapy schools without the baggage of their jargons. His approach was stated in common language and emphasized the ways in which action produces feedback that can modify what he called "procedures" or strategies that people use to interact with the world. Using an object relations theory that is translated into common language, Ryle also drew from the thinking of George Kelly (1955) in his description of how people actively construct their own reality, and how the structure of these realities prevents them from learning from experience. Ryle's approach is one of the most carefully developed integrations to date, and it has led to research and innovations in clinical practice (cf. Ryle, 1995). Although Ryle's approach has not received the attention it deserves outside of the United Kingdom, it is an important development in theoretical–assimilative integration, and one whose impact will likely grow.

For several years, Wolfe has been developing a psychoanalytic–behavioral integrative approach to understanding and treating anxiety disorders (Wolfe, 1989, 1992, 1993). In Wolfe's approach, anxiety is not only a distressing symptom that often leads to avoidance behavior, but it is also a sense of self-endangerment that reflects more enduring beliefs and unresolved conflicts about the self, anchored in past experiences. In order to treat anxiety problems and accomplish enduring changes, Wolfe has recommended a combination of exposure therapy and helping the patient confront these underlying issues of self-experience.

Wolfe's approach is noteworthy for its problem-specificity, along with its development of etiological theory and clinical strategies. The specificity of Wolfe's approach to anxiety disorders has allowed him to go beyond general universal theories and strategies of change to draw from the literature on psychopathology and psychotherapy relating to the anxiety disorders. Elsewhere (Arkowitz, 1993), I have discussed the importance of focusing integrative proposals on specific problem areas. Just as the common factors may not be so common, general principles of change may not be so general. By developing theories and treatments of specific classes of disorders and problems, we can draw from what we know about the factors that cause and maintain problems to develop specific interventions appropriate for that problem. In addition to a "top-down" approach (e.g., P. L. Wachtel's psychodynamic–behavioral integration) that starts with general principles of change, I think that a "bottom-up" approach can be useful as well, starting with specific problems and disorders.

Although integrations primarily involving various psychoanalytic and cognitive–behavioral approaches still dominate the literature on theoretical–assimilative integration, the past few years have seen a growing interest in other integrations as well. There has been considerable interest in the development of integrative therapies for personality disorders (Gold & Stricker, 1993; Linehan, 1993a; Millon, Everly, & Davis, 1993; Westen, 1991). Because such disorders affect virtually every mode of functioning and pervade one's life, integrative strategies have seemed more appropriate to many than do single-school strategies. Linehan's Dialectical Behavior Therapy (DBT; 1993a) is the most highly developed and researched of these proposals. This therapy draws from both cognitive–behavioral approaches to change and Zen concepts relating to acceptance. Heard and Linehan (1994) suggested that both cognitive–behavioral approaches and Zen deal with change, but in different ways. As an illustration, they described how this integrative approach is used with suicidal patients: "While behavioral procedures can reduce suicidal behavior by teaching the client how to actively reduce suicidal urges, Zen practice can reduce suicidal behavior by teaching the client how to allow and observe the urges without acting on them" (Heard & Linehan, 1994, p. 65). Linehan has published extensively on this approach, including a major book (Linehan, 1993a) and a treatment manual (Linehan, 1993b). In addition, DBT has been evaluated in research that has supported its effectiveness (Linehan, Armstrong, Suarez, Allmon, & Heard, 1991; Linehan, Heard, & Armstrong, 1993).

The possibility of integrating Gestalt or experiential therapy with other therapies is more likely today largely because of the sophisticated theoretical and clinical conceptualizations of Leslie Greenberg and his associates (e.g., Greenberg et al., 1993; Greenberg, Elliott, & Lietaer, 1994). Rather than presenting a narrow "school" of experiential therapy, Greenberg et al. (1993) have developed an integrative approach that draws from a number of sources, most notably modern cognitive psychology and emotion theory. With such a common language for experiential therapies, integration with other approaches is facilitated. For example, in an important convergence with cognitive therapy, the experiential therapy of Greenberg et al. (1993) emphasized accessing and correcting what they call "schemes," or what are more commonly called "schemas" in cognitive psychology and cognitive therapy. However, the experiential approach emphasizes the importance of accessing them through methods that enhance emotional arousal rather than in more purely cognitive modes. Other examples of cognitive–experiential integration include Arkowitz and Engle (1995), Bohart (1993), and Reeve, Inck, and Safran (1993).

Is the increase in integrative proposals a positive development? In my view, it is. However, Lazarus (Lazarus & Messer, 1991) has taken a different stand. Of the diversity of integrative proposals, he wrote,

> Does this sound like progress? One particularly unfortunate trend is what appears to be a rather capricious bimodal melding which I have called 'fusionism'.... Suffice it to say that when a psychotherapist identifies himself or herself as an integrationist, this conveys nothing of meaning or substance. Differences among various integrationists may even surpass those of the most rigid school adherents. (p. 145)

Lazarus' critique raises a question about the goal of psychotherapy integration. If the goal is to develop a single fixed integrative approach that is all-encompassing, then the diversity we are seeing may lead to an affirmative answer to the question raised by Lazarus and Messer (1991): Does chaos prevail? However, if we think of psychotherapy integration as seeking an evolving framework as proposed by P. L. Wachtel (discussed earlier in this chapter), then we are more likely to look with favor on this diversity.

The majority of writers in psychotherapy integration have argued *against* the goal of a single integrative theoretical framework that will be all-encompassing, along with a single "integrative therapy" that goes along with it. Most, like Messer (1992) believe that there is not one truth to be discovered, but many different ways of looking at our complex world. In fact, many integrative writers have pointed toward a pluralistic world in which different approaches exist, with convergences and differences coexisting, and with each posing healthy challenges for the others (Mahoney, 1993; Neimeyer, 1993; Omer & Strenger, 1992).

Common Factors

Whereas there has been considerable progress on the theoretical–assimilation front, there has been much less in the area of common factors. This discrepancy may be because there are a number of unresolved questions in the area, including: What are the common factors that may account for change in psychotherapy? How shall we conceptualize them? How can we conduct meaningful research on them?

What are the common factors? There has been continued interest in trying to describe what may be important common factors across different psychotherapies. In this regard, the therapeutic relationship has attracted a great deal of interest, both conceptually and empirically (e.g., Horvath & Luborsky, 1993; Gaston et al., 1995).

Goldfried's work on common factors remains one of the most significant research programs in psychotherapy integration, noteworthy for the careful definition of the factors under study and the data that he and his associates have begun to accumulate. With careful attention to measurement and to empirical examination of how feedback and other factors may operate in different therapies, Goldfried and his associates (Castonguay, Goldfried, Wiser, Raue, & Hayes, 1996; Goldsamt, Goldfried, Hayes, & Kerr, 1992; Kerr, Goldfried, Hayes, Castonguay, & Goldsamt, 1992; Raue, Castonguay, & Goldfried, 1993; Wiser & Goldfried, 1993) have generated a number of interesting findings in their recent research.

For example, Wiser and Goldfried (1993) considered the possible common factor of emotional experiencing. They found that psychodynamic–interpersonal therapists viewed tapes containing higher affective experiencing as more critical to the change process, whereas cognitive–behavioral therapists viewed lower levels of experiencing as being more significant. It may well be that the emotional experiencing plays rather different roles in different therapies and interacts with different therapies in different ways. In a recent and related study, Castonguay et al. (1996) studied the role of three variables in the cognitive therapy of depressed patients. Two of these variables (the therapeutic relationship and the client's emotional experiencing) were presumed to be common to other therapies, whereas a third (therapist focus on the impact of distorted cognitions on depressive symptoms) was assumed to be specific to cognitive therapy. Although the two common factors correlated positively with outcome, the presumed specific factor actually correlated negatively with outcome. Various explanations of this surprising finding were proposed. In a recent study of cognitive therapy, Hayes, Castonguay, and Goldfried (in press) found that cognitive therapists treating depressed patients did indeed maintain a primarily cognitive focus, but it was interventions that addressed the interpersonal and developmental domains that were associated with improvement. These are but a few of the provocative findings from this program of research on common and specific factors in psychotherapy.

Several relatively new proposals for common factors have also appeared. For example, Weinberger (1995) has paid special attention to the therapeutic relationship, expectations, confronting problems, mastery, and attribution of problems. Other proposals have included acceptance (Hayes et al., 1994), therapeutic impact (Omer, 1992), and experiencing (Bohart, 1993).

The cross-theoretical concept of *acceptance* seems to be attracting interest. A fascinating book by Hayes et al. (1994) examined the role of acceptance in different therapies (e.g., family therapy, experiential therapy, and cognitive therapy), and in different problems (e.g., addictions and alcohol, paraphilias, problems of the elderly, and physical and sexual abuse). Hayes (1994) defined acceptance as "experiencing events fully and as they are" (1994, p. 30).

Hayes (1994) pointed to a number of instances in which acceptance is useful, such as when the process of change contradicts the outcome. He suggested that "it is not possible to earn self-acceptance by criticism and deliberate change, or to learn peace of mind by rejecting negative thoughts, or to eliminate disturbing thoughts by thinking of how to get rid of them" (p. 28). In such instances, Hayes recommended acceptance rather than change strategies. Acceptance is also a central part of Linehan's DBT, discussed earlier, and of the integrated behavioral couples therapy being developed by Christensen, Jacobson, and Babcock (1995).

Although much work is needed in defining, measuring, and studying the role of acceptance in psychotherapy, the construct of acceptance is a very appealing one that captures an important aspect of all psychotherapies. Hayes (1994) pointed out that acceptance is neither a simple nor a unitary construct. Acceptance can be something that therapists "do," that clients "receive," and that leads to an outcome involving client "self-acceptance." Although many questions remain about this intriguing area, the recent work on acceptance points toward a potentially important factor in all psychotherapies, and one that has been reincarnated from earlier approaches to psychotherapy (e.g., the work of Carl Rogers) with the blessings of modern cognitive science.

How shall we conceptualize common factors? Most of the problems in studying common factors that I discussed earlier in the chapter remain. These include measurement problems, degree of specificity, the interactions between common factors and particular problems (e.g., that the provision of support may be important for depression but not necessarily other problems), the unidimensional and linear view of causality in most common factors proposals, and the consideration that there are most likely *both* common and specific factors in therapy.

Weinberger (1995) has presented an interesting analysis of how we need to think about common factors and endorsed a view that emphasizes reciprocal interaction rather than linear causality. Although this is a valuable suggestion, I have argued that we need to go beyond even this level of complexity for a full understanding of common factors in psychotherapy (Arkowitz, 1995). The term *common factors* obscures the fact that we are dealing with "change processes" rather than with the fixed and static entities.

In most publications on common factors in psychotherapy, the potentially causal role of one or more factors is typically discussed. Usually, these factors are taken out of the context of other variables in the therapy situation and without regard to possible changes over the course of therapy.

This point can be illustrated by reference to the relationship in psychotherapy. Should we consider "the relationship" as a relatively static "factor" that we need to measure to predict change (e.g., with a relationship questionnaire), or as a complex, interactive, and multivariate process that may play different roles at different times in different therapies? I believe the latter is a more accurate portrayal. If so, the "relationship" may better be considered as a *process* that has mostly eluded our understanding of its role in change, perhaps because we have tended to treat it as a relatively static and unidimensional variable. Instead of asking *whether* the relationship causes change, and, if so, *what* about the relationship causes change, I think that we would do better to develop a model or theory of those interactional and relational processes that may influence session-by-session outcomes as well as end-of-therapy outcomes.

The relationship may play a different role in different contexts (e.g., forced vs. voluntary therapy; group vs. individual therapy; cognitive vs. psychoanalytic therapy) and may also play a different role over time. For example, in the early stages of therapy, relationship "rapport" may be a necessary prerequisite for all therapies. However, in later stages, the relationship may be the main source of change in some instances (e.g., the corrective emotional experience), may serve as a source of identification for the client in other instances, and may serve as a motivator for further attempts at change in still others. Alternatively, it may serve all of these functions to differing degrees at different times. Rather than static measures of "relationship," I believe that for most if not all common factors, we would make more progress by considering them as change processes rather than as static factors. As processes, we need to discover what relationship variables are of interest, how we define them, how they interact with other variables, how they change over time, and how they influence the process of therapy at different points in therapy. Shoham-Salomon & Hannah (1991) made a similar point and stressed the need for studying interactions over the course of therapy and not just single variables in order to understand change.

I believe that an important challenge for future work in common factors is the development of theories of the processes of change that include a variety of factors and their interactions. Although such theory development makes our task more complicated, I think it can also bring us closer to the realities of change.

How can we conduct meaningful research on common factors? This may be the most important challenge facing the area of common factors, and there are no clear answers on the horizon. However, if we do try to understand dynamic processes of change rather than static common factors, there is a new research method that seems ideally suited to this undertaking.

Greenberg and his associates (Greenberg, 1984, 1986, 1991; Rice & Greenberg, 1984) have proposed a *process analytic approach*, in which a particular type of episode in therapy is defined and good and bad resolutions of the episode are studied in different sessions and across different people. On the basis of these observations, a process model is constructed and tested through further observations. For example, Greenberg (1986) compared people who showed resolution in episodes of two-chair Gestalt work and those who did not. He developed a model that suggested that successful resolvers went through stages of separation, contact, expression of wants and needs, and resolution, whereas nonresolvers did not. This clinical research strategy holds promise for the study of such other factors as hopefulness and morale in psychotherapy, emotional arousal, conflict, and a variety of relationship factors such as anger and dependency.

Technical Eclecticism

This approach continues to be a significant one in the literature on integration. Various chapters and articles have updated and elaborated on strategies for such an approach (e.g., Beutler & Consoli, 1992; Beutler, Consoli, & Williams, 1995; Beutler & Hodgson, 1993; Clarkin, Frances, & Perry, 1992; Lazarus, 1992).

As I suggested earlier, one of the main problems confronting technical eclecticism is the almost limitless number of interactions possible among variables relating to patients, therapists, therapies, and problems. Without a theory to guide our search, it is unlikely that we will discover the important interactions. It does appear, however, that technical eclectics do rely on theory, although their theoretical preferences tend to be fairly minimal compared with theoretical—assimilative integrationists.

During the past few years, several initial findings have appeared from client—therapy interaction research that have been based on low-level theory and that point to matching variables relating to treatment outcome. For example, Beutler and his associates (Beutler, 1991; Beutler, Engle, et al., 1991; Beutler, Mohr, et al., 1991) have examined several patient variables but have focused on the role of reactance and impulsivity in the outcome of different treatments.

Their findings on reactance are provocative. In this work, *reactance* represents the tendencies of people to resist authoritative influence. This program of research has already yielded some promising results. Beutler, Engle, et al. (1991) hypothesized and found that reactant clients did worse in more directive treatments such as cognitive therapy, and better with less directive approaches. This held true even though the less directive approach (supportive/self-directive) was a fairly minimal form of therapy.

Beutler, Engle, et al. (1991) also studied client impulsivity and found that depressed clients high on impulsivity did better in cognitive therapy than in supportive/self-directive therapy, whereas the reverse was true for clients low on impulsivity. These results suggest that the relatively high structure of cognitive therapy may be especially useful for people who are lacking in impulse control.

Shoham, Bootzin, Rohrbaugh, and Urry (in press) studied insomnia and found that highly reactant clients benefited more from paradoxical instructions than from a straightforward behavioral intervention. In addition, several studies have pointed to possible interactions in the treatment of alcoholism (Kadden, Cooney, Getter, & Litt, 1990; Longabaugh et al., 1994; Woody, Luborsky, McLellan, & O'Brien, 1990).

Thus, results are beginning to accumulate pointing to some client–therapy interactions that may be useful in treatment planning. There is still a long way to go, however, before technical eclecticism demonstrates the predictive power to which it aspires. The studies of aptitude–treatment interactions have begun to show that such interactions exist. The next question that needs to be addressed is whether these variables can be used a priori to assign people to treatments in ways that lead to better treatment outcomes than does random treatment assignment, as is the case in most psychotherapy studies.

Shoham and Rohrbaugh (1995) have acknowledged that the promise of the interactional approach of technical eclecticism remains largely unfulfilled, and have made some valuable suggestions for future work in the area. One of their most interesting suggestions is that we widen the scope of client variables (which thus far have accounted for relatively little of the outcome variance) to include relational variables. Thus, in addition to such person variables as client reactance, impulsivity, severity of problem, and so on, they have directed our attention to relationship variables such as the presence, extent, and quality of intimate relationships outside of therapy.

It is apparent that there has been significant progress in all three areas of psychotherapy integration. In addition, there have been a number of thoughtful articles on the problems facing each area, with suggestions for the future that may help to solve them.

As mentioned earlier, a number of recent developments in psychotherapy have pointed to the possibility that these categories have lost some of their power to capture significant trends in the field. In the next section, I will briefly survey what I consider to be some additional promising developments that do not readily fit into any of these three categories.

Promising New Directions

The Transtheoretical Approach

Prochaska, Norcross, DiClemente, and their associates (e.g., Prochaska, 1995; Prochaska & DiClemente, 1992; Prochaska, Norcross, & DiClemente, 1994) have been developing a transtheoretical model of change for more than 15 years. This work has focused on stages, processes, and levels of change. The central idea is deceptively simple: Change will be most likely to occur when there is a correspondence between stages and processes of change. Their research has revealed that certain processes of change are maximally effective only when used at certain stages of change and that when there is a mismatch between processes and stages, change is less likely to occur. Furthermore, their stage model suggests that we need to understand the sequence of stages that people must pass through in order to accomplish enduring change—not just whether they change or not. Much of their earlier work has dealt primarily with addictions (Prochaska, DiClemente, & Norcross, 1992), and so the broader field of psychotherapy seems to have been slow in seeing the more general applicability and importance of the transtheoretical model. However, more recent work has shown applicability of the model to psychotherapy and health-related changes and to self-directed changes without therapy. Because it is a useful model to understand how and why people change, systematically incorporates techniques from different therapies, and is supported by an impressive body of research, the transtheoretical model is clearly one of the most important new directions in psychotherapy integration today.

The Generic Model of Psychotherapy

Orlinsky and Howard (1995) have been developing what they call a "generic model" of psychotherapy for a number of years, based largely on their exhaustive reviews of psychotherapy research for several editions of the *Handbook of Psychotherapy and Behavior Change*. This model has been generated from psychotherapy research and is designed to facilitate psychotherapy research—to help identify important variables and hypotheses in the study of psychotherapy. It is an integrative model in the truest sense, cutting across all approaches to therapy. In this model, six aspects of the therapeutic process are proposed: the therapeutic contract, the therapist's treatment model, the therapeutic bond, self-relatedness, in-session impacts, and sequential events during therapy. Each of these is hypothesized to interact with the others in ways that can facilitate or interfere with the occurrence of change in psychotherapy.

The Self as an Integrative Construct

Largely stimulated by recent developments in the cognitive sciences, concepts of "self" and "schema" have become central ones in many different areas of psychotherapy (once again) and psychotherapy integration. In addition to the work of Greenberg and his associates discussed earlier (e.g., Greenberg et al., 1993), many others have also been developing concepts of self and schema and exploring their relevance for both research and practice in psychotherapy (e.g., Horowitz, 1991b; Segal & Blatt, 1993; Stein, 1992). An entire recent issue of the *Journal of Psychotherapy Integration* was devoted to this topic (Wolfe, 1994). More recently, Wolfe (1995) synthesized much of the literature on the self, demonstrating that "self pathology" represents an integrative treatment focus for different approaches to psychotherapy. He also described integrative treatment principles to address these self pathologies. Wolfe's excellent article highlighted the tremendous potential of the self as an integrating construct for the field of psychotherapy.

Integrative Approaches to Resistance to Change

A number of researchers and writers have been interested not only in understanding change but also in understanding obstacles to change. This work is based on the assumption that an understanding of obstacles to change can further understanding of the change process itself. In the single-school approaches, the phenomena have been referred to as "resistance" or "noncompliance," often reflecting different phenomena, processes, theories, and interventions. These differences, as well as convergences, were highlighted in a recent issue of the journal *In Session* that was devoted entirely to an examination of resistance to change in different approaches to psychotherapy, including integrative perspectives (Arkowitz, 1996a).

In addition, progress has been made in theory, research, and practice in dealing with obstacles to change: Safran and his associates (Safran & Muran, 1995b) have described and studied what they call "ruptures" in the therapeutic alliance; Omer (1995) has described a "pluralistic" approach to understanding impasses in psychotherapy; and Arkowitz (1992b, 1996b; Arkowitz & Engle, 1995) has been developing an integrative model of resistance to change in psychotherapy. As Mahoney (1991) has pointed out, we cannot meaningfully talk about change without also understanding stabilization and the often-neglected complementarity that, together, they form. The work on obstacles to change can be important in understanding how change occurs, why it does not occur, and how we can more effectively work with our patients' obstacles to change.

Integrative Approaches to Couples, Children, and Families

For reasons that are not clear, most writers in psychotherapy integration have limited their focus to individual adult therapy. Until recently, integrations that involve work with children, families, and couples have been relatively ignored. However, there have been some promising movements in these directions, as evidenced by the work of Addis and Jacobson (1991); Christensen et al. (1995); Fauber and Kendall (1992); Feldman and Powell (1992); Kirschner and Kirschner (1993); Pinsof (1995); E. F. Wachtel (1992, 1994); and Wachtel and Wachtel (1986). We can hope the future will see more development in these areas.

CONCLUSION

The quantity *and* quality of the work just reviewed is a testament to the field of psychotherapy integration. Integrative workers have made significant contributions to theory, research, and practice, and they are continuing to do so at an accelerating pace.

Some who hear about psychotherapy integration are puzzled to find out that there is no single overarching theory of psychotherapy integration that is emerging and that neither is there a single well-defined integrative therapy that characterizes the field. To them, the very term *psychotherapy integration* implies the search for a single integrative theory that ties all of the existing schools of therapy together, along with a well-defined brand of integrative therapy. They are wrong. Such grand integrations in theory and practice are most definitely *not* the goal of most authors in the field of psychotherapy integration. Perhaps the term *psychotherapy integrations* better captures where the majority see it going. Psychotherapy integration is a way of thinking about and doing psychotherapy that reflects an openness to points of view other than those with which one is most familiar. This has led to many versions of theoretical–assimilative integration, common factors proposals, systems of technical eclecticism, and other integrative approaches. Integrative thinking in psychotherapy has generated new ways of thinking about psychotherapy and change, new ideas that can be tested, and new and useful clinical approaches. In recent years, it has come a long way toward fulfilling its promise.

REFERENCES

Addis, M. E., & Jacobson, N. S. (1991). Integration of cognitive therapy and behavioral marital therapy for depression. *Journal of Psychotherapy Integration*, 4, 249–264.

Alexander, F. (1963). The dynamics of psychotherapy in light of learning theory. *American Journal of Psychiatry, 120,* 440–448.

Alexander, F., & French, T. M. (1946). *Psychoanalytic therapy: Principles and application.* New York: Ronald Press.

Alford, B. A. (Ed.). (1995). "Psychotherapy integration" and cognitive psychotherapy [Special issue]. *Journal of Cognitive Psychotherapy: An International Quarterly, 9*(3).

Alford, B., & Norcross, J. C. (1991). Cognitive therapy as an integrative therapy. *Journal of Psychotherapy Integration, 1,* 175–190.

Alloy, L., Acocella, J., & Bootzin, R. (1996). *Abnormal psychology: Current perspectives* (7th ed.). New York: McGraw-Hill.

Andrews, J. (1991a). *The active self in psychotherapy: An integration of therapeutic styles.* Boston: Allyn & Bacon.

Andrews, J. (1991b). Interpersonal challenge: The second integrative relationship factor. *Journal of Psychotherapy Integration, 1,* 267–288.

Appelbaum, S. A. (1976). A psychoanalyst looks at gestalt therapy. In C. Hatcher & P. Himmelstein (Eds.), *The handbook of gestalt therapy* (pp. 215–232). New York: Aronson.

Appelbaum, S. A. (1982). Challenges to traditional psychotherapy from the "new therapies." *American Psychologist, 37,* 1002–1008.

Arkowitz, H. (1984). Historical perspective on the integration of psychoanalytic therapy and behavior therapy. In H. Arkowitz & S. B. Messer (Eds.), *Psychoanalytic therapy and behavior therapy: Is integration possible?* (pp. 1–30). New York: Plenum.

Arkowitz, H. (1985, May). *A behavioral-psychodynamic approach to depression.* Paper presented at the annual meeting of the Society for the Exploration of Psychotherapy Integration, Annapolis, MD.

Arkowitz, H. (1989). The role of theory in psychotherapy integration. *Journal of Integrative and Eclectic Psychotherapy, 8,* 8–16.

Arkowitz, H. (1992a). A common factors therapy for depression. In J. N. Norcross & M. R. Goldfried (Eds.), *Handbook of psychotherapy integration* (pp. 402–431). New York: Basic Books.

Arkowitz, H. (1992b). Psychotherapy integration: Bringing psychotherapy back to psychology. *The General Psychologist, 28,* 11–20.

Arkowitz, H. (1993). Introduction to the special issue: What can the field of psychopathology offer to psychotherapy integration? *Journal of Psychotherapy Integration, 3,* 295–296.

Arkowitz, H. (1995). Common factors or processes of change in psychotherapy? *Clinical Psychology: Research and Practice, 2,* 94–100.

Arkowitz, H. (1996a). Introduction to series: Resistance to change in psychotherapy. *In Session: Psychotherapy in Practice, 2,* 1–3.

Arkowitz, H. (1996b). Toward an integrative perspective on resistance to change in psychotherapy. *In Session: Psychotherapy in Practice, 2,* 87–98.

Arkowitz, H., & Engle, D. (1995, April). *Working with resistance to change in psychotherapy*. Paper presented at the annual meeting of the Society for the Exploration of Psychotherapy Integration, San Diego, CA.

Arkowitz, H., & Hannah, M. T. (1989). Cognitive, behavioral, and psychodynamic therapies: Converging or diverging pathways to change? In A. Freeman, K. Simon, L. Beutler, & H. Arkowitz (Eds.), *Comprehensive handbook of cognitive therapy* (pp. 144–167). New York: Plenum.

Arkowitz, H., & Messer, S. B. (Eds.). (1984). *Psychoanalytic therapy and behavior therapy: Is integration possible?* New York: Plenum.

Babcock, H. H. (1988). Integrative psychotherapy: Collaborative aspects of behavioral and psychodynamic therapies. *Psychiatric Annals, 18,* 271–272.

Bandura, A. (1969). *Principles of behavior modification.* New York: Holt, Rinehart, & Winston.

Bandura, A. (1977). *Social learning theory.* Englewood Cliffs, NJ: Prentice-Hall.

Beck, A. T. (1991). Cognitive therapy as *the* integrative therapy. *Journal of Psychotherapy Integration, 1,* 191–198.

Beck, A. T., Rush, A. J., Shaw, B. F., & Emery, G. E. (1979). *Cognitive therapy of depression.* New York: Guilford Press.

Beckham, E. E. (1990). Psychotherapy of depression at the crossroads: Directions for the 1990s. *Clinical Psychology Review, 10,* 207–228.

Beitman, B. D. (1987). *The structure of individual psychotherapy.* New York: Guilford Press.

Beitman, B. D. (1989). Why I am an integrationist (not an eclectic). *British Journal of Guidance and Counselling, 17,* 259–273.

Beitman, B. D., Goldfried, M. R., & Norcross, J. C. (1989). The movement toward integrating the psychotherapies: An overview. *American Journal of Psychiatry, 146,* 138–147.

Bergin, A. E., & Garfield, S. L. (1994). *Handbook of psychotherapy and behavior change* (4th ed.). New York: Wiley.

Beutler, L. E. (1979). Toward specific psychological therapies for specific conditions. *Journal of Consulting and Clinical Psychology, 47,* 882–892.

Beutler, L. E. (1983). *Eclectic psychotherapy: A systematic approach.* New York: Pergamon.

Beutler, L. E. (1986). Systematic eclectic psychotherapy. In J. C. Norcross (Ed.), *Handbook of eclectic psychotherapy* (pp. 94–131). New York: Brunner/Mazel.

Beutler, L. E. (1989). Differential treatment selection: The role of diagnosis in psychotherapy. *Psychotherapy, 26,* 271–281.

Beutler, L. E. (1991). Have all won and must all have prizes? Revisiting Luborsky et al.'s verdict. *Journal of Consulting and Clinical Psychology, 59,* 226–232.

Beutler, L. E., & Clarkin, J. (1990). *Differential treatment selection: Toward targeted therapeutic interventions.* New York: Brunner/Mazel.

Beutler, L. E., & Consoli, A. J. (1992). Systematic eclectic psychotherapy. In J. C.

Norcross & M. R. Goldfried (Eds.), *Handbook of psychotherapy integration* (pp. 264–299). New York: Basic Books.

Beutler, L. E., Consoli, A. J., & Williams, R. E. (1995). Integrative and eclectic therapies in practice. In B. Bongar & L. E. Beutler (Eds.), *Comprehensive textbook of psychotherapy: Theory and practice* (pp. 274–295). New York: Oxford University Press.

Beutler, L. E., Engle, D., Mohr, D., Daldrup, R. J., Bergan, J., Meredith, K., & Merry, J. (1991). Predictors of differential and self-directed psychotherapeutic procedures. *Journal of Consulting and Clinical Psychology, 59,* 333–340.

Beutler, L. E., & Hodgson, A. (1993). Prescriptive psychotherapy. In G. Stricker & J. R. Gold (Eds.), *Comprehensive handbook of psychotherapy integration* (pp. 151–163). New York: Plenum.

Beutler, L. E., Mohr, D. C., Grawe, K., Engle, D., & MacDonald, R. (1991). Looking for differential treatment effects: Cross-cultural predictors of differential therapeutic efficacy. *Journal of Psychotherapy Integration, 1,* 121–141.

Birk, L. (1970). Behavior therapy: Integration with dynamic psychiatry. *Behavior Therapy, 1,* 522–526.

Birk, L. (1988). Behavioral/psychoanalytic psychotherapy with overlapping social systems: A natural matrix for diagnosis and therapeutic change. *Psychiatric Annals, 18,* 292–308.

Birk, L., & Brinkley-Birk, A. (1974). Psychoanalysis and behavior therapy. *American Journal of Psychiatry, 131,* 499–510.

Blanck, G., & Blanck, R. (1976). *Ego psychology* (Vol. 1). New York: Columbia University Press.

Bohart, A. C. (1993). Experiencing: The basis of psychotherapy. *Journal of Psychotherapy Integration, 3,* 51–68.

Brady, J. P., Davison, G. C., DeWald, P. A., Egan, G., Fadiman, J., Frank, J. D., Gill, M. M., Hoffman, I., Kempler, W., Lazarus, A. A., Raimy, V., Rotter, J. B., & Strupp, H. H. (1980). Some views on effective principles of psychotherapy. *Cognitive Therapy and Research, 4,* 269–306.

Brown, G. W., & Harris, T. (1978). *Social origins of depression: A study of psychiatric disorder in women.* New York: Free Press.

Budman, S. H. (Ed.). (1981). *Forms of brief therapy.* New York: Guilford Press.

Caspar, F. (1995). *Plan analysis: Toward optimizing psychotherapy.* Göttingen, Germany: Hogrefe & Huber.

Castonguay, L. G., Goldfried, M. R., Wiser, S., Raue, P. J., & Hayes, A. M. (1996). Predicting the effect of cognitive therapy for depression: A study of unique and common factors. *Journal of Consulting and Clinical Psychology, 64,* 497–504.

Christensen, A., Jacobson, N. S., & Babcock, J. C. (1995). Integrative behavioral couple therapy. In N. S. Jacobson & A. S. Gurman (Eds.), *Clinical handbook of couples therapy* (pp. 31–63). New York: Guilford Press.

Clarkin, J. F., Frances, A., & Perry, S. (1992). Differential therapeutics: Macro and micro levels of treatment planning. In J. C. Norcross & M. R. Goldfried (Eds.), *Handbook of psychotherapy integration* (pp. 463–502). New York: Basic Books.

Cohen, S., & Syme, S. L. (1985). *Social support and health.* New York: Academic Press.

Cornsweet, C. (1983). Nonspecific factors and theoretical choice. *Psychotherapy: Theory, Research, and Practice, 20,* 307–313.

Davis, J. D. (1983). Slaying the psychoanalytic dragon: An integrationist's commentary on Yates. *British Journal of Clinical Psychology, 22,* 133–144.

Davison, G. C., & Neale, J. (1996). *Abnormal psychology* (6th ed. rev.). New York: Wiley.

Dawes, R. M. (1971). A case study of graduate admissions: Application of three principles of human decision making. *American Psychologist, 26,* 180–188.

Dollard, J., & Miller, N. E. (1950). *Personality and psychotherapy: An analysis in terms of learning, thinking, and culture.* New York: McGraw-Hill.

Dryden, W., & Norcross, J. C. (1989). Eclecticism and integration in counselling and psychotherapy: Introduction. *British Journal of Guidance and Counselling, 17,* 225–226.

Elkin, I., Shea, M. T., Watkins, J. T., Imber, S. D., Sotsky, S. M., Collins, J. F., Glass, D. R., Pilkonis, P. A., Leber, W. R., Docherty, J. P., Fiester, S. J., & Parloff, M. B. (1989). National Institute of Mental Health Treatment of Depression Collaborative Research Program: General effectiveness of treatments. *Archives of General Psychiatry, 46,* 971–982.

Eysenck, H. J. (1960). Learning theory and behaviour therapy. In H. J. Eysenck (Ed.), *Behaviour therapy and the neuroses* (pp. 67–82). London: Pergamon.

Eysenck, H. J. (1970). A mish-mash of theories. *International Journal of Psychiatry, 9,* 140–146.

Fauber, R. L., & Kendall, P. C. (1992). Children and families: Integrating the focus of interventions. *Journal of Psychotherapy Integration, 2,* 107–125.

Feather, B. W., & Rhoads, J. M. (1972a). Psychodynamic behavior therapy: I. Theory and rationale. *Archives of General Psychiatry, 26,* 496–502.

Feather, B. W., & Rhoads, J. M. (1972b). Psychodynamic behavior therapy: II. Clinical aspects. *Archives of General Psychiatry, 26,* 503–511.

Feldman, L. B., & Pinsof, W. M. (1982). Problem maintenance in family systems: An integrative model. *Journal of Marriage and Family Therapy, 8,* 295–308.

Feldman, L. B., & Powell, S. L. (1992). Integrating therapeutic modalities. In J. C. Norcross & M. R. Goldfried (Eds.), *Handbook of psychotherapy integration* (pp. 504–532). New York: Basic Books.

Fensterheim, H. (1983). Introduction to behavioral psychotherapy. In H. Fensterheim & H. I. Glazer (Eds.), *Behavioral psychotherapy: Basic principles and case studies* (pp. 3–23). New York: Brunner/Mazel.

Fiedler, F. E. (1950a). The concept of the ideal therapeutic relationship. *Journal of Consulting Psychology, 14,* 239–245.

Fiedler, F. E. (1950b). Comparisons of therapeutic relationships in psychoanalytic, nondirective, and Adlerian therapy. *Journal of Consulting Psychology, 14,* 436–445.

Fitzpatrick, M. M., & Weber, C. C. (1989). Integrative approaches in psycho-therapy: Combining psychodynamic and behavioral treatments. *Journal of Integrative and Eclectic Psychotherapy, 8,* 102–117.

Frances, A., Clarkin, J., & Perry, S. (1984). *Differential therapeutics in psychiatry.* New York: Brunner/Mazel.

Frank, J. D. (1961). *Persuasion and healing.* Baltimore: Johns Hopkins Press.

Frank, J. D. (1973). *Persuasion and healing* (2nd ed.). Baltimore: Johns Hopkins University Press.

Frank, J. D. (1974). Psychotherapy: The restoration of morale. *American Journal of Psychiatry, 131,* 271–274.

Frank, J. D. (1982). Therapeutic components shared by all psychotherapies. In J. H. Harvey & M. M. Parks (Eds.), *The Master Lecture Series. Vol. 1. Psychotherapy research and behavior change* (pp. 73–122). Washington, DC: American Psychological Association.

Frank, J. D. (1985). Therapeutic components shared by all psychotherapies. In M. Mahoney & A. Freeman (Eds.), *Cognition and psychotherapy* (pp. 39–80). New York: Plenum.

Franks, C. M. (1984). On conceptual and technical integrity in psychoanalysis and behavior therapy: Two fundamentally incompatible systems. In H. Arkowitz & S. B. Messer (Eds.), *Psychoanalytic therapy and behavior therapy: Is integration possible?* (pp. 223–248). New York: Plenum.

Freeman, A., Simon, K., Beutler, L., & Arkowitz, H. (Eds.). (1989). *Comprehensive handbook of cognitive therapy.* New York: Plenum.

French, T. M. (1933). Interrelations between psychoanalysis and the experimental work of Pavlov. *American Journal of Psychiatry, 89,* 1165–1203.

Garfield, S. L. (1973). Basic ingredients or common factors in psychotherapy? *Journal of Consulting and Clinical Psychology, 41,* 9–12.

Garfield, S. L. (1980). *Psychotherapy: An eclectic approach.* New York: Wiley.

Garfield, S. L. (1982). Eclecticism and integration in psychotherapy. *Behavior Therapy, 13,* 610–623.

Garfield, S. L. (1986). An eclectic psychotherapy. In J. C. Norcross (Ed.), *Handbook of eclectic psychotherapy* (pp. 132–162). New York: Brunner/Mazel.

Garfield, S. (1995). *Psychotherapy: An eclectic–integrative approach. Second Edition.* New York: Wiley.

Garfield, S. L., & Kurtz, R. (1976). Clinical psychologists in the 70s. *American Psychologist, 31,* 1–9.

Gaston, L., Goldfried, M. R., Greenberg, L. S., Horvath, A. O., Raue, P. J., & Watson, J. (1995). The therapeutic alliance in psychodynamic, cognitive–behavioral and experiential therapies. *Journal of Psychotherapy Integration, 5,* 1–26.

Gill, M. M. (1984). Psychoanalytic, psychodynamic, cognitive behavior, and behavior therapies compared. In H. Arkowitz & S. B. Messer (Eds.), *Psycho-*

analytic therapy and behavior therapy: Is integration possible? (pp. 179–188). New York: Plenum.

Gold, J. R., & Stricker, G. (1993). Psychotherapy integration with character disorders. In G. Stricker & J. R. Gold (Eds.), Comprehensive handbook of psychotherapy integration (pp. 323–337). New York: Plenum.

Gold, J. R., & Wachtel, P. L. (1993). Cyclical psychodynamics. In G. Stricker & J. R. Gold (Eds.), Comprehensive handbook of psychotherapy integration (pp. 59–72). New York: Plenum.

Goldfried, M. R. (1980). Toward the delineation of therapeutic change principles. American Psychologist, 35, 991–999.

Goldfried, M. R. (1982a). Converging themes in psychotherapy: Trends in psychodynamic, humanistic, and behavioral practice. New York: Springer.

Goldfried, M. R. (1982b). On the history of therapeutic integration. Behavior Therapy, 13, 572–593.

Goldfried, M. R. (1991). Research issues in psychotherapy integration. Journal of Psychotherapy Integration, 1, 5–25.

Goldfried, M. R. (1995). From cognitive–behavior therapy to psychotherapy integration: An evolving view. New York: Springer.

Goldfried, M. R., Greenberg, L. S., & Marmar, C. (1990). Individual psychotherapy: Process and outcome. Annual Review of Psychology, 41, 659–688.

Goldfried, M. R., & Newman, C. (1986). Psychotherapy integration: An historical perspective. In J. C. Norcross (Ed.), Handbook of eclectic psychotherapy (pp. 25–61). New York: Brunner/Mazel.

Goldfried, M. R., & Robins, C. J. (1983). Self-schema, cognitive bias, and the processing of therapeutic experiences. In P. C. Kendall (Ed.), Advances in cognitive-behavioral research and therapy (Vol. 2). New York: Academic Press.

Goldfried, M. R., & Safran, J. D. (1986). Future directions in psychotherapy integration. In J. C. Norcross (Ed.), Handbook of eclectic psychotherapy (pp. 463–483). New York: Brunner/Mazel.

Goldsamt, L. A., Goldfried, M. R., Hayes, A. M., & Kerr, S. (1992). Beck, Meichenbaum, and Strupp: A comparison of three therapies on the dimension of therapist feedback. Psychotherapy, 29, 167–176.

Goldstein, A. P. (1962). Therapist-patient expectancies in psychotherapy. New York: MacMillan.

Goldstein, A. P., Heller, K. H., & Sechrest, L. B. (1966). Psychotherapy and the psychology of behavior change. New York: Wiley.

Greenberg, L. S. (1984). A task analysis of intrapersonal conflict resolution. In L. N. Rice & L. S. Greenberg (Eds.), Patterns of change: Intensive analysis of psychotherapy process (pp. 67–123). New York: Guilford Press.

Greenberg, L. (1986). Change process research. Journal of Consulting and Clinical Psychology, 54, 4–9.

Greenberg, L. (1991). Research on the process of change. Psychotherapy Research, 1, 3–16.

Greenberg, L. S., Elliott, R. K., & Lietaer, G. (1994). Research on experiential therapies. In A. E. Bergin & S. L. Garfield (Eds.), *Handbook of psychotherapy and behavior change* (4th ed., pp. 509–542). New York: Wiley.

Greenberg, L., Rice, L., & Elliott, R. (1993). *Facilitating emotional change: The moment-by-moment process.* New York: Guilford Press.

Greenberg, L. S., & Safran, J. D. (1987). *Emotion in psychotherapy: Affect, cognition, and the process of change.* New York: Guilford Press.

Greenberg, L. S., & Safran, J. D. (1989). Emotion in psychotherapy. *American Psychologist, 44,* 19–29.

Grencavage, L. M., & Norcross, J. C. (1990). Where are the commonalities among the therapeutic common factors? *Professional Psychology: Research and Practice, 21,* 372–378.

Gurman, A. S. (1981). Integrative marital therapy: Toward the development of an interpersonal approach. In S. Budman (Ed.), *Forms of brief therapy* (pp. 415–457). New York: Guilford Press.

Haaga, D. A. (1986). A review of the common principles approach to the integration of psychotherapies. *Cognitive Therapy and Research, 10,* 527–538.

Hayes, A. M., Castonguay, L. G., & Goldfried, M. R. (in press). The effectiveness of targeting the vulnerability factors of depression in cognitive therapy. *Journal of Consulting and Clinical Psychology.*

Hayes, S. C. (1994). Content, context, and the types of psychological acceptance. In S. C. Hayes, N. S. Jacobson, V. M. Follette, & M. J. Dougher (Eds.), *Acceptance and change: Content and context in psychotherapy* (pp. 13–32). Reno, NV: Context Press.

Hayes, S. C., Jacobson, N. S., Follette, V. M., & Dougher, M. J. (1994). *Acceptance and change: Content and context in psychotherapy.* Reno, NV: Context Press.

Heard, H., & Linehan, M. (1994). Dialectical Behavior Therapy: An integrative approach to the treatment of Borderline Personality Disorder. *Journal of Psychotherapy Integration, 4,* 55–82.

Heilizer, F. (1977). A review of theory and research on Miller's response competition (conflict) models. *Journal of General Psychology, 97,* 227–280.

Held, B. (1995). *Back to reality: A critique of postmodern theory in psychotherapy.* New York: Norton.

Higginbotham, H. N., West, S. G., & Forsyth, D. R. (1988). *Psychotherapy and behavior change: Social, cultural, and methodological perspectives.* New York: Pergamon.

Hobbs, N. (1962). Sources of gain in counseling and psychotherapy. *American Psychologist, 17,* 741–747.

Horowitz, M. J. (1988). *Introduction to psychodynamics: A new synthesis.* New York: Basic Books.

Horowitz, M. J. (1991a). New theory for psychotherapy integration. *Journal of Psychotherapy Integration, 1,* 85–102.

Horowitz, M. J. (1991b). *Person schemas and maladaptive interpersonal patterns.* Chicago: University of Chicago Press.

Horvath, A., & Luborsky, L. (1993). The role of the therapeutic alliance in psychotherapy. *Journal of Consulting and Clinical Psychology, 61,* 561–573.

Izard, C., Kagan, J., & Zajonc, R. (Eds.). (1983). *Emotion, cognition, and behaviour.* New York: Cambridge University Press.

James, J. R., Mulaick, S. A., & Brett, J. M. (1982). *Causal analysis: Assumptions, models, and data.* Beverly Hills, CA: Sage.

Jones, E. E., Cumming, J. D., & Horowitz, M. J. (1988). Another look at the nonspecific hypothesis of therapeutic effectiveness. *Journal of Clinical and Consulting Psychology, 56,* 48–55.

Kadden, R. M., Cooney, N. L., Getter, H., & Litt, M. D. (1990). Matching alcoholics to coping skills or interactional therapies: Post treatment results. *Journal of Consulting and Clinical Psychology, 57,* 698–704.

Karasu, T. B. (1986). The specificity versus nonspecificity dilemma: Toward identifying therapeutic change agents. *American Journal of Psychiatry, 143,* 687–695.

Kazdin, A. E. (1984). Integration of psychodynamic and behavioral psychotherapies: Conceptual versus empirical syntheses. In H. Arkowitz & S. B. Messer (Eds.), *Psychoanalytic therapy and behavior therapy: Is integration possible?* (pp. 139–170). New York: Plenum.

Kelly, E. L. (1961). Clinical psychology—1960. Report of survey findings. *Newsletter, Division of Clinical Psychology, 14,* 1–11.

Kelly, G. A. (1955). *The psychology of personal constructs.* New York: Norton.

Kendall, P. C. (1982). Integration: Behavior therapy and other schools of thought. *Behavior Therapy, 13,* 559–571.

Kerr, S., Goldfried, M. R., Hayes, A. M., Castonguay, L. G., & Goldsamt, L. A. (1992). Interpersonal and intrapersonal focus in cognitive–behavioral and psychodynamic–interpersonal therapies: A preliminary analysis of the Sheffield Project. *Psychotherapy Research, 2,* 266–276.

Kiesler, D. J. (1966). Some myths of psychotherapy research and the search for a paradigm. *Psychological Bulletin, 65,* 110–136.

Kilbourne, B. K., & Richardson, J. T. (1988). A social psychological analysis of healing. *Journal of Integrative and Eclectic Psychotherapy, 7,* 20–34.

Kirschner, S., & Kirschner, D. A. (1993). Couples and families. In G. Stricker & J. R. Gold (Eds.), *Comprehensive handbook of psychotherapy integration* (pp. 401–412). New York: Plenum.

Klein, M., Dittman, A. T., Parloff, M. B., & Gill, M. M. (1969). Behavior therapy: Observations and reflections. *Journal of Consulting and Clinical Psychology, 33,* 259–266.

Kleinke, C. (1994). *Common principles of psychotherapy.* Pacific Grove, CA: Brooks/Cole.

Kohlenberg, R. J., & Tsai, M. (1991). *Functional analytic psychotherapy: Creating intense and curative therapeutic relationships.* New York: Plenum.

Kubie, L. S. (1934). Relation of the conditioned reflex to psychoanalytic technique. *Archives of Neurology and Psychiatry, 32,* 1137–1142.

Lambert, M. J. (1986). Implications of psychotherapy outcome research for eclectic psychotherapy. In J. C. Norcross (Ed.), *Handbook of eclectic psychotherapy* (pp. 436–462). New York: Brunner/Mazel.

Lambert, M. J. (1989, May). *Contributors to treatment outcome.* Paper presented at the annual meeting of the Society for the Exploration of Psychotherapy Integration, Berkeley, CA.

Lambert, M. J., Shapiro, D. A., & Bergin, A. E. (1986). The effectiveness of psychotherapy. In S. L. Garfield & A. E. Bergin (Eds.), *Handbook of psychotherapy and behavior change* (3rd ed., pp. 157–211). New York: Wiley.

Langs, R. (1976). *The bipersonal field.* New York: Aronson.

Lazarus, A. A. (1967). In support of technical eclecticism. *Psychological Reports, 21,* 415–416.

Lazarus, A. A. (1971). *Behavior therapy and beyond.* New York: McGraw-Hill.

Lazarus, A. A. (1973). Multimodal behavior therapy: Treating the BASIC ID. *Journal of Nervous and Mental Disease, 156,* 404–411.

Lazarus, A. A. (1976). *Multimodal behavior therapy.* New York: Springer.

Lazarus, A. A. (1981). *The practice of multimodal therapy.* New York: McGraw-Hill.

Lazarus, A. A. (1986). Multimodal therapy. In J. C. Norcross (Ed.), *Handbook of eclectic psychotherapy* (pp. 65–93). New York: Brunner/Mazel.

Lazarus, A. A. (1989). Why I am an eclectic (not an integrationist). *British Journal of Guidance and Counselling, 19,* 248–258.

Lazarus, A. A. (1992). Multimodal therapy: Technical eclecticism with minimal integration. In J. C. Norcross & M. R. Goldfried (Eds.), *Handbook of psychotherapy integration* (pp. 231–263). New York: Basic Books.

Lazarus, A. A., & Messer, S. B. (1988). Clinical choice points: Behavioral versus psychoanalytic interventions. *Psychotherapy, 25,* 59–70.

Lazarus, A. A., & Messer, S. B. (1991). Does chaos prevail? An exchange on technical eclecticism and assimilative integration. *Journal of Psychotherapy Integration, 1,* 143–158.

Lebow, J. L. (1984). On the value of integrating approaches to family therapy. *Journal of Marital and Family Therapy, 10,* 127–138.

Levis, D. (1970). Integration of behavior therapy with dynamic psychiatry: A marriage with a high probability of ending in divorce. *Behavior Therapy, 1,* 531–537.

Linehan, M. M. (1993a). *Cognitive–behavioral treatment of borderline personality disorder.* New York: Guilford Press.

Linehan, M. M. (1993b). *Skills training manual for treating Borderline Personality Disorder.* New York: Guilford Press.

Linehan, M. M., Armstrong, H. E., Suarez, A., Allmon, D., & Heard, H. L. (1991). Cognitive-behavioral treatment of chronically parasuicidal borderline patients. *Archives of General Psychiatry, 48,* 1060–1064.

Linehan, M. M., Heard, H. L., & Armstrong, H. E. (1993). Naturalistic follow-up of a behavioral treatment for chronically parasuicidal borderline patients. *Archives of General Psychiatry, 50,* 971–974.

London, P. (1964). *The modes and morals of psychotherapy.* New York: Holt, Rinehart, and Winston.

London, P. (1986). *The modes and morals of psychotherapy* (2nd ed.). New York: Hemisphere.

London, P., & Palmer, M. (1988). The integrative trend in psychotherapy in historical context. *Psychiatric Annals, 18,* 273–279.

Longabaugh, R., Rubin, A., Malloy, P., Beattie, M., Clifford, P. R., & Noel, N. (1994). Drinking outcomes of alcohol abusers diagnosed as antisocial personality disorders. *Alcoholism: Clinical and Experimental Research, 18,* 778–785.

Luborsky, L. (1984). *Principles of psychoanalytic psychotherapy: A manual for supportive-expressive treatment.* New York: Basic Books.

Luborsky, L., & DeRubeis, R. J. (1984). The use of psychotherapy treatment manuals: A small revolution in psychotherapy research style. *Clinical Psychology Review, 4,* 5–14.

Mahoney, M. (1991). *Human change processes.* New York: Basic Books.

Mahoney, M. J. (1974). *Cognition and behavior modification.* Cambridge, MA: Ballinger.

Mahoney, M. J. (1984). Psychoanalysis and behaviorism: The yin and yang of determinism. In H. Arkowitz & S. B. Messer (Eds.), *Psychoanalytic therapy and behavior therapy: Is integration possible?* (pp. 303–326). New York: Plenum.

Mahoney, M. J. (1993). Diversity and the dynamics of development in psychotherapy integration. *Journal of Psychotherapy Integration, 3,* 1–14.

Malan, D. H. (1976). *The frontier of brief psychotherapy.* New York: Plenum.

Marks, I. M., & Gelder, M. G. (1966). Common ground between behavior therapy and psychodynamic methods. *British Journal of Medical Psychology, 39,* 11–23.

Marmor, J., & Woods, S. E. (Eds.). (1980). *The interface between the psychodynamic and behavioral therapies.* New York: Plenum.

Meichenbaum, D. (1977). *Cognitive behavior modification.* New York: Plenum.

Mendelsohn, E., & Silverman, L. H. (1984). The activation of unconscious fantasies in behavioral treatments. In H. Arkowitz & S. B. Messer (Eds.), *Psychoanalytic therapy and behavior therapy: Is integration possible?* (pp. 255–294). New York: Plenum.

Messer, S. B. (1983). Integrating psychoanalytic and behavior therapy: Limitations, possibilities, and trade-offs. *British Journal of Clinical Psychology, 22,* 131–132.

Messer, S. B. (1986). Behavioral and psychoanalytic perspectives at therapeutic choice points. *American Psychologist, 41,* 1261–1272.

Messer, S. B. (1989). Integrationism and eclecticism in counselling and psychotherapy: Cautionary notes. *British Journal of Guidance and Counselling, 19,* 275–285.

Messer, S. B. (1992). A critical examination of belief structures in integrative and eclectic psychotherapy. In J. C. Norcross & M. R. Goldfried (Eds.), *Handbook of psychotherapy integration* (pp. 130–168). New York: Basic Books.

Messer, S. B., & Winokur, M. (1984). Ways of knowing and visions of reality in psychoanalytic therapy and behavior therapy. In H. Arkowitz & S. B. Messer (Eds.), *Psychoanalytic therapy and behavior therapy: Is integration possible?* (pp. 63–100). New York: Plenum.

Millon, T., Everly, G., & Davis, R. D. (1993). How can knowledge of psychopathology facilitate psychotherapy integration? A view from the personality disorders. *Journal of Psychotherapy Integration, 3,* 331–352.

Mischel, W. (1973). Toward a cognitive social learning reconceptualizaton of personality. *Psychological Review, 80,* 252–283.

Murray, E. J. (1983). Beyond behavioral and dynamic therapy. *British Journal of Clinical Psychology, 22,* 127–128.

Murray, N. E. (1976). A dynamic synthesis of analytic and behavioral approaches to symptoms. *American Journal of Psychotherapy, 30,* 561–569.

Neimeyer, R. (1993). Constructivism and the problem of psychotherapy integration. *Journal of Psychotherapy Integration, 3,* 133–158.

Norcross, J. C. (Ed.). (1986). *Handbook of eclectic psychotherapy.* New York: Brunner/Mazel.

Norcross, J. C., & Goldfried, M. R. (1992). *Handbook of psychotherapy integration.* New York: Basic Books.

Norcross, J. C., & Grencavage, L. M. (1989). Eclecticism and integration in counselling and psychotherapy: Major themes and obstacles. *British Journal of Guidance and Counselling, 19,* 227–247.

Norcross, J. C., & Prochaska, J. O. (1982). A national survey of clinical psychologists: Affiliations and orientations. *The Clinical Psychologist, 35,* 1–2, 4–6.

Norcross, J. C., & Prochaska, J. O. (1983). Clinicians' theoretical orientations: Selections, utilization, and efficacy. *Professional Psychology: Research and Practice, 14,* 197–208.

Norcross, J. C., & Prochaska, J. O. (1988). A study of eclectic (and integrative) views revisited. *Professional Psychology: Research and Practice, 19,* 170–174.

Omer, H. (1992). Theoretical, empirical, and clinical foundations of the concept of "therapeutic impact." *Journal of Psychotherapy Integration, 2,* 193–206.

Omer, H. G. (1994). *Critical interventions in psychotherapy.* New York: Norton.

Omer, H. (1995). Troubles in the therapeutic relationship: A pluralistic perspective. *In Session: Psychotherapy in Practice, 1,* 47–58.

Omer, H., & Strenger, C. (1992). The pluralistic revolution: From the one true meaning to an infinity of constructed ones. *Psychotherapy, 29,* 253–261.

Orlinsky, D. E., & Howard, K. I. (1986). Process and outcome in psychotherapy. In S. L. Garfield & A. E. Bergin (Eds.), *Handbook of psychotherapy and behavior change* (3rd ed., pp. 311–381). New York: Wiley.

Orlinsky, D. E., & Howard, K. I. (1987). A generic model of psychotherapy. *Journal of Integrative and Eclectic Psychotherapy, 6,* 6–27.

Orlinsky, D. E., & Howard, K. I. (1995). Unity and diversity among psychotherapies: A comparative perspective. In B. Bongar & L. E. Beutler (Eds.), *Comprehensive textbook of psychotherapy: Theory and practice* (pp. 3–23).

Papajohn, J. C. (1982). *Intensive behavior therapy: The behavioral treatment of complex emotional disorders.* New York: Pergamon.

Paul, G. L. (1969). Behavior modification research: Design and tactics. In C. M. Franks (Ed.), *Behavior therapy: Appraisal and status* (pp. 29–62). New York: McGraw-Hill.

Pinsof, W. M. (1983). Integrative problem centered therapy (IPCT): Toward the synthesis of family and individual psychotherapies. *Journal of Marriage and Family Therapy, 9,* 19–35.

Pinsof, W. M. (1995). *Integrative problem-centered therapy: A synthesis of family, individual, and biological therapies.* New York: Basic Books.

Powell, D. H. (1988). Spontaneous insights and the process of behavior therapy: Cases in support of integrative psychotherapy. *Annals of Psychiatry, 18,* 288–294.

Prochaska, J. O. (1984). *Systems of psychotherapy: A transtheoretical analysis* (2nd ed.). Homewood, IL: Dorsey.

Prochaska, J. O. (1995). An eclectic and integrative approach: Transtheoretical therapy. In A. S. Gurman & S. B. Messer (Eds.), *Essential psychotherapies: Theory and practice* (pp. 403–440). New York: Guilford Press.

Prochaska, J. O., & DiClemente, C. C. (1986). The transtheoretical approach. In J. C. Norcross (Ed.), *Handbook of eclectic psychotherapy* (pp. 163–200). New York: Brunner/Mazel.

Prochaska, J. O., & DiClemente, C. C. (1992). The transtheoretical approach. In J. C. Norcross & M. R. Goldfried (Eds.), *Handbook of psychotherapy integration* (pp. 300–334). New York: Basic Books.

Prochaska, J. O., DiClemente, C. C., & Norcross, J. C. (1992). In search of how people change: Applications to addictive behaviors. *American Psychologist, 47,* 1102–1114.

Prochaska, J. O., & Norcross, J. C. (1994). *Systems of psychotherapy: A transtheoretical analysis* (3rd ed.). Pacific Grove, CA: Brooks/Cole.

Prochaska, J. O., Norcross, J. C., & DiClemente, C. C. (1994). *Changing for good.* New York: William Morrow.

Prochaska, J. O., Rossi, J. S., & Wilcox, N. S. (1991). Change processes and psychotherapy outcome in integrative case research. *Journal of Psychotherapy Integration, 1,* 103–120.

Raimy, V. (1975). *Misunderstandings of the self.* San Francisco: Jossey-Bass.

Raue, P., Castonguay, L. G., & Goldfried, M. R. (1993). The working alliance: A comparison of two therapies. *Psychotherapy Research, 3,* 197–207.

Reeve, J., Inck, T. A., & Safran, J. (1993). Toward an integration of cognitive, interpersonal, and experiential approaches to therapy. In G. Stricker & J. R. Gold (Eds.), *Comprehensive handbook of psychotherapy integration* (pp. 113–124). New York: Plenum.

Rhoads, J. M. (1984). Relationships between psychodynamic and behavior therapies. In H. Arkowitz & S. B. Messer (Eds.), *Psychoanalytic therapy and behavior therapy: Is integration possible?* (pp. 195–212). New York: Plenum.

Rhoads, J. M. (1988). Combinations and synthesis of psychotherapies. *Annals of Psychiatry, 18,* 280–287.

Rhoads, J. M., & Feather, B. W. (1972). Transference and resistance observed in behavior therapy. *British Journal of Medical Psychology, 45,* 99–103.

Rice, L. N., & Greenberg, L. S. (Eds.). (1984). *Patterns of change: Intensive analysis of psychotherapy process.* New York: Guilford Press.

Robertson, M. H. (1995). *Psychotherapy education and training: An integrative perspective.* New York: International Universities Press.

Rogers, C. R. (1951). *Client-centered therapy.* Boston: Houghton-Mifflin.

Rogers, C. R. (1957). The necessary and sufficient conditions of therapeutic personality changes. *Journal of Consulting and Clinical Psychology, 21,* 95–103.

Rosenzweig, S. (1936). Some implicit common factors in diverse methods in psychotherapy. *American Journal of Orthopsychiatry, 6,* 412–415.

Ryle, A. (1978). A common language for the psychotherapies. *British Journal of Psychiatry, 132,* 585–594.

Ryle, A. (1990). *Cognitive–analytic therapy: Active participation in change.* New York: Wiley.

Ryle, A. (Ed.). (1995). *Cognitive analytic therapy: Developments in theory and practice.* New York: Wiley.

Safran, J. D., & Muran, C. (1995a). Introduction. *In Session: Psychotherapy in Practice, 1,* 3–5.

Safran, J. D., & Muran, C. (1995b). Resolving therapeutic alliance ruptures: Diversity and integration. *In Session: Psychotherapy in Practice, 1,* 81–92.

Safran, J. D., & Segal, Z. V. (1990). *Interpersonal process in cognitive therapy.* New York: Basic Books.

Schacht, T. E. (1984). The varieties of integrative experience. In H. Arkowitz & S. B. Messer (Eds.), *Psychoanalytic therapy and behavior therapy: Is integration possible?* (pp. 107–132). New York: Plenum.

Schafer, R. (1983). *The analytic attitude.* New York: Basic Books.

Schofield, W. (1964). *Psychotherapy: The purchase of friendship.* Englewood Cliffs, NJ: Prentice-Hall.

Schwartz, G. E. (1984). Psychobiology of health: A new synthesis. In B. L. Hammonds & C. J. Scheirer (Eds.), *Psychology and health.* Washington, DC: American Psychological Association.

Schwartz, G. E. (1991). The data are always friendly: A systems approach to psychotherapy integration. *Journal of Psychotherapy Integration, 1,* 55–69.

Sears, R. R. (1944). Experimental analysis of psychoanalytic phenomena. In J. McV. Hunt (Ed.), *Personality and the behavior disorders* (pp. 297–323). New York: Ronald Press.

Segal, Z. V., & Blatt, S. J. (1993). *The self in emotional distress.* New York: Guilford Press.

Segraves, R. T. (1982). *Marital therapy: A combined psychodynamic–behavioral approach.* New York: Plenum.

Shengold, L. L. (1979). Child abuse and deprivation: Soul murder. *Journal of the American Psychoanalytic Association, 27,* 533–539.

Shoben, E. J. (1949). Psychotherapy as a problem in learning theory. *Psychological Bulletin, 46,* 366–392.

Shoham, V., Bootzin, R. R., Rohrbaugh, M. J., & Urry, H. (in press). Paradoxical versus relaxation treatment for insomnia: The moderating role of reactance. *Sleep Research.*

Shoham, V., & Rohrbaugh, M. (1995). Aptitude × treatment interaction: Sharpening the focus, widening the lens. In M. Aveline & D. Shapiro (Eds.), *Research foundations for psychotherapy research* (pp. 73–95). New York: Wiley.

Shoham-Salomon, V., & Hannah, M. T. (1991). Client–treatment interaction in the study of differential change processes. *Journal of Consulting and Clinical Psychology, 59,* 217–225.

Silverman, L. H. (1974). Some psychoanalytic considerations of non-psychoanalytic therapies: On approaches and related issues. *Psychotherapy: Theory, Research, and Practice, 11,* 298–305.

Sloane, R. B., Staples, F. R., Cristol, A. H., Yorkston, N. J., & Whipple, K. (1975). *Psychotherapy versus behavior therapy.* Cambridge, MA: Harvard University Press.

Smith, M. L., Glass, G. V., & Miller, T. I. (1980). *The benefits of psychotherapy.* Baltimore: Johns Hopkins University Press.

Sponsel, R. (1995). *Handbuch integrativer psychologischer psycotherapie.* Germany: IEC Verlag.

Stein, D. J. (1992). Schemas in the cognitive and clinical sciences: An integrative construct. *Journal of Psychotherapy Integration, 2,* 45–64.

Steuer, J. L., Mintz, J., Hammen, C. L., Hill, M. A., Jarvik, L. F., McCarley, T., Motoike, P., & Rosen, R. (1984). Cognitive–behavioral and psychodynamic group psychotherapy in treatment of geriatric depression. *Journal of Consulting and Clinical Psychology, 52,* 180–189.

Stiles, W. B., Shapiro, D. A., & Elliott, R. (1986). "Are all psychotherapies equivalent?" *American Psychologist, 41,* 165–180.

Stricker, G. (1994). Reflections on psychotherapy integration. *Clinical Psychology: Research and Practice, 1,* 3–12.

Stricker, G., & Gold, J. R. (1993). *Comprehensive handbook of psychotherapy integration.* New York: Plenum.

Stricker, G., & Gold, J. R. (1996). Psychotherapy integration: An assimilative psychodynamic approach. *Clinical Psychology: Research and Practice, 3,* 47–58.

Strupp, H. H. (1973). On the basic ingredients of psychotherapy. *Journal of Consulting and Clinical Psychology, 41,* 1–8.

Strupp, H. H., & Binder, J. L. (1984). *Psychotherapy in a new key: A guide to time-limited dynamic psychotherapy.* New York: Basic Books.

Thoresen, C. E. (1973). Behavioral humanism. In C. E. Thoresen (Ed.), *Behavior modification in education* (pp. 98–122). Chicago: University of Chicago Press.

Truax, C. B., & Mitchell, K. M. (1971). Research on certain therapist interpersonal skills in relation to process and outcome. In A. E. Bergin & S. L. Garfield (Eds.), *Handbook of psychotherapy and behavior change* (1st ed., pp. 299–344). New York: Wiley.

Wachtel, E. F. (1992). An integrative approach to working with children and their families. *Journal of Psychotherapy Integration, 2,* 207–224.

Wachtel, E. F. (1994). *Treating troubled children and their families.* New York: Guilford Press.

Wachtel, E. F., & Wachtel, P. L. (1986). *Family dynamics in individual therapy.* New York: Guilford Press.

Wachtel, P. L. (1975). Behavior therapy and the facilitation of psychoanalytic exploration. *Psychotherapy: Theory, Research, and Practice, 12,* 68–72.

Wachtel, P. L. (1977). *Psychoanalysis and behavior therapy: Toward an integration.* New York: Basic Books.

Wachtel, P. L. (1982). What can dynamic therapies contribute to behavior therapy? *Behavior Therapy, 13,* 594–609.

Wachtel, P. L. (1983). Integration misunderstood. *British Journal of Clinical Psychology, 22,* 129–130.

Wachtel, P. L. (1984). On theory, practice, and the nature of integration. In H. Arkowitz & S. B. Messer (Eds.), *Psychoanalytic therapy and behavior therapy: Is integration possible?* (pp. 31–52). New York: Plenum.

Wachtel, P. L. (1987). *Action and insight.* New York: Guilford Press.

Wachtel, P. L. (1991). From eclecticism to synthesis: Toward a more seamless psychotherapeutic integration. *Journal of Psychotherapy Integration, 1,* 43–54.

Wachtel, P. L. (1993). *Therapeutic communication: Principles and effective practice.* New York: Guilford Press.

Wachtel, P. L. (1994). Cyclical processes in personality and psychotherapy. *Journal of Abnormal Psychology, 103,* 51–54.

Wachtel, P. L. (1997). *Psychoanalysis, behavior therapy, and the relational world.* Washington, DC: American Psychological Association.

Wachtel, P. L., & McKinney, M. K. (1992). Cyclical psychodynamics and integrative psychodynamic therapy. In J. C. Norcross & M. R. Goldfried (Eds.), *Handbook of psychotherapy integration* (pp. 335–374). New York: Basic Books.

Walborn, F. S. (1996). *Process variables: Four common elements of counseling and psychotherapy.* Pacific Grove, CA: Brooks/Cole.

Wandersman, A., Poppen, P. J., & Ricks, D. F. (Eds.). (1976). *Humanism and behaviorism: Dialogue and growth.* Elmsford, NY: Pergamon.

Weinberger, J. (1995). Common factors aren't so common: The common factors dilemma. *Clinical Psychology: Science and Practice, 2,* 45–69.

Weitzman, B. (1967). Behavior therapy and psychotherapy. *Psychological Review, 74,* 300–317.

Westen, D. (1991). Cognitive–behavioral interventions in the analytic psychotherapy of borderline personality disorders. *Clinical Psychology Review, 11,* 211–230.

Wills, T. A. (1982). *Basic processes in helping relationships.* New York: Academic Press.

Wilson, G. T., Nathan, P. E., O'Leary, K. D., & Clark, L. A. (1996). *Abnormal psychology.* Boston: Allyn & Bacon.

Wiser, S., & Goldfried, M. R. (1993). Comparative study of emotional experiencing in psychodynamic–interpersonal and cognitive–behavioral therapies. *Journal of Consulting and Clinical Psychology, 61,* 892–895.

Wolfe, B. E. (1989). Phobias, panic, and psychotherapy integration. *Journal of Integrative and Eclectic Psychotherapy, 8,* 264–276.

Wolfe, B. E. (1992). Integrative psychotherapy of the anxiety disorders. In J. C. Norcross & M. R. Goldfried (Eds.), *Handbook of psychotherapy integration* (pp. 373–401). New York: Basic Books.

Wolfe, B. E. (1993). Self-experiencing and the integrative treatment of the anxiety disorders. *Journal of Psychotherapy Integration, 2,* 29–44.

Wolfe, B. E. (1994). Introduction to the special issue. *Journal of Psychotherapy Integration, 4,* 285–289.

Wolfe, B. E. (1995). Self pathology and psychotherapy integration. *Journal of Psychotherapy Integration, 5,* 293–312.

Wolfe, B. E., & Goldfried, M. R. (1988). Research on psychotherapy integration: Recommendations and conclusions from an NIMH workshop. *Journal of Consulting and Clinical Psychology, 56,* 448–451.

Wolpe, J. (1958). *Psychotherapy by reciprocal inhibition.* Stanford, CA: Stanford University Press.

Wolpe, J., & Rachman, S. (1960). Psychoanalytic "evidence": A critique based on Freud's case of Little Hans. *Journal of Nervous and Mental Disease, 131,* 135–148.

Woody, G. E., Luborsky, L., McLellan, A. T., & O'Brien, C. P. (1990). Corrections and revised analyses for psychotherapy in methadone maintenance patients. *Archives of General Psychiatry, 47,* 788–789.

Yates, A. J. (1983). Behavior therapy and psychodynamic therapy: Basic conflicts or reconciliation or integration. *British Journal of Clinical Psychology, 22,* 107–125.

AUTHOR INDEX

Numbers in italics refer to listings in the reference sections.

Abend, S. M., 45, *87*
Abraham, K., 45, *87*
Abueg, F. R., 168, *173*
Ackerman, N., 182, 207, *222*
Acocella, J., 258, *273*
Addis, M. E., 272, *272*
Adler, A., 182, 206, *222*
Alexander, F., 53, 54, 59, 74, *87*, 231, 241, 260, *273*
Alford, B. A., 255, 258, *273*
Allmon, D., 263, *281*
Alloy, L., 258, *273*
Allport, G. W., 44, *87*
Altman, I., 147, *172*
Amenson, C. S., 18, *30*
American Psychiatric Association, 4, 19, *30*
Anderson, S. A., 216, *222*
Andrews, J., 238, 239, *273*
Angel, E., 103, *127*
Antonuccio, D. O., 18, 19, *30*
Appelbaum, S. A., 229, 233, *273*
Applebaum, A. H., 75, *92*
Arkowitz, H., 227n, 229, 230, 235, 237, 241, 243, 244, 246, 253, 255, 258, 260, 263, 264, 266, 271, *273*, *274*, *277*
Arlow, J., 43–45, *88*
Armenti, N. P., 161–163, *172*, *174*
Armstrong, H. E., 263, *282*
Atwood, G. E., 78, *95*
Azrin, N. H., 149, 153, *172*

Baars, B. J., 132, 140, 149, *172*
Babcock, H. H., 237, *274*
Babcock, J. C., 266, *275*
Baer, D. M., 164, *172*
Baker, L., 209, *224*
Baker, M., *31*
Balint, M., 40, 56, *88*
Bandura, A., 136, 142, *172*, 232, 233, *274*
Barber, J. P., 15, *30*
Barbrack, C. R., 171, *172*
Barkley, R. A., 161, *172*

Barlow, D. H., 2, 30, 149, 153, 156, 157, 161–163, *172–174*
Bass, D., 23, *33*
Bateson, G., 184, 185, *222*, *224*
Beattie, M., *282*
Beavers, W. R., 217, *222*
Beavin, J., 185, *225*
Beck, A. T., 254, 255, *274*
Beckham, E. E., 227, 239, 240, *274*
Beitman, B. D., 21, 30, 237, 246, *274*
Belar, C. D., 7, *30*
Bell, J. E., 194, 195, *222*
Bellack, A. S., 2, *30*
Bellah, R., 2, *30*
Bellak, L., 11, *30*
Bemis, K. M., 143, 166, *176*
Bennett Johnson, S., *31*
Bergan, J., *275*
Bergin, A. E., 2, 22, 26, 33, 118, *123*, 227, 258, *274*, *281*
Bergman, A., 72, 73, 88, *93*
Bergman, J. S., 10, *30*
Berman, J. S., 27, *36*
Beutler, L. E., *31*, 115, *124*, 229, 237, 244, 246, 250–252, 255, 261, 268, 269, *274*, *275*, *277*
Bibring, E., 53, 54, *88*
Bierman-Ratjen, E., 119, *124*
Binder, J. L., 9, 25, 30, 31, 32, 61, 95, 254, *287*
Binswanger, L., 99, 103, 106, *123*
Birchler, G. R., 152, *173*
Birk, L., 232, 237, *275*
Bishop, D., 217, *223*
Blake, D. D., 168, *173*
Blanck, G., 233, *275*
Blanck, R., 233, *275*
Blatt, S. J., 24, 30, 271, *286*
Bloom, B. L., 8, *30*
Blum, H. P., 47, 53, *88*
Bohart, A. C., 121, *123*, 264, 266, *275*
Bootzin, R. R., 258, 269, *273*, *286*
Borduin, C. M., 217, *223*
Bornstein, R. F., 20, *32*
Boss, M., 99, 103, 106, *123*
Boszormenyi-Nagy, I., 193, 194, 216, *222*

Bowen, M., 196, 198, 200, *223*
Bower, G. H., 117, *123*
Bowlby, J., 55, 88
Bozarth, J. D., 115, *123*
Brady, J. P., 241, 244, *275*
Brenner, C., 43–45, 51, 70, 88
Brett, J. M., 247, *280*
Breuer, J., 41, 42, 42n2, 88
Brinkley-Birk, A., 232, *275*
Brodley, B. T., 115, *124*
Broskowski, A. T., 161, *173*
Brown, G. W., 248, *275*
Buber, M., 101, 112, *124*
Bucci, W., 80, 88
Budman, S. H., 11, *31*, 70, 88, 255, *275*
Bugental, J. F. T., 17, *31*, 98, 104, *124*
Buhler, C., 98, *124*
Burden, S., 203, *223*
Burnham, W. H., 137, *173*
Butler, S. F., 25, *32*

Campbell, D. T., 150, *173*
Cantor, N., 151, 152, *173*
Cardin, V., 161, *177*
Carr, A. C., 75, *92*
Carter, E. A., 203, *223*
Caspar, F., 258n2, *275*
Caston, J., 80, 88
Castonguay, L. G., 265, *275*, *279*, *280*, *284*
Cattell, R. B., 147, *173*
Cautela, J. R., 151, *173*
Chabot, D. R., 181n
Chaiklin, S., 17, *31*
Chambless, D. L., 2, 23, *31*, 162, *173*
Charcot, J. M., 41, 88
Chevron, E., 61, *92*
Christensen, A., 266, 272, *275*
Cicchetti, D. V., 18, *38*
Clark, L. A., 258, *288*
Clarkin, J. F., 229, 250, 252, 268, 274, *275*, *277*
Clifford, P. R., *282*
Cloutier, P., 119, *125*
Cohen, S., 248, *276*
Collins, J. F., 26, *33*, *276*
Consoli, A. J., 261, 268, 274, *275*
Cooney, N. L., 269, *280*
Cooper, A. M., 51, 52, 64, 88
Cooper, H. M., 217, *223*
Cornsweet, C., 244, *276*
Craig, E., 112–113, *124*

Craik, F. I. M., 117, *124*
Craine, M. H., 11, *34*
Cristol, A. H., 227, *286*
Crits-Christoph, P., 18, *31*, *36*
Cumming, J. D., 244, *280*
Cummings, N. A., 161, 162, *173*
Curtis, H. C., 46, 88
Cushman, P., 6, *31*

Dahl, H., 80, 88
Daldrup, R., 115, *124*
Daldrup, R. J., *275*
Danton, W. G., 18, *30*
Davidson, N., 211, *223*
Davis, J. D., 237, *276*
Davis, R. D., 263, *283*
Davison, G. C., 162, *173*, *175*, 258, *275*, *276*
Dawes, R. M., 162, *176*, 241, *276*
DeBattista, C., 19, *31*
Delisle, G., 120, *124*
Delprato, D. J., 168, *173*, *179*
DeNelsky, G. Y., 18, *30*
Depression Guideline Panel, 19, *31*
DeRubeis, R. J., 254, *282*
de Shazer, S., 10, *31*
DeWald, P. A., *275*
Dickter, D., *34*
DiClemente, C. C., 245, 258n2, 270, *284*
Diguer, L., *34*
Dittman, A. T., 232, *280*
Docherty, J. P., *276*
Dollard, J., 136, 138, *173*, 230, *276*
Dompierre, L., 115, *125*
Dougher, M. J., 165, *176*, 258n2, *279*
Dryden, W., 237, *276*
Dunlap, K., 137, *173*
Dymond, R. F., 100, 114, *128*

Eagle, M. N., 39n, 56, 58, 59, 65, 79, 81, 86, 88, 89
Eckert, J., 119, *124*
Edelson, M., 79, 89
Efran, J. S., 16, *31*
Egan, G., *275*
Ehrenberg, D., 64, 89
Eifert, G. H., 142, 167, *173*, *179*
Eissler, K. R., 45, 46, 89
Elkin, I., 26, *33*, 227, 240, 248, 260, *276*
Ellenberger, H., 41, 89, 103, *127*
Elliott, R. K., 2, 10, 27, *31*, *37*, 117, 118,

120, *124*, *125*, 227, 258n2, 263, *279*, *286*
Ellman, S., 72, 88
Emery, G. E., 254, *274*
Emmelkamp, P. M. G., 171, *174*
Engle, D., 115, *124*, 246, 268, 269, 271, *274*, *275*
Epstein, N. B., 217, *223*
Epston, D., 13, 14, 38, 219, *225*
Erle, J., 48, 89
Erwin, E., 136n2, 144, 149, 150, *173*
Eshelman, S., 33
Evans, C., 161, *177*
Evans, I. M., 142, 167, *173*
Everly, G., 263, *283*
Eysenck, H. J., 133, 136, 139, 144, *173*, *174*, 231, 249, *276*

Fadiman, J., *275*
Fagan, J., 103, *124*
Fairbairn, W. R. D., 40, 55–60, 73, 75, 76n5, 81, 86, 89
Falloon, I. I., 161, *177*
Fauber, R. L., 272, *276*
Fay, L., 203, *223*
Feather, B. W., 232, 236, *276*, *285*
Felder, R., 204, *225*
Feldman, L. A., 10, *35*
Feldman, L. B., 229, 238, 272, *276*
Fensterheim, H., 24, *31*, 162, *174*, 237, *276*
Ferenczi, S., 48, 74, 89
Fiedler, F. E., 83, 89, 241, *276*
Fiester, S. J., *276*
Fine, E., 82, 89
Fine, S., 82, 89
Fisch, R., 10, *31*, 190, *225*
Fisher, S., 20, *32*
Fishman, D. B., 131, 132, 144, 145, 147–150, 153, 159, 162–164, 167, 171, *174*, *178*
Fishman, S. T., 4, *31*, 162, *174*
Fitzpatrick, M. M., 237, *277*
Foa, E. B., 171, *174*
Fogarty, T. F., 201, 202, *223*
Follette, V. M., 16n1, *32*, 162, 164, 165, *176*, 258n2, *279*
Follette, W. C., 16n1, *32*, 164, 165, *176*
Forsyth, D. R., 248, *279*
Foster, S. L., 153, *179*
Foulds, M., 115, *124*
Fox, R. E., 7, *32*, 161, *174*

Framo, J., 193, 216, *222*
Frances, A. J., 19, 34, 250, 268, *275*, *277*
Frank, E., 19, 21, *32*
Frank, J. D., 1, 3, *32*, 89, 229, 241–243, 260, *275*, *277*
Frankl, V., 17, *32*, 99, 109, 113, *124*
Franks, C. M., 131, 132, 135, 138n3, 139, 141, 142, 144, 145, 147, 149, 167, 169, 171, *174*, *175*, 178, 180, 236, *277*
Freeman, A., 255, *277*
French, T. M., 59, 74, 87, 230, 241, 260, *273*, *277*
Freud, A., 40, 44, 53, 54, 89
Freud, S., 39–42, 42n2, 44, 46, 47, 49, 52, 54, 58, 59, 65, 88–90, 147, *175*, 182, *223*
Friedlander, S., 102, *124*
Friedman, L., 48, 70, 90
Fromm, E., 61, 90
Fromm-Reichmann, F., 61, 90

Gabriel, T., 117, *126*
Gantt, W. H., 135, *175*
Garfield, S. L., 10, *32*, 118, 123, 227, 237, 243, 244, 249, 250, 258, 258n2, *274*, *277*
Garske, J. P., 11, *32*
Gaston, L., 265, *277*
Gelder, M. G., 232, *282*
Gendlin, E., 101, 107, 110, 115, 120, 121, 123, *124*
Gendlin, G. T., 101, 114, *128*
Gergen, K. J., 147, 148, 150, *175*
Getter, H., 269, *280*
Giannetti, V. J., 8, 38, 144, *180*
Gilbert, T. F., 140, *175*
Giles, T. R., 2, *32*, 161–163, *174*, *175*
Gill, M. M., 40, 43, 49, 51–54, 64, 70, 80, 85, 86, 90, 93, 232, 233, 235, *275*, *277*, *280*
Giorgi, A., 113, 115, *124*, *125*
Glass, D. R., *276*
Glass, G. V., 79, 94, 227, *286*
Glenwick, D., 161, *175*
Glick, I. D., 18, 19, *32*, 37
Glover, E., 79, 90
Gold, J. R., 22, 25, *32*, 37, 258, 259, 261, 263, *278*, *286*
Goldenberg, H., 182, 215, *223*
Goldenberg, I., 182, 215, *223*

Goldfried, M. R., 24, 25, 32, 162, *175*, 229, 230, 237–239, 243–245, 247, 248, 255, 257, 258, 258n2, 265, *274, 275, 277–280, 283, 284, 288*
Goldiamond, I., 168, *175*
Goldman, R., 119, *125*
Goldsamt, L. A., 265, *278, 280*
Goldstein, A. P., 242, 243, *278*
Goldstein, K., 101, 108, *125*
Goodman, P., 103, *127*
Gordon, S., 211, *223*
Gordon-Walker, J., 119, *125*
Gorman, J. M., 2, *35*
Grady, K., 162, *176*
Grawe, K., 12, *35*, 246, *275*
Gray, P., 87, *90*
Greaves, D. W., 22, *33*
Greenberg, J. R., 40, 45, 61, *91*
Greenberg, L. S., 10, *31*, 97n, 109, 115, 117–123, *123–129*, 229, 238, 239, 258n2, 263, 264, 268, 271, *277–279, 285*
Greenberg, M. D., 20, *32*
Greenberg, R. P., 20, *32*
Greenson, R. R., 46, 50, 51, 53, 54, *91*
Grencavage, L. M., 237, 244, 246, *279, 283*
Gross, M. L., 2, *32*
Grunbaum, A., 79, *91*
Guerin, P. J., Jr., 181n, 182, 203, *223*
Guevremont, D. C., 164, *179*
Guntrip, H., 40, 60, 78, *91*
Gurman, A. S., 11, *31*, 152, *175*, 229, 238, *279*
Gustafson, J. P., 11, *32*

Haaga, D. A., 244, *279*
Haigh, G., 100, *125*
Haley, J., 188, 222, *223*
Hall, M. J., 21, *30*
Hammen, C. L., *286*
Hampson, R. B., 217, *222*
Hannah, M. T., 241, 243, 244, 246, 267, *274, 286*
Hannigan, M., 115, *124*
Harris, S. L., 161, *179*
Harris, T., 248, *275*
Harter, S., 15, *35*
Hartley, D., 8, *37*
Hartmann, H., 40, 43, 44, 55, *91*
Harvey, D., 11, *32*

Hayes, A. M., 9, 36, 265, 275, *278–280*
Hayes, L. J., 165, *176*
Hayes, S. C., 16n1, *32*, 144, 149, 162, 164–166, *172, 175, 176*, 258n2, 265, 266, *279*
Hazelrigg, M. D., 217, *223*
Heard, H., 263, *279*
Heard, H. L., 263, *282*
Hefferline, R. F., 103, *127*
Heidegger, M., 97, *126*
Heilizer, F., 231, *279*
Held, B. S., 14, 15, 17, *32*, 258n2, *279*
Heller, K. H., 242, *278*
Henry, W. P., 25, *32*
Hersch, L., 163, *176*
Hersen, M., 2, 5, 30, *32*, 149, 162, *173, 176*
Higginbotham, H. N, 248, *279*
Hill, M. A., *286*
Hobbs, N., 243, *279*
Hodgson, A., 268, *275*
Hoffman, I., *275*
Hoffman, I. Z., 78, 80, *91*
Hoffman, L., 16, *33*, 184, 194, 204, 207, *223*
Hollon, S. D., 19, *36*
Horney, K., 4, *33*, 61, *91*
Horowitz, M. J., 9, *33*, 239, 244, 258n2, 271, *279, 280*
Horvath, A., 260, 265, *280*
Horvath, A. O., *277*
Houts, A. C., 148, *177*
Howard, G. S., 13, *33*
Howard, K. I., 12, *35*, 244, 246, 247, 253, 270, *283, 284*
Hoyt, M. F., 8, 11, *33*
Hughes, M., *33*
Hurvich, M., 44, *91*
Husserl, E., 97, *126*
Hutterer, R., 123, *126*

Imber, S. D., *276*
Inck, T. A., 264, *284*
Izard, C., 239, *280*

Jackson, D. D., 185, 186, 190, *222, 224, 225*
Jacobson, E., 70, 71, *91*
Jacobson, N. S., 165, *176*, 210, *224*, 258n2, 266, 272, *275, 279*
Jacoby, R., 2, *33*
James, J. R., 247, *280*

Jarvik, L. F., 286
Jason, L., 161, *175*
Jaspers, K., 97, *126*
Jeger, A. M., 161, *176*
Jensen, J. P., 22, 25, *33*
Johnson, B., *31*
Johnson, M., 107, 118, *126*
Johnson, S., 119, *125, 126*
Johnson-Laird, P. N., 117, *126*
Jones, E. E., 244, 245, 248, *280*
Jones, H. S., 139, *176*
Jourard, S. M., 98, *126*

Kadden, R. M., 269, *280*
Kagan, J., 239, *280*
Kaltreider, N., *33*
Kanfer, F. H., 132, 144, 153, 158–160, 162, 163, *176*
Kantor, J. R., 168, *176*
Kantrowitz, J., 85, *91*
Karasu, T. B., 2, *33*, 227, 244, 254, *280*
Karon, B. P., 161, *176*
Karp, J. F., 19, *32*
Kaslow, F., 182, *224*
Katz, A. L., 85, *91*
Kautto, J., 203, *223*
Kazdin, A. E., 23, *33*, 236, *280*
Keane, T. M., 168, *173*
Keith, D., 204, *225*
Keitner, G., 217, *223*
Kelly, E. L., 249, *280*
Kelly, G. A., 262, *280*
Kempler, W., *275*
Kendall, P. C., 143, 166, *176*, 237, 272, 276, *280*
Kendler, K. S., *33*
Kepner, J., 120, *126*
Kernberg, O. F., 40, 45, 64, 70, 71, 74–76, *91, 92*
Kerr, S., 265, 278, *280*
Kessler, R. C., 18, *33*
Kierkegaard, S., 97, *126*
Kiesler, D. J., 101, *128*, 260, *280*
Kilbourne, B. K., 246, *280*
Kimble, G. A., 133, 149, *176*
Kirschner, D. A., 272, *280*
Kirschner, S., 272, *280*
Klein, M., 40, 56, 74, 75, 76n5, *92*, 232, *280*
Kleinke, C., 258n2, *280*
Klerman, G. L., 61, *92*
Knight, R. P., 45, *92*

Kniskern, D. P., 152, *175*
Koenigsberg, H. W., 75, *92*
Koffka, K., 102, *126*
Kohlenberg, R. J., 16n1, *33*, 164–166, 177, 258n2, *280*
Kohler, W., 102, *126*
Kohut, H., 40, 47, 64–69, 69n4, *92*
Korman, R. J., 161, *179*
Koss, M. P., 8, *33*
Krasner, L., 136, 137, 148, 167, 169, 177, 178, *180*
Kratochwill, T. R., 164, *177*
Kris, E., 43, 50, *91, 92*
Krupnick, J., 21, 26, *33*
Kubie, L. S., 230, *281*
Kuhn, T., 68, *92*
Kuhn, T. S., 131, *177*
Kurtz, R., 227, 249, *277*

Lachmann, F. M., 83, *92*
Lambert, M. J., 2, 26, *33*, 227, 240, 244, 246, 254, *281*
Lang, P. J., 117, *126*
Langs, R., 50, *92*, 233, *281*
Lasch, C., 2, *33*
Lazarus, A. A., 11, *33*, 143, 162, *173*, 177, 229, 236, 237, 250–251, 259, 261, 264, 268, 275, *281*
Leary, K., 17, *34*
Lebow, J. L., 229, 238, *281*
Lederer, W., 185, 186, *224*
Lee, R., 120, *126*
Leger, W. R., *276*
Lehman, A. K., 10, *34*
Levenson, E., 62, 63, 65, *92*
Leventhal, H., 117, *126*
Levine, M., 8, *37*
Levis, D., 231, *281*
Lewin, K., 98, 102, *126*
Lewinsohn, P. M., 18, *30*
Liberman, R., 161, *177*
Liberman, R. P., 211, *224*
Liddell, H. S., 137, *177*
Lietaer, G., 115, 120, 123, *125, 126*, 263, *279*
Limentani, A., 53, *92*
Lindsley, O. R., 143, 151, *179*
Linehan, M. M., 165, *177*, 258n2, 259, 263, *279, 281, 282*
Litt, M. D., 269, *280*
Lockhart, R. S., 117, *124*
Loewald, H., 47, 70, 78, *92*

London, P., 2, 3, *34, 229, 232, 237, 255, 282*
Longabaugh, R., 269, *282*
Lowenstein, R. M., 43, *91*
Lubetkin, B. S., 4, *31, 162, 174*
Luborsky, E., *34*
Luborsky, L., 2, 9, *34, 55, 79, 80, 92, 93, 254, 260, 265, 269, 280, 282, 289*
Lukens, M. D., 16, *31*
Lukens, R. J., 16, *31*
Lusterman, D.-D., 215, *224*

Macalpine, I., 51, *93*
Macchia, P., 161, *177*
MacDonald, R., 246, *275*
Mace, F. C., 164, *177*
Madsen, R., 2, *30*
Mahler, M., 40, 58, 70–74, *93*
Mahoney, M. J., 11, 13, 15, 16, *34, 117, 126, 132, 150, 151, 177, 233, 236, 264, 271, 282*
Mahrer, A., 116, 120, 123, *127*
Malan, D. H., 233, *282*
Malloy, P., *282*
Mann, J., 9, *34*
Manning, D. W., 19, *34*
Manyon, I., 119, *125*
Marafiote, R. A., 161, *175*
Marcel, S., 97, *127*
Margolin, G., 210, *224*
Mark, D., 9, *34*
Marks, I. M., 232, *282*
Marmar, C., *33, 238, 278*
Marmor, J., 237, *282*
Marshall, W. L., 149, *177*
Martin, E., 80, 88
Maslow, A. H., 17, *34, 98, 127*
Masserman, J. M., 137, *177*
Mateer, F., *177*
May, R., 17, *34, 98, 99, 103, 104, 109, 110, 114, 115, 120, 123, 127, 129*
Mays, D. T., 171, *178*
McCarley, T., *286*
McCullough, L., 11, *34*
McCurry, S., *31*
McDaniel, S. H., 215, *224*
McFarlane, W. R., 213, *224*
McGill, C., 161, *177*
McGoldrick, M., 203, *223*
McGonagle, K. A., *33*

McKinney, M. K., 261, *287*
McLellan, A. T., 269, *289*
McWaters, B., 98, *127*
Meichenbaum, D., 16, *34, 233, 282*
Meissner, W. W., 45, *93*
Mendelsohn, E., 236, *282*
Meredith, K., *275*
Merry, J., *275*
Messer, S. B., 6, 8, 10–12, 15, 17, 24, 25, 35–36, 38, 80, *93, 148, 161, 178, 233, 235–237, 250, 259, 264, 274, 281–283*
Mikesell, R. H., 215, *224*
Miller, I., 217, *223*
Miller, J. G., 147, *178*
Miller, N. E., 136, 138, *173, 230, 276*
Miller, T. I., 79, *94, 227, 286*
Millon, T., 263, *283*
Mintz, J., *286*
Minuchin, S., 147, *178, 182, 209, 224*
Mischel, W., 151, *178, 233, 283*
Mitchell, K. M., 242, *287*
Mitchell, S. A., 40, 45, 61, 81, 86, *91, 93*
Modell, A. H., 40, 47, 51, 64, 70, 78, 81, *93*
Mohr, D. C., 246, 251, 252, 268, *275*
Molnar, A., 10, *31*
Molteni, A. L., 11, *32*
Moras, K., 8, *37*
Morell, J. A., 147, 149, *178*
Moretti, M. M., 10, *35*
Motoike, P., *286*
Moustakas, C., 113, *127*
Mowrer, O. H., 137, *178*
Mowrer, W. M., 137, *178*
Moyer, J., *33*
Mulaick, S. A., 247, *280*
Muran, C., 258, 271, *285*
Murray, E. J., 237, *283*
Murray, N. E., 233, *283*
Muslin, H., 64, *93*

Nathan, P. E., 2, *35, 258, 288*
Neale, J., 258, *276*
Neigher, W. D., 147–149, *174, 178*
Neimeyer, R. A., 15, 16, 27, *35, 36, 264, 283*
Neisser, U., 116, 117, *127*
Nelson, C. B., *33*
Nelson, R. O., 149, 162, *172*
Nevis, E., 120, *127*

Newman, C., 230, 255, *278*
Nezu, A. M., 162, 164, *178*
Nezu, C. M., 162, 164, *178*
Nichols, M. P., 182, 184, 185, 218, *224*
Noel, N., *282*
Norcross, J. C., 227, 237, 238, 240, 244, 246, 249, 250, 255, 258, 258n2, 270, *273, 274, 276, 279, 283, 284*

O'Brien, C. P., 269, *289*
O'Donahue, W., 25, *35*, 167, 169, *178*
O'Leary, K. D., 140, 145, 146, *178, 180,* 258, *288*
Olfson, M., 7, *35*
Ollendick, T. H., 162, *178*
Olson, D. H., 217, *224*
Omer, H. G., 13–15, *35, 37,* 258n2, 264, 266, 271, *283*
Orlinsky, D. E., 12, *35,* 244, 246, 247, 253, 270, *283, 284*
Ornstein, P., 66, *93*

Packer, M. J., 148, *178*
Paivio, S., 118, 120, *125, 127*
Palmer, M., 237, 255, *282*
Paolitto, F., 85, *91*
Papajohn, J. C., 237, *284*
Parks, B. P., 12, *35*
Parloff, M. B., 232, *276, 280*
Parry, A., 14, *35*
Pascual-Leone, J., 121, 122, *125*
Paul, G. L., 250, *284*
Pepper, S. C., 150, 170, *178*
Perls, F. S., 99, 102, 103, *127*
Perry, S., 250, 268, *275, 277*
Persons, J. B., 18, 19, 21, 24, *35, 36,* 153, 154, 154n4, 155–157, 162, *178*
Peterfreund, E., 58n3, 83, *93*
Peterson, D. R., 151, 152, *179*
Petronko, M. R., 161, 163, *179*
Phillips, E. L., 7, *36*
Pilkonis, P. A., *33, 276*
Pincus, H. A., 7, *35*
Pine, F., 39, 40, 70, 72, 73, 84, 87, *93, 94*
Pinsof, W. M., 229, 238, 258n2, 272, *276, 284*
Plaud, J. J., 167, *179*
Polkinghorne, D. E., 12, 14, *36,* 148, *179*
Polster, E., 17, *36,* 103, 110, *127*

Polster, M., 17, *36,* 103, 110, *127*
Pope, K. S., *31*
Poppen, P. J., 229, *287*
Porder, M. S., 45, *87*
Powell, D. H., 237, *284*
Powell, S. L., 272, *276*
Prochaska, J. O., 227, 240, 244, 245, 249, 258n2, 270, *283, 284*
Prouty, G., 120, 122, *127*
Pulver, S., 84, *94*
Putnam, H., 150, *179*

Rabkin, R., 207, *224*
Rachman, S., 231, *288*
Racker, H., 64, *94*
Raimy, V., 243, *275, 284*
Rangell, L., 54, *94*
Rank, O., 48, 74, *89*
Raskin, N. J., 100, 101, *127*
Raue, P. J., 265, *275, 277, 284*
Raw, S., 24, *36*
Raw, S. D., *31*
Reeve, J., 264, *284*
Reich, W., 4, *36,* 54, *94*
Reid, W. J., 11, *36*
Rennie, D. L., 115, 117, 122, *125, 128*
Rhoads, J. M., 232, 236, 237, *276, 285*
Rice, L. N., 97n, 115, 117, 118, *125,* 128, 258n2, 263, 268, *279, 285*
Richards, A. D., 82, 83, *94*
Richards, A. K., 82, 83, *94*
Richardson, F. C., 132, *180*
Richardson, J. T., 246, *280*
Ricks, D. F., 229, *287*
Ricoeur, P., 16, *36*
Rieff, P., 2, *36*
Risley, T. R., 164, *172*
Robertson, M. H., 258n2, *285*
Robin, A. L., 153, *179*
Robins, C. J., 9, *36,* 243, *278*
Robinson, L. A., 27, *36*
Robinson, P., 161, *179*
Rogers, C. R., 99–101, 104, 108, 111, 114, *127, 128,* 147, *179,* 242, *285*
Rogoff, B., 147, *172*
Rohrbaugh, M. J., 269, *286*
Rombauts, J., 115, *126*
Rorty, R., 13, *36*
Rosen, R., *286*
Rosenau, P. M., 14, *36*
Rosenbaum, M., 169, *175*

Rosenzweig, S., 241, 243, *285*
Rosman, B., 209, *224*
Rossi, J. S., *284*
Rotgers, F., 131, 132, 145, 149, 167, 171, *174*
Rotter, J. B., *275*
Rounsaville, B., 61, *92*
Ruben, D. H., 168, *179*
Rubin, A., *282*
Ruesh, J., 184, *224*
Rush, A. J., 19, *32*, 36, 254, *274*
Russell, B., 184, *225*
Russell, C. S., 217, *224*
Ryan, C., 217, *223*
Ryle, A., 258n2, 262, *285*

Sabatelli, R. M., 216, *222*
Safran, J. D., 11, *36*, 117, *125*, 229, 238, 239, 258, 264, 271, 278, 279, *285*
Salovey, P., 10, *34*
Sampson, H., 9, *38*, 40, 70, 71, 76, 77, 80, 86, *96*
Sanderson, W. C., 25, *31*, 36
Sandler, J., 58, 70, 84, *94*
Sartre, J.-P., 97, 111, *128*
Sass, L. A., 12, 17, *35*, 36, *38*, 106, *129*, 148, *178*
Satir, V., 204, 205, *224*
Scarr, S., 148, *179*
Schacht, T. E., 25, *32*, 235, 236–237, 262, *285*
Schafer, R., 17, *36*, 50, 53, 57, 70, 78, *94*, 233, *285*
Schatzberg, A. F., 19, *31*
Schefft, B. K., 132, 144, 153, 158–160, 162, 163, *176*
Schimek, J. G., 51, *94*
Schmidt, K. A., *34*
Schmidt, P., 123, *126*
Schneider, K., 120, 123, *129*
Schofield, W., 242, *285*
Schwaber, E., 50, *94*
Schwartz, G. E., 238, 239, *285*
Schwartz, R. C., 218, 219, *224*
Sears, R. R., 230, *285*
Sechrest, L. B., 242, *278*
Seeman, J. A., 100, *129*
Segal, H., 45, *94*
Segal, L., 10, *31*
Segal, Z. V., 238, 239, 271, *285*, *286*

Segraves, R. T., 11, *36*, 229, 237, 238, *286*
Selekman, M. D., 214, *224*
Seligman, M. E. P., 8, 20, 24, *37*
Selzer, M. A., 75, *92*
Settle, E. C., 19, *37*
Shaffer, L. F., 137, *179*
Shapiro, D. A., 2, 4, 27, *31*, *37*, 227, 281, *286*
Shapiro, F., 168, *179*
Shaw, B. F., 10, *35*, 254, *274*
Shaw, F. J., 137, *179*
Shea, M. T., *276*
Shengold, L. L., 233, *286*
Shepherd, I. L., 103, *124*
Shiang, J., 8, *33*
Shoben, E. J., Jr., 137, *179*, 230, *286*
Shoham, V., 22, 25, *31*, *37*, 269, *286*
Shoham-Salomon, V., 267, *286*
Silverman, D. K., 40, 84, *94*
Silverman, L. H., 233, 236, 282, *286*
Silverman, W. H., 25, *37*
Simkin, J. S., 103, *129*
Simmens, S., 26, *33*
Simon, K., 255, *277*
Singer, B., *34*
Skinner, B. F., 104, *128*, 137, 143, 151, *179*
Sledge, W. H., 8, *37*
Sloane, R. B., 227, 240, 251, *286*
Slotnick, R. S., 161, *176*
Smith, M. B., 113, *129*
Smith, M. L., 79, *94*, 227, 240, 251, 254, *286*
Smuts, J., 102, *129*
Solomon, H. C., 143, 151, *179*
Sommers-Flanagan, J., 20, *37*
Sommers-Flanagan, R., 20, *37*
Sotsky, S. M., 26, *33*, *276*
Spark, G., 194, *222*
Spence, D. P., 13, 16, *37*, 80, *94*
Spiegler, M. D., 153, 164, *179*
Spillman, A., 80, *93*
Spinks, S., 153, *173*
Sponsel, R., 258n2, *286*
Sprenkle, D. H., 213, 217, *224*
Staats, A. W., 142, 167, 169, *179*, *180*
Staples, F. R., 227, *286*
Stein, D. J., 271, *286*
Stein, M. H., 53, *94*
Sterling, M. M., 17, *31*
Steuer, J. L., 251, *286*

Stiles, W. B., 2, 27, 31, 37, 227, 240, 248, 254, 286
Stolorow, R. D., 78, 94
Stone, L., 45, 47, 49, 54, 95
Storr, A., 67, 95
Strachey, J., 47, 59, 95
Strenger, C., 13–15, 35, 37, 264, 283
Stricker, G., 23, 25, 37, 258, 259, 261, 263, 278, 286
Strosahl, K. S., 161, 166, 176, 180
Strupp, H. H., 9, 25, 30, 32, 61, 95, 241, 254, 275, 286, 287
Stuart, R., 211, 224
Suarez, A., 263, 281
Sue, S., 31
Sullivan, H. S., 50, 61–63, 95
Sullivan, W., 2, 30
Sutich, A. J., 98, 129
Swidler, A., 2, 30
Syme, S. L., 248, 276
Szymanski, J., 25, 35

Tageson, W. C., 98, 114, 129
Task Force on Promotion and Dissemination of Psychological Procedures, 21, 37
Taylor, C., 123, 129
Thase, M. E., 18, 19, 36, 37
Thoresen, C. E., 229, 238, 287
Thorndike, E. L., 135, 180
Tipton, S., 2, 30
Tishby, O., 80, 93
Tomarken, R., 117, 126
Toukmanian, S. G., 115, 122, 125, 128
Truax, C., 101, 128
Truax, C. B., 242, 287
Tsai, M., 16n1, 33, 164–166, 177, 258n2, 280

Ullmann, L. P., 136, 180
Urry, H., 269, 286

Van Balen, R., 115, 126
Van Kaam, A., 115, 129
Vich, M., 98, 129
von Glasersfeld, E., 16, 37

Wachtel, E. F., 221, 224, 225, 229, 237, 238, 272, 287

Wachtel, P. L., 6, 25, 29, 37, 38, 54, 95, 221, 225, 229, 233–235, 237, 238, 258n2, 259, 261, 262, 272, 278, 287
Waelder, R., 44, 45, 95
Walborn, F. S., 258n2, 287
Wallerstein, R. S., 33, 40, 48, 52, 55, 82, 83, 87, 95
Wampold, B. E., 38
Wandersman, A., 229, 238, 287
Warkentin, J., 204, 225
Warner, M. S., 120, 121, 129
Warren, C. S., 6, 8, 10, 15, 35, 161, 178
Watkins, J. T., 33, 276
Watson, J. B., 118, 120–123, 125, 129, 134, 137, 151, 180, 277
Watzlawick, P., 185, 190, 225
Weakland, J. H., 10, 31,185, 190, 222, 224, 225
Weber, C. C., 237, 277
Webster, M., 115, 125
Weinberger, J., 260n3, 265, 266, 287
Weinshel, E. M., 48, 55, 85, 95
Weiss, J., 9, 38, 40, 70, 71, 76, 77, 80, 86, 96
Weissman, M., 61, 92
Weitzman, B., 231, 288
Wells, R. A., 8, 38, 144, 180
Wertheimer, M., 102, 129
West, S. G., 248, 279
Westen, D., 263, 288
Wexler, B. E., 18, 38
Wexler, M., 51, 91
Wheeler, G., 120, 126, 129
Whipple, K., 227, 286
Whitaker, C., 204, 225
White, M., 13, 14, 38, 219, 225
Whitehead, A. N., 184, 225
Widmeyer Group, 161, 180
Wilcox, N. S., 284
Wile, D. B., 83, 96
Williams, D. A., 31
Williams, R. E., 268, 275
Willick, M. S., 45, 87
Wills, T. A., 246, 248, 288
Wilner, N., 33
Wilson, G. T., 9, 24, 25, 38, 140–142, 144–146, 149, 178, 180, 258, 288
Wilson, K. G., 166, 176
Winnicott, D. W., 40, 47, 60, 61, 70, 78, 96

Winokur, M., 236, *283*
Wiser, S., 265, *275, 288*
Witenberg, E. G., 63, 64, 96
Wittchen, H., *33*
Wolf, M. M., 164, *172*
Wolfe, B. E., 24, 25, *32, 237, 238, 257, 262, 271, 288*
Wolitzky, D. L., 39n, 79, 89
Wolpe, J., 136, 139, *180,* 231, *288*
Woods, S. E., *237, 282*
Woodward, B., 21, *30*
Woodward, S. H., 168, *173*
Woody, G. E., 269, *288*
Woody, S. R., 25, *31, 36*

Woolfolk, R. L., 12, 17, *35, 38,* 132, 148, *178, 180*

Yalom, I., 17, 38, 99, 103, 104, 109–111, 113–115, *127, 129*
Yates, A. J., *237, 288*
Yontef, G. M., 103, 112, 116, 120, *129*
Yorkston, N. J., 227, *286*

Zajonc, R., 239, *280*
Zborowski, M. J., 20, *32*
Zetzel, E. R., 45, 96
Zhao, S., *33*
Zucker, H., 62, 96

SUBJECT INDEX

AABT. *See* Association for Advancement of Behavior Therapy
Abreaction, 41–42
Abstinence, 46, 49–50
Acceptance and Commitment Therapy (ACT), 166
Acceptance (common factor), 266
Ackerman, Nathan, 182, 206–208
ACT. *See* Acceptance and Commitment Therapy
Active techniques, 48
Actuarial matrix, 252–253
Adler, Alfred, 182
Adult Children of Alcoholics, 182
Age of Grand Theory, 149
Agoraphobia, 58, 73
Alcoholics Anonymous, 219
Alexander, Franz, 231
Allport, Gordon, 113
American Psychiatric Association, 19–20
American Psychological Association (APA), 21, 100, 167, 169, 215
American Psychological Society, 167
Anderson, Carol, 220
Anderson, Harlene, 218
Antidepressant medication, 18–21
Anxiety, 43–44, 62
APA. *See* American Psychological Association
Applied behavior analysis, 141–142, 164–166
Assimilative integration, 259–260
Association for Advancement of Behavior Therapy (AABT), 140, 165–167
Association for Behavior Analysis, 141
Auerswald, E. H., 207
Autistic psychoses, 72–73
Autonomy, primary vs. secondary, 44

Balint, M., 56
Bandura, A., 142
Barlow, D. H., 156–157
Bateson, Gregory, 183–186, 191
Bateson Project, 182–186
Beavers, W. R., 217

Beckham, E. E., 239
Beels, Christian, 219
Behaviorism, behavioralism vs., 135–136
Behavior therapy, 131–172. *See also* Cognitive–behavioral therapy
brief, 9–10
case formulation approach, 154–156
cognitive-behavioral therapy vs., 132
constructive change as goal of, 132
contextual, 166
defining, 143–146
epistemological paradigms of, 147–150
family therapy, behavioral, 210–211
and learning theory, 133–136
and managed care, 160–164
marital therapy, behavioral, 211
metatheoretical framework for, 146–147
multimodal therapy, 250–251, 261
original focus of, 4–5
origins of, 133–143
panic disorder, packaged therapy for, 156–157
process model of, 158–160
radical, 16n1
in Russia, 140–141
theoretical developments within, 164–169
theoretical submovements within, 141–143
worldviews of, 150–153
Beliefs, pathogenic, 77
Bell, John, 194–195
Beutler, L. E., 251–252
Bohart, A., 121
Bootstrapping, 240–241, 247
Borderline personality organization, 74–76
Boundaries (in family therapy), 208–210
Bowen, Murray, 189, 195–201, 203, 211–212, 220
Bowlby, J., 56
Breathing retraining, 156–157
Breuer, J., 42n2
Brief psychotherapy, 5–11
in behavior therapy, 9–10

Brief psychotherapy (*continued*)
  defining, 7–8
  effectiveness of, 8–9
  in family therapy, 10
  focus in, 8
  in humanistic/experiential therapy, 10
  in integrative approaches, 10–11
  and managed care, 7
  motivations for, 5–6
  origins of, 6–7
  prevalence of, 7
  in psychoanalytic approaches, 9
Brief Therapy Project, 183, 190, 191, 218
Buber, Martin, 101, 102, 112
Bugental, J. F. T., 116

Cantor, N., 151–152
Carrol, Lewis, 2
Carter, Betty, 201, 203
Case formulation approach (behavior
    therapy), 154–156
Center for Family Learning (CFL), 201,
    219–220
CFL. *See* Center for Family Learning
Character, 4
Character disorders, 4
Child Guidance Movement, 182
Children, integrative approaches with,
    272
Circular questioning, 189
Circumplex Model, 217
Client-centered therapy, 17
  and construction of new meaning, 110
  discovery focus of, 104–105
  growth focus of, 107–108
  origins of, 99–101
  recent developments in, 114
  relationship in, 111–112
  therapeutic process in, 104–105, 107–
    108, 110–112
Client-Centered Therapy (Carl Rogers),
    100–101
Client suitability, for brief psychotherapy,
    8
Clinical psychologists, 136, 167
Clinton, W., 161
Cognitive–behavioral therapy, 132, 143,
    165, 166. *See also* Behavior ther-
    apy
  constructivist approach, 16
  as integrative therapy, 255
Cognitive restructuring, 157

Cognitive therapy, constructivist ap-
    proach to, 15–16
Common factors approach, 10–11, 240–
    249
  definition, 229
  depression, treatment of, 260
  early history, 241–244
  evaluation of, 246–249
  recent developments, 244–246, 264–
    268
Common features of psychotherapy, 2
Communications approach to family
    therapy, 183–192
  Bateson's theories, 183–187
  Brief Therapy Project, 189–191
  Haley's theories, 187–188
  Milan Associates, 189
Complementary models of psychotherapy,
    236
Concentration therapy, 102
Conditional reflex, 135
Conflicts, neurotic, 44–46
Constructivism, 13–17
Contextual behavior therapy, 166
Contextualism, 16n1
Cooper, A. M., 52
Corrective emotional experiences, 241
Corrective symbiotic experiences, 74
Cost effectiveness, 28–29, 161
Counseling and Psychotherapy
    (Carl Rogers), 100
Countertransference, 50, 64–65
Couples, integrative approaches to, 272
Crisis intervention, 163
Cyclical psychodynamics, 235

Daseinanalyse, 103
Davidson, N., 211
DBT. *See* Dialectical Behavior Therapy
Defense hysteria, 42
Defense mechanisms, 44
Demoralization, 243
Demystification, 63
Depression, psychopharmacological treat-
    ments for, 18–21
Depression Guideline Panel (Agency for
    Health Care Policy and Re-
    search), 19–20
de Shazer, Steve, 10, 218
Developmental defects, 68
Dewey, John, 100

Diagnostic and Statistical Manual of Mental Disorders (DSM), 4, 24–25
Dialectical Behavior Therapy (DBT), 263
Differentiation, 197–199
Disease model of mental illness, 138
Division of Clinical Psychology (American Psychological Association), 21, 22, 27
Dollard, J., 230–231, 233
Dose-effect studies, 8
Double bind, 184–185, 220
Drive theory. *See* Freudian drive theory
DSM. *See Diagnostic and Statistical Manual of Mental Disorders*
Dunlap, K., 137
Duquesne University, 115
Dynamic hypothesis, 76–77

Early intervention, 163
Eclecticism, 228. *See also* Integration, psychotherapy; Technical eclecticism
Economic factors, 28–29
Effectiveness of psychotherapy
  behavior therapy, 162
  brief psychotherapy, 8–9
  cost effectiveness, 28–29, 161
  empirically validated treatments, 22–24
Efficacy of psychotherapy, 23–24, 26
Efficiency, 28
Ego, 39, 42, 44, 45, 66, 74
Ego psychology, 40, 43–55
  analytic interpretation in, 53–54
  autonomy of ego functions in, 44
  contribution of, 44
  and object relations theory, 55
  and psychoanalysis vs. psychoanalytic psychotherapy, 54–55
  technical neutrality in, 49–50
  therapeutic framework of, 44–45
  and traditional Freudian theory, 45–50
  transference in, 50–52
  wish and anxiety in, 43–44
EMDR. *See* Eye Movement Desensitization and Reprocessing
Emotion, in humanistic psychotherapy, 117
Emotional experiencing (common factor), 265
Emotional pursuer/distancer, 201–202
Empathy of therapist, 47–48, 50

Empirically validated treatments (EVTs), 21–27
  conceptual aspects of, 23–26
  criteria for (exhibit), 23
  methodological aspects of, 26–27
  political aspects of, 22
Empiricism, 133
Enlightenment, 11, 132, 133
Epistemology, 147
Erickson, Milton, 187
Erikson, E., 234
Erwin, E., 146
Esalen Institute, 102
European Association for Behaviour Therapy, 141
EVTs. *See* Empirically validated treatments
"Exceptions," looking for, 10
Existential approaches to psychotherapy
  and construction of new meaning, 111
  growth focus of, 109–110
  origins of, 103–104
  person-centeredness of, 112–113
  phenomenological aspects of, 106
  recent developments in, 114, 115
  therapeutic process in, 106, 109–112
Experiential family therapy, 203–206
Eye Movement Desensitization and Reprocessing (EMDR), 168
Eysenck, H. J., 136, 139, 143, 249

Fairbairn, W. R. D., 55–58, 63, 193, 194
False self, 61
Families, integrative approaches to, 272
Families and Family Therapy (Salvador Minuchin), 209
Family Systems Training (FST), 219
Family therapy, 181–222
  behavioral approach, 210–211
  brief psychotherapy, 10
  collaborative–conversational model of, 218–219
  communications approach, 183–192
  constructivist approach, 16
  deconstruction model of, 219
  development of, 211–212
  experiential, 203–206
  internal family systems model of, 219
  multigenerational approach, 192–206
  and normalcy of family functioning, 217–221
  psychoeducational approach, 219–220

Family therapy (continued)
    recent developments in, 212–221
    solution-focused model of, 218
    strategic, 185, 188, 190
    structural, 187, 206–210
    "uncovering" vs. "containment" models of, 213–214
FAP. See Functional Analytic Theory
Feedback, providing patients with, 244–245
Ferber, Andrew, 201, 218, 219
Ferber, Jane, 219
Ferenczi, S., 56
Fiedler, F. E., 241–242
Fisch, Richard, 186, 190
Fishman, D. B., 144–145, 150
Fluoxetine (Prozac), 20–21
Focus, in brief psychotherapy, 8
Fogarty, Thomas, 201–203
Forgetting, 42
Foundationlessness, 12, 14
Fragmentariness, 12–14
Framo, James, 193–194
Frank, Jerome, 1–4, 242, 243
Frankl, Victor, 99, 103
Franks, C. M., 236
Free association, 42
Freud, Sigmund
    and behavior therapy, 150
    drive theory of, 39–43, 61, 81
    "dynamic hypothesis" of, 76–77
    instinct theory of, 67
    "Little Hans" case of, 182
    on neuroses, 45
    and object relations theory, 56, 57
    and pluralism, 80
    and psychology as profession, 4
    on self love, 66
    signal anxiety concept of, 62
    on transference, 52
Freudian drive theory, 39–43, 61, 81
Friedlander, S., 102
Fromm, Erich, 103
FST. See Family Systems Training
Functional Analytic Theory (FAP), 165–166
Functional autonomy, 44

Gantt, W. H., 135
Gendlin, Eugene, 101, 110
Generic model of psychotherapy, 270–271

Georgetown University, 196, 201
The Gestalt Approach and Eyewitness to Therapy (Frederick Perls), 103
Gestalt therapy, 17
    and construction of new meaning, 110–111
    discovery focus of, 105–106
    growth focus of, 108–109
    origins of, 102–103
    person-centeredness of, 112
    recent developments in, 115
    therapeutic process in, 105–106, 108–112
Gestalt Therapy Integrated (Frederick Perls), 103
Gibbon, Edward, 67
Gill, M. M., 51–52, 80–81, 81, 235–236
Goals, in brief psychotherapy, 8
Gold, J. R., 259
Goldfried, M. R., 244–245, 265
Goldstein, Kurt, 101, 102
Goldstein, Michael, 220
Good breast/bad breast, 193
Goodman, P., 102
Goolishan, Henry, 218
Gorbachev, M., 140
Gordon, Ed, 201
Gordon, S., 211
Greenberg, Leslie, 116, 263–264, 268
Guerin, Katherine, 201
Guerin, Philip, 200–203, 219
Guilt, 44
Guntrip, H., 56
Guthrie, 149, 170

Haley, Jay, 184, 185, 187–189, 207, 220
Hayes, S. C., 164–166, 266
Hefferline, R. F., 102
Heidegger, Martin, 103
Hermann, 56
Hoffman, Lynn, 207
Holding environment, 47
Hope, arousal of, 247
Horney, Karen, 102, 103, 234
Hull, 149, 170
Humanistic approaches to psychotherapy, 97–123
    brief psychotherapy, 10
    client-centered approach, 99–101, 104–105, 107–108, 110–112, 114
    emotion in, 117

existential approaches, 103–104, 106, 109–112, 114, 115
future of, 116–117
Gestalt approach, 102–103, 105–106, 108–112, 115
growth orientation of, 98, 107–110
and mainstream psychology, 113–114
person-centeredness of, 99, 111–113
and phenomenology, 98, 104–107
postmodernism in, 17
practical developments in, 119–120
recent theoretical developments in, 115–116, 120–121
research in, 118–119
self-determination as theme of, 99, 110–111
Husserl, Edmund, 103
Hysteria, 41, 42

Id, 44
Id psychology, 40
IFS model. *See* Internal family systems model
Impulsivity, 269
Infant–mother dyad, 61, 63
Insomnia, 269
Integration, psychotherapy, 227–272
  brief psychotherapy, 10–11
  common factors approach, 240–249, 260, 264–268
  contributions of, 256
  defining, 228
  and focus on self, 271
  generic model, 270–271
  goal of, 264
  growing interest in, 254–256
  problems with, 256–257
  recent developments in, 258–272
  and resistance to change, 271
  scope of, 229
  technical eclecticism, 249–253, 261, 268–269
  theoretical integration approach, 230–240, 259–264
  transtheoretical approach, 270
Intellectualization, 44
The Intensive Theory of Schizophrenia (Nagy & Framo), 193–194
Interactional theories, 152–153
Internal family systems (IFS) model, 219
Internalized objects, 56–57, 59, 60
Interoceptive exposure, 157

Interpersonal psychoanalysis, 61–70
  and Kohut's self psychology, 65–70
  Sullivan's theory of, 62–65
Interpretation, in ego psychology, 53–54
Invisible Loyalties (Nagy & Spark), 194
I–Thou relationship, 101, 112, 116

Jackson, Don, 184–186, 189–190, 204
Jacobson, N., 210
Janet, P., 42
Jaspers, Karl, 103

Kanfer, F. H., 158–160
Kantor, J. R., 168
Kelly, George, 113
Kernberg, O. F., 71, 73–76
Kerr, Michael, 201, 203
Kierkegaard, Soren, 103, 117
Kilpatrick, W. H., 100
Klein, Melanie, 56, 193
Kohlenberg, R. J., 165–166
Kohler, Wolfang, 114
Kohut, H., 65–70, 73, 81, 121
Krasner, L., 136–137

Langley Porter Institute, 184
Language, fragmentariness of, 14
Lazarus, Arnold, 250–251, 264
Learning theory, 133–136
Liberman, R. P., 211
Libido, 56, 66
Lindsley, O. R., 151
Linehan, M. M., 263
"Little Hans," 182
Live modeling, 142
Logical positivism, 147, 148
Logotherapy, 103
London, P., 232

Madanes, Cloé, 188
Mahler, M., 70–74
Managed care, 27–29
  and behavior therapy, 160–164
  and brief psychotherapy, 7
  and values, 28
Managed care organizations (MCOs), 7, 22
Manuals, use of
  for behavior therapy, 162
  in empirically validated treatments, 25–27

Marcel, Gabriel-Honoré, 103
Margolin, G., 210
Mateer, F., 137
Maudsley Hospital, 136, 138, 139, 143–144
May, Rollo, 99, 103–104, 112, 113, 116
McFarlane, William, 219, 220
McGoldrick, Monica, 201, 203
McMaster Model, 217
MCOs. *See* Managed care organizations
Meaning, creation of, 14, 17, 103, 110–111
"Medicalization" of psychotherapy, 3–5
Menninger Clinic, 183, 196
Menninger Foundation, 55
Mental Research Institute (MRI), 10, 186, 190, 191, 204, 218
Messer, S. B., 233, 236, 259
Metatheories, 146
Milan Associates, 183, 189
Miller, N. E., 230–231
Minuchin, Salvador, 182, 187, 189, 202, 207–210, 212
Mischel, W., 151
Modeling, 142
Modernist approach to psychotherapy, 11–12
Montalvo, Braulio, 187, 207
Mother–child dyad, 197
Mowrer, O. H., 137, 142
Mowrer, W. M., 137
MRI. *See* Mental Research Institute
Multigenerational approach to family therapy, 192–206
    Bowenian family systems therapy, 195–201
    experiential family therapy, 203–206
    Fogarty's theories, 201–202
    group focus in, 194–195
    Guerin's theories, 202–203
Multimodal therapy, 250–251, 261
Murphy, Gardner, 113
Murray, Henry, 113

Nagy (Boszormenyi-Nagy), Ivan, 193–194, 214
Narcissism, 66–68
Narrative psychotherapy as, 13–15
National Institute of Mental Health (NIMH), 26, 183, 196, 238
National Medical Expenditures Survey, 7

Neobehavioristic mediational S–R model, 142
Neopragmatism, 13, 15
Neurotic conflicts, 44–46
Neutrality, in psychoanalytic approach, 49–50
New experiences, providing patients with, 244
New York Institute for Gestalt Therapy, 102
Nichols, M. P., 218
Nietzsche, Friedrich, 103
NIMH. *See* National Institute of Mental Health
Nodal events, 198
Normal autism, 71–72
Normal symbiosis, 72

Object, 39, 66
Object love, 66–67
Object relations theory, 55–61, 73, 192–194
    basic tenets of, 56–57
    and ego psychology, 55
    treatment implications of, 57–61
Oedipal conflicts, 45, 48, 84
O'Hanlon, William, 218
Olson, D. H., 217
On Becoming a Person (Carl Rogers), 101
Optimal failures, 69
Ordeal therapy, 188
Overt difficulties, 154

Panic disorder, packaged therapy for, 156–157
Papp, Peggy, 207
Paradigmatic behaviorism, 142–143
Paradoxical injunction, 185
Participant-observer, therapist as, 50, 63, 64, 80
Pathogenic beliefs, 77
Paul, Gordon, 250
Pavlov, Ivan, 134–135, 139, 142
Pendagast, Eileen, 201, 219
Perls, Frederick (Fritz), 99, 102–103, 108, 112
Perls, Laura, 102
Personality and Psychotherapy (Dollard & Miller), 230
Personality disorders, 4
Person-centered therapy, 101
Persons, J. B., 154–157

Persuasion, psychotherapy as, 242–243
Persuasion and Healing (Jerome Frank), 1–4, 242
Peterson, D. R., 151, 152
Pharmacotherapy, 5, 17–21
  compared with psychotherapy, 18–19
  with or without psychotherapy, 19–20
  placebos, use of, 20–21
Philadelphia Child Guidance Clinic, 182, 187
Pine, F., 84
Placebos, 20–21
Pluralism, 12, 40, 78–82, 80
Positive expectancies, 247
Postmodernist approach to psychotherapy, 12–17
  constructivism in, 14–17
  foundationless in, 14
  fragmentariness in, 14
  neopragmatism in, 15
  pluralism in, 12
Pragmatic paradigm, 148–150
Pragmatics of Human Communication (Watzlawick, Beavin, & Jackson), 185–186, 190
Prevention, 163
Primary autonomy, 44
Problem-Solving Therapy (Milton Erickson), 187
Process analytic approach, 268
Process model of therapeutic change, 158–160
Process question, 189
Prochaska, J. O., 245
Projective identification, 193
Prozac (fluoxetine), 20–21
Pseudomutuality, 195
Psychoanalysis
  definition of classical, 49
  psychoanalytic psychotherapy vs., 54–55
Psychoanalytic approaches to psychotherapy, 39–87. *See also* Multigenerational approach to family therapy
  brief psychotherapy, 9
  constructivist approach, 16–17
  ego psychology, 43–55
  Freudian drive theory, 41–43
  interpersonal psychoanalysis, 61–70
  Kernberg's theory, 71, 74–76
  Mahler's theory, 70–74
  object relations theory, 55–61

theoretical pluralism in, 40, 78–82
theory vs. technique in, 82–85
unconscious-control theory, 71, 76–78
"widening scope" of, 45
Psychodynamic–behavioral integration, 233–239
The Psychodynamics of Family Life (Nathan Ackerman), 207
Psychodynamic Therapy and Behavior Therapy (Arkowitz & Messer), 235
Psychopharmacology, 138
Psychoses, autistic vs. symbiotic, 72–73
Psychosomatic Families (Minuchin, Rosman, & Baker), 209
Psychotherapy integration. *See* Integration, psychotherapy
Psychotherapy Research Project (Menninger Foundation), 55
Psychotherapy (Schofield), 242
Pulver, S., 84

Rabkin, Richard, 207
Radical behavior therapy, 16n1
Raimy, V., 243
Random assignment, 26
Rank, Otto, 100, 102
Reactance, 268
Recursive patterning, 65
Regression, in treatment, 60
Regressive transference neurosis, 51
Relaxation, in behavior therapy, 139–140
Repression, 42
Resistance, 53–54, 69, 271
Rogers, Carl, 11–12, 99–101, 104, 107, 108, 111, 114, 121, 242
Rossman, Bernice, 207
Ruesch, Jurgen, 184
Russia, behavior therapy in, 140–141
Ryle, A., 262

Sampson, H., 76–78
Sartre, Jean-Paul, 103, 111
Satir, Virginia, 204–206
Schacht, T. E., 235–237
Schefft, B. K., 158–160
Scheflen, Albert, 201
Schizophrenia, and family communication, 184, 219–221
Schofield, W., 242
Schools of psychotherapy, 2–3, 83
Schwartz, R. C., 218

Sechenov, Ivan, 135
Secondary autonomy, 44
Self
    as integrative construct, 271
    in psychoanalytic theories, 39–41
Self-efficacy, 142
Selfobjects, 67–68
Self pathologies, 165
Self psychology, 40, 65–70
    and object love, 66–67
    and selfobject, 67–68
    and traditional Freudian theory, 65–66
    treatment implications of, 68–70
Self-regulation, in Gestalt therapy, 108
Selvini-Palazoli, Maria, 189
SEPI. *See* Society for the Exploration of
        Psychotherapy Integration
Sherman, Randy, 219
Skinner, B. F., 136, 149, 151, 165, 170
Smuts, Jan, 102
Social behaviorism, 142–143
Social constructivism, 80–81, 147, 148
Social interaction, 152
Social learning theory, 142
Society for the Exploration of Psycho-
        therapy Integration (SEPI), 255–
        256
Solomon, H. R., 151
Spark, Geraldine, 194
Spence, Kenneth, 114
Splitting, 193
S–R theory. *See* Stimulus–response the-
        ory
Staats, A. W., 142–143
Stimulus–response (S–R) theory, 138,
        139, 142, 167, 169
Story construction, psychotherapy as, 13–
        15
Strategic family therapy, 185, 188, 190
Stricker, G., 261
Structural family therapy, 187, 206–210
Structuralism, 134
Structural neuroses, 65
Stuart, R., 211
Sullivan, Harry Stack, 61–64, 64, 103,
        184, 234
Superego, 44, 57, 59–60
Symbiotic psychoses, 72–73
Symbolic modeling, 142
Symptoms, treatment of, 3–6
Synergistic models of psychotherapy, 236
Systematic desensitization, 140

Systematic eclectic psychotherapy, 251–
        252

Tavistock Group, 194, 195
Technical eclecticism, 249–253
    definition, 229
    early history, 249–250
    evaluation and current status of, 252–
        253
    Lazarus' theory of, 250–251
    recent developments, 268–269
    role of theory in, 261
    systematic eclectic psychotherapy, 251–
        252
Technical neutrality, 49–50
Test-passing/-failing, 77–78
Theoretical–assimilative integration,
        261–264
Theoretical integration, 230–240
    and assimilative integration, 259–260
    definition, 229
    early history of, 230–232
    evaluation of, 239–240
    in 1970s, 232–233
    psychodynamic–behavioral integration,
        233–239
    recent developments, 237–239, 261–
        264
Therapeutic alliance, 46
Therapeutic double bind, 185
Think rules, 158
Thorndike, E. L., 135–137
Tillich, Paul, 102
Titchener, Edward, 133–134
Tolman, 149, 170
Transference, 46, 50–54, 69
Translational models of psychotherapy,
        236
Transtheoretical approach, 270
Treatment manuals. *See* Manuals, use of
Triangles, relationship, 199–200, 202,
        203
Triangulation, 199–200
Truax, C. B., 242
Twelve-Step programs, 219

Unconscious-control hypothesis, 76, 77
Unconscious-control theory, 71, 76–78
Underlying psychological mechanisms,
        154
United States
    ego psychology in, 40

logical positivism in, 148

Values and psychotherapy, 3, 5–6, 28
Verbal meaning, 164

Wachtel, Ellen, 221
Wachtel, P. L., 233–235, 237, 238, 259–262
Wallerstein, W. S., 82–83
Wampold, B. E., 26–27, 27
Washington Family Institute, 187, 188
Watson, Goodwin, 100
Watson, J. B., 134, 149, 151, 169–170
Watzlawick, P., 190
A *Way of Being* (Carl Rogers), 101
Weakland, John, 184, 186–187, 189–191
Weiner-Davis, Michelle, 218
Weiss, J., 76–78
Weitzman, B., 231–232

Whitaker, Carl, 204, 207, 208, 218, 219
White, Michael, 219
William Alanson White Institute, 103
Wiltwyck Project, 207–208
Winnicott, D. W., 56, 63
Winokur, M., 236
Wish, 43–44
Witmer, 167
Wolfe, B. E., 262–263, 271
Wolpe, J., 139–140, 142, 143
Working alliance, 50, 53
World Congress in Behaviour Therapy, 141
Worldviews in psychology, 150
Wundt, Wilhelm, 133
Wynne, Lyman, 195

Yale University, 138
Yalom, Irvin, 99, 116

Zen, 102, 259, 263

ABOUT THE EDITORS

Paul L. Wachtel is CUNY Distinguished Professor at City College and the Graduate Center of the City University of New York. He completed his undergraduate work at Columbia University, received his PhD in clinical psychology from Yale University, and is a graduate of the post-doctoral psychoanalytic training program at New York University. He is the author of *Psychoanalysis, Behavior Therapy, and the Relational World* (1997), *Therapeutic Communication: Principles and Effective Practice* (1993), *Action and Insight* (1987), and *The Poverty of Affluence: A Psychological Portrait of the American Way of Life* (1983), among other books, and is the coauthor of *Family Dynamics in Individual Psychotherapy* (with E. F. Wachtel, 1986). Dr. Wachtel has lectured and given workshops throughout the world on psychotherapy, personality theory and development, and the applications of psychological perspectives to social issues. He has served on the editorial boards of numerous journals spanning a variety of perspectives and concerns, including *Psychoanalytic Psychology*, *Journal of Marital and Family Therapy*, *Political Psychology*, and the *Journal of Social Distress and Homelessness*. He was a cofounder of the Society for the Exploration of Psychotherapy Integration.

Stanley B. Messer is professor and chairperson in the Department of Clinical Psychology at the Graduate School of Applied and Professional Psychology, Rutgers University. He received a BSc in honors psychology from McGill University, MA and PhD degrees in clinical psychology from Harvard University, and he completed a psychotherapy fellowship program at Hillside Hospital in Glen Oaks, New York. He is coauthor of *Models of Brief Psychodynamic Therapy: A Comparative Approach* (with C. S. Warren, 1995); associate editor of *History of Psychotherapy: A Century of Change* (with D. K. Freedheim et al., 1992); and coeditor of *Essential Psychotherapies: Theory and Practice* (with A. S. Gurman, 1995), *Hermeneutics and Psychological Theory* (with R. L. Woolfolk and L. A. Sass, 1988), and *Psy-*

choanalytic Therapy and Behavior Therapy: Is Integration Possible? (with H. Arkowitz, 1984), among other works. He has written extensively on topics such as psychotherapy integration, brief psychotherapy, and case formulation in relation to psychotherapy, and he has conducted empirical research on the process of psychotherapy. He was an associate editor of *American Psychologist* and is on the editorial board of several other journals. Dr. Messer maintains a clinical practice in Highland Park, New Jersey.